D1598303

For Church and Confederacy

THE LYNCHES OF SOUTH CAROLINA

EDITED BY Robert Emmett Curran

THE UNIVERSITY OF SOUTH CAROLINA PRESS

Published by the University of South Carolina Press
Columbia, South Carolina 29208

www.sc.edu/uscpress

Manufactured in the United States of America

28 27 26 25 24 23 22 21 20 19
10 9 8 7 6 5 4 3 2 1

Library of Congress Cataloging-in-Publication Data can be found at
http://catalog.loc.gov/.

ISBN: 978-1-61117-917-0 (hardcover)
ISBN: 978-1-64336-021-8 (ebook)

This book was printed on recycled paper with 30 percent postconsumer waste content.

Contents

ILLUSTRATIONS

Acknowledgments

In the course of collecting this material, I have incurred many debts, nowhere more so than with the Catholic Diocese of Charleston Archives, where the archivist, Brian Fahey, and his associate, Melissa Bronheim, did the invaluable work to make this volume possible: from locating materials, directing me to others, scanning documents, confirming sources, securing permissions, and much other assistance that greatly facilitated the production of this edition. Others to whom I would like to express my appreciation include Tricia Pyne, director, and Alison Foley, associate archivist, of the Associated Archives of St. Mary's Seminary and University; Constance Fitzgerald, OCD, archivist of the Baltimore Carmel; William Kevin Cawley, senior archivist, and his assistant, Joseph Smith, of the University of Notre Dame Archives; George Rugg, curator of the University of Notre Dame Special Collections; Martha Jacob, OSU, and Sr. Cabrini, OSU, of the Ursuline Sisters of Louisville Archives; Edie Jeter of the Diocese of Richmond Archives; Timothy Meagher, director, and W. John Shepherd of the Catholic University of America Archives; Debbie Lloyd, OSU, archivist of the Ursuline Sisters of Brown County (Ohio) Archives: Gillian M. Brown, of the Catholic Diocese of Savannah Archives; and Stephanie Brooks, Library Express Leader, Eastern Kentucky University, especially for securing documents from the Library of Congress Manuscripts Division.

At the University of South Carolina Press I am particularly indebted to the anonymous reviewers. Their critiques and recommendations greatly improved this volume. Especially valuable was their identification of a number of persons who had escaped my recognition. But most of all I am grateful to Linda Fogle, assistant director for operations at the press, who inherited my manuscript in very difficult circumstances. Her experience, sound judgment, and steady encouragement were primarily responsible for bringing it into print.

Grants from the Graduate School of Arts and Sciences of Georgetown University provided me with the funds to make several visits to the archives of the Roman Catholic Diocese of Charleston, as well as to have hundreds of documents scanned for my transcribing and annotating back in central Kentucky.

For this assistance I am most grateful. Finally, to my wife, Eileen, who has graciously endured, for more than a decade now, a life she hardly anticipated when we moved here for our retirement, that of being a scholar's widow, I can only offer an appreciative love for all she has put up with and for all she has meant to me and continues to mean.

Introduction

Many summers ago I was looking for a text on the Civil War to use in the History of the American South course I was preparing to offer the following spring semester. So I packed away a number of possibilities as I headed off on vacation to the deep woods of Maine, just across from Mount Desert Island. One of the volumes was *The Children of Pride,* Robert Manson Meyers's collection of letters of the Charles Colcock Jones family in Georgia during the Civil War era.[1] I knew that *Children* had won a National Book Award but had no particular expectations about the work. But as I got into the story of the Joneses, it more and more swept me up. Even in high summer, the days proved too short (we had no electricity in the cabin we were renting) in keeping up with Charles Colcock Jones and his family as the Civil War played out through their correspondence. I remember saying to myself: This reads just like *Gone With the Wind,* only better! Only later did I learn that Margaret Mitchell had spent a great deal of time with the Jones collection at Tulane University when she was preparing to write her bestseller. Needless to say, I added *Children* to my booklist.

Three decades later I was researching a book that I hoped to write about Catholics and the American Civil War. That research took me to Charleston, South Carolina, to the Archives of the Catholic Diocese on Broad Street in the old district of the city. While looking through the papers of Patrick Lynch, Charleston's bishop during the war, the archivist, Brian Fahey, asked whether I had ever seen the correspondence of the Lynch family. He thought I might find it quite useful in tracing Catholic involvement in the war. He proceeded to bring out a calendar of Lynch family correspondence that seemed to go on and on and on. There were in fact more than 1,600 letters written over a forty-year period. Since I had but one day in Charleston, I could not really give them any attention just then, but Brian steered me to the Lowcountry Digital Library, where the South Carolina Historical Society had very conveniently scanned the correspondence between 1858 and 1866, which is where I finally had the opportunity to peruse them. It was like reliving that special summer long ago as I followed the Lynches up to the war and through it, in the many different ways in which they participated and felt the war's impact.

THE JONESES AND THE LYNCHES

The parallels between these two prominent families were immediately evident. Both the Joneses and the Lynches operated multiple plantations, in Georgia and South Carolina respectively, on which scores of enslaved African Americans labored. Both families were extraordinarily involved within their respective faith communities, with the Joneses counting three ministers in their extended family and the Lynches a bishop as well as three nuns within two generations of the nuclear family. Both counted notable members of the medical profession in their communities. Both families in their political affiliation were staunchly Democratic, but whereas political issues tended to be in the Joneses' bloodstream, for the Lynches they were very much confined to the epidermis of their social lives. As the volume and frequency of their correspondence suggest, both the Joneses and Lynches were close-knit families, the Joneses encompassing a network of extended relatives, the Lynches a more intimate clan of siblings. For both families, the matriarchs were the ones providing cohesion and final authority.

If there were striking parallels between the two families, there were also important differences. The Joneses were a small nuclear family with a large network of relatives throughout Georgia. The Lynches were a typically large Irish-American family (parents and a dozen children), but they had no other kin (at least within a recognizable degree of affinity) within a thousand miles. The Joneses had deep roots in America, having been in the country for at least six generations, about as native as any Anglo-Americans in the Deep South could be.

Among the landed aristocracy of the South, wealth was a given for them. The three plantations and 130 slaves that Charles Colcock Jones possessed in Liberty County had come to him through inheritance and marriage. That wealth enabled him and his sons access to the finest academies and colleges in the North for their education and professional training. It insulated them from the need to use their professions as moneymaking operations. So Joseph Jones, a doctor, could easily boast that "making money . . . is not the end and aim of my life."[2]

The Lynches were unmistakably immigrants, even though all but one of the second generation had been born in this country or on the way to it (Eleanor Lynch had given birth to her son John during the Lynches' crossing from Ireland to Newfoundland in 1819). As Irish Catholics, they were doubly "strangers in the land." Their lineage was as rich as any Irish could claim, numbering Gaelic and Old English chieftains as well as primates of Ireland. But if it was a proud heritage, it was also one in which ethnic and religious oppression had stripped them of their traditional wealth and position in society. At least, that was what they remembered. From the time that Eleanor Nieson was cut out of her father's will for marrying a *déclassé* Lynch, the family eye was on regaining the place that by history and justice should have been theirs. The Lynches had a keen consciousness of their outsider status in both Ireland and America, a status chiefly attributable, in both societies, to their religion. But if America represented a continuation to some extent of the discrimination that had marginalized them in Ireland, it also gave them the opportunity to regain the place in society they had been accustomed to having in Ireland, before the British.

In both Georgia and South Carolina, slaveholding was the indispensable means to social mobility and the accumulation of wealth. The peculiar institution had been part of the Joneses' way of life for generations. Although as a young Presbyterian minister in Philadelphia, Charles Colcock Jones had been an advocate for emancipation, he came to regard slavery as an institution that the Scriptures confirmed to be ordained by God and dedicated his life to the evangelization of bonded blacks.[3] Jones was the very epitome of the paternalistic owner, considering the proper care and treatment of his slaves a sacred obligation. The "servants" were clearly regarded as members of the Jones family, distinctly lower, to be sure, but part of them. Even when he deemed it necessary to sell some of their slaves for bad behavior, he made every effort to keep families intact. When his wishes were not honored by the buyer, he attempted to buy back his former bondspeople. His lawyer son, Charles Colcock Jr., fell short of the father's example. For the son, who was an absentee owner of a plantation in southwest Georgia, slave labor was ultimately a commodity that could be sold when it became impractical to oversee its management.

Slavery was also integral to the economy of the upcountry of South Carolina. Slaves provided a major portion of the work force both for the staple agriculture as well as the industry of the area. In 1840 slaves constituted over a third of the total population of Chesterfield County.[4] The Town Market Hall, built by Conlaw Peter Lynch, served in part as a slave mart. Lynch, once he found his economic footing in Cheraw, began to acquire slaves on a very modest scale. He lacked the capital to acquire enough to meet all his labor needs for farm, shop, and household. By 1840 he had seven slaves, four of whom provided labor in his shop and mill. The elder Lynches continued to depend on their children, particularly the females, to compensate for the household labor slaves ordinarily provided. The older sons, by contrast, were quick to effectively utilize the peculiar institution to fulfill their labor needs on their plantations as well as in their industrial operations. Francis had ten slaves in 1850, twenty-two a decade later. Patrick, thanks to legacies he received as the legal heir of the Diocese of Charleston, by 1860 was by far the largest slaveholder in the family, with more than a hundred slaves in Charleston and on upcountry plantations. For Bishop Lynch slavery was an integral part of the natural order ordained by God. In practice the Lynches treated their slaves humanely but more as disposable servants than as members of the family, even inferior ones. Patrick, whose episcopal residence was in Charleston, was, like C. C. Jones Jr., of necessity an absentee owner. His slaves' condition and treatment fluctuated according to the overseer the bishop appointed.

As the correspondence of both families reveals all too well, health was a constant concern, one could say the default topic of their written conversations. One could not take it for granted. Fever and disease were common features of life in the Old South, death a too frequent consequence. One approached life with a sharp awareness of its utter contingency. A fever could take a member of the family, particularly the young, in the blink of an eye. Within a few July days of 1861, Charles Colcock Jr. lost both his wife and daughter to puerperal and scarlet fevers respectively. Chronic health problems plagued both patriarchs (an insidiously spreading palsy in C. C. Jones's case, an undiagnosed condition in Peter Lynch). For the Lynches there was the specter of consumption hanging over the family. The younger half of the Lynch offspring all succumbed to the disease. The older ones somehow avoided its deadly reach, although there persists throughout the letters an unspoken fear that Patrick Lynch, with his chronic "indisposition," coughs, sore throats, and general weaknesses, might have it as well (indeed, when Patrick was a youth, the doctor attending him expected tuberculosis to soon claim his life). Ellen, too, complained rather habitually of her neuralgia and other ailments. Despite their supposed "delicate" health, both Patrick and Ellen lived vigorous lives well into their sixties.

Religion functioned as a major bonder for both families, particularly through daily communal prayer and shared liturgies. If religion was of central importance to Joneses and Lynches alike, it was a highly significant differentiator as well. The Joneses were staunch Old-Side Presbyterians, on the periphery of the evangelical Protestantism that was redefining Southern society in the antebellum period, chiefly through the revivals that swept the region.[5] The sacred cosmos of these traditional Presbyterians was one in which the personal conversion (or turning to God) experience was the crux of one's faith, indeed the sine qua non of one's making a success (by the divine standard) of earthly life. So the recurrent urging of the elder Joneses to their sons to take the necessary steps to experience the metanoia that would make them Christians. "When, my son, will you seek the Lord?" the father pleaded with his namesake. "Why are you not a Christian?"[6] All depended on Charles Colcock Jr.'s response to the promptings of the Holy Spirit, whom the elder Jones firmly believed was ever working upon his unsaved offspring, in the same way that God in his unfathomable way was directing the course of the war to chasten his people into the acceptance and repentance that would ensure victory and independence.

For the Lynches, genuine religion was corporate Catholicism in which one's faith manifested itself in obedience to an authority rooted in scripture and tradition, as well as in living a grace-filled life, particularly through prayer and the sacraments. What mattered most for Catholics was not the conversion experience but the practice of their faith. So Baptista Lynch worried that her younger brothers were not "practical" Catholics, faithfully attending church to share in its prayer and sacraments. Prayer, for Catholics, is a fundamental activator of grace for oneself and others. Constituting a mystical body, Catholics are not only dependent on each other to reap the fullness of God's blessings but also bear responsibility for praying for others, within and outside the formal church itself. Group prayer involves a concentration of spiritual energy: "storming heaven," as Ellen Baptiste liked to describe the blitzkrieg of corporate petitioning by nuns and students in a convent school.

As the second generation of Lynches came of age, immigration was transforming the Catholic Church in the United States from exotic outcast to the largest organized Christian body in the country. Along with the sharp spike in immigration there was a revival of nativism, which in the antebellum era was primarily anti-Catholic since Catholics made up a majority of the immigrants, with Ireland being the largest source of the immigrant traffic. Although the South was the destination of less than 10 percent of the immigration that flooded the country from the mid-1840s to 1861 (Catholics in South Carolina constituted less than 3 percent of the state's population in 1860), nativism infected the politics of that region as well. In both Charleston and Columbia nativist stirrings threatened Catholic interests in which the Lynches had deep commitments.

Despite Roman Catholicism's rather precarious presence in a South Carolina society that was becoming ever more evangelical Protestant in the antebellum era, the two Lynches in leadership positions within the state's Catholic community, especially Ellen Baptista Lynch, had what can only be termed audacious goals for the Catholic Church in the region. It was "the utopia of my youth," Baptista once confessed to her bishop brother. "It was to me always as a charming fancy, that I never expected to see fulfilled."[7] She was referring to nothing less than the conversion of high Carolina society to Roman Catholicism. A fulcrum of this transformation in her vision was the Ursuline Academy that she founded in Columbia in 1858. Her dream was to build an educational institution whose reputation for excellence would attract the cream of Southern society, from South Carolina and beyond. In turn the academy would become a nursery of conversions and subsequent religious vocations, which would provide an ongoing pool of Ursulines to staff and conduct the school. With her brother Patrick at the head of the diocese, Baptista envisioned bold institutional expansion that would include a male orphanage (the Sisters of Mercy already had one for females in Charleston), a college, and a model community for emancipated blacks. Toward attaining this goal, the annual local and regional fairs became venues for showcasing the many attractive aspects of Catholicism. Bishop Lynch's acquisition of Protestant Churches, as part of the expansion plan, also served as a symbol of this Catholic moment, in which Rome's church was making powerful inroads upon the religious landscape.

A conflux of developments over the first half of the century radically changed the prospects for fulfilling Baptista's dream from utopian to propitious. The evangelical tide that had been sweeping over America since the beginning of what became known as "the Great Revival" in Cane Ridge, Kentucky, in 1801 had produced an era of extreme religious instability. That state of flux was the primary precondition for what one historian has recently termed "the critical period for conversions" to Roman Catholicism in the United States.[8] Of no region was this more true than the South. As the area arguably most impacted by the Second Great Awakening, the South also ironically became the most fertile ground for a Catholic harvest of converts. None were more disposed to take the road to Rome than the Episcopalians, who were experiencing not only the effects of the Great Revival but also the American equivalent of the Oxford Movement, whose quest to recover the more Catholic elements of the Anglican tradition was producing a stream of converts to Roman Catholicism in Great Britain and America. Escaping the anarchy that seemed to many within American Protestantism to be the chief fruit of revivals and a yearning for "catholicity" were the principle factors driving conversions. Potential converts were deeply struck by the contrast between the "one, holy, catholic, and apostolic" Church of Rome and the utterly centrifugal nature of American Protestantism, with its seemingly endless splitting of denominations and the creation of new ones claiming to be the authentic restoration of the church. In this age of democratic Christianity, in which the individual was seemingly placed at the center of the religious universe, those questing for security and authority (an authority beyond the self), were very susceptible to the appeal of Roman Catholicism. Within this circle of orthodox believers looking amid all the spiritual turmoil for a religiously safe place for their children, enrolling them in a convent school became a culturally fashionable thing to do; for a good number of the daughters, entering the religious community itself as novices became even more fashionable. Ellen Baptista Lynch had a keen awareness of this cultural trend and calculated the best ways to maximize it.

The War

As the more politically engaged family, the Joneses realized long before 1860 the crisis that was building between the two sections. "There is no place left for forbearance—no ground for compromises," Charles Colcock Jones wrote in the wake of John Brown's shocking raid at Harpers Ferry. "Such sparks as these, struck to produce a universal conflagration, should be stamped out immediately."[9] Brown was quickly hanged, but his soul went marching on through his apotheosis by abolitionists and other Northern sympathizers with the movement. By the first month of 1861, Jones's older son had concluded that the South had no other recourse than to depart from the Union they had once thought perpetual: "I have long since believed," he wrote his father, "that in this country have arisen two races which, although claiming a common parentage, have been so entirely separated by climate, by morals, by religion, and by estimates so totally opposite of all that constitutes honor, truth, and manliness, that they cannot longer coexist under the same government."[10] The events of the last two years, culminating with Lincoln's election, had borne out the painful truth that the physical and cultural pathways in North and South (including climate, moral tradition, religious worldview, and linguistic meanings) had become so starkly different as to constitute distinct peoples who could no longer form one nation. Once the war came, the elder Jones believed that the churches too must necessarily reflect the sectional division of the political order.[11]

The Joneses did all they could for the cause: the two sons and their brother-in-law saw military service, as officers and chaplain respectively; the father and the women served on the home front. Charles Colcock Jones Jr. even opted to join his artillery battery rather than stand for reelection as mayor of Savannah, because, as he explained to his parents, "a graver duty calls me into the field with my company."[12] C.C. Junior eventually rose to command the artillery in a critical area of Charleston's defenses. His brother, Joseph, made valuable contributions to the improvement of sanitary conditions for the Confederate army as well as to the medical care for the wounded. Throughout the highs and lows of the war's progress, the Joneses kept up their trust that the Lord, in his justice, would somehow grant victory and independence to the Confederacy.

Once he became involved in the political debate preceding the war in late 1860, Patrick Lynch made a strong case justifying secession to his counterpart in the North, John Hughes, a defense that elevated his reputation as the chief Catholic voice of the Confederacy. Until the first cannons were fired upon Fort Sumter in the predawn of April 12, 1861, both the Joneses and the Lynches expected a peaceful resolution of the crisis brought on by the secession of the states in the Deep South. War, for both families, at first was unthinkable; then, it was seen as a one-battle prospect that would determine, once and for all, the matter of secession. With the possible exception of C. C. Jones Jr., none sensed a conflict that would pit armies of Napoleonic size against each other in horrific battles producing mind-numbing casualties—"a gigantic war," as Martin Spalding, the Catholic bishop of Louisville, precociously fathomed it to be in the first month of the conflict, indeed a war in which the scale of the armies and the carnage rose relentlessly from one cruel year to the next.

When it became painfully evident that the war would not be won in one grand battle, nor in the ninety days that marked the term of enlistment for many of the soldiers, nor indeed in the foreseeable future, both families nonetheless remained fervent supporters of the "cause." They could all have said, with Baptista Lynch, "I am a very strong secessionist."[13] She and the rest of the family all made their contributions to the war effort: some symbolic, such as the flags that the Ursulines made for the Irish volunteers of Columbia and other military units; others more material, such as the thousands of pairs of shoes that Francis Lynch produced for Confederate soldiers. Several Lynches of the second and third generations joined the army, including Hugh, whose short service was ended by terminal tuberculosis. But it was the eldest, Patrick, who played the largest role in the war, when in early 1864, the Confederate government commissioned him to secure the favor of the Catholic powers of Europe, particularly the Holy See, toward a mediated settlement of a conflict increasingly turning against the South. Patrick needed little persuasion to undertake the mission. Like the Joneses, the Lynches manifested a persistent faith in the Confederacy's ability to strike a peace accord and survive as a nation. Compounding this delusion was the expectation that slavery would continue to anchor the Southern economy, even as the institution was slowly collapsing around the families. That blind optimism surely led Bishop Lynch, while in Europe, to pen the trilingual pamphlet on American slavery, the exposition of which, he was sure, would enlighten the Italians, Germans, and French to recognize the peculiar institution as a Christian one worth maintaining.

The war for both families culminated in a leg of Sherman's march through Georgia and the Carolinas: the Joneses, in the lush lowlands south of Savannah; the Lynches, in the supposedly secure upcountry of South Carolina. Both found themselves in the destructive path of Sherman's grand army as it burned and "foraged" its way, first to the sea, then to rendezvous with Grant in Virginia. For the Joneses and the Lynches alike, Sherman's march brought devastating loss, including buildings, slaves, possessions, and (for the Lynches) human life. In the end both the Presbyterian Joneses and the Catholic Lynches reconciled themselves to their losses and the agony of defeat through their abiding faith in God's providence. For both families a firm trust in providence's wisdom in ordering all things aright enabled them to resign themselves to the loss of virtually all their earthly possessions and the new nation they had tried so hard to create.

THE LETTERS

The correspondence and other writings of the Lynches tell the story, over a period of a quarter of a century, of how the members of three generations took very different avenues of social mobility to achieve success in America. They tell as well of their relationship with the two institutions that came to dominate the family's life in the 1860s: the Roman Catholic Church and the Confederate States of America. Of the more than 1,600 Lynch family letters I have located, not only in the archives of the Catholic Diocese of Charleston but also in those of a number of dioceses, religious communities, and institutions of higher education, I have transcribed and annotated approximately a third of them (561); for this edition I have reproduced selected letters dating from the year 1858— the year in which both Patrick and Baptista became religious superiors, the former as ordinary of Charleston, the latter as the head of the newly established Ursuline community in Columbia, South Carolina, to the end of the year in which peace, of a sort, finally came to the nation. Among the many members of the extended Lynch family, I have focused on six of the bishop's siblings— John, Francis, Mary, Ellen (Baptista), Catherine (Antonia), and Anna, who were the most frequent correspondents of Patrick Lynch. The first five had very consequential lives, whether within the business or medical world, on the Texas frontier, or behind convent walls. Anna, the sixth, served an important family role as the epistolary voice of their parents. I have included those letters of other Lynches or Lynch relatives that, in my estimation, contribute to our understanding of the family experience during this critical period.

In addition I have included three other documents either written by or based on information provided by a Lynch: Ellen Baptista Lynch's "Account of the Lynch Family,"[14] for the Irish background of the family; the narrative of the events surrounding the burning of the Ursuline Convent and Academy in Columbia in the Annals of the community (for which Baptista Lynch was clearly the source); and excerpts from Patrick Lynch's 1864 pamphlet on domestic slavery in the Confederacy.

The search for Lynch family correspondence took me to a number of depositories beyond Charleston: in Baltimore, Baltimore County, the District of Columbia, Louisville, Richmond, Savannah, South Bend, Indiana, and Brown County, Ohio. By far most of the surviving letters are in Charleston. There are very few of them there or elsewhere from Patrick Lynch to his siblings or relatives. The wonder is that there are so many letters from family members to the bishop, who was an exasperatingly dilatory correspondent. His siblings cajoled, pleaded, threatened, shamed, even commanded their unresponsive brother to write ("answer this letter"), but nothing seemed to increase his output of family correspondence. As one of the evaluators of this manuscript noted, this life-long procrastination was something that those who had to work most closely with the bishop were also not above criticizing, most notably John Moore, his diocesan administrator during the bishop's Confederate mission. Moore not only rebuked him for his nonresponse, but complained to his metropolitan, Francis Kenrick, that such silence amounted to a serious neglect of his diocese in a very critical time.[15]

Despite their perennial frustration over his abysmal record as a correspondent or visitor, Patrick Lynch's brothers, sisters, nephews, and nieces continued to write to him regularly, for which we can be grateful. Two of his most frequent correspondents were his nun sisters, Baptista and Antonia. As cloistered religious, traveling was closed to them as a means of keeping in contact with family; but letter writing was not, and they used the mails to their full advantage, despite their brother's habitual failure to reciprocate. Even during the war, Catherine managed to get letters from Baltimore through the lines to her brother in Charleston by utilizing friends as personal couriers.

Ironically, it is the mother, Eleanor Lynch, the one illiterate member of the family, who most lives through the correspondence of her children. She emerges as a strong, irreducible figure, who, in the Irish tradition, continues in America to be the central force in the family. By contrast her semiliterate husband seems ever removed from the family's doings and calculations, a shadow on the sidelines. Chronic illness may account, at least in part, for this peripheral status.

The Lynches opened and closed their correspondence in variations of a formula that transmitted love, invoked prayers and (when writing to the bishop, the recipient of most of the extant correspondence) begged the episcopal benediction. My practice has been to include this formulaic salutation and sign-off the first time a letter from a particular Lynch family member is presented. Thereafter I omit them, unless one or both represent a significant departure from their habitual style. Some of the writers were prone to abbreviating, often with the result of obscuring the meaning of the shortened word. So I have provided in the front matter a list of abbreviations for guidance. As for spelling, I have honored the original as far as possible. In a few cases I have felt the necessity to insert a *sic* for clarification. Persons mentioned in the correspondence I have attempted to identify wherever appropriate. Ellipses (. . .) indicate portions of the letters that I have deemed repetitive or insignificant.

The letters are, for the most part, remarkably preserved. Physical defects that render parts of the text inaccessible are rare indeed. A greater problem is deciphering the hand of some of the writers (this being a pre-typewriter era). Of none is legibility more of a challenge than with the letters of Ellen Baptista Lynch, who had a maddening tendency to let her words trail off into squiggly lines after the initial few letters. Baptista was aware of this; indeed she was informed by her episcopal brother, for one, of how difficult a task it was to read her letters. This poor penmanship was made all the worse by the pressing circumstances that all too often forced her to write in haste. For an editor it has meant reconstructing many words and phrases as best as one could, relying on the context and habits of expression to make sense of what she wrote. Where all else has failed, I have indicated those places where her writing is simply unintelligible. Fortunately, those instances have proved relatively rare. And fortunate as well is the overall clarity of the handwriting of Ellen Lynch's siblings. Her manuscripts stand in comparison to theirs like murky objects in a clear sea.

Lynch Family Genealogy

❧

Conlaw Peter Lynch	Eleanor Neison
(1790–1870)	(1796–1877)

Patrick Lynch	John Lynch	Francis Lynch	Mary Lynch
(1817–1882)	(1819–1881)	(1820–1901)	(b. ca. 1822)

Ellen* Lynch	James Lynch	Catherine+ Lynch	Conlaw Lynch
(1825–1887)	(1825–1860)	(1827–1873)	(1830–1856)

Hugh Lynch	Bernard Lynch	Anna Lynch	Julia Lynch
(1833–1863)	(1835–1859)	(1835–1870)	(1838–1861)

*name in religion: Baptista
+name in religion: Antonia of the Purification

❧

Children of John Lynch and Elizabeth Steele Macnamara (1823–1903)

Robert Lynch	Conlaw Lynch	Elizabeth Lynch	John Lynch
(1843–1928)	(1845–1880)	(1847–1929)	(1848–)

Mary Lynch	Eleanor Lynch	Anastasia Lynch	Louisa Lynch
(1851–)	(1852–1943)	(1855–1924)	(1857–1938)

James Lynch	Julia Lynch
(1860–)	(1862–1944)

❧

Children of Francis Lynch and Henrietta Mulligan Blain (1830–1888)

Marie Lynch	Conlaw Lynch	Eleanor Lynch	James Lynch
(1856–1930)	(1857–1930)	(1859–1897)	(1864–1865)

Henrietta Lynch
(1866–1875)

❧

Children of Julia Anna Lynch and Eustice Bellinger Pinckney (1835–1925)

Conlaw Pinckney | Sarah Bellinger Pinckney
  (1858–1932)   (1860–1940)

❧

Children of Mary Lynch and Charles Spann (1812–)

Bernard M Spann | Eleanor Spann | Martha Spann | John Spann
  (1842–)   (1843–1863)   (1844–)   (1846–)

Ellen Spann | James Spann | Caroline Spann | Marian Spann
(1847–1865)   (1850–)   (1852–)   (1855–)

William Spann | Maschal Spann
  (1857–)   (1858–)

ABBREVIATIONS

Abp, Archbp	Archbishop
Acad	Academy
Acct	account
Affec	affectionate
A.M.D.G.	Ad Majorem Dei Gloriam (For God's Greater Glory)
Amt	amount
BVM	Blessed Virgin Mary
Ch, Chston	Charleston
Chk	check
Con.	Confederate
D G	Deo Gratias
Disct(s)	discount(s)
Doll	dollar
DV	Deo Volente [God Willing]
Mt	market
M.S.	Mother Superior
Pymt	payment
Prs	pairs
Recd, reced, rced	received
Rcpt, rct	receipt
Spr, Super	Superior
TG	Thank God
V G	Vicar General
wd	would

Prologue

"For their Faith and Country"

Catholic Ireland in the nineteenth century still could be divided into the two blocs that had constituted it since the thirteenth century: the Gaelic majority and the Old English minority. The MacMahons and the Lynches represented the finest families of the two respective communities that had joined forces in the revolution against England in 1641 and paid the terrible price in lives and land that the victorious Cromwell imposed upon them. The MacMahons were an old Gaelic family with a number of distinguished branches in the Ulster Province, one of which was the tribe of Fermanagh. Like most of the Gaelic tribes, Fermanagh had sent some of its finest young males to the continent to serve in the armies of Catholic monarchs.[1]

The Lynches had come to England with William the Conqueror in 1066; one of William's generals at the Battle of Hastings was a Lynch. Two centuries later another Lynch was among the first English transplants in Galway. Over the next four centuries the Lynches became the most powerful of the thirteen merchant families ("the thirteen tribes"), the oligarchy that controlled the political and economic life of the region. No fewer than eighty-four Lynches served as mayor of Galway City. All that ended with Cromwell's invasion of Ireland and the Punic peace that he imposed, with massive land confiscations and deportations that swept up the Lynches along with the rest of the Thirteen. One of the family, Peter Lynch, was forced in the 1650s to relocate to Fermanagh, where the MacMahons had traditionally ruled. Conlaw Peter Lynch was the great-great-grandson of this internal exile. His marriage to Eleanor McMahon Neison joined the histories of these two remarkable families.

Internal evidence suggests that Ellen Baptista Lynch was the author of this family biography, written in the late 1870s, with her mother as her chief source. Eleanor Neison Lynch, following her husband's death in 1870, spent the final seven years of her life at Valle Crucis, the Ursuline convent and academy outside

Map of Ireland, with outset of Counties Fermanagh and Monaghan depicting the town of Clones. The parish of Clones split the two counties. Map created by Lynne Parker.

of Columbia, South Carolina, where her daughter was superior. Much of the information and perspective in this essay, it would seem, could only have been provided by the mother: the pride in their storied Irish roots with the Lynch and McMahon clans, together with the deep-seated resentment of English oppression that had survived the Atlantic passage to shape the memory of a new generation of Irish exiles in America. Of note as well is the family tradition of consecrating their firstborn male to the service of the Church; both the Lynches and the McMahons boasted a long line of priests and bishops, including one who became Primate of Ireland. This tradition of church service is one that the Lynches would carry to South Carolina and beyond.

Not all of the text has survived; we are not told what happened when Eleanor Lynch brought her newly baptized firstborn to her father's house. But the foreshadowing of final rejection has been clear enough. Presumably that failure to secure a financial underpinning was a factor in setting their course for America, if not in making the decision itself, at least in confirming it.

[ELLEN BAPTISTA LYNCH], ACCOUNT OF THE LYNCH FAMILY

Mrs Eleanor McMahon lived a retired life in the town of Magheraveely Ireland —diverting herself to the care & education of her only little daughter & visiting the poor.[2]

She was a widow . . . & never ceased to mourn for her noble husband (the cousin of the present Duke of Magenta & President of France)—who had been struck down while yet in the prime of life—never did she grow weary of recounting his many noble traits of character to her little fatherless daughter, until . . . the child budded into woman hood possessing her father's characteristics.

Many were the suitors who solicited the hand in marriage of Miss Sue McMahon—but most of them were *parvenus* & a cold refusal from the mother decided that point however rich the suitor was in this worlds goods.

[In] 1773, the memories of English protestant bigotry were too fresh & frequent for any of the noble old families of Ireland, to look with favor on the tools of a government, which had confiscated their estates & given them over to its minions, had taxed them for every luxury, aye even necessity of life, & either driven them as aliens from the native homes, or reduced them to become the hewers of wood & drawers of water for these venturers—these usurpers— Therefor a McMahon could not, would not, form an alliance which would demand a sacrifice of principle & set at naught the sufferings of ancestors for the *"pro aris et focis"*[3]—Sue McMahon looked with a favorable eye on a Catholic suitor who presented himself in the person of young Patrick Neillson. This young man was esteemed by all as being steady, industrious & intelligent. he was remarkable for his integrity in all business transactions—& although poor —claimed to be a descendant of the great O'Neill—.[4]

Mrs. McMahon gave her consent to the marriage of her only child Sue & moreover, out of her wealth, established her son in law in business & lived to see her daughter most happily settled in life—

Upon her death which occurred soon after[,] Mr. & Mrs P. Neillson were sole heirs to a handsome property, [from] which he was not long in turning . . . profits—In those days of English persecution over Irish Catholics, they could not purchase real estate, but could lease it for "99 years & a day"—

An elegant property with large stone wall dwelling—several offices & every desirable improvement on the place—with larger & well built Barns & Byres for a stock farm, were offered for Lease—& taken by young Mr Neillson—Here he set up looms for spinning & weaving flax—there he started a farm dairy—soon could be seen a village of industrious laborers under his intelligent supervision—Providence seemed to smile on him & although many of his neighbors were envious of his good fortune—& some even pronounced him money loving & exacting, yet the poor, all were received kindly at his door, & often, . . . travellers found a comfortable nights lodging . . . on his premises—& early with the dawn was Mr Neillson up & saw that the weary traveller had his morning meal & gave a god speed you on your way.

Two sons & a daughter were born to these happy parents, when Mrs. Sue McMahon Neillson was sent for to visit a sick family of one of her husbands operatives—She found on entering the cottage a little boy about the age of one of her own darlings lying at the point of death—unsparing of herself—she exhausted her strength in fruitless exertion to save the life of the little person—& in doing so contracted the sickness of which the little boy died—& herself became the martyr of charity at the early age of 22—leaving her three babes motherless & her husband heartbroken— (R.I.P.)

From a bright & cheerful spirit Mr Neillson became sad, growing even morose—he endeavored to conquer grief by attending to his still prosperous business—But what was now the sound of spindle—what the dash of those monster churns, the play of whose massive beams his loving wife had so often watched with him—Her presence was missed everywhere, & the merry sound of the dear childrens voices seemed but to embitter his grief—. . . . Their only remembrance of their devoted mother was of the pretty lady whom they were taken to kiss in the coffin—. He could not bear of their prattle—

The same faithful family servants of Mrs McMahon took care of the little motherless ones—& good old Peggy McDonough—who had been early friend & house keeper— . . . She had confided to her maternal care Mr Neillsons only little daughter Eleanor.

This little old woman, with plain countenance sat beside her little Flax-wheel spinning, & with the bright little Eleanor by her side watching the motions of both foot & wheel—would recount to dear little one the many domestic virtues of her saintly Mother & grandmother—until in the mind of little Eleanor the McMahons & O'Neills were unequalled for goodness & bravery—. Time rolled on & although prosperity had ripened into great wealth, under the intelligent business management of Patrick Neillson & his Brother- in Law Mr. Patrick McMahon— . . .

The penal laws prohibited Catholic education—How were his children to be educated at home—True, he could send them to their relatives in France—the

McMahons—or to their relatives in England the Neillsons—But he preferred to keep them near himself—they were his all—To avoid the government agents & tools, he employed a tutor for his Boys—who also took his seat at a loom to weave flax—the Boys sat near him, as if to learn the Flax & loom, on the approach of footsteps, lest some government spy or tool would betray the secret & subject the teacher to death or transportation—.[5]

Little Eleanor could not be sent with her brothers nor exposed as they—She was the pet of the household . . . —She was promised a grand treat— "Fair-day" was approaching & she who had never been to Clones was to be taken there by her father—It was a grand occasion to all the country—as well as to little Eleanor —for her Uncle Hugh McMahon was to speak.

The mighty O'Connell[6] had not then aroused the nation & with legal skill "split the hairs" of persecution— . . . but his predecessors were agitating the subject & one of the most powerful & acceptable orators of the day was Mr Hugh McMahon—In personal appearance Mr McMahon was very imposing —tall, handsome erect, with broad & sloping shoulders he appeared a man of about 30 years of age, he possessed a clear sonorous voice & an animated countenance.

An immense crowd was assembled around & near the platform to hear his speech—& the little Eleanor upheld on the shoulders of a faithful employee enjoyed the scene vastly—As her uncle ascended the steps of the platform & his fine manly form became visible to the crowd below—shout after shout of huzzahs rent the air—

But as if in an instant & before he had opened his mouth to speak while with uplifted hand he acknowledged the triumphant welcome—a man from the crowd rushed up after him, & drove into his heart the knife of the assassin—& rushing down was lost in the crowd & confusion.

McMahon staggered & would have fallen had not a dozen brave arms supported him—& carried him at once into the nearest Hotel—surgeons declared it a mortal wound—

Then the murmur of anger & revenge stirred the crowd—the murderer was hunted in vain for what of law or justice was meted out to a Catholic—? None whatever.

Yet such was the universal respect entertained for Mr Hugh McMahon that his remains were laid out in state—his Bier decorated with (crimson) heavy rosettes & sashes of crimson & no horse was allowed the honor of drawing it—For three miles the Bier was borne by detachments of friends until they reached the family burial ground.

It was a moving spectacle to the immense crowd as they saw the crimson streamers from the Bier & arms of the Pall -bearers pass on into the chapel & rest before the altars for the rights of which, this noble young mans life had been sacrificed—. The Holy Mass was offered—the remains consigned to the tomb, amid the prayers & tears of some, & the threats & murmurs of others— Little Eleanor saw and heard all & nestled close to her uncle Patrick McMahon — (the Brother of the deceased) as if to shelter herself & at the same time soothe his great grief—

Her elder brother John & younger Brother Hugh McMahon Neillson led on by their father shared the indignation glowing in every honest breast, at the fearful deed, & that shelter provided by the minions of English Protestant Rule over Catholic Ireland—These children early learned that the enemies of the Irish were to be distrusted—They saw the precautions taken to conceal from the oppressive agents of Government all that could in any way offer them an excuse to tithe & tax & confiscate—as they prowled around day & night or hired spies to do the mean work for them—Mr Patrick Neillson saw it was to his interest to appear as neutral as possible—his wealth was too tempting a bait—, could these "Valentine McClutchys"[7] by any pretext lay hold on it—His desire to save his property activated him in dissembling much that he felt—. On one occasion he heard the tramp of horses on the pavement in the court-yard & could perceive the glitter of arms—soon entrance was demanded in a loud familiar voice of the leader of a band of Orangemen—but before the door could be opened—"Caesar," a splendid mastiff—paid the forfeit of his life, for defending his Masters premises—

How the master chafed with anger when on opening the door at that unseemly hour he heard the dying groans of his faithful "Caesar," now lying there welling in his blood—An apparently friendly greeting passed & Mr. Neillson had a hot supper prepared for the party en route—who left apparently satisfied, though their concealed intent was to surprise Mr Neillson & his employees if possible in some act, however trivial against the government, which could be made a plea for laying hold on some of the gold which report said he had conceald—

These golden charms together with others brought many suitors for the hand of Mr Neillsons only daughter Eleanor McMahon—but so rigid had he been in rearing her, that her face was known to but few. This was of little importance however, where such marriage arrangements are perfected by parents & based on the fortune & social position of each party.

Mr Neillson was very difficult to please but . . . Finally [he] engaged his young daughter to the son of an old friend. The young man was handsome, wealthy, sensible—but unfortunately an Orangeman—[8]

Eleanor was told of this—& when she mentioned it to her uncle McMahon, whom she loved devotedly & made the *confidante* of all her little secrets—she observed the rigid pressure of his lips, the cloud on his brow & his ominous silence—He paced the room after she left him—. No, said he this must not be—The daughter of Sue McMahon & the heir of my murdered Brother Hugh can never marry a "Sassanach"[9] I must speak with Neillson about this matter, painful though it be. While revolving in his mind how to address one so reticent as his brother-in-law on the subject, so dear to the hearts of both—all were startled by the news of a skirmish between the "crosses" & orangemen in which the fiancé was accidentally killed—

Eleanor was unconcerned—The servants congratulated her on a lucky escape—& her Uncle McMahon was relieved in mind—

No one ever knew the sentiments of Mr. Neillson on the subject—but soon he proposed to his daughter a rich young Catholic—of whom she would not listen—Meantime she met at the chapel a remarkably handsome youth, a stranger from the mountain—Conlaw Peter Lynch—The young gentleman was evidently attracted to her, & on her return home she sought "Uncle McMahon" (to narrate all that had passed)—Oh! said he, there's a young man I would like to see—One of the Lynches of Galway, one of "Ireland's true sons—& sons of the Faith for which they have nobly fought & suffered—Yes, they sacrificed for their Faith & Country everything they possessed of power & wealth & comforts of life—but never would they sacrifice principle & betray the Faith—They are a noble family, those Lynch's of Galway—"

Soon it reached the ears of Eleanor's brother, that at last she was interested in a suitor for her hand—Her younger brother Hugh McMahon was a gentle blue eyed boy who so loved his bright-gay sister, as to think every thing she did perfect—but her elder brother John, a dark-eyed pale young man had mourned the death of her Orangeman lover—& now made all manner [of] threats against this "poor Mercutio," as he derisively called young Conlaw Peter Lynch

Being the oldest son his influence over his father was considerable & John lost no time in misrepresenting to Mr Neillson that this poor Catholic young man was a fortune hunter, who sought more the wealth of his sister than her affection—

Mr Neillson had placed in Bank prior to his second marriage—the fortune of each of his children with the proviso that it was theirs if they married to please him—but he would cut any one off with a shilling, who would marry against his will—. John knew it would revert to him if his sister married against the will of his father, & he saw she was determined—therefore his part was to prevent her father's consent—which was not difficult to do, given the young man was poor.—

Eleanor's advisor & friend was Uncle McMahon—Young Mr Lynch made every honorable proposal to Mr Neillson but the old gentleman was so embittered by his son & his misrepresentations & his daughter's silent persistence, that he was unreasonable—Finally it was arranged that on the following Sunday, May 5th 1816 Eleanor McMahon Neillson accompanied by her faithful attendant—an old family servant—woman would attend Mass at Clones Chapel —there meet young Conlaw Peter Lynch—& after Mass she would not return home but go arm in arm with him—still attended by her . . . woman to the house of distant relatives of her & send word to her father by a servant man— This is called a run-away match in Ireland—

Mr Neillson seeing further opposition useless, sent for the young people & for Rev. Father Firnan—They were married in the Brides father's house & he had the relatives assembled—gave them a handsome dejeuner—the Bridal party took leave & the old gentleman & his son John never would see them after—

Eleanor's young heart, full of love & hope expected her father to relent, & waited day after day for some indication—& she would not have waited in vain perhaps, were it not for the mercenary elder son.

Mr Conlaw Peter Lynch was the youngest of eight sons. His venerable Mother gave a loving welcome to the young bride, who had honored her boy above all other aspirants for her hand & she made her feel for the first time in her life the happiness of possessing a loving mother. The family of "Lynch" or as it was anciently spelt "Loingseach" of Galway & of Tara's Hall, was renowned in Irish history—

It was one of those noble brave clans, whose love of the faith & country gave martyrs & heroes to old Ireland, in the days of her persecution by the English government & finally after their overthrow & the confiscation of their estates, they retreated to the mountains, where unmolested they practised the Faith & concealed their honorable poverty—The venerable widow Mrs Lynch enjoyed in the midst of her children & grand-children an undisturbed peace—she was esteemed & beloved one might say revered by every one, & the poor found in her a tender & compassionate friend—The mountain scenery was beautifully new to the young Bride—All nature was charming, in this lovely month of May —& from the eminence on which their dwelling stood could be seen the dwelling of the several sons of the old lady—to each of which she made frequent visits—Since the death of her husband, one of her sons had brought his wife & children to console his devoted Mother—now, her youngest son & the pet of the family had brought his bride—& all endeavoured to make her happy & enable her to forget her father's stern treatment, & assure her he would relent—

Her "Babies" as she fondly termed Conlaw & his young wife were now her special object of affectionate solicitude—& often would she come herself to the dear child Eleanor with some tempting delicacy & kind of loving cheerfulness —to which the bright spirit of Eleanor warmly responded—The cloud above darkened ever & anon the first years of their marriage—Eleanor tried in vain to get some word from her father—She employed faithful family servants—& also relatives, but the stern relentless old gentleman admitted no approach— . . .

March 10th 1817 was born a son to them, according to the pious Catholic custom of the Lynch family, the first born in each family is consecrated to the service of the altar. . . . What a fine Boy—a splendid little fellow—God bless him—! Was the exclamation of every one as member after member of the family came to offer congratulations—And when at Mass the following Sunday the news was circulated among friends, the faithful servants came to see their young mistress & her babe— "Surely now, the old master will be proud—do send the fine looking little fellow on his first visit to his grandfather & see what he will do for him—!

The young mother's heart beat with joy & pride, & she resolved to follow the suggestion; secretly hoping that her father would give to her eldest son the fortune he had refused to herself—Grandma dressed Babe for his Baptism & many assembled to rejoice in the event, & the child was called after his grandfather, "Patrick Neillson".

A few days after with a young mother's love & pride of her first-born Mrs Conlaw Peter Lynch placed her little Patrick Neillson in the arms of good faithful nurse—adjusted his dress with care & with a cheerful smile & loving kiss sent him to see her father. Something whispered within her—surely he will now relent, he cannot look into those eyes & not love the child of his only daughter —& he will prove his love of a father for me & mine—How her imagination pictured her Father's pleasure in hearing the name of his only grandson—how proud he would . . . [text ends]

Antebellum Years

"Everyone must have their own troubles."

Having failed in her attempt to reconcile with her father, Eleanor Neison Lynch and her husband, Conlaw Peter Lynch, set sail with their son, Patrick, in the late fall of 1818 for the New World. The first week of the new year, while still at sea, Eleanor gave birth to a second son whom they named John. Like so many of the Irish immigrants to America, the Lynches' first port was a Canadian one, St. John's, Newfoundland. From there they made a difficult, storm-filled passage down the coast of the Maritime Provinces and the eastern United States to Georgetown, South Carolina, where they intended to settle. A chance contact there quickly changed those intentions. John Lyde Wilson, a local lawyer and soon-to-be governor of the state, recommended an upcountry town, Cheraw, as the best prospect in the state for newcomers. Wilson, a native of Cheraw, was then serving on the Internal Improvements Committee of the state legislature. Aware of an ongoing project to clear silt and other debris from the Great Pee Dee River, whose navigable portion terminated at the town, Wilson had an insider's vision of Cheraw's ideal fall-line location for tapping the commercial opportunities of the industrial and transportation revolutions that steam power was creating in the first decades of the century.[1]

Wilson's optimistic projection of Cheraw's future moved the Lynches to cast their fortunes with the rising town. They made the seventy-five mile trip up the Great Pee Dee on the first steamboat to ply that vital waterway. The site proved to have all the potential that Wilson had promised. Cheraw itself was one of the oldest developments in South Carolina, having by 1750 become important enough as a trading center with water mills to be among the six settlements shown on a contemporary map of the colony. In the years immediately before the Revolution, a grid of broad streets and town green had been laid out. In that civil conflict the village found itself in the midst of the savage fighting between local Patriots and Tories, which by war's end left much of Cheraw devastated. When the Lynches arrived in 1819, the town had recovered enough to be on the cusp of a new era of development, as its legal incorporation a year later signaled. Cheraw grew rapidly as a shipping center for the various staple crops grown in the region (tobacco, rice, indigo, cotton). The town also became an important producer of leather goods, the home of a curing industry, and by the 1850s the largest market for cotton between Charleston and Wilmington. Merchants' Bank by the 1850s was the largest one in the state outside of Charleston, a testimony to the scale of commerce in the area, which the advent of the Cheraw and Darlington Railroad in 1853 only increased.

This was the fertile environment the Lynches found upon docking in Cheraw in 1819, one in which Conlaw Lynch quickly put his artisan skills to productive use. As the economy boomed in the 1820s, Peter Lynch was among those meeting the need for both public and private structures. While practicing his trades as carpenter and millwright, Lynch was responsible for the construction of several residences, including one for his family, which by 1838 numbered thirteen. He also designed and built the Town Market Hall (1837) and St. Peter's Catholic Church (ca. 1843). As the head of the first Catholic family in the area, Peter Lynch served as site provider, fund-raiser, architect, and builder of the church. Located on a substantial lot at High and Market Streets, diagonal to the modest, two-story upcountry farmhouse of the Lynches, St. Peter's mirrored the earlier Lynch project, Market Hall, without the elevated first floor of the town building, and with its central tower bearing a cross rather than a weather vane.

Over the course of their first six years in Cheraw, Eleanor Lynch gave birth to four children, two boys (Francis and James) and three girls (Mary and Ellen, and Catherine). Then, in the decade of the 1830s, there were five more successful births: three boys (Conlaw, Hugh, and Bernard) and two girls (Anna and Julia). In all there were a dozen children, hardly conducive to the reacquisition of wealth and social prestige that had brought them to America. As patriarch of his ever-growing family, Peter more often than not found himself living on the edge of being able to provide for his family. In 1848 he had to pull his son Conlaw out of school in Charleston because the family needed the income the son could provide by clerking for a merchant in Cheraw. Seven years later, when his daughter Catherine wanted to enter the Carmelite order, he did not have the wherewithal to furnish an appropriate dowry for her. But if the Lynches lacked the substantial wealth to provide generously for their many children, they very effectively implanted in their children this fundamental drive to accumulate it. By the time they reached maturity, the pursuit of money as a life goal had been embedded in the cultural genes of the Lynch children. All, as Francis noted, developed "a taste for business," which the males indulged, including those with professional training, be it the law, medicine, or even the ministry. Most of the younger males entered the business world by apprenticing

Peter's Church, Cheraw. Conlaw Peter Lynch became a major builder in Cheraw, constructing its Market Hall (1837) as well as St. Peter's Church (ca. 1843), the first building for Catholic worship in the area. Courtesy of the Roman Catholic Diocese of Charleston Archives.

themselves as clerks. All the Lynch men at one time or other were involved with business and investment ventures.

True to classical American expectations, the five Lynch children who escaped consumption's grip surpassed their parents in their achievements, although only one realized the riches of family dreams and that for a very brief time. The firstborn, Patrick, had honored the family's tradition of consecrating the firstborn to the Lord's service by becoming a priest. John England, who had arrived in South Carolina from Ireland a year after the Lynches to become Charleston's first Catholic bishop, regularly stayed with them when making his episcopal visits to the upcountry. Seeing in the young Lynch extraordinary intellectual and spiritual promise, England had brought him to Charleston to the classical academy/seminary he had established there, then in 1834 sent him, along with another gifted Charlestonian, James Corcoran, to the Urban College in Rome for theological studies. Ordained there in 1840, Lynch, with doctorate in hand, had returned to Charleston, where Bishop England made him his personal secretary and appointed him to the faculty at St. John's Seminary. When England died in April 1842, Patrick Lynch became editor of the *United States Catholic Miscellany* and, despite his extreme youth, was one of the three names submitted to Rome by the prelates of the Province of Baltimore as candidates to succeed England.

That Patrick Lynch, at twenty-five, could have so impressed the bishops of the eastern dioceses was likely due to the learning and skills he had displayed in the polemical duel he had been waging since 1841 with James Henley Thornwell, the leading Presbyterian theologian and president of South Carolina College. For four years Thornwell and Lynch, products of upcountry Carolina (both had attended Cheraw Academy), engaged in an ongoing published exchange of letters over controversial theological issues such as papal infallibility and the canon of the scriptures. Thornwell was notorious for his slash-and-burn rhetoric. His contempt for "anti- Christian popery" and his dismissal of Lynch's arguments as "puerile sophisms" could not have stood in sharper contrast with Lynch's detached, scholarly defense of Catholic doctrines.[2] For the gatekeepers of organized intellectual life in Charleston, Lynch's closely followed debate with Thornwell indelibly established his credentials as "one of the best-educated people in Charleston," even though he was yet in his mid-twenties, and gained him a position within the circle of Charleston's intellectual elite.[3] He was John England *revividus*.

Patrick Lynch was a big man, over six feet in height, increasingly prone to stoutness as he aged, with the receding hairline and spectacles befitting a scholar. He carried himself with the stately air of someone descended from the highest Irish chieftains. Like his mentor, Patrick Lynch developed a reputation for preaching that reached far beyond Charleston.[4] His multilingual fluency, rhetorical skills, and broad learning in the arts and sciences (the latter knowledge mostly self-acquired) made him the kind of polymath that knowledge societies coveted for members. By the mid-1850s Lynch held membership in virtually all of the local and national associations that defined America's intellectual community, from the Charleston Library Society, to the Elliott Natural History Society, to the Conversation Club, to Russell's Bookstore Club and the Philadelphia-based American Association for the Advancement of Science, to which group of the nation's leading scientists Lynch was elected in 1849, a year after its founding.

For Lynch the informal meetings of the Bookstore Club may have been the most significant for him, owing to the contacts he was able to establish through them with the finest minds of Charleston's intellectual cohort. None proved more productive than the relationship he struck with the club's best-known member, the novelist and editor William Gilmore Simms. Simms was so taken with Lynch's intellectual breadth that he made him an associate of his *Southern Quarterly Review*. The priest wrote several articles related to science for the journal in the late 1840s.

In 1849, when the municipal government abandoned its effort to construct artesian wells as the principal water source for the city, Lynch, who had taken a keen interest in the project from its beginnings in the early 1840s, assumed the role of public intellectual with a series of articles in the *Charleston Evening News,* in which he undertook to persuade Charlestonians of the need for such deep wells. Despite the daunting challenges their construction presented, Lynch showed how they could be built to ensure an adequate supply of potable water. Lynch's newspaper lobbying proved decisive in the city's renewing the project. The priest himself was named one of its principal managers. As such, he oversaw the collection of fossil species from the several strata uncovered by the drilling for the scientific information they contained about the corresponding geological periods. All in all, the artesian project gained Lynch a national reputation as a geologist.

John England had envisioned as his cathedral a magnificent Gothic structure whose spire would proclaim to city and state God's glory according to the Roman Catholic tradition. He never lived to realize this grand dream, so it was fitting that Bishop Ignatius Aloysius Reynolds chose Patrick Lynch, England's protégé, to put England's dream into stone. Lynch chose as architect the Irish-born Patrick Charles Keely. The young Keely did not disappoint. The neo-Gothic Cathedral of St. John and St. Finbar was dedicated in 1854, the first of sixteen cathedrals that would establish Keely as the leading Catholic architect in America.

In March 1856 Ignatius Reynolds, at age fifty-six, succumbed finally to the ravages of his chronic medical disabilities. Rome appointed Patrick Lynch to administer the diocese until it named a new bishop. That fall he found himself caught up in the wave of revived nativism that had brought violence, political disruption, and anti-immigrant/anti-Catholic legislation throughout the nation in the mid-1850s. The xenophobic American Party peaked in 1856, questing for power at the municipal, state, and national levels. Charleston did not escape its reach, with American candidates in elections for sheriff and mayor. During campaigns in that year, Patrick Lynch broke his rule of skirting politics by utilizing the diocesan paper, the *United States Catholic Miscellany,* where James Corcoran had succeeded him as editor, to rebut nativist charges that voting abuses and other corrupt Catholic practices had produced Democratic victories. He no doubt contributed to the Irish-led counteroffensive that produced decisive Democratic triumphs at the polls.[5] For Patrick Lynch the two campaigns marked the beginning of his involvement in the political sphere that would ultimately carry him to the highest diplomatic circles of Europe.

Patrick's siblings were sure that his appointment as administrator of the diocese was prelude to his consecration as Charleston's next bishop. Then came reports that Rome had appointed John McCaffrey, the president of Mount St. Mary's College and Seminary in Maryland. Throughout 1857 Patrick Lynch continued to govern the diocese, all the while awaiting the official notice of "Bishop" McCaffrey's appointment.

The Lynches' second oldest brother, John, graduated from the Medical College of Charleston and took up practice in Cheraw. In September 1842 he married Elizabeth Steele Macnamara of Salisbury, North Carolina, the daughter of a prosperous, well-connected Irish Catholic merchant, and the descendant, on her mother's side, of one of North Carolina's first families.[6] The marriage dramatically enhanced John's social credentials, and by extension his family's, within Carolina society. Whether status and/or monetary concerns entered into Lynch's marital choice we do not know, although such concerns were clearly at play in the courtship a younger Lynch conducted a decade later. We do know that, in the practice of medicine, John Lynch always had an eye out for anything that would give him an edge. In 1842 it was phrenology to which he was strongly drawn as a scientific means of gauging human character. Six years later animal magnetism was the latest obsession to which he admitted to Patrick he had become "a full convert," with its potential for curing psychosomatic illnesses.[7] When smallpox struck Cheraw in the winter of 1854, he had Patrick secure some "genuine and fresh" vaccine in Charleston so that he could be the first physician in Cheraw with the antidote and "hold the trump cards" in establishing his reputation.[8]

Despite a constant search for medical innovations that would enable him to stand out among local doctors, John's practice never came close to producing the lucrative revenue he described as one of his "grand objects" when he was starting his medical career in the early 1840s.[9] Adventures into real estate to get out from under his mounting debts went nowhere. He continued to struggle to build up a practice sufficiently remunerative to support his ever-growing family, including eight children of his own, as well as an illegitimate son of his wife's deceased brother. Compounding John's predicament was the sectarianism in the area that moved persons to select physicians of their own faith. There were simply too few Catholics in Cheraw to constitute a strong cohort of clients for a doctor. His mounting debts led to severe economic pressures, which his significant real estate ventures failed to reduce. By 1849 he was contemplating a move out of Cheraw to an area with more promising economic prospects. Charleston was his first choice, with its diverse population, opportunities for engaging in a joint practice, and the rising image of Catholicism, thanks in no small part to the status his brother has achieved there. That rising reputation was another asset that John hoped to tap in securing patients in Charleston.

For most of the next decade John Lynch soldiered on in Cheraw, never shaking the economic burdens of overextended borrowing and lending, as well as a growing mass of uncollected medical fees (dunning patients for payment not being in John's character). His brother Patrick's financial assistance provided some relief, but the unpromising situation in Cheraw revived, at the prodding of his wife, his plans to move family and practice to a more favorable location. In the end John stayed in the upcountry but relocated in late 1856 to the more highly populated Columbia, the state capital as well as the site of a medical school and asylum for the insane. He failed, initially, to secure a position at either of these institutions but managed through a closely managed practice to do better than just earn a living. In the fall of 1857 his oldest child, Robert, upholding the family's Irish tradition, began studies for the priesthood at the Sulpicians' minor seminary in Maryland.

The third brother, Francis, had read law in Charleston but chose to go into business as a tanner in Cheraw. Francis, ever seeking to improve his tanyard and dry-goods operations through innovative technology and efficient management, enjoyed early success in building up his business but in the process accrued a heavy debt, which he struggled to keep from dragging him into bankruptcy. To escape his bondage to creditors, Francis resorted to various schemes, from speculating in the California gold fields to investing in local coal mines. But his boldest plan to get out from under his financial albatross was to gain solvency by securing tanning supplies himself, thus eliminating middlemen.

Francis gradually concentrated his tanyard on the production of shoes. To publicize his products, he entered some models in the annual Charleston Fair where he hoped a ribbon or two would bring the recognition that would elevate him to the top tier of shoe manufacturers in South Carolina. To prepare for the expanded production that such a prestigious position would necessitate, Francis went on a recruiting trip to New York and New England, where the skilled shoemakers were.

While Francis was making his debut as a mass producer of shoes, he married, at the rather advanced age of thirty-four, Henrietta Blain, the daughter of a Charleston widow. To Francis's dismay, Henrietta, for unknown reasons, a few months into their marriage returned to her mother's home. With Patrick's aid, Francis managed to persuade his bride to resume her married life in Cheraw with her husband. She apparently never regretted her return. Over the next decade they had five children. That steady increase in Francis's household only made his precarious financial condition more of a threat to take down his burgeoning business in the latter fifties. His not-so-adroit juggling of debts and revenues eventually made banks wary of continuing to treat him as a dependable investment. As with John, Patrick proved to be his savior as the priest's voucher and loans enabled Francis not only to keep his debts under control but finally to turn some profit.

The oldest daughter, Mary, at nineteen had married Charles Spann, a struggling farmer with a controlling mother in Sumter County, about forty-five miles due east of Columbia. In 1847 Spann sought to better his fortunes in Galveston, the Gulf port city of the recently annexed state of Texas on the frontier of the still rapidly expanding cotton kingdom. In that hub of east Texas's cotton trade, Spann saw opportunity, not in raising cotton but in practicing the law in which he had trained. So he struck out for Texas in the midst of the war the United States was waging with Mexico to prepare the way for his family's removal there. (If Charles had hoped to get out from under his mother by migrating to Texas, he failed. She moved there as well.) A sluggish economy and the high cost of living in Galveston forced Spann, less than two years after relocating, to move once again. They purchased land in Washington County in the upcountry of East Texas. "[O]ur home is better than the generality of country houses," Mary wrote her siblings in September 1847. "The logs are of cedar and hewed squares[;] between the log is plastered as it belonged to a Baptist preacher [so] of course it is somewhat aristocratic[.]"[10] Once more Spann worked the land for his living, this time with corn and cotton, which proved much more productive than any of the staples he had planted in Sumter County. Mary returned home by herself to Cheraw in May 1854 for an extended stay; her parents cajoled her into lengthening it until the beginning of the new year. It was the last time she saw them, as well as most of her siblings. By 1857 Mary and John Spann had nine children.

Ellen, the second-oldest daughter, had long desired to follow Patrick in embracing the religious life. In Charleston in the early 1840s there were two possibilities for women: the Sisters of Our Lady of Mercy and the Ursulines. The former was a diocesan community that Bishop England had founded in 1829 when he invited three Irish immigrants living in Baltimore to establish a religious group in his see city and to conduct both a school and an orphanage. Five years later the bishop extended an invitation to another group of Irish women to establish an academy for the higher education of young women in Charleston. This group, however, were already members of a well-established religious order, the Ursulines. It was to their Broad Street institution that Ellen Lynch had come down from Cheraw for her higher education. Returning to Cheraw as a graduate of the Ursuline Academy, in mid-1845 Ellen applied to enter the community as a postulant. The mother superior kept putting off her entrance, only finally to confess that "affairs of great consequence" to the community must be first resolved before the nuns could receive any further women for the novitiate. This was an apparent reference to their ambivalent relationship with Bishop England's successor, Ignatius Reynolds. The bishop had evidently asked the nuns, in light of their declining numbers, to exchange their current convent for a smaller facility. To the nuns this request simply confirmed their long-standing suspicion that Reynolds did not accord them the same preference over the Sisters of Mercy that his predecessor, John England had, despite England's special relationship to the Mercy community. In December 1845 the Ursuline superior in Charleston privately informed the bishop that they had decided to relocate their academy in another diocese.[11] For the next year and a half, the Ursulines sought a bishop who would receive them. John Purcell, the Irish-born bishop of Cincinnati, finally agreed in the spring of 1847 to have them open an academy. All this time, Ellen Lynch was becoming increasingly frustrated by the Ursulines' opacity, particularly since she had made quite public her intention to become a nun and feared raising the impression, by remaining at home, that she had somehow been rejected by the order.

At some point in the spring or early summer of 1847, Ellen Lynch entered the community of the Sisters of Mercy in Charleston. She apparently had acted only after learning from the Ursuline superior that she and her fellow nuns were leaving Charleston. It is probable that Mother Borgia had advised her that, given their unsettled situation, it was best that Ellen join the sole remaining Catholic religious community for women in South Carolina. Whatever brought her to the Mercy Community, Ellen Lynch's stay there proved a short one. Within the year she journeyed west, across the Alleghenies to northern Kentucky where the former Charleston Ursulines had relocated in the Ohio River city of Covington. Her parting from the Sisters of Mercy was, by all signs, an amicable one. One can only surmise that, upon the extended self-reflection that novitiates promote, Ellen had second thoughts about her decision to make her religious life with the Sisters of Mercy, rather than the Ursulines, her former teachers and the community she had originally intended to enter. She reached Covington in June 1848 and entered the novitiate, where a fellow Charleston alumna, Mary Maloney, and Nora England, the Irish-born niece of the late bishop, were preparing for their professions. She had barely settled in when she learned that the community was moving across the river to Bank Street in Cincinnati, a much better location for their academy. In the new convent that October, she made her own profession, taking the religious name of Baptista.

The following year proved to be especially challenging. Sister Baptista managed to avoid the cholera and other summer plagues that struck Cincinnati but had her own spiritual demons to wrestle with, triggered by the decision of the founding group of nuns to return to Ireland. That loss left the remaining community in a kind of limbo that Baptista at least experienced as a profound spiritual depression. The remnant of the former Charleston Ursulines painfully concluded that they could continue no longer as a separate community.

Debts—the result of a mortgaged academy building, an inability to manage their financial affairs, and stagnant enrollment—were one pressure on them to disband. A greater one was the failure of the individual nuns to blend as a community, something Archbishop Purcell recognized as the root cause of their disbanding. When the nuns accepted his offer to merge with the Ursulines of Brown County, Purcell excluded from the merger several Bank Street Ursulines, including Nora England, now Sister Augustine.

In August 1854 the chosen Ursulines traveled the forty miles northeast from Cincinnati to Brown County to spend a week at their future home and work out plans for their union. It all went badly. Differences arose during the discussions that many of the Bank Street Ursulines judged irreconcilable. The result: those Irish-born members who had chosen not to join their countrywomen in returning to Black Rock in Ireland now did so. Others, including Baptista, chose to go to the oldest Ursuline community in the United States, that in New Orleans. The upshot was yet another change in community for Baptista Lynch, her fourth in seven years.

It took Baptista Lynch a very short time to discover that the New Orleans Ursuline community was far from what she had anticipated. The rules and customs seemed totally different from what she had known in South Carolina and Ohio. Particularly bothersome were the grates that separated the members of the community from the outside world, an ancient tradition that she deemed much too confining and isolating for nineteenth-century American women. Then there was the non-French-speaking Baptista's jarring realization that French was still the language of the community and classroom, even though New Orleans had been part of the United States for nearly a half century. With the local superior's encouragement, Baptista approached the Brown County community, which to her surprised delight, welcomed her to make her life with them. Returning up the Mississippi, she found the riverboat awash with "gamblers, rogues &c &c . . . I was obliged to keep my room almost altogether," particularly since she had decided to pack her habit in her trunk and pass as a civilian.[12] That unpleasant voyage made all the sweeter the warm welcome she received from the Brown County Ursulines upon her arrival in April 1855. And topping her joy was the discovery that Mother Joseph and her companions were back from Ireland as well, having reconciled with their Ursuline hosts.

Baptista Lynch early on had a particularly keen eye for potential candidates for a school or vocation to the religious life or both, even within one's family. In 1857 she lobbied her sister Mary in Texas to enroll her oldest girl Ellen in the Ursuline Academy in Brown County, but found that water can be thicker than blood when accessibility became the chief consideration in her sister's family choosing the Mercy Sisters' school in Charleston over the Ursuline academy in rural Ohio.

In 1853 Ellen's younger sister Catherine startled her by expressing her intention of joining the Baltimore Carmel. The stay-at-home sibling who had effectively taken on the responsibility of caring for their parents had finally sought her own path for the spiritual vocation she had long harbored. Two obstacles stood in her way: the Carmel had the maximum twelve nuns that their rule allowed, and her family lacked the means to provide an appropriate dowry. Once again Patrick saved the day for a sibling but only after occasioning some extreme frustration in his sister. Catherine, hearing nothing from her brother, after having sought his aid in securing entry into the Carmelites, attributed Patrick's inaction to his congenital procrastination. In reality, her brother, unbeknownst to Catherine, had persuaded the superior of the Baltimore Carmel to admit his sister. In lieu of a dowry, Patrick had agreed to pay a substantial interest rate semiannually for a loan to be redeemed within a relatively short period.[13]

Catherine, while overjoyed with the unexpected acceptance she finally heard about in December, could not abandon her parents until her younger sisters returned from the Mercy Sisters' school in Charleston in July to relieve her. She made the mistake of asking her brother to respond in her behalf, explaining her inability to take up the offer until sometime late in the summer of 1854. May came and Catherine had heard nothing from Baltimore. Finally in June she awkwardly wrote the mother superior to inquire whether her offer still stood and to assure her of her continuing desire to join them as early as that summer. Delay, however, begot delay. A year and a half passed before Catherine received a second offer from the Baltimore Carmel. This time she herself accepted the invitation and made the difficult arrangements of leaving the homestead she had been responsible for managing for so long. In the spring Patrick accompanied his twenty-seven-year-old sister to Baltimore. She brought with her a token dowry of sixteen dollars, but her brother's loan arrangement with Mother Superior Teresa had already ensured an appropriate level of revenue that the community could expect to receive with Catherine's entrance.[14] In light of the extraordinarily protracted process, the community waived the usual postulancy period. Catherine immediately donned the novice's habit of the order. Less than a year later, on the Feast of the Annunciation, March 25, 1857, she was professed as a choir member of the Baltimore Carmel, with the given name of Antonia of the Purification.

Navigating the perilous economic waters of the late antebellum period was a challenge for all the Lynches. As Catherine Lynch confessed to her brother, Patrick, "the great object of our family at present is money." That need impelled Conlaw Peter to recall his fifteen-year-old son, Hugh, from school in Charleston to secure his income as a clerk for a local merchant. For the Lynches, money, or its prospect, affected not only schooling but virtually everything, including courtship. Catherine's remark about "the great object of our family" was in reference to James Lynch's pursuit of the daughter of a Charleston merchant.

It was, in fact, a perennial concern for the Lynches, one that peaked in 1857. In late August the New York Branch of the Ohio Life Insurance and Trust Company collapsed, setting off a chain of failures of thousands of banks and businesses that wreaked havoc with the economy across the country, its rippling effects reaching the South after it had devastated the financial and commercial infrastructure of the northeast. The "hard times" of the Panic of 1857, as it subsequently became known, persisted for two years, the very time when the younger Lynch males—James, Conlaw, Hugh—were all following their brother Francis into the business world. James, perhaps because of his precarious health, was a restless young man who abandoned his position as a clerk for the Cheraw Post Office because he found it too confining. In its stead James concocted various ventures—operating a sawmill, running a store on the Texas frontier—before he cut his entrepreneurial teeth, too cautiously in the eyes of Francis, as a merchant and speculator in cotton. Conlaw, at twenty, clerked for a merchant, as did his younger sibling, Hugh, in whom his nun sister, Ellen, had not yet given up hope of nurturing a religious vocation.

Poor health continued to stalk the younger siblings. Conlaw and Anna both showed disturbing symptoms of consumption, as tuberculosis was then called. Conlaw by the beginning of 1856 had become so enfeebled that Patrick took his brother to a spa in Orange Springs, Florida, with the hope that the milder winter climate and the greater opportunity for exercise would improve his health, if not restore it. It proved to be an unusually wet winter in central Florida, which Conlaw experienced as a kind of drop-by-drop poisoning. Neither body nor soul seemed to benefit from the semitropical venue. After two months, Conlaw had had enough. Patrick, along with John, returned to Florida to escort him home to Cheraw, where his doctor brother took charge of his care, relying mainly on massages of several hours a day. "I feel quite confident now," Baptista wrote Patrick in late April, "that he will soon be much better, & that home nursing will quite restore him, as it did Brothers John & James." That plus the prayers and communions she had been steadily offering for his recovery.[15] Despite John's efforts and Baptista's prayers, Conlaw died two weeks later of tuberculosis. He was twenty-six.

The Lynches, proud of their distinguished Irish past, understandably had high social aspirations in South Carolina, despite being relative newcomers and Catholics. The scarcity of Catholics in Cheraw made certain that their social network there would not be confined by religion. Statewide their social network consisted primarily of non-Irish Catholics. The schooling of the Lynch daughters in Charleston, first with the Ursulines, then with the Sisters of Mercy, provided a venue for the Lynches, through their daughters, to form friendships and eventually alliances with their Catholic peers, who in fact were mostly converts, especially from the Episcopal Church: the Pinckneys, Bellingers, Blaines, Spanns, Rices, and so on. Mary, Francis, James, and Julie all married within this circle. The exception was Hugh Lynch, the only one to have an endogamous wedding. When he announced his engagement to Cornelia Reilly, the daughter of a ne'er-do-well father and a mother whose legitimacy of birth was in question, he occasioned bitter opposition within his extended family. Eliza Macnamara Lynch, with her privileged background, found such a proposed alliance threatening the Lynches' social and moral standing in the community (one suspects that Eliza felt she had already taken a step downward in marrying a Lynch). Ellen Neison Lynch asked her first-born to assay the rumors and determine if it was all smoke. Patrick finally satisfied his mother's concerns, and the wedding took place in July 1857 at St. Peter's Church in Columbia. All the Lynches, with the possible exception of Eliza, in time came to esteem Cornelia highly, no matter her dubious lineage.

Two other weddings soon followed: James's and Julie's to offspring of one of South Carolina's first families: Eustice Bellinger Pinckney and his sister, Mary Augustus, of Walterboro. The Lynches' genteel poverty put them in no position to stage an elaborate wedding. Eleanor Lynch had to ask her bishop son for fifty dollars to buy a suitable going-away dress for Julie. Unsurprisingly, they made her wedding a private affair, despite her fiancé's social status, and had it take place a week before James married Mary Augustus Pinckney in an all-frills ceremony, no doubt to mitigate the contrast between the two. Nonetheless, the back-to-back weddings were a double coup for the Lynches' social aspirations.

"After the usual salute of the Big Gun . . . and the hoisting of the Flag of the Stars and Stripes," Francis reported to his brother Patrick about Cheraw's celebration of the Fourth of July in 1850, "all was quiet as a summer day until about 10 o'clock [when the] . . . procession was formed at the City Hall [and] . . . marched to the Baptist Meeting House and heard a very good though somewhat nullifying oration from Mr. Prince[.] After which all was again so quiet that it almost seemed two Sundays had come within a week[.] A faint display of Fireworks came off after night but was rather a failure."[16]

This lethargic observance of the Fourth, normally the biggest patriotic celebration of the year, reflected just how widespread was the Deep South's dismay over the compromise struck by Congress earlier that year over the territory acquired from Mexico in the late war. Despite growing signs to the contrary, many Southerners still feared that the antislavery forces in Congress would prevail in making the Wilmot Proviso, which forbade any of the territory to become open to slavery, the law of the land. The "nullifying oration" Francis referred to was an appeal to the state legislators of South Carolina and elsewhere in the South to invoke their states' right to nullify national laws, such as the anticipated proviso, which they judged to be unconstitutional. Beyond that radical step lay the ultimate one of secession.

The Compromise of 1850 set in motion a polarization of North and South that intensified four years later with the Kansas-Nebraska Act, leading to civil war in Kansas and culminating with the *Dred Scott* decision at the close of 1857. That Supreme Court opinion seemed to shocked Northerners to open the entire country to the legal spread of slavery. It revitalized the abolitionist movement, which in turn convinced Southerners all the more of a Northern conspiracy to destroy their constitutionally protected peculiar institution. None of these ominous events found their way into the correspondence of the Lynches. Yet one can see their effects at work upon even this nonpolitical family, if only by the cultural contrasts the Lynches increasingly drew between themselves as Southerners and "Yankees," an ominous indication of the South's rising antipathy toward the North.

1858

"The honor and dignity you have received"

Some individuals seem so inextricably bound to a particular place that it is impossible to imagine them apart from it. John McCaffrey (1806–1881), from all indications, was one of them. With the exception of a year in Baltimore, he lived his entire life in the foothills of the Blue Ridge range in Emmitsburg, Maryland, by far the most of it on the foothill that students and alumni of Mount St. Mary's fondly called "the Mountain." That rolling terrain was his sea anchor, providing security and identity. That bonding between person and place, one suspects, was the reason that John McCaffrey twice declined Rome's appointment as the third bishop of Charleston, the second time despite the "clear wish" of Pope Pius IX that he submit. That deeply ingrained sense of those hills as home may best account for the "repugnance" he felt about the prospect of heading up a diocese six hundred miles removed.[1] Ultimately Rome let him remain in his native hills.[2] In December 1857 the Congregation of the Propagation of the Faith issued a decree naming Patrick Lynch bishop of the diocese that he had already been governing for the past three years. Greater Charleston was delighted with the choice. In a testament to the bishop-elect's high civic standing, the Chamber of Commerce invited him to their annual banquet, where they toasted him as "The scholar, the gentleman, the American Bishop." In this appointment, the toaster proclaimed: "we are all Catholic."[3]

Catherine, from her convent in Baltimore, joked to her brother Patrick that perhaps her sister nuns would pressure the bishop-elect into establishing a Carmelite monastery in Charleston. "Stranger things have happened," she noted. When she wrote, the wheels were already in motion for a new foundation of a woman's religious community in the diocese. That addition, however, involved not the Carmelites but the Ursulines. The previous year Baptista Lynch had half-jokingly told her brother that, should he become the bishop of Charleston, she and the Ursulines would return to his see city. Subsequent events quickly demonstrated how earnest she had been in anticipating their future.

Indeed, convinced that the Holy Spirit was inspiring her to bring about the restoration of the Ursulines to Charleston, Baptista deftly facilitated developments toward this end, which the naming of her brother as bishop and the extraordinary request of his dying predecessor were serendipitously making possible.

Even before his consecration as bishop, Patrick Lynch had invited the Ursulines of Brown County to establish a new foundation in the diocese. According to the *Annals of the Ursuline Community*, Bishop Reynolds, shortly before his death, had made Patrick Lynch promise that, if he succeeded Reynolds, he would bring the Ursulines back into the diocese. Whatever the cause for the Ursulines' departure a decade earlier, the dying bishop had clearly regretted it. Once having received the appointment, Lynch wasted no time in carrying out the late bishop's request.[4] Initially the new convent and academy were to be located in the village of Edgefield in upcountry South Carolina, fifty miles southwest of Columbia, where the diocese had begun under Bishop Reynolds, to construct facilities for a girls' academy. Baptista, appointed superior of the new community, seemed happy enough about heading an academy and convent in Edgefield, as rural a setting as the one she was leaving in Brown County. Then she learned that they would be taking over the academy that the Mercy Sisters had been conducting in Columbia, the state capital. The bishop transferred the Mercy Sisters to Charleston to operate the boys' orphanage that the diocese was opening there.[5] The displaced sisters, who had learned of the changes several months after the Ursulines knew of them, resented what they considered to be high-handed nepotism on the bishop's part, a community sentiment that would vex relations among bishop, Mercies, and Ursulines in the ensuing years.

On August 26, 1858, Patrick Lynch himself led a group of six Ursulines (Baptista, four professed nuns—all from the Charleston and/or Cincinnati communities—and one novice) on their journey from Brown County to Columbia. The trip by coach and steamer took six days, with stops at Cincinnati and Baltimore. In the latter city they were able to stay at the Carmelite monastery, where the three Lynches—Antonia, Baptista, and Patrick—had a reunion. Once in Columbia, Baptista immediately set out to make the academy they were taking over worthy of the Ursuline tradition. This was to be an academy that educated the daughters of the elite, Catholic and not. To make it so, the new mother superior set for herself an ambitious program of aggressive recruiting of both students and postulants. In student recruitment the daughters of upper-class Protestants were especially sought, with conversion and a subsequent religious vocation always in sight. As for attracting postulants, Baptista had a twofold strategy for the two categories of potential religious she needed to bring into the community: the choir and lay sisters. For the candidates to be

choir sisters, she looked to friends and relatives, as well as students and alumnae
of the various academies taught by religious women, especially the Sisters of
Mercy school in Charleston (despite fears that she would be accused of poaching
upon, if not betraying, her own former teachers and coreligionists there). For the
candidates to be lay sisters, her recruiting was much less direct, relying instead
on bishops and priests to secure appropriate individuals, often Irish immigrant
women or their daughters.

The persistent economic recession compounded the challenge of securing all
the necessities for conducting the Ursuline Academy in Columbia as Baptista
envisioned it. She immediately became dependent on Patrick's supplying the
financial assistance for keeping in check their mounting bills, despite efforts
to economize by buying food and coal wholesale. The continuing shortage of
money in the depressed economy affected all the family. John Lynch's finances
were so stretched that he contemplated selling some of his slaves in a desperate
attempt to raise cash. Peter Conlaw's as well as Francis's debts to the bank were
such that they could draw no further credit. In the midst of this financial crisis,
Patrick, while in Baltimore on business, learned that his nephew Robert was

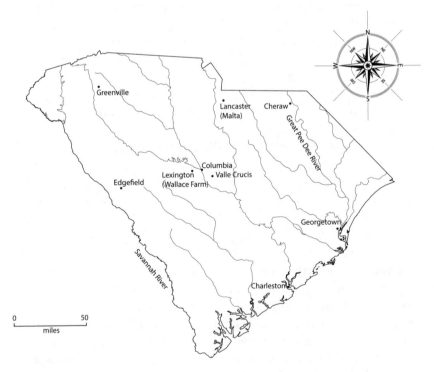

Map of eastern South Carolina, depicting area between North Carolina and
Georgia borders.

seriously sick at the nearby minor seminary.[6] *After a hasty trip to the college confirmed his nephew's poor physical condition, the bishop wired his brother John, who quickly came to bring his son back to Columbia.*

For the two youngest male Lynches of the second generation, 1858 proved to be one of scant blessings. Hugh's attempts to present himself as a man of substance in order to gain his economic footing were undone by what seems to be a drunken spree that embarrassed and angered his siblings, and left his career prospects looking bleak. Bernard, through no fault of his own, was forced to give up his clerking and take to his bed in his parents' home. With the symptoms of consumption all too evident, Bernard continued to decline, slowly but undeniably, all under the helpless watch of his twin sister, Anna.

JOHN LYNCH, CHERAW, TO PATRICK LYNCH, JANUARY 5TH[7]

Dear Brother,

Yours of 1st came to hand in due time. We are obliged to you for the New Years gift, to the little stranger (Louisa) and for your kind wishes. The baby was baptized last Sunday. Miss Mary Montague[8] & Master Jno Bauskett[9] sponsors. It was Eliza's first Sunday out, herself & child are doing first rate. We recd a letter from Robt soon after you left, he was quite well. The other day we recd an envelope with some pictures for the children from him.

I was called to Cheraw last week to a court of reference in which I was concerned. Father, mother & all the family are quite well except Bernard & Anna. Anna looks pretty well, but I am afraid she is induced to *nurse* her sickness from too much sympathy. Bernard is something in the same way, father is uneasy about him; he has promised to come over and remain under my care for a month or so if I can get him employment during the time. As yet I have been unsuccessful but will continue trying.

While in Cheraw I tried very hard to raise some money, but entirely failed. I even offered to sell a negro (from which offer I am to hear yet) but from all appearances there was not a thousand dollars in the district outside of the Banks. . . .

I am besides offering my house, offering to sell a negro woman about twenty one years of age very likely, & without children, a good cook washer and ironer. I offer her for one thousand for the purpose of meeting my first installment on my house which falls due 14th this month. I don't wish to lose the advantage I have gained so far, by letting my first note be protested. If in all my efforts I should fail is there no one of your acquaintance from whom I could borrow for a while $6000 say till I could force a sale of my house, or if it comes to the pinch I can sacrifice a negro. I will enclose you a rough statement showing you about how I stand with the world, you will see from it what is my prospect for meeting a lone [*sic*].

Lieber[10] has not yet returned from New York.

Pray for your affectionate brother,

John

␥

Baptista Lynch, Ursuline Convent BC, to Patrick Lynch, February 27th[11]

My dearest Brother,

I leave it to others, to congratulate you on the honor & dignity you have received if any I will bless God for having extended your sphere of usefulness, & placed you in a position where you may effect the good which hitherto you could only desire, without possessing the authority of executing it.

How is your cold & cough? I am very anxious about it, for none of us have stentorian lungs, & I am afraid you will not resort to effectual remedies—let me beg of you my dearest Brother, not to delay having the uvula of your palate cut, if necessary—you know, you recommended it for me, & to it, under God's goodness, I am indebted for the prolongation of my life—If such a remedy be not necessary for you, perhaps to wash your throat in a weak solution of nitrate of silver, would remove whatever irritates it, & produces the cough—Do my dear Brother endeavor to get rid of it, as soon as you can.

. . . I am very happy to hear that our dear Parents & family are all well (TG) What a subject of grateful joy your consecration must be to our dear Mother & Father—to have you for their Bishop—to see you chosen for the diocese, in which we have all been reared, with those clergymen sustaining you, who have known us from childhood. . . . I thank God for having chosen you for the Charleston diocese, it is the only one I wish to *see* you Bishop of—if Bishop at all & now we need no longer fear your being sent to any of those out of the way places—. And so "little Ellen Spann" my favorite niece is with you at the good Sisters. I am very glad of it—I will enclose a note to her—I suppose that Caroline & Judge Rice have returned to Charleston.[12] I hope they are quite well—remember me kindly to them please—Has Louise McNamara returned?[13] (Feb 24th) I have just received a letter from dear Sr Ambrose who answers the above questions, & tells me much that really gratifies me—I wonder if we could count upon Louisa, for our Noviciate? You see I am looking to number one—it seems to me I have heard something of her having a latent vocation for our Order & as the Irishman said "I'll take her & the *Nagers* too."[14]

. . . I am truly glad to hear that you are going to make your retreat in St. Augustine, where the mildness of the climate will agree so well with you—You

Portrait of Patrick N. Lynch in episcopal robes. Courtesy of the Roman Catholic Diocese of Charleston Archives.

must not attempt to preach while there, but pray as much as you like & take care of your health—& I will pray with & for you, with all my heart—I think it is providential for us, that you are going there; because Mother Superior told me she thought it likely we could get some candidates for our Noviciate there, since the pastor of that place wrote to her some time ago, saying that there were some young ladies desirous of becoming Ursulines. So you can use your influence AMDG.[15] It would however cost those hot-blooded Spanish dames something to conform to our Rules—but all things are possible with God's grace—I

am very glad to hear my dear Brother that the house in Edgefield[16] is so small
& indifferent a one—I was afraid [if] it was such a nice one, that you would
think it unnecessary for us to build a convent; which I so much desire for the
reasons I have before mentioned—& Edgefield I am sure answers our purpose
quite as well as Father's [illegible blot] did, when very different to what it now is.
Our good Mother & S^rs at first used it for their convent and when we build, it
can be refitted for the chaplain's, or if you prefer the "Bishops house" & serve too
for those friends to whom we may with your approbation—show hospitality—
such as the parents of some of the pupils, . . . the Pinckneys & Rices—& more
than all our dear Parents when they come to see us—

What a happiness to them it will be, to see us engaged in so good a work for
the propagation, & preservation of our Holy Faith to many— . . .

I understand very well my dearest Brother what you felt when the time
came to say *yes* or no—When things come to a point, it is not easy to assume
a responsibility without a *positive* certainty that it is for the best; & in those
instances when all seems to devolve on ourselves, we feel as Father Faber[17] says
"that no man is sufficient for himself" This refers to many things I think, as
well as offices &c, but I always throw myself headlong in to the ocean of God's
mercy, & depend on its powerful waves to buoy me up—I suppose you have
written to Sr. Antonia & will have the fervent prayers of her good Mothers &
Sisters—so that with those of the good Sisters of Mercy, & all our friends especially those of our dear Parents I trust that every blessing & grace you need for
your office, may be fully bestowed at the time of your Consecration—

I hope [you] will write to me soon after your Consecration. Let me know all
the particulars—if our dear parents were present—& how many of the family
—who officiated &c . .

Pray for your own sister Ellen, Sr. Baptista

ᕦ

BAPTISTA LYNCH, URSULINE CONVENT—BC, TO SR. AMBROSE,
MARCH 1ST[18]

My very dear Friend and Sister,

I am very much obliged to you, for your truly gratifying & interesting letter, & your kindness in giving me an account of the different members of *our
family.* We have reason to be truly grateful to Almighty God, for His many
blessings to us—

I cannot help feeling anxious about the health of my good Brother, Bernard,
& Anna—I think Anna, like myself will with care, grow stronger & stronger
but gentlemen can not endure what we can in the way of sickness, & I especially
dislike a cough in our family—

I am glad that Bernard has placed himself under brother Johns care, for he has hitherto proved skillful in such cases— . . .

I am very glad my dear Sister that you write to Anna, it will stimulate her in the path of duty, & we both know what up hill work it is, to live so exclusively apart from Catholic Society, & deprived of the comfort & aids of our holy Religion— . . . You must get Augusta to bring James to see you—I think you will like him very much—(Tho' he never forgave me for being a Religious) I am told he is a remarkably fine looking man—but he promised to be a little—"a la Lucius Northrop"[19] in his manner—I cannot say however what changes time has wrought in him—when I left home, he was only about twenty years of age, extremely delicate, suffering with coughs &c—& very tall & slight in figure— quite a contrast to what he is now I believe.

Our family is so much pleased with Augusta, that I could not be otherwise *especially if she is anything like her sister Maria*—& I assure you I do not think your description of Eustace at all too partial— . . . Were you not amazed at good Dr Bellingers[20] marriage—Has Eleanor done well ? I heard she wished to become a Religious—When you see Caroline Rice please give her my aff love & compliments to the Judge—I am happy to hear he is better.

And after all my dear Sister, you have *my favorite niece Ellen* with you—you see our penchant for "the institution of the good Sisters of Mercy," which began when her mother was a pupil under the first Superioress, Miss Julia Doty, still continues—for I wrote to Sister Mary, to send Ellen to our Convent as I had always looked forward with pleasure to teaching her, but she preferred sending her to Charleston. She thinks I am too far away & among strangers—I hope she will prove a docile & good child (for she was a *very mischievous* one when I knew her).

Your very affectionate Sr in J C^t,
Sr. M Baptista

ॐ

Antonia Lynch, Mount Carmel, Baltimore, to Patrick Lynch,
6th March[21]

My very dear Brother,

The Archbishop[22] very kindly offered to take care of this Mitre which Rev. Mother has with so much affection . . . sent you. I don't think I took more interest in it than she did every spare moment that she could steal from her duties she would spend working on your Mitre and so often she would make a fervent aspiration for your future welfare. Indeed all the Community have shown so much pleasure at the fact of your having a Mitre worked in the Convent that it is with greater pleasure that Rev. Mother now offers it to you We were only two weeks working on it. On last Tuesday evening the Arch-Bishop very kindly wrote me a letter saying that he would leave on Friday. Then Rev. Mother gave me all the assistance she could . . . Rev Mother *the six novices* including myself with the *Sacristan* S[r] Joseph, all busy at work upon it. . . . The outSisters have also with so much cheerfulness this cold weather gone out at all times to buy the materials.[23] When I told them I would ask you to say beads for them they were so delighted. But we will all expect much of that from you for all the Community pray so much for you, and on your Consecration Day, they are also going to offer their Communion for you perhaps they will pray you into giving us a Foundation. *Stranger* things have happened. I received a letter from Anna last week and was glad to learn that so many of the family would be present at your Consecration, I am in hopes that Mother will accompany Father at that time at all events I guess she will soon make an opportunity of seeing some of our Carmelite work when you go up to give Confirmation. It gave me so much happiness when I would see Rev Mother working so intently, even so late last night at twelve oclock that we might have it done in time for the Arch-Bishop today. I am sure when she showed so much interest, a great grace must accompany this Mitre for I think she is a great favorite of Heaven. She is so self-sacrificing. She often puts one in mind of our own dear Mother she is so kind to me. She sends you her *wish* that your *Crown* in *heaven* may have as many *spangles* as your Mitre is now covered with, and were the Community able to afford it, with *as great pleasure* would she have sent you a suit of Vestments. . . .

Pray for us all,
Antonia of the Purification, D. Carm. [Discalced Carmelite]

Bernard Lynch, Columbia SC, to Patrick Lynch, April 5th[24]

Dear Brother,

As I have the presumption to entertain the idea of making application for the position of Superintendent of the Gas works in this place, if you can get for me a little work from which I can derive some information on the subject I will be obliged to you

I have very little idea I can get the situation but if I should chance to be so fortunate of course I would like to be pretty well posted as I would have to enter on the duties immediately.

Pray for your aff bro,
Bernard Lynch

Baptista Lynch, Ursuline Convent B.C., to Patrick Lynch,
April 27th[25]

... It has occurred to me my dear Brother that if we could possibly go down
in the latter part of July, or in August while the exercises of the Academy are
suspended, & the greater part of the children at home it would be advisable, &
more satisfactory both to our good Mother Superior & ourselves than to delay
until the return of the children &c—We would be glad too to have a month to
prepare before opening our school, & I think the sooner now that we begin our
work, the better—. What do you think?

It seems to me also that if you could either after the Council[26] come &
arrange matters satisfactorily—or at least as soon as you know the decision of
the Springfield community,[27] which I suppose when the Bishop returns will be
given, we could then see our way more clearly, & make the necessary preparation, which we will want some time for—then at the time of our going down
you could send some one to take care of our baggage, which is all that will be
necessary—

But should you delay coming until you intend us to return with you (which
may be the best) you will be detained here at least a week for we can do nothing
decisive until you come.

I never intend to disguise myself as a secular again when traveling, so I
think I will assume the costume of the Sisters of Mercy of Charleston, which is
so universally known & respected throughout the U. States.

What do you think of it—I will reserve until I see you my dearest Brother
all that I would say of your consecration.—Good Archbishop Hughes' valuable
gift—the amiability & kindness of the clergy of the diocese—of Venerable Father O'Neill—of good Bishop Barry &c &c all of which is truly gratifying—I am
sorry you did not extend your invitation to the far west, as I perceive you have
given umbrage—in a certain quarter by this omission—It is always the way, as
at weddings &c somebody gets offended—but I need not assure you that I pray
for you now if possible more than ever, for I know that your responsibility is
greater, & moreover I see that no sooner is any one clothed with an imaginary
dignity, than they become targets for others ...

John Lynch, Columbia, to Patrick Lynch, May 18th[28]

I will trouble you only with a few lines, knowing you must be very busily
engaged, but I think you may be of service in accomplishing what I think would
afford both yourself & myself pleasure, viz. the procuring an employment for

Bernard here which will not be fatiguing, but will be respectable, the pay corresponding to the work. (light)—$500—a year, it is a situation at the state house in the gift of Genl Jones[29] now filled by a son of Dr. Lee of Camden, it will be vacant so the Genl told me on the 1st of next month, but he had several applications ahead from the Citadel in Charleston (beneficiaries I believe) towards whom he feels a little leaning, but from what little I have said to him and his knowledge of Bernard, I do not think it would take a great deal of persuasion for him to give B. the place. I have been thinking if you will not be up before the time, if you would write to him, mentioning I had intimated such a thing to you, and expressing a wish on the subject, he would not hesitate a moment. I have consulted Father & Mother & the family. They are anxious that B. should remain where he is and take the situation, on account of his health, for my part I believe it would be better for him, than remaining idle as he is, write me if you have time, and let me know your views, and what you have done (if any thing)—Send our love to Louisa & Ellen & remember us to our friends—Eliza has been quite sick since Louisa left, but is getting much better, and I think all things are turning out for the best. . . .

Tell us about Robert, how he looks, his health, spirits, &c &c.

⚓

Anna Lynch, Cheraw, to Patrick Lynch, May 21st[30]

My dear Brother,

Presuming that you have returned from the North, I will write you a few lines, to let you know how we all are. As it is after night-prayers, I cannot do more, Father & the family are quite well but Mother seems quite sick today. Suffering from severe headache & sick stomach & has had chills. Her symptoms are so similar to those she had when so ill with congestive chills, some years ago, that I am afraid she is going to have an attack of the same kind, but as I am naturally disposed to look at the dark side of the clouds, I sincerely hope I will be mistaken. She took cold last night & was complaining a little all day with soreness in her bones but did not give up until tonight. Tell Ellen we heard from her mother two or three days ago & all were well. Brother Francis, Sister Henrietta & family are well too, Annie was a little sick last week, but has recovered. The [illegible] was up here to-night & said he would return early in the morning and if mother was no better, send for Brother John. I did not mention to him or Father either that I intended writing to you & they may think I am causing you unnecessary uneasiness.— . . .

Pray for your affect. Sister,
Anna

SATURDAY MORNG 22D 1858

Rt Revd [Right Reverend] & Dear Bro.

Mother suffers much yet, having had headache continuous & little sleep. This morning she will take an emetic, and if not very much relieved will send for Doct Mallory. I am sanguine she will be better, because disposed to vomit and I think the headache is from sympathy.

I have sent a renewal note for 12000$ to Thos [Thomas] R Waring Cash Bk of State, please call them & endorse it on the 24th; the date of maturity for my note now in Bk. I wd have enclosed it to you, but was uncertain of your return to the city in time. . . .

Francis

ANNA LYNCH, CHERAW, TO PATRICK LYNCH, MAY 23RD[31]

I am happy to inform you that mother is much better to-night & escaped her chill today. She was quite sick all day yesterday—we called in Doctor Malloy, who gave her a good deal of medicine & said it was a billious attack. She is so much better this evening that she speaks of getting up to-morrow, but I don't think that would be prudent. . . .

JULIA LYNCH PINCKNEY, WALTERBORO, TO PATRICK LYNCH, MAY 27TH[32]

Dearest brother,

You must excuse this very short letter as I have not time to write a longer one & this is principally on business. It is to ask you to send up a priest if there is one to spare; if not, to come yourself, as soon as possible. Eustace has a very severe attack of fever which he has had off and on for the last three weeks but this last few days it has got much worse. Don't know if there is any thing serious yet but there is no knowing when a change may take place for the worse & it is always best to be on the surer side. Do comply with *my request as soon as possible* & Pray for your ever affectionate Sister, Julia

☙

My Dear Brother,

I have concluded to take the liberty to ask you (if possible for you to do so) to do a favor for me. I am sorry to have to trouble you with it, but the nature of the case must be my apology for doing so. Mr. Reidy promised last summer when he was over here to give me this fall $1000 towards a mark for me to commence business with: which amt I expect to get when I go over to Columbia —but as I did not want to go empty handed I made arrangement (as I thought) to get $1000 from the Bank at 90 d/a[y]s time. With Father & Bro Francis securities to be paid ½ at the time it was due & renew the balance & pay the whole at second payment but this week the note was presented and did not pass the Bank which has rather broken all my calculations up—as I had promised Cornelia before she left that I would take Isaac with me when I went over to Columbia—Now at the suggestion of Mother I write to ask you cannot you let me have $1000 at either 60 or 90 d/as time. If you possibly can. I will pay either the whole or half of it when it is due—as I wish & more to have it & for appearance sake than to use. If you can let me have it or get it for me the whole of them at home will take it as a great favor and to me it will amount to treble the amt in the end. Will you please be so kind as to write by tomorrow's mail. So that I can get your letter on Friday morning whether I can get it or not and *if I can* please send me the amount by as soon a mail as you can. The reason why I mention Fridays morning mail is that if I can not get it and have to [go] on a *begging expedition* to Columbia—the sooner I go over will be the better and if I can't get it I will leave on Friday morning for Columbia. But if I can I would defer my trip until sometime the week after but the sooner I can go over I would like it as Cornelia is getting rather impatient for me to go over. If you can send me the amt you can send me either a check—certificate of Deposit on the amt in SC Bank Bills and if you can't spare it only for a short time I will take it and not use it at all, but if possible for me to do so I want to have that much with me when I go to Columbia.

All the Family at home are quite well and were half way looking for you up last night. Mrs. Blain[34] & Daughter arrived all safe. . . .

Pray for your aff. Brother,

Hugh P. Lynch

❧

Baptista Lynch, Ursuline Convent, Columbia SC, to Patrick Lynch, Sept 12th[35]

Mr dearest Brother—excuse me—
Rt Rev Father in God—

I thank you very much for your kindness in writing & sending our prospectus which we will publish as you advise, tho I fear it will cost a "pretty penny" You must be very much pressed by duty & anxious for the sick—I need scarcely say we pray constantly for *yourself* the clergy, the Sisters & people, sincerely hoping that the blessed sickness may soon cease. Besides our private prayers we say in choir the "Stella coeli"[36] in which we have great faith—

Our sisters in general are well T.G. & often express their gratitude for the blessings we enjoy—

Mother arrived on the Thursday evening & came to see me about 8 oclock at night—She spent Friday with me, & I expect her again today after Mass—I think her very much changed in appearance, but the more I see her—the more natural she appears—(the doorbell rings)

(Monday) I wish you could come up before she leaves for Cheraw, which she intends doing about Friday I think. Don't you think you might manage to do so?—I have reced a letter from Miss Eliza Riordan of Lexington Ky, telling me that her mother has at length consented to let her come to our convent, & asks a prospectus—her guardian is Maj Breckinridge,[37] vice-President of U.S. —I will send a prospectus but I suppose should she come the Brown County nuns would never forgive me for depriving them of a pupil. We recd Ellen Spann as our first Boarder but for our convenience she is still at Johns with Mother where all are well (TG) except for Robert & our dear Bernard whose cough is troublesome—we have one boarder in the house—Rose Gallagher whose parents urged so pressingly that we would take her from a sickly home that I did not like to refuse, tho' I am not at all satisfied with their arrangements, which I will write to Mother Teresa about & explain when I see you— On Tuesday, we will receive three more the "Gaffneys" procured for us by Rev. J. J. O'Connell—so with the blessing of the Almighty we will get on by Sept.

We have had seven applicants for day scholars since you left & at our Sunday school yesterday had quite an interesting class.

Please my dearest Brother, give my respects to the Rev Clergy particularly to our friend & brother in JC—Rev Dr Corcoran, & good Father Sullivan, to whose prayers & sacrifices I commend our infant community—I will be glad to hear immediately from "our postulants" we are very much pleased with "Sister Rosa" alias Miss Reilly—Mother says Louisa Blain[38] will be a treasure. I have written to Revd Mother of Baltimore & asked about those she mentioned—I have been too busy to write as yet to any one else but got Srs Ursula & Augustine to do so—

Believe me Rt. Rev Father in God, with much esteem & regard,
Your truly grateful child,
Sr. M Baptista Sup—

෪

BAPTISTA LYNCH, URSULINE CONVENT, COLUMBIA, TO PATRICK LYNCH,
SEPT 18TH[39]

It is past bed time for us Saturday night, but I cannot go to sleep without saying a few words to you, which I would not have leisure to write tomorrow— We are all well TG, & doing well—Mother left today at 1½ oclock for Cheraw & Bernard with her—we were very sorry that you could not come—but there is a good time coming, & after all, it is such a blessing to me to be near enough to you as to get a letter in so short a time, that I would reproach myself with ingratitude if I murmured in the least.

Mother is quite well, as were all at our dear home yesterday—John's family too, as well as usual—Bernard has been poorly, but is better & will recreate at home for a fortnight or so—

Mother did not believe the reports about Julia—James has a daughter. Eliza was told today about Louisa, & cried almost as much as if she were not better— How are the S[rs]? It was reported here that Sr. Flavian was dead & several other sick—& that several of the orphans from this place, had died of yellow-fever. Is it true or not—?

I sincerely trust the fever will soon abate, & that the good Priests with you at their head, & the good Srs will preserve your strength in the midst of your labors, by every means possible—by wholesome & frequent nourishment. My dearest Brother, if you are not too busy, please ask about *our boxes,* we want our blankets these chilly nights, & would be glad to have other things in them too—

Monday Morning 20th I had not time my dearest Brother to finish or send my letter as I wished—Sr Ursula says you will be very much pleased with us *we are all so busy,* & you said you would [be] pleased when we were so—Sr. Augustine begs you will spare of blushes, *calling us Apostolic missionaries (!)* O I wish L Blain or E Condy would come to us—Mother says Louisa Blain is a treasure, so the sooner we get the treasure the better—

We have our two sets of instruction every Sunday, an interesting class of girls in the morning from 8 to 8¾—& in the evening the negroes from 4 to 5—What is Mary Brownfield[40] thinking of? I suppose the yellow fever engrosses every ones thought at present—I would be glad she thought of becoming a Nun, as she never intends getting married— . . .

Sr. Augustine wishes to write to Rosie but I told her not to venture, until we were certain—John got a letter from Anna yesterday, written before Mother & Bernard had left here. Father & all well quite well T G—James has a daughter & Julie a son.

I am very much pleased with my little pupils especially Ellen Spann. They will come to school today & Ellen will not return to Johns, but remain a boarder —Mr Bollin's oldest daughter will enter today also, & his second as a day boarder—$165. per Session—The bell is ringing persistently by the children coming to school, so I must stop tho I have *plenty to say as usual*—I think it was providential that you did not come up to Columbia when Mother was here, as by sleeping a night out of Charleston, I am told you would expose yourself to fever—We are happy to hear that Louisa is better, & hope all the good S^{rs} & Clergy are quite well—If our poor prayers will do them any good they have them. . . .

❦

FRANCIS LYNCH, CHERAW, TO PATRICK LYNCH, 21 SEPT[41]

Bro Hugh arrived home on Friday night, since when he has been confined to his room, I have not yet seen him. He was surely unfortunate, it is with sorrow I learn of his course. I think this the first accident of the kind that has occurred to him since opening business on his own account. It is a pity his wife did not accompany him, to the city, her influence perhaps would have restrained him—As a young merchant, mishaps of this kind have anything but an encouraging influence—I fear he has lost much in that way, as in others. A strict attention & promptness may restore confidence, if shaken—It will require good resolutions, which I sincerely hope he will have strength to keep, for the others.

❦

MARY LYNCH SPANN, WASHINGTON COUNTY [TEXAS], TO PATRICK LYNCH, SEPT 24[42]

My dearest Brother,

I am really ashamed when I remember the time that has passed without my having replied to your most welcome letter, but I will not offer you apologies. I know you do not require them. I was expecting your letter so long that I was prepared for it at any moment & you may be sure it did not require a second glance to recognize the hand-writing. I think you are determined that we shall value your letters very much and that is the reason why you are so precious with them. Mrs Rice & Emily were also delighted at receiving their letters at the same time—upon reflection my dear Brother I believe this is the first time I have written to you since your promotion to the See of Charleston, we are thinking & speaking of you so frequently that I can scarcely realize that my pen could have been silent, however you know well that no one could have felt more interest & pleasure than I did at the honors conferred on you & trust that you will be blessed with continued good health & all the other helps to enable you to perform well your important duties—I cannot tell you the delight with which we read in the last Miscellany of the arrival of the Ursulines in Columbia, the news is almost too good to be true—there must have been a general rejoicing throughout our family, & our dear Father & mother must really feel thankful & feel that they are now being rewarded for the sacrifices they have made. The Catholics throughout the Diocese will feel that they are under obligations to you for the re-establishment of such an institution as the Convent is known to be—I hope it will be appreciated & liberally patronized—I suppose Father & Mother have been over to welcome Sister Ellen & that all of the family will go by turns [;] the younger members of the family would really require an introduction for 10 or 11 years makes quite a difference in their appearance—brother John & Eliza must be delighted—I long to hear from Sister Ellen to know how she feels on her return & how she finds the different members of the family looking—I hope too that you both had the pleasure of seeing sister Catharine on your return & left her in good health—she could almost imagine that she was in the family circle when you & sister Ellen were both with her—My dear Brother, Mr Spann & I feel very thankful to you for your care & kindness to our Ellen. She seems to be so happy among her relations that I have never been able to perceive the least touch of home sickness & to have associated herself with all at home as if she had always lived with them, which of course is greatly owing to the affection shown towards her, it is a great qualification to us—from Sr Ellen's letter to me some time ago my dear Brother I conclude that you have both arranged that as soon as the School is opened Ellen will be placed at the Convent, which arrangement of course suits our wishes exactly. We are too happy to think that she will have the double advantage of being with her Aunty Ellen & at the Convent at the same time—it seems strange that what I have been wishing for, for so many years past, but saw no possibility of putting in practice, will now be effected so easily, quietly.

I hope, Father, Mother & all at home are well. I have not heard very recently, we regret to hear that the Fever is an epidemic in Charleston & trust that it will soon be decreasing—you must try my dear Brother and not expose yourself unnecessarily. I know you have already had the Yellow fever, but you might take some other sickness that would be just as bad—the Yellow fever is very bad in Galveston, as well as in N. Orleans. I think most of the cases prove fatal in

Galveston—we all feel anxious as the old Lady is there & her two oldest Grandsons
—the old Lady however never fears it & is an excellent nurse.

I suppose my dear Brother you have received a number of the "Texas Monthly
Magazine" edited by the old Lady. I heard that she had sent you a number—it
is certainly a great undertaking for a Lady of her age & for that reason her children were averse to her commencing but she is so energetic that she may succeed at least she seems determined to be—the clergy are opposed to her French
translations but I suppose she thinks as she has taken the trouble to translate
them it is a pity that the world should not have the benefit of them—We were
favored last week with a visit from our first Pastor who has just returned from
France with three nephews, from 13 to 21 years of age. On reaching Galveston
he found the Yellow fever & knowing how dangerous it would be for them,
brought them up here & begged the favor as to board them until after the sickly
season would be over. He left a few days ago, so you may imagine what an interesting family we have, as they don't speak a word of English, it puts Mr Spann
& myself to our trumps to make out a French sentence we have both become
so rusty in what we formerly knew a little of—but in charity to them we are
obliged to try to speak some—We still have Father Gounard for our Pastor,
he is a model of piety . . . Our little congregation is very fortunate in having two
Clergymen stationed with us this summer. One was recently ordained and the
Bishop allowed him to remain some months with Father Gounard that he might
learn more of the language and the ways of the people before going on the
Mission. . . . We all regretted much to hear of R. Macnamara's state of health.[43]
It must be a great consolation to his sisters to see him in such a good frame of
mind; it is a great trial to Eliza to see him suffering so long. I hope Louisa is
quite well & I have no doubt is very happy; she must have given you all as well
as ourselves quite a surprise by joining the Sisters—I had the pleasure of a letter
from Julia not very long since. I think she bids fair to be a better correspondent
than formerly altho' she has followed my worldly example I trust she will do
well. I think our old home place must have quite a comfortable appearance
with so many of our Brothers settled around Father & Mother, all thriving. I
hope living happily together. I suppose my dear Brother you can run up home
more frequently than formerly as it takes so short a time to make the journey
& probably you will have to visit Columbia often, in order to see the new Convent well under way. I shall feel very anxious for its success but I think the
Community ought to try to have a good stock of patience to begin with, as it so
often takes time before a good Institution is well patronized. I have written you
a pretty long letter my dear Brother—without telling you anything of our own
little family—in the first place we are all blessed with good health. Mr Spann
looks very much as in old times & altho on his last birthday he saw 50 years,

every one says they never would suppose that he was more than 40, he is both spiritually & corporally as far as I can judge in good health—we often think that everything would go well if we only had a little more of this world's goods but the crop this year is turning out better than it ever did before—Conlaw & Cara are learning well & seem to give great satisfaction to Father Gounard. They are often speaking of you. Conlaw remembers you perfectly. Cara speaks of you as her Uncle Bishop—little Catharine is a second edition of Ellen only where Ellen used to be bad Catharine is good. So you may imagine that she is something of a little pet. Judge Rice's health continues about the same. I cannot see any improvement. . . .

Your affectionate Sister,
Mary

Baptista Lynch, Ursuline Convent, Columbia S. Carolina, to Patrick Lynch, Sept 29th[44]

We were very agreeably surprised this morning on receiving your welcome letter, to learn that we might expect the pleasure of seeing you so soon, but this evening, since the arrival of the dispatch, we were disappointed, & a little anxious lest illness has detained you—I trust you have not overexerted yourself, or brought on indisposition by going up to Walterboro.—I hope also that it is not illness among the clergy or Religious which has prevented your coming—but I am not sorry that you are spared your trip to Norfolk at this sickly season—it is too much for you just now—Revd J. J. O Connell has been unable to say Mass for us for the past week, but I believe he is up again today—

We are happy to hear that Julia is better—when Mother passed thro on Sunday she spent the day with us—I cheered her up the best I could & she promised herself the gratification of meeting you in Charleston—She intends remaining until Julie can return to Cheraw with her—John & family are well, & all at home are as usual.

. . . —With your permission Right Revd Father we will accept Miss Payne of whom Bishop O Connor[45] writes, & will answer him to that effect—enclosed you will find a copy of a letter which you will please comment—approve or annul as you think best—Should you telegraph & say "yes" I will send it, or "No" & I will not send it—But do not telegraph for that specially—Our school is progressing & please God we will get on very well. . . .

BAPTISTA LYNCH, URSULINE CONVENT, COLUMBIA SC, TO PATRICK LYNCH, OCT 26[46]

I am somewhat disappointed today at not hearing of your safe arrival in Charleston & that you are quite well—please write & let me knew if your rest has entirely relieved you of your indisposition.

I sincerely trust you are free from any danger of contracting fever or illness of any kind—We are all quite well TG exception Sister Ursula. I am glad for her sake especially that next Monday, we begin to keep school only until two o'clock—She asked me to remind you of those two Sisters or rather Candidates you spoke of for Laysisters, especially the one who would be so clever & saving in marketing, Housekeeping &c—as it would be better perhaps to have another than to have to pay servants here—which will not do if we can avoid it—Sister Agnes (Miss Coffey) has been quite indisposed since you left but is well as ever again— . . .

Bernard called to see me this evening for the first time since you left; he is better & scarcely coughs at all—he recd a letter from our dear home yesterday where Father Mother & all were well TG— Julie is improving also—I recd a long letter from Sister Mary a few days since, she was quite well as were her family—Judge Rice is no better, if anything he is worse—they are going to Galveston for this winter—Bernard told me that John had telegraphed from Baltimore on Monday, & is expected home with Robert tonight—I miss him & his kind services very much—

I wrote to Mr. Baker Commission Merchant Charleston, & asked to forward us two tons of coal—two thirds anthracite & one third bituminous. I hope he will send it soon, & if it is perfectly correct he may call on you for payment & you can *charge* us.

I told him you had recommended me to get our winters supply from him, & assured us that he would let us have it at a moderate price, so I hope he will be both generous & civil—

Please let me know my dearest Brother when you send the box & provisions if you think it well to get them—Just now we have a little supply, by buying at retail—Mr Reilly paid us $48—forty-eight dollars today which was quite acceptable—

JOHN LYNCH, CHERAW, TO PATRICK LYNCH, OCT 29TH[47]

Robt & myself arrived here yesterday morning. safely after having been detained in Raleigh from want of connexion which threw us back 24 hours. I arrived in Baltimore Sunday morning, saw Catherine, quite well. Went to the

College found Robt doing tolerably well, started back with him after dinner, called on Dr. McLauchlin, at Ellicotts Mills, left him pretty well pleased with himself, ran over to Washington and returned in time to take the 5 oclock boat, traveled strait on till the interruption at Raleigh &c as above, while in Baltimore called to see the naval ship and was kindly treated by Mr N—who took me through the whole or rather hole of it. It will work, but when that is said, all is said, it is amusing oneself to a strong tune, for mere amusement sake, I think. The representation you saw is very correct and gives a correct idea, except it looks smaller than I expected to find it. I had H. W. Conner & family as traveling companions as far as Charlotte. At Raleigh he introduced himself to me saying he knew you very well, I found him very agreeable but rather inclined to egotism especially when talking of rail roads or engines—he don't like Winans.[48]

Robt had two severe attacks of bleeding from the nose while on his return, one on the boat and one after leaving Weldon, he was also threatend again in Raleigh, the one on the boat I let continue till it stopt itself as I knew it would be beneficial to him, the one on the cars commenc[e]d so freely I thought it best to stop it, so went into a forward car looking for something to make a plug, found some nice sponges cut a few plugs, had some sugar lead [?] in pocket made a strong solution and saturated the plugs, went back and found the carfull prescribing this this and the other thing some quite alarmed, I quietly went to him and placed a plug in each nostril gave his nose a squeeze and of course forced the solution up, left the plugs in and told him to keep his handkerchief to his nose; the bleeding stopped at once, and Robt seeing I did not mind it was not the least harmed by the remarks of his neighbours, one a gentleman from Charleston, came to me and asked if the young man was under my charge and began telling some remedies. I told him I was obliged to him for the interest he showed. The remedies were very good, but I was then using another, that I was the boys father, that of course put a stop to all further solicitations about doing this or that as the sponge did to the hemorrhage. I removed them after a few minutes washed his face and he was himself again, a renewal of the same application in Raleigh checked it at once, his eyes & skin since has nearly cleared his bowells are rather free, I see nature has commenced so well I will wait and let her try her hand. She and I are particularly good friends in sickness, and is one reason why she does not often deceive me. Tell Louisa if I possibly can I will write to her today but if I don't I will do so tomorrow. Eliza is as well as could be expected and will go to see Louisa as soon after frost as it will be perfectly safe.

Ellen is quite well but complains that she is afraid they will break down as there are not enough of them for their work, I expect it is so. She was as glad to see me almost as [much as] Eliza was. Bernard is looking pretty well and has given notice to General Jones that if his salary cant be raised that he will leave as soon after 15th of next month as he can get one to fill the post.

⚜

Baptista Lynch, Ursuline Convent, Columbia, to Patrick Lynch,
Nov 6th[49]

I choose this blotted sheet to write on thro' economy, not disrespect for
your lordship, hoping you will have the kindness to excuse me.

I thank you very much indeed for your promptitude & kindness in attending to *the box* which we recd yesterday,—John told me it must have wine in it for
the Altar, or something of the sort, as he heard the bottles—I have not opened it
yet, but I am sure everything is very nice—Have you received my letter written
on the reception of the beautiful harmonium? The tones of it are delightful—
The keys were knocked out of place—at least two octaves, but between John,
Mr Caldwell & Mr. Gardiner it is all rectified now—one of the most essential
stops does not work well however—It is the "Diapason stop"—John has cob-
bled it for the present—I only mention these things that you may not pay too
much for it—. We are all very well T.G. I hope that the yellow fever has totally
disappeared since the cold has set in, & that the Revd Clergy & good Sisters have
quite recruited [*sic*] from their labors—. John tells me Louisa is to be recd on
the 21st. We recommend ourselves to her fervent prayers & I will pray for her.—
Eliza is not at all pleased, nor do I blame her, in one sense, for I would be sorry
to see a sister of mine enter in such an institution, worthy tho it is—How much
does Mr Baker charge for the three bbls of coal which we have received from
him—? I told him that you had advised me to procure our winter supply from
him, assuring me that he would let me have it, at a moderate price—so I hope
he will do so, & let you have yours cheaper for getting him some customers—I
am clearing up all my accounts up to the 1st Nov—& am astonished to find
how much money I have to pay out—you must not be surprised if I call on you
about January—but if I can avoid it, you may be sure I will—We are storming
heaven for more pupils & Sisters—which I suppose God will send in His own
good time, if we only have a little patience—our trust is in Him & our Blessed
Mother—I have not heard from Miss Reynolds or Bishop O'Connor—& the
quasi postulant of Cincinnati, wrote me word a few days ago, that she could not
come as soon as she expected, because her sister who had promised to help her,
had joined the Good Shepherd Nuns, & left her without the means of travelling
—she asked me what the price would be of travelling from Cinc to Columbia—
which you will oblige me by letting me know—. She also expressed a wish to be
a Choir Sister, or at least said she would not like to be a Lay Sister—thereupon
I think it probable she may not come at all. —How are Lizzie Condy? Louisa
Blain—Mary Brownfield, Margaret Pauck? and as many others as you think
might have latent vocations—I am trying to win Miss Garnett & Miss Cullen
who visit us often. Have you heard anything of the Virginia & North Carolina

ladies?—I suppose my dearest Brother you will think me a perfect traitresse—but I do not mean to be such—I am much pleased with Revd Joseph "O'Connell —& tho' I never liked the idea of having a young confessor, I prefer him to his brother; he seems to me altogether better suited for our convent ways—but perhaps "a new broom sweeps clean"—

Sr Augustine wrote to Rosie Jones not long since—I have engaged Miss Cullen to give lessons in drawing to Miss Griffin in colored pastels—I will send my letter to Mr. Murphy[50] as soon as I can, & think if you have no objection of paying for our books—partially, by allowing the Ladies of the Congregation to join our "circulating Library" which we always have for our pupils—It will be advantageous both to them & to us—We will also let them join our "Children of Mary" Society—We will have inside of the chapel door a small box, for— "the poor of Christ" for the benefit of giving something to our destitute sacristy & altars. We wish very much to get up a little Bethlehem for Xmas.

I forgot to say that I thought of offering Mr Murphy the copyright (?) on two manuscripts for publication, which he might give us something for—what do you think of it?—they are "The Terrestrial Paradise" translated from the French—& a little drama of Sr. Charles' Composition, together with a little anecdote of my own, called the first communicant—my hand is so tired that I can scarcely guide my pen.

In our last accounts from our dear home all were as well as usual T G– ... I expect Bernard will soon go home, & Francis come to the fair. John says that Catharine does not seem at all changed. Donald McKay is coming to see me soon. I suppose thro' curiosity more than anything else.

ଈ

JAMES LYNCH, CHERAW, TO AUGUSTA LYNCH, NOV 16[51]

Dear Gus,

As I expect you are in Charleston or will be soon I will write to let you know that Bro Patrick has something over $400 for you which he will pay you & you can buy such furniture as we will need. . . . —what you buy ship by NER Road.[52] I think you had better buy yourself a Bonnet also altho I never liked the Charleston made Bonnets but suit yourself. If you will be economical we may have blinds put to the windows but they will cost about as much as the furniture all will.

Your husband,

Jas Lynch

Make good bargains & buy cheap

☙

BAPTISTA LYNCH, URSULINE CONVENT, COLUMBIA, TO PATRICK LYNCH, NOV 17TH[53]

These few collarets made so hastily that I have not leisure to mark them, are at present all we have to send as a little testimony of gratitude for all your kindness & solicitation on our account—when we get rich & have more sisters we will do better—this only to gratify ourselves & to let you see we do not forget you— ...

We recd a letter from a young lady in the West who wishes to join us & requested an immediate reply. We know her very well, & by the advice of our Sisters I presumed on your permission & have accepted her—I trust you will approve of what I have done—

One of our Laysisters is unable to work at present—& Sr. Rose is suffering a little too—I am sorry to see that the Prioress of Carmelite Convent has resigned her charge—I wrote to her last night— ... We want to have a procession on Sunday & wish you were here. We will have day scholars & all—

I have not time to say anything more unless to enquire for our dear Mother & Father & why Francis did not come to the Fair—I feel anxious & hope that sickness did not prevent—My respects to Revd Dr. Corcoran & friends of our Comty [Community]—Rev. Father O Connell's has kindly offered to be the bearer of this to you or I would write longer & write more legibly. I like him very much as a Confessor & trust our Lord will preserve him in the spirit which he now manifests.

☙

JOHN LYNCH, COLUMBIA, TO PATRICK LYNCH, NOV 17TH[54]

I recd a long letter from Louisa the other day begging Eliza & myself to be present at her reception next Saturday, and this morning recd another with the same request; and tickets for several of her friends of this place, Eliza & myself would have been down, but unfortunately yesterday the baby was taken sick, it has Erysipelas on the leg—Lucinda & Mary, the two principal house servants are sick in bed, which makes it utterly impossible for Eliza to leave home, neither can I unless a change takes place, as Louisa writes she is going into retreat, and will not come out until Saturday. I cannot of course write to her, I have therefore to ask you to make our excuse to Louisa if I do not come down, I know if I am able to go down my expences in the city would be light, if I would accept of the hospitalities of D𝑟 Carey (who was sick in Col. this fall, I attended him gratuitously.)

Eliza begs me to remind you of a promise or rather offer you made her *last* year, regarding the ladies fair. She has concluded to assist in getting up a table, how, for the life of me, I can't see; the fair will come off I believe the first or second week of the sitting of the legislature, and Eliza begs you to let her have all you can, that was left over from the fair in Charleston at as cheap a rate as possible, with the privilege of returning what is not sold. She also requests that you *beg* for her as it is in a good cause, any and everything will be thankfully received; please let me know if you can do anything for her. If I go down I can bring up the gleanings.

Robert has continued steadily to improve since coming home. I think him perfectly well now. I see very little change in Bernard, he is no worse, eats heartily, and shows it agrees well with him. Still the cough remains, the same as when you saw him.

I suppose I need not say anything of how the Convent, school & inmates are getting on as I suppose from the number of letters I post to you, you must be kept better posted than I am, although I am there nearly every day.

～ઈ

Baptista Lynch, Ursuline Convent, Columbia SC, to Patrick Lynch, Nov 19th[55]

I begged Brother John to apologize to you for my sending you that miserable & hurried scrawl by Rev. Dr O Connell, which I was ashamed of—. I hope that you are quite well, & have left our dear Mother, Father, & all the family quite well at home.

Our Sisters were like myself expecting the pleasure of a short visit from you on your return, until we heard that it would be altogether inconvenient. You see how ignorant we are about the world's doings & how much happens . . . than those who are worldly-wise. We are all well thank God—or at least pretty well—I refer you to John for particulars & for news about our three new boarders—the Misses Gaffney. We are preparing for a procession which we want to have in honor of our Blessed Mother on Sunday. I suppose you would laugh at our banners &c if you saw them, but I assure you, we are quite pleased with our efforts —& hope the children may be impressed by it—& that it may be A M D G— Our Sisters say that they are expecting another visit from you most anxiously, but that you must stay for the evening recreation when you do come, as that is the only time we can assemble together—If I could have written this before Johns departure for Charleston, I would have done so, but it was not until after he left, that I had time to see what I should write to Mr Bernard O Neale for— & now, if he will have the kindness to select these groceries for us, & attend to their being conveyed to Columbia I will feel most obliged to him—I am sorry that I spoke of the coldness of our home as I did, the morning on which he left, for I am sure we are thankful to get it, as it is even—It is only poor human nature shrinks from the suffering & inconvenience sometimes, but a little reflection teaches us to goad it on—So do not mind anything I may have said about the female Academy, or involve yourself in any difficulty for us—You have already a plenty of debt. I would rather aid you to get out of it—than ask you sink deeper in it on our account. What would you think of going to Cuba or Mexico begging—or of sending some one of your clergy for *our poor diocese or especially for the poor Ursulines*—I think it would be both pleasant, & profitable—I will send you the list for Mr. O Neale, but if you think it well or prudent, please retract anything you wish. I only seek to economize by getting a quantity at one time—John says, I am *penny-wise* & pound foolish & I suppose I am. I must not forget to tell you that I *keep a day-book* in obedience, but I am not much improved—Please give my love to Sister Ambrose who I think will join us yet —& if I were to listen to my inspirations, I would ask you to encourage her to come, for you know I think it is with us she ought to be—I am so sleepy that it behooves me to seek my pillow—but I will continue my charitable messages of affection to L[ouisa] Macnamara, for whom we will pray & to all the good Sisters whose prayers we beg—

[P.S.] I have not seen Father J O C__ since his return from Charleston, tho I think it would only have been polite in him to call & let me know how you were today—Its no use looking for extra compliments I presume but only take everything kindly as meriting

I'm glad however the better man came back in time to hear our children's confessions, for I prefer him to "Rough & Ready: alias ____" I am afraid to write the name, lest some one else might see it & that would never do. . . .

᪥

Baptista Lynch, Ursuline Convent, Columbia SC, to Patrick Lynch, Dec 4th[56]

I am so careless myself that it would ill become me to find fault with you for losing "our report." However precious on account of its scarcity—I will try & copy from one Sister Ursula has, & send it in time for the time specified in our prospectus. Please see to the printing of them for us & forward as soon as convenient—I was sorry that Dr. Corcoran was detained so long in Columbia since it was an inconvenience to you, I hope that you will have an agreeable time in Raleigh, & be instrumental in doing much good.—We will do the part of the Jesuit Lay Brothers, & pray for the people as well as your dear self.

It is now my turn to express mortification which I feel about my management of affairs—I have received from Mr B. O Neill the provisions sent for, but altho' I cannot in the least censure him, it will I think be the last time I will deal in *wholesale business*—I have not his letters near me now, but the bill, to my astonishment, exceeds somewhat $1000—It seems to me if John had selected them as I asked, we would have done better as we would have chosen a less expensive material—I will write to Mr O Neale acknowledging the receipt of them as soon as the molasses comes to hand, which I expect today, & I will be obliged to refer him to you for payment, for if I were to send him what money I have in hand, I should be obliged to call on you to pay our bills here—Whatever you wish, I will do—I felt almost dispirited this morning about our money affairs— but I afterward reproached myself for any distrust in the good providence of God who has done so much for us & will continue to do so if we are only faithful to Him—At the foot of the Altar I learn where to place my trust & how we should confide in Him—I will show you a letter when you come which I received from Madam S__ of New Orleans whose daughter has been for eight of ten years in B C Convent & thinks of becoming a Nun—she is well educated— respectable & rich—but exceedingly delicate &c &c &c—And asks my advice— which I cautiously gave with an interpretation to come to us—if &—&—

I have heard nothing more of Miss Reynolds but fancy at each ring of the door bell it is she who has arrived—Neither have I had time to hear from our former pupil Miss Maguire of Kentucky—so that for the present patience & prayer are very necessary—The Children are quite well & happy TG—I wish I could say as much for all of our Sisters—Sister Ursula has been suffering & unable to go to class since yesterday evening—& Sister Augustine & our good laysister are as well & laborious as ever—as for Sister Rose[57] she is a blessing to us—& a very *great assistance* altho not able to hear the recitations—I would be very badly off without her cheerful aid—Should Sr. A put into execution her repeated threats of leaving & Sr. Ursula become so delicate as she sometimes sees—we would be in a fix, but I feel that our Blessed Mother will draw to herself other followers in our convent, & we will have the happiness of effecting much good yet with God's assistance—M[rs] Monroe passed thro' Columbia last week & called to see us twice—I believe we were mutually pleased with each other, & will correspond—I wish you would either visit her at Conwayboro or send some clergyman occasionally—I pity her, so removed from the sweet influence of Catholic society—we talked all about Cin [Cincinnati] Abp Purcell— the Sisters of Notre Dame &c &c She told me of having awakened you in the cars to—.

. . . —I am so angry with Hugh, that I do not trust myself to say much—But I believe I will write soon—Enclosed you will find the *Model Report*—

❧

BAPTISTA LYNCH, URSULINE CONVENT, COLUMBIA, TO PATRICK LYNCH,
DEC 15TH[58]

I have just finished a letter to Miss Eliza Ryan of Halifax saying we have
accepted her demand to enter our Noviciate—& we trust she will prove a good
& useful sister—which is more than bringing either talents or dowers, as experience has proved.

I thank you very much for so promptly & kindly attending to our Reports
& Mr O Neills acct. . . . I have had an attack of the neuralgia pain to which I
ought to be accustomed but am able to do my duties after a fashion.—Sister
Ursula who is I am happy to say better is anxious that you should be here for
Benediction on the octave of the Imm. Con. [Immaculate Conception][59] & admire her prettily arranged altar—it is really tastefully arranged, & we feel truly
grateful for having Benediction of the Most Blessed Sacrament every evening
at 5 PM—I have very recently heard from Sister Mary—Sister Antonia & our
dear home all were as well as usual TG—Sister Antonia suffers from the change
of Sup^r Mr Spann to whom I sent a Prospectus but offered to teach Ellen gratuitously, only charging for board & clothing—has promised to send a cheque—
Mother sent me various wearing articles & eatables from home the other day.
Which were very acceptable & for which our Srs expressed their gratitude . . .

When will Dr Corcoran's work come out? Col John Ryan[60] called on us a
few days since & expressed how much pleasure it would afford him to see Sr.
Charles associated with us & that he thought our chances of success better than
that of the Springfield Community—But perhaps he spoke to please present
company—I have not seen Charles Pinckney. I have a notion of writing to Lizzie
Condy, but I am afraid her mother & sister may not like it & I suppose she does
not feel hurt at my silence—Please give our charitable remarks to the good S^{rs}
particularly to M Teresa & Sr. Ambrose—I suppose I should add Louisa—

❧

ANNA LYNCH, CHERAW, TO PATRICK LYNCH, DEC 22ND[61]

I suppose you heard. . . of Brother Bernard's sickness. He is some better
today but was quite unwell on Monday & Tuesday, suffering with acute pains in
his stomach which prevented him from eating without increasing them greatly.
I believe he suffers from them, in a measure, all the time. In regard to his trip
to Cuba, he does not fancy the idea of going among strangers in the state, he
is to be indebted to them alone for the attention he requires, & which he will
never ask for, & consequently not receive, unless given gratuitously, & persons
not interested, are not apt, to be as observant as necessary. As Matanzas is on

the sea shore, will it not be injurious, to stay there? Many persons say that just the exposure in travelling will be bad, but you are the best judge of that.

I suppose Brothers John, Francis, & yourself talked the matter over when together.

Brother Bernard stopped me here to write himself, so I will only add that Mother would not be willing to see him leave unless you would accompany him to his destination . . . on your way to those islands you intend to visit.[62] He has felt the changes for so far so sensibly I don't know how he can possibly stand the winter & spring. He is remarkably thin already & expectorates freely— . . . I feel very anxious about Brother Bernard & hope you will remember us both frequently in your prayers—

Bernard Lynch, Cheraw, SC, to Patrick Lynch, 22d Dec[63]

I have just read Anna's letter to you about myself, and although she has given you my reasons and surmises on the subject very well, I will take occasion to express myself more to the point. In addition to my cough which is rather worse now than it was in the summer, I am troubled with weakness of the digestive organs—This I have felt growing on me for several months but it has proved more troublesome within the last, especially for a few days back.

My appetite is tolerably good but as a general thing I am afraid to give it full scope else pay the piper for it afterwards. I do not think that this is exactly the state for a man to be in when he has to form and cultivate the acquaintance & friendship of polite society & I guess my embryo friends in Cuba would think they had met a semi-savage if I was often troubled as I have been latterly. For I assure you nothing knocks the politeness out of one sooner than a colic. The truth of the business is if I knew I would derive any permanent benefit from the trip of course I would very gladly go (take my chance as to getting along when there—I know nothing of Spanish yet).

The sea sickness might probably be a good thing for me but I have not much strength to spare just now & don't fancy the idea of facing it.

On the whole it would probably be best for me to give up the trip as I have never been professionally advised to take it & as an essential to my health, though brother John said he thought it would benefit me . . .

1859 January–June

"This mustard seed, this tiny nut"

Baptista and her sister nuns quickly discovered that the Columbia site they had taken over from the Sisters of Mercy was an impossible one in which to conduct an academy for the formation of young ladies. Not only was the building too small for the Ursulines and the number of students they hoped to attract, but the neighborhood—teeming with grog shops and the like—was as undesirable as one could imagine. And so Patrick Lynch undertook a search to relocate convent and academy, either in the city or on an estate in the country. Given the atmosphere that Baptista was trying to create for the convent-academy community—one of quiet and controlled isolation in which contemplation and creativity could flourish and in which the convent/academy community could become the center of the students' world and sustain a culture that nurtured vocations— one would expect her to strongly favor a rural setting. But if one could somehow preserve a rural environment even within the confines of the city, she was open to that as well.

Within his own extended family, Patrick was planning out and paying for the seminary education of his nephew Robert, in spite of the latter's precarious health. In 1859 he sent him abroad to France to resume his studies for the priesthood. Robert left a family that was stumbling. John Lynch's practice continued to recover from the low patient load that the recession had brought about. He had much less success in dealing with the demon of intemperance, a failure that put severe strains on his marriage. His fragile wife, Eliza, sought a safe haven with her mother in Charleston.

John, together with his sister Baptista, found himself at odds with the three O'Connell brothers, all of whom were more or less based at St Peter's. John refused to go to Confession to any of them. The oldest of the three brothers, and the pastor of St. Peter's, refused to give Communion to parishioners who were attending Mass not at their parish Church but at the nuns' chapel. Baptista was sure this petty behavior stemmed from the brothers' resenting the Ursulines' *dislodgement of the Sisters of Charity from their school in Columbia. This bad feeling, she concluded, was aggravated in the oldest O'Connell when Baptista had the youngest O'Connell, not the resident pastor who would seem the natural choice, made chaplain of the girls at the Ursuline Academy.*

South Carolina was in a perpetual state of fevers, some seasonal, some chronic; the risk of contracting one of them was just part of the cost of living in the South in the mid-nineteenth century. The Lynches were hardly immune to them, but their far greater concern was consumption, which seemed to be the lot of, if not imminent threat to, the younger tier of siblings. Conlaw already had succumbed to the disease the previous May. Now Bernard, the youngest brother at age twenty-four, seemed well on his way to being its next victim within the family. As winter turned to spring, Bernard lingered in a near-death condition.

Baptista Lynch, Ursuline Convent, Columbia, to Patrick Lynch
Jan 16th[1]

I have opened the box of books & am somewhat disappointed with Mr Murphy. I will wait enclosing a check to him for them, & politely let him know that I did not wish some of the books which he has sent & wished another edition of some of what he did—But do not fear that I will offend him—shall I offer to return the *catechism of history* which he has sent me a great quantity of, instead of Religious Catechisms. I have this morning recd a very pleasing letter from Miss Ryan, who wrote that she will be in Columbia DV the first or second week in February & should anything occur to prevent, she will write & let us know.

Thanks to our Lord & the Blessed Lady, we seem to be getting on very well indeed. We will now start our "Circulating Library." I hope under the protection of our Blessed Mother to enrol as members, some of the most intelligent of the Community here—Yesterday we had a visit from Mrs Thomas Taylor, & her Sister Miss Elmore, a maiden lady, with whom I was much pleased. We are also anxious to start *at once* our society of the "Sodality of the B. V. M. for the Ladies of the Congregation, but find in the manual for which we sent, no rules of any importance—seeing in the Miscellany of today, an article on "The children of Mary" I thought perhaps you would have the kindness to give me its rules, manner of proceeding &c &c since it is adapted to persons in the world, & would suit them better than any we could give . *Please send me this information as soon as convenient*—as Mrs Bauskett[2] has asked me about it several times & I think it might do some good to the Ladies of the congregation. John & his family are quite well (TG) he presented me with a very nice pair of alabaster candlesticks, which we use on our Communion table. I think he was ashamed of his manner that evening, & I suppose you spoke to him—of course I made no further allusion to it—He is on his best behavior at present—I had quite a long talk with "the old Doctor"³ & I trust I may be instrumental in removing any uncharitable [feelings] that may exist between them—*this is entre nous* for John would be *out & out vexed with me* if he knew it—so we mutually requested that our conversation should be confidential. Of course that does not exclude you who are my superior, Bishop, Brother, & spiritual father so when you come, I will tell you what we said.

Rev. Father Joseph⁴ has gone, I am told, to Greenville & will be away *for a month*—I hope this is not the case—for he may go as much as he likes (which I think is not at all) for a week at a time—but I do not like his being away on our confession day—we are not willing to consider it *all in the family* & go to the other brothers—but would be glad that he was always convenient for that duty both for ourselves & our pupils.

At the same time, I am afraid of paining the others⁵ by showing too decided a preference, or of spoiling the "little Padre:"—a word from you perhaps would do better—what do you think— . . .

Mrs Bauskett told me yesterday that if Bernard would get some powders from Adams Springs in Virginia, & take them regularly, he would no doubt find great relief, & then next spring if he would go to the Sulphur Springs Va he might like Col Bauskett, be restored to health.

. . . —Sr. Augustine, whose spirits are as good as usual, will write one of her agreeable epistles, which I hope will amuse you. . . .

🐀

John Lynch, Columbia, to Patrick Lynch, Jany 31st⁶

Eliza tells me you intend visiting Cheraw soon and taking Robert to Charleston with you & intend sending him to France next month sometime, if you say so I will bring him home at once, and get him ready, but of course you intend him to see his family before sending him off. Eliza arrived safely and appears to have enjoyed herself very much considering the weather, since she has been home Anna (the largest child she had with her) has been quite sick, and continues so, what is the matter I can't exactly say, symptoms of worms, for which I am treating her, I wish brother that you would make out a statement of what I am due the Sisters & yourself, up to date, and I will try and pay it during the coming month.

. . . .

P.S. I have not tasted so much as a glass of wine for better than a week and if possible will continue the same regimen, but trials and temptation are strong & the flesh is weak.

Baptista Lynch, Ursuline Convent, to Patrick Lynch, Feb 26th[7]

I suppose if I were to wait until tomorrow or the next day, I might say something of Miss Ryan's arrival, but I feel as if I would like a little "chat" with you, so I will obey the impulse & talk on—I was called to the parlor a few evenings since to accept a very pretty present of the "Lives of the Saints" from a little French woman of Aach who said she bought them in Paris last summer, & begged my acceptance of them in pretty good English—I soon perceived that the books were a mere pretext, & learned that "Marie Charlotte Fehrenbach" wished to be a Religious, & was willing to do all she might be told. She only feared she could not be received because she was not good enough, or might be sent away. She is twenty-eight years of age, I think she said; healthy & has learned *embroidery* as a trade together with millenary—& for the last three years has been a sort of ladies-maid, & work-woman in respectable families, to avoid boarding among all sorts of people, since her sister's death.

I like her merry countenance, & her capacity for embroidery, *& with your permission* will give her a trial—I gave her no decided answer, but told her to pray & consult Father Joseph who is her confessor—He says she is as good a Catholic as is in Columbia— . . . We are all very well thank God—I felt a little alarmed about Ellen Spann yesterday, & sent for John in a great hurry, fearing she had the Scarlet fever which is so prevalent. Happily my fears were groundless, & she is better today— . . .

My dearest Brother would you not think it well to speak to Henrietta, for her neglect of duty, as a wife & housekeeper. It is really a shame for her to act as she does. I don't know what kind of a conscience she has to approach the sacraments & neglect her duties as she does—A lady from Cheraw told me this evening that she never was at home—some one else asked if Francis & his wife were separated—and she does not hesitate to say that her mother & sister wish her to remain in Charleston, & she never would return to Cheraw, if she was not obliged to do so—I feel very much tempted to write her a *lecture*—the opinion of her!

If I were in Francis' place, I would not pay a cent for her while in Charleston, but while in Cheraw she should have every comfort, & she should be at her post of duty—she never will like it, as long as she remains absent from it—. I suppose you think my dearest Brother it is time to stop after this tirade — Well, the finale with me is "Deo Gratias, I am a Religious" & we feel this especially after being in the parlour & hearing the details of every day life— . . .

❧

BAPTISTA LYNCH, URSULINE CONVENT COLUMBIA SC, TO PATRICK LYNCH,
27TH FEB[8]

... John would be glad if Revd Mr Quigley[9] has not yet gone to N Carolina,
if he would stop in Columbia on his way—he told John when in Charleston,
that he would do so if he had permission—I suppose you will readily grant that
rather than have John remain without Confession. Which you know must be a
matter of perfect liberty—I am sorry he will not go to any of the Revd Fathers
here, but his confidence is not sufficient in them—

Time perhaps will produce a change which cannot be effected now.—

When you have time to write my dearest brother, please let me know about
our observance of Lent—& give me your answer about "little Frenchy" as we
term the little woman from Aach—Miss Ryan has not yet come, & I am not
sorry since the gutter has not yet been cleaned, & the weather has been so very
rainy—we have prevented some of the rain from coming in, by placing a board
near the window, but it is still too damp for [a] sleeping room—John will see
about it tomorrow— ...

❧

BAPTISTA LYNCH, URSULINE CONVENT, COLUMBIA, MARCH 4TH
(THURSDAY)[10]

This morning at 5 o clock Miss Ryan arrived—TG We are quite pleased with
her, & trust our Lord may give her the grace of perseverance—

On Monday DV the little French woman will come in—I gave her our answer this evening, not thinking well under the circumstances, to defer longer.
She will bring $200. We have rced another boarder for $100. Jumpers, washing
& bedding supplied—

❧

BAPTISTA LYNCH, URSULINE CONVENT COLUMBIA, TO PATRICK LYNCH,
MARCH 14TH[11]

The Sisters are all quite well & happy T G—We are praying hard about our
temporal as well as spiritual affairs—the house for sale & all—A.M.D.G.—&
free from anxiety, leaving all to the good Providence of God—. I am very much
pleased with Sister Eliza (Ryan). Sr Raymond's troubles are over for the present
but—The little French woman is very good & will be very useful, if she can ever
get used to our self-denying life, but poor little thing she finds it very hard—
Dr & Mrs Jarvis sent me word yesterday, that they were much pleased with her,

& sorry she had left them—Dr. Jarvis said he would be glad to see "*the Lady Abbess*" himself if allowed—I suppose he wants to pay what he owes to the little French woman—about $140. I expect him today or sooner—I answered Miss Weeds' letter & hope she will come to us—I will expect an answer soon which will let us know something of her inclination—

It is time for us to think of who will give us our spiritual exercises this year. Could we have *Father Sourin S.J.*?[12]—We would prefer a quiet Jesuit father who was a man of prayer, rather than a preacher. Such as I imagine Father Sourin or *Father Superior*[13] of the Jesuits in Baltimore—I forget his name he is I believe an Italian—I think at the same time we may have the profession of Sister Loretta the lay sister & the reception of two of our postulants—do not mention this please, but think about it—

In our last letters from home all was as well as usual T G—I believe John expects Father this week—Has *the beauty* Henrietta gone home yet—? Cornelia's Mother & sisters begged her to come & meet her Sister Cecilia here—but she did not—& I admire her for it—Eliza is still in Salisbury— . . .

Anna Lynch, Cheraw, to Patrick Lynch, St. Patrick's day[14]

For fear that you should feel uneasy, after hearing of Mother's indisposition, I will write to let you know, that she is so much better as to be up, attending again to household affairs, but is still weak, & shows plainly in her appearance that she has been sick. Brother Bernard is not so well today, as he has been, for the last week. I expect he feels lonely, as well as badly, since Mr Stafford left: he remained long enough with us, for all the family to become attached to him and we too, & will miss him greatly. Company, especially when good, like Mr. Stafford's, serves Brother Bernard by diverting his mind from his sickness & making him cheerful. I fear the loss of it will have the contrary effect, for a while at least. . . . I feel very anxious about him sometimes & hope my dear Brother, you will pray for his recovery—which M[r] Stafford gave us great hopes of—Brother Hugh got home safely—saw Sister Catherine who was well. . . . Sister Henrietta has got over her fatigue & she, the children all well. . . .

Baptista Lynch, Ursuline Convent, to Patrick Lynch [n.d.][15]

. . . I suppose you know that we are enjoying a visit from Father at present— He is looking very well Thank God & comes every day to the Convent—He will return home D V on Tuesday or Wednesday—I am sorry to hear that Augusta is quite indisposed or perhaps ill—Father is anxious about her—I am so glad

that you have sent Rev. Mr Cullinane[16] to spend the summer in Cheraw especially on poor Bernard's account—

I suppose from what I heard that you have just visited home—John, who is
well & doing well at least spiritually, begs me to say that he has written to you,
enclosing a letter, which he has to answer, & without which he cannot act—If
you have the kindness to forward it to him, & give him your views on it, he will
be most obliged—.

I wonder he did not think to mention to you a letter which was enclosed to
him by Mr Northrop[17] I believe, & which he spoke to me of—Of course you
have seen it, & know long before this all about the McKenna will—

Was it not a shocking thing for Mrs Kennedy to have her infant poisoned?

. . . I lent John a hundred dollars to put in the Bank a few days since, just to
keep up appearances—as he was obliged to draw out nearly all he had in it.

☞

BAPTISTA LYNCH, URSULINE CONVENT, COLUMBIA SC, TO PATRICK LYNCH,
APRIL 8TH[18]

I am happy to say we are all quite well, & doing well TG—The weather is
fair, the *clouds have all disappeared*, & all is right.

We have four hundred & odd dollars in hand, & hope soon to hear from
Mrs Gaffney— . . .

I was so annoyed by S____[19] the night you were here; & your indisposition
served to make me anxious so that I do not remember what advice you gave
her about answering the letters of Miss Weed, & Miss Fisher. I thought of urging both to more immediate action—If I can help you out of any little difficulty,
by at any time making you *partial* payments—you know how happy I would
be to do it—but if you are rich—I will wait until the exhibition[20] is over, to
straighten our accounts, if I can only do it then, for I find so many wants at the
end of the year—each mistress claiming something for her pupils—I make a
poor mouth, but give, trusting it may all be A.M D G— . . .

[P.S.] Please let me know how your cold is—we wish to decorate the altar
with taste on Holy Thursday—but will not have a *reposoire*[21]— I intend to have
the Mandatum[22] much to the annoyance of the Sisters—You will too will you not?

☞

BAPTISTA LYNCH, COLUMBIA, TO PATRICK LYNCH, SUNDAY MORNING
[APRIL 10][23]

This morning Father Lawrence[24] said Mass for us, & as often heretofore did
not give Holy Communion to those who wished to go in our Chapel, but told

them after Mass they must go down to the Church to communion—I wonder if they persisted on requiring people to attend mass & go to H. Communion in the *parish church*, for the *sake of good example*, when the Sisters of Mercy were here—?

The beauty of it is that while they are apparently driving the people off from the Convent, we appear in blissful ignorance & are succeeding in drawing them to it, in every way we can—so that Miss Cullen told me not long since, that she never witnessed such a reaction as among the Catholics of C[olumbia]—since we came—At first, the pupils would say they never could like the Nuns after losing the dear Sisters—now, they all agree in saying they never loved & respected the Sisters as they do the Nuns—With the Ladies, it is she says the same—even Mrs Comerford, who she told me got on her knees, to beg that the sisters might remain in C[olumbia], now says, she *loves* the Nuns, & thinks a great deal more of them than she ever did the Sisters—*that Mrs Kean* that gave me such a rating when we first came, told me yesterday that her daughter said, the school is conducted now, very differently from what it was—that the poor Sisters did all they could but—&c &c.

I think too, I have won Mrs McGuiness by a little amiability—Of course, I do not forget "omnes homines me deserent" nor, the lesson of Palm Sunday—.[25] & I tell you this just to let you *see how the land lies*.

I need not say that charity—duty & interest combine to make me both silent & guarded with these externs [laity], lest anything may give them room to make mischief, & be the *agents of Satan* as Father Faber would say. The *Novena* will finish Tuesday

JOHN LYNCH, COLUMBIA, TO PATRICK LYNCH, 13TH APRIL[26]

Enclosed I send you a note that arrived the day you left here for Greenville which I intended to give to you, on your return. I mentioned to you at the depot, there was something else I wanted to say to you, but could not think of it. I had the note in my pocket at the time, but being hurried so could not think of it. The letter I gave to you with the copy, I would be obliged if you would send back as soon as you can, after Louisa has seen it, as I have since you were here, rced a long letter from Louisa, which with the one from Mr Spann I wish to answer but cant do so, until I have the copy before me. I have told Eliza all about it. She has taken it much more quietly than I expected, and is only a little angry. She is anxious to see the letters and document. I also forgot to give you my manuscript, & suppose I had best send it on for publication and send you a copy which you can look over at your leisure. Tell Louisa I will write a *long* letter to her soon and that Eliza is much better. It has been some time since I heard from Cheraw directly. M^rsReilly told Eliza today that she heard that Bernard was confined to his bed and had lost his voice. I hope it is not so, but fear it may be. I shall look anxiously for a letter from home. . . .

&

BAPTISTA LYNCH, URSULINE CONVENT, COLUMBIA, SC, TO PATRICK LYNCH, EASTER SATURDAY[27]

. . . I wish you could have seen our altar & sanctuary on Holy Thursday & Good Friday it was, & I may still say is beautifully arranged—a great many persons visited it both Catholic & Protestant We exposed your precious relic for adoration all day Good Friday & had it surrounded with twelve lights.

Alice Reilly will enter as a Boarder on Wednesday next when the studies will recommence.

On Wednesday morning when I was seated in the parlor with Father, Mrs Malony (Sister Charles' Mother) from Barnwell arrived—of course we received the old Lady very cordially—she reminds me somewhat of Mother—. She had her trunk left in our hall since it contained clothes for her little granddaughter, & asked me to recommend her to some good private boarding house. I told her of M^rs McCarthy's—& sent at once to ask them to prepare a room, but much to our discomfort they had none to spare that day—We then did the best we could—moved a bed down into the back parlor, & gave her possession of it with the best grace possible—The old Lady will remain until after Easter & seems delighted with the convent & says that she thinks all of Col^n Ryans daughters will be our pupils even the one who is [at] Georgetown [Visitation Convent] perhaps—She will interest herself for us—She seems to think my dearest Brother that their pastor does not visit them often enough or stay long enough at a time—She also said very politely that she had not seen you since your consecration—

Mrs Keitt[28] sent me word yesterday that she intended calling, in a few days I told her of M^rs McCarthy's. . . (an alarm of *fire, the second today!*) The stables of the American Hotel have just been burnt—John hastened to assure us that there was no danger—the wind is very high, but in our favor—

. . . Wednesday . . . we finished our Easter Examinations—Father left for home—Mrs Malony arrived— . . . I am sorry to say that sister Agnes is quite sick tho' better than she was yesterday. John says she is his first case here—She had the fever & inflammation of the bowel I think—She has begun to take quinine this evening & I hope will soon be able to leave her bed—John thinks it is from overexertion.

Our sister washwoman is partly knocked up too—but I hired Uncle Cits wife to help her at present. . . .

HUGH LYNCH AND FRANCIS LYNCH, CHERAW, SC, TO PATRICK LYNCH
25TH APRIL[29]

Anna & myself have concluded we had best write you of Bernard's care as we consider he can't live much over a week and I would not be surprised to hear of his death at anytime but as in such cases I generally write too strong a letter you must form your own judgment of the case from the following. At any rate if any sudden or important change should take place I will telegraph you from Florence. Bernard remained until Thursday night about the same as he was when you left. On Thursday night he was quite sick and very weak and remained so. Only gradually getting weaker until yesterday when he was very sick for a while suffering with severe pains all through the system. Today he has not been able to be up at all and looks very weak. I noticed at dinner time that his breathing was short and sometimes stopping for a short time as if with difficulty he could breath and once I heard a pretty sharp rattle which I took to be in his throat—No one knows that I am writing to you but Anna but as we both considered he can live but a short time concluded it best to write you. . . .

[Francis Lynch], Tuesday morning 7½ o clock

. . . Bro Bernard had for a short while omitted the usual dose of Brandy & morphine and became so weak yesterday, that he appeared sinking, he made an attempt to take a ride, but returned almost immediately. Doct. Wilson gave him his normal anodyne & after resting tolerably well last night, says he feels much easier this morning. Revd Mr Cullinan administered the Sacrament of Extreme Unction about 10 o'clock last night. I think his bowels are disposed to be free, the morphine may restrain their action to some extent.

FRANCIS LYNCH, CHERAW, TO PATRICK LYNCH, 8 OCLOCK A.M. THURSDAY,
28 APR[30]

Thinking you must needs be anxious about the state of Bro Bernard, it is due that I should say, that since resuming the usual treatment of anodyne he is getting on easier and is very much in same condition as when you were here, though somewhat weaker.—Yesterday afternoon he sat up awhile and last night rested tolerably well.

This morning he was sleeping when I was at home.

Bro Hugh has recd for him from Paxton's a box of Oil tar & inhaling tubes yesterday, the effect of which is said to be soothing.

ᢒᢖ

Baptista Lynch, Ursuline Convent, to Patrick Lynch,
Sunday Morning [May][31]

It occurred to me that for two motives it would be well to get one of the
Pastors here to preach to the children during their retreat—in the first place it
might seem to *heal the wound* & create a more charitable feeling—& secondly it
might prevent an increase of that foolish jealousy which already exists—

You then could come up for their Confirmation, & remain with us on the
feast of St. Angela—Revd Father O'Connells niece was withdrawn from our
school on last Monday—under the pretext that she is not improving—I spoke
to Father Lawrence about her & he said she would return—as yet she has not
done so—I have not pretended to our Sisters what I think is the cause but I suspect you know—.

This morning I received a very pleasing letter from Josephine Griffin who
wishes very much to return. Her father sent me $15.00 the amt due for her
Board &c—She may perhaps come back next year, & says she hopes we may
have a large house soon, for she thinks we shall have a great many boarders
next year.

ᢒᢖ

Baptista Lynch, Ursuline Convent, Columbia, SC. to Patrick Lynch,
May 3rd[32]

Two things contribute to put me in a good humor while writing this letter
—One is my pen is good—the other is—more important—today we received
from Mrs Gaffney through her cousin "Mr G. K. Williams of Gadsden" the
sum of one thousand dollars for the board & tuition of the Misses Gaffney—
which I gave John to deposit in Bank—Now you may as well have the use of it,
as to have it lying there & if you will only come to see us it will give us a great
deal of pleasure to pay our debts—& also to pay the good Sisters of Mercy what
we owe them, as theirs is a debt I would be glad to liquidate as soon as ever
we can—.

I am sorry to say one of our Laysisters has given me a good deal of trouble
this week—I wish very much Father Joseph were at home—This is the first
time he has left since I requested him to be our chaplain—Columbia is *now
desolate* for this morning. Father Lawrence was kind enough to send me a note
saying "he was suddenly summoned to Orangeburg (Mr Birminghams mission) & could not give us Mass tomorrow morning, but would return if possible in the evening—I do not know whether Father O Connell is at home sick
or has left since Sunday. I suppose for the latter—

Father Birmingham's parishioners are loud in their compliments I believe, from what I hear. I hope he is meeting with good success—we have not heard from home of Bernard since I wrote—today, we did not forget the *anniversary* of the finding of the cross—I went to Holy Communion for poor dear Conlaw —RIP. We have the precious relic[33] exposed for adoration all day on the altar. Our "Month of Mary" devotions are at 6 P.M. but I think we will probably change to some morning hour for the benefit of the day pupils. St. Agnes is up at work again. TG tho still weak. I am afraid Sr Raymond will follow her example, she has her symptoms—The weather seems to affect several among the children & nuns—I believe after all, I am one of the strongest—However we have no reason to complain, on the contrary, we have every reason to be most grateful for so many blessings.

ↄ

BAPTISTA LYNCH, URSULINE CONVENT, COLUMBIA, SC, MAY 12TH[34]

Yesterday afternoon John called to tell me all about our dear home, & let me know exactly how dear Bernard was when he left. He was so fortunate to be surrounded with every spiritual & temporal blessing—may our Blessed Mother & Saint Joseph be with, & protect him—I am glad to hear that our dear parents, Anna & all the family are so submissive to the Divine Will—

We propose that all our pupils will enter upon their annual retreat on the feast of St. *Philip Neri*, & come out on Sunday, the feast of St. Catharine of Sienna—on which day we will have them all confirmed who have not been before—if you have the kindness to come for that time—I wish very much too that you would give them their retreat—I did intend asking Father Joseph to give it, since he is their director, but Father O Connell has sent him off to Fennell Hall, to remain during the month of Mary—*Rough-&-ready* has supplied his place as far as possible—If the worst comes to the worst we will give it ourselves, but would prefer a clergyman of course—

My dearest Brother, Mrs Cass has placed her daughter here, & paid me two hundred dollars in gold, for the session & vacation time; which is at your disposal if you will call for it—

You know we have Mrs Gaffney's one thousand in Bank untouched. We shall have many little or perhaps great expenses at the winding up of the session— but D G—we will get on very well—

I am having the Sisters & Children to say a novena to St. Joseph, before next Sunday, the feast of his protection, for our intention about a house &c if it be A.M.D.G—

[PS] Father O Connell (the oldest one) is so angry with us, ever since we expressed the wish that Father Joseph would be our Chaplain, that he has never crossed our threshold, even to say Mass, or give us benediction—we have been dependent on Father Lawrence who evinces a much better disposition, & when he was absent, on a stranger clergyman named Rev. Peter McLaughlin, from Maine who was on a questing expedition—Sunday last we had no Benediction & today no Mass—

That is the way with poor human nature—We all are saints, until we are knocked out of the groove we are running in so smoothly—. But when we are, it is like the locomotive being dashed off the track—

❧

BAPTISTA LYNCH, URSULINE CONVENT, COLUMBIA SC, TO PATRICK LYNCH, MAY 16TH[35]

I thank you very much for kindness & promptitude in writing to me while you are still suffering,[36] . . . what you heard me say to brother John was, I would wish to *hire* a piano for *two months*—that is from now until after our Distribution[37] —this we can do for six or seven dollars a month—would prefer if we had the money to spare, getting a *Harp* by the next session—It is such a "genteel" instrument & thanks to Mother Joseph I can teach it—. I forgot to tell you, that last week Mr J. F. Browne, harp manufacturer, sent me his card or rather a large sheet describing his instruments. We had two of them when in the west, & know their merit—I am trying to make up a class for the next session & if I see that we can safely venture the expense, will try & get one for the next session. But I am afraid of being extravagant. . . .

Ellen Spann & Celia Bollin are complaining. Ellen had a chill & some fevers tonight but I hope will be quite well in a few days—

[PS] I hope you have already engaged Father Dr McNeal to give us our annual retreat—or some other good Jesuit father—I prefer one who is or has been Superior or Master of Novices—I think somebody came into our yard last night & stole Carl [the convent dog]—Good night my dearest Brother 10 oclock

❧

BAPTISTA LYNCH, URSULINE CONVENT, COLUMBIA, S.C. TO PATRICK LYNCH, JUNE 2ND[38]

I am glad to have an excuse for writing to you, so Mrs Martin's visit affords me one—I have *three* things to speak of—*first*, I have quite an interest in "*Philip Neri Reilly*" one of Sister Rose's brothers—a lad of about fifteen years of age, who despite the contradiction of a stepmother, & the labors of a blacksmith shop, still remembers the good instructions given him in Philadelphia by Revd Mr Dunn, & thinks of becoming a priest—He *thirsts* for an education, & begs

Sr. Rose to intercede with his father that he may go to school somewhere—
second you will be pleased to hear that John had a call to Revd Fathers O Connell, to see old Mr Gallager—their gardener. I hope this is a salve to heal the
wound & *thirdly* what about Mrs Martin? She has [been] enquiring for a small
room to rent for a store—a place in a family as housekeeper or upper servant
&c &c and this evening called to see me—She told me how good a friend you
were to her, & had been to her husband, & said *you* had other views for her
beside that of living in the world—so, I asked her, what *her own* views were on
the subject—? She said, she thought a person might save her soul very well in
the world, if she did all she ought—I answered undoubtedly, & it was not every
one that was blessed with a religious vocation—. Seeing nothing about her
which seemingly would make her very desirable for us—since she is not sufficiently educated for the class[room], & I feared would not be willing to wash,
iron, & do the labor of a lay Sister, I left her *very* free, & represented our life as
a very self-sacrificing & hard one—After we talked longer, I liked her better, &
she, finding I was your sister, spoke more plainly—I do not know what to
think of her, but it occurred to me that one who had seen as much of the *ups &
downs* of life as she has, might prove a very useful member to our inexperienced
community—I told her that we would pray about this affair, & that she could
do the same, but I did not think she could make up her mind properly, until she
had approached the sacraments & prayed with a composed & peaceful mind—
Is she very vacillating in her character?

I also told her that if she intended entering our convent (which she said she
would do if ever she entered any) that I preferred her not getting a situation
here first, but rather that she would come in immediately, or return to Charleston, until she had decided what step to pursue—which latter she will do—In my
opinion she only awaits another offer to become Mrs Somebody Else but, perhaps I am mistaken.

I am pleased to say that Eliza is growing better tho slowly—John is very well
& busy. T. G—

. . . We are as busy as possible—as former Bishop Reynolds used to say
"Making labor for ourselves" & planning about the DeBruhl[39] house—I had
the "Quarterly Educational Messenger" sent to me, & subscribed twelve cents
for the year. It shows very plainly, what a powerful impetus Satan is giving to
the educational system of the present day it makes me almost covetous, that we
might rival them—Who is this Henry Barnard LL D.?[40]

∽

BAPTISTA LYNCH, URSULINE CONVENT COLUMBIA, S.C., TO
PATRICK LYNCH, JUNE 6TH[41]

Since I wrote to you, I saw again Mrs Martin, who told me of her engagement to Mr Hewstead—so good bye to her—at least I told her to go to her duty,
pray, & await the return of the (*fugitive* lover), whose conversion probably she
was destined to effect—If not time would tell, & we would see—& you & I
would confer about her—Tonight, I am tired settling Sr. Eliza's scruples—such
a time of it—dear me—! Well, no cross no crown—She has been talking about
returning to her mother for the last month, for now she thinks she did wrong
in leaving her, & that it is her duty to return to the world for her support—she
also hints about becoming a Sr of Mercy—I have considered this painful state
of mind, is in her, either a temptation to test her vocation, or that she has no
vocation for our Order & has for the Congregation of the Srs of Mercy—I have
said & done all I could to ease her mind but to no effect, yesterday she asked
my permission to write & ask her mother for money to pay her travelling expenses back to her—I asked [her] to remain until after the close of the session,
which she consented to do—I hope that by prayer & reflection she may become
more satisfied by that time, but of course, we leave her perfectly free to act as
the Spirit of God may suggest—My own experience at the Srs, teaches me to
feel for her—& Providence may have some special designs over her, as I believe
it had over me for the restoration of the Ursulines to the diocese—Happily her
loss will not be much felt by us—but I regret exceedingly any one leaving us—I
would like it to be as quiet as possible—Mr McCulley paid me twenty dollars
Saturday, & today M^rs McCulley called to see me—expressed great pleasure at
the improvement in her children, & the wish that I would let them stay with us
during her absence of a few weeks—she would be content if they slept on the
floor—She also said she wished very much that we would buy their place, which
they are very anxious to sell—I told her we did not like the situation &c &c—
But after she left, I began to reflect that if we could get their place for about one
third of what DeBruhl's would cost—it would be better to get it & buy the lots
back of us, which would secure a large yard & garden where we could build a
convent with some of the funds sunk in the purchase of DeBruhl's as it is &
knock down the house in which we now live in course of time—. I have not
seen John today to *consult* about it—I *suspect* but do not *know* why he did not
come around—Eliza is better, & speaks, I am told, of going to Charleston—but
John wants Miss Ann Sullivan to come up first & take charge of the housekeeping & children—. He says that you said you would see her, & I think get her to
come— . . . I received a very satisfactory letter from Julie on yesterday, in which
she said all were well—She asked me for a *Gospel*[42] for her little Conlaw who

she says is dedicated to the Blessed Virgin—Mother told her *you* wore one when an infant—I suppose she wished him to be "born of God" & follow in your footsteps—.

I have told Sr. Eliza, that since Revd Dr Ryan has more influence over her than any one else, & was instrumental in keeping her here, I would be glad after some weeks of prayer & reflection she would write & ask his advice, if her mind continued in that state in which she now is—she does not wish to do it, after all her fair promises to him—she has mentioned it to you she says, but I see that Dr Ryan would have more influence over her—I do not wish to accuse her of making her mothers condition a pretext for going out, but it looks to me very like it—. Tho she expresses her gratitude to us—respect & admiration &c &c — . . . I hear that Dr. Marks[43] will begin vacation 15th of June—The College of Columbia for young men on the 28th of June—Most of the schools will continue their schools until the end of July & give the months of August & Sept for vacation—But I prefer to have our distribution on the 1st of July & let the children go home for the 4th . . . —& give the months of July & August for vacation —What do you think?

◀

Baptista Lynch, Ursuline Convent Columbia, to Patrick Lynch,
   [Feast of] St Margaret [June 10][44]

Yesterday our little Cincinnati postulant arrived. T.G.—& appears a cheerful promising Sister & I hope well calculated to take Sister Rose's place in going out.

Every body seems well & happy—Emily Buel will leave in a few days but goes quite pleased with the Academy—her father the same—Yesterday, Dr. Duncan called to see his niece Mary Ryan, at first I did not go to the parlor but sent the child—but he sent a message requesting her to go out with him—so I went to refuse him *amiably*.

If I may judge by his loquacity & the length of his visits, he is as much pleased as Dr. Buel—I hope so, if it is A. M.D. G.— . . .

Have you read the prospectus of the Wesleyan Institution cunningly termed "Columbia Female College?

I have not heard of the DeBruhl plan—I wrote John one *awful scolding*, because Eliza wrote me a note complaining of him—since then, I think he is better—but I am sorry to see he does not tell the truth when he is drinking— Uncle Cito is sick—Eliza is better & preparing to go to Charleston—I wish you would send Miss Ann Sullivan up as soon as you can. Some such pious person would do good in John's family, & is needed to relieve both John & Eliza of the care of their children— . . .

MICHAEL AND LUKE LYNCH, KIBERIDOGUE, NOSLEA, CO. FERMANAGH, TO
PATRICK LYNCH, JUNE 15TH[45]

Right Revd Nephew,

It is with the greatest emotions that I address a few lines to you, Uncle Michael often urged me to write a few lines to you but when I thought of the correspondence that was between you and my dear Son Bernard when you were in Rome and him in Paris my resolution failed but now as I am the eldest of the family ... being born the 17th of November 1772. The most of my family are in America. I have not got a letter from any of them since I got a letter from your father when he was in New York. I suppose they think that I am dead. Uncle Michael's wife died last year he is a widower without any family[;] the failure of the crops in Ireland since the year 46 hurted [*sic*] him more than any of the family Uncle Hugh Neeson and family are well. I saw him in his own House on the 27th ult, he told once that he got a letter from you and that it mentioned one of the family being married to a descendant of one of the ancient chiefs of America.[46] I thought that no wonder for if your Father knew his own genealogy he could trace his own family to the best or greatest families in Tyrone Cavan and Monaghan viz. Oneil Oreilly & McMahon if you have any curiosity to know it I can give it you in detail[.] ... I hope you will offer a Prayer for me as I don't expect to be here long by the course of nature. . . . Your Father had 3 Granduncles priests Edward Bernard and Conlaw Cassidy their Granduncle Hugh McMahon Bishop of Clogher first next Archbishop of Dublin afterwards ArchBishop of Armagh and Primate of all Ireland.

The said Hugh McMahon the Primate it was his uncle Arthur Augustine McMahon Provost of St. Peters in the City of Cassell in Flanders that left the money to establish the McMahons burses in the Irish College Paris for students to be priests of the Dioces [*sic*] of Clogher or Kilmore in the Province of Ulster in Ireland . . .

We remain Right Revd dear Nephew Your most affectionate uncles

FRANCIS LYNCH, CHERAW, TO PATRICK LYNCH, 16 JUNE[47]

. . . I received your kind letter yesterday, and am glad to be able to dispel all apprehensions as to my health D.G.

Last week I did take a little medicine to work off a bilious attack that was accompanied by chills, but it was soon over, and 'Richard' is himself again—
. . . I may go to your city to see Messrs I & Webb on business relations, if so, it

will be a running visit. I have kept along so far very well, at an increased rate in production of shoes. But may want to draw on them after a little.

ᑫ

BAPTISTA LYNCH, URSULINE CONVENT, COLUMBIA SC, TO PATRICK LYNCH, FEAST OF ST. ALOYSIUS [JUNE 21][48]

Anna is here & will remain until after the Distribution. She was always a favorite of mine & is more so now than ever— John is very busy— . . . About a week ago I recd a *long* letter from Miss Weed, who seems desirous to become an Ursuline—but is not seemingly settled on the point—she is very desirous to see, or at least *hear from you*, & begs me to ask you to answer her last letter— . . . I was pleased with her candor, & would be glad you wrote to her—I will send her letter to you if you wish it, in my next— . . . I was speaking to John about the Elmore property—he says we will lose all our Catholic day pupils if we go out there, excepting such as can ride in carriages that is, we may, we shall lose all—This would of course never do, either in a Religious or pecuniary point of view which I am very sorry for, since the sooner we can remove from this location, I think the better, we are now in the midst of *grog shops* & *large beer houses* & such profane language & midnight carousals as disturb us are frightful—. We have reason to wonder at, & admire the Divine Patience.

Mrs Keitt called lately, & wished either we or the Jesuits would purchase her place, but I do not think it would suit— . . .

I hope the Orphan Asylum is getting on well, & satisfactorily to you— . . .

When will Eliza return?

I hope she is much better.

ᑫ

BAPTISTA LYNCH, URSULINE CONVENT COLUMBIA SC, TO PATRICK LYNCH, SUNDAY 26TH JUNE[49]

Before I begin to give you an account of how I spent my *feast day* let me thank you most sincerely for your congratulations, & still more for your prayers & offerings—I expected you to come that morning, but had not reason to do so I am sure—Did you remember that you arrived in Brown County on the feast of St. John the Baptist last year—? Our Sisters imitated the examples they had seen elsewhere, & put themselves to a great deal of trouble, especially the novices. . . .

The day passed off as happily to every one else, as it did to myself seemingly & we blessed God for His goodness to us—. On Friday morning we held our examinations as usual . . . The performance of the evening lasted from seven o clock until nine, & the tableux were as prettily got up, as in Brown County—I wish you could have witnessed them— . . .

Our Lord, who watches over me, & knows how good humiliation is for me, sent me a very good one, in the midst of all this, thro' John—who came after Anna, & was seen by our Srs in a condition most painful for us to witness—This evening he & Anna called for the first time since, when he was quite well, but annoyed with me—& I do not blame him.

Today, I received a letter from Mother Theresa, who tells me that she will have her "distribution" on the 14th, consequently we will have ours on the 16th & under the protection of "Our Lady of Mt Carmel"—It's being Saturday makes no difference to us— . . . I am very much afraid you are giving yourself a great deal of anxiety & trouble to get the means requisite for purchasing a convent for us—& I would not have you suffer five minutes on our account—You told me to trust in the good providence of God, & so I do—The good disposition of our Sisters too, in that regard, is a great support to me—today, when at recreation we were planning for the erection of a chapel &c—I said if you allowed me, I would beg thro' the streets of Columbia for means to accomplish our designs, & three of the Postulants begged as a favor, that they might share in the humiliation—I feel tempted to ask your permission to imitate our Sisters of St. Louis in that way, after the Distribution; perhaps such an act of public humiliation, might bring a blessing on the house, & do much good—. I fear our Distribution this year will be too trifling a thing to ask persons of distinction to, the greater number of the children being so small—& the house so unfit—. Should you not visit us before the 16th of July, I will tell you that it will terminate with a short address to you, which you will have the goodness to make some reply to, & give your Episcopal benediction to *this mustard seed, this tiny nut,* which is we trust to germinate & yield a hundred fold—.

I hope Eliza will soon return. I think John misses her a good deal—Anna too speaks of returning to Cheraw—

. . . Mrs De Bruhl, not yet returned, but expected every day. A man who lives next door to Mrs Bausketts, called & requested John to buy his place, saying he thought the next property could be got too—A most eligible situation I am told by him if only enough of ground. We are awakened at all hours, by the inmates of these establishments near us— . . .

1859 July–December

"'Tempest in a tea-pot'"

The year 1858 had seen two of the Lynches assume major leadership roles: Patrick as the bishop of the Charleston diocese, Baptista as the foundress of a new community of Ursulines conducting an academy. The diocese, with its array of institutions scattered over two states, was, by far, a larger responsibility than a community and academy. But, given the resources of personnel, facilities, and money that Patrick Lynch inherited as the third Bishop of Charleston, the challenges he faced in accepting miter and crozier were far less than the ones confronting his sister in establishing the Ursulines' new foundation in Columbia. Baptista was heading up an academy whose faculty consisted of herself and two other nuns; two lay sisters and a novice made up the staff. The building they inherited from the Sisters of Mercy was too old, too small, and located in too seedy a neighborhood for the prestigious institution of higher learning that Baptista envisioned. Then, too, the locals who sent their daughters to the academy resented the Ursulines' displacing the well-loved Sisters of Mercy who had begun the school. In brief, Baptista had too few personnel, an outmoded facility, a terrible setting, and unwelcoming parents and students. Her ambitious designs for the upgrading of the modest academy the Ursulines had taken over (she wanted it called "The St. Charles Institute for the Education of Young Ladies") only aggravated the scope of the challenges she faced.

From the time of their arrival in Columbia, Baptista had focused on the recruitment of candidates for the Ursulines, as well as students for the academy. To augment the meager staff that she had brought from Brown County, she concentrated especially on securing lay sisters through supportive prelates such as John Purcell of Cincinnati and James Wood of Philadelphia. For enlarging the faculty, she had a longer-range plan: cultivating vocations among the academy's pupils to develop a homegrown faculty for the future. Key to this was the creation of a pool of potential candidates for the Ursulines made up of the daughters of affluent Catholics, especially converts, as well as émigrés from

Maryland now scattered throughout the Deep South, such as the Semmes family. But for Baptista, the top priority was the acquisition of a facility that would provide the wherewithal for the development of a female institution of higher learning. In meeting that goal, Baptista turned to her bishop brother. Patrick Lynch, within the first year of the Ursulines' arrival, purchased a property Baptista considered a vast improvement over their inherited site, only to reactivate the nativism that had recently been dormant in the region.

The Know-Nothing wave that had swept across much of America in the mid-1850s had been ebbing in most places, South Carolina included, since the elections of 1856. But if nativism as a political movement was in steep decline, anti-Catholic feelings persisted, a reality the Lynches knew too well. In July Bishop Lynch bought from the Bauskett family the American hotel in Columbia for $40,000. When the identity of the buyer and the projected use of the former hotel became public knowledge, the bishop's fears about a hostile reaction were realized. The hotel might have been in a wretched state of neglect, but business owners in the neighborhood brought a suit against the bishop for damaging their economic interests by depriving them of the customers they could regularly expect to attract from a hotel, even a fleabag like the American. Bishop and nuns finally prevailed in the court, kept the property, and the Ursulines moved into their new home on the corner of Richland and Blanding Streets. Soon after the nuns occupied the hotel, a mob threatened building and occupants, but city authorities provided protection to the convent and academy that ended the protest. Still, the fear remained of another attack. That worry led them to hire a night watchman and to depend on family and friends in the community, including the mayor,[1] for protection.

In the summer, as Patrick Lynch pondered what to do with the contested property in Columbia, John Brown, notorious for his cold-blooded execution of proslavery settlers in Kansas three years earlier, was secretly gathering men and supplies in an isolated cabin five miles east of the Potomac River in the hills of western Maryland. On a dark Sunday evening in mid-October, "Captain" Brown and twenty-two black and white abolitionists descended on the river road to a town on the Virginia side of the Potomac, Harpers Ferry, which housed both the largest armory in the country as well as a major arsenal of the U.S. government. Brown's band seized both facilities, liberated slaves from nearby plantations, and sent out word that the war to end slavery had begun. Then, over the next day, they waited for those who would respond to their cry and join their fight: free men committed to rooting out the national sin that was slavery and the slaves themselves. The only respondents, as it turned out, were the local militia from Virginia and Maryland, as well as a company of marines, led by a former commandant of West Point, brought in by train from Washington. After a day and a half of sporadic fighting, followed by a siege of the engine house within the armory grounds, where the majority of the surviving raiders had taken refuge, the marines, at Robert E. Lee's command, stormed the building and captured Brown and the seven followers who were still alive. Ten of Brown's band were dead, as were a marine and three townspeople.

John Brown's raid, as it came to be known, sent shock waves through the country, especially south of the Mason-Dixon Line. Here was the frightening confirmation of the conspiracy theories Southerners had been harboring about abolitionist intentions of inciting slave insurrection and providing the arms to carry it off. One prominent Southerner, the agricultural reformer Edmund Ruffin, during the presidential campaign of the following year, sent each Southern governor a pike that had been part of the array of weapons Brown had either brought with him or commandeered in Harpers Ferry. On each pike Ruffin attached a label that read, "Sample of the Favors Designed for US by our Northern Brethren."[2]

Over the past decade, beginning with the Compromise of 1850, the differences between the sections had been growing ever wider. Events ranging from the publication of Harriet Beecher Stowe's novel Uncle Tom's Cabin to the Kansas-Nebraska Act, the civil war in Kansas, the Dred Scott decision, and now John Brown's raid had seriously disturbed the national fault line of slavery and split the sections, each quake worsening the fissure. After the shock of Brown's raid, the country got a glimpse of the abyss. Some Southerners, like Ruffin, avid for secession, could barely contain their glee at the destabilizing event: "it really seemed now most probable," he noted in his diary, "that the outbreak was planned & instigated by northern abolitionists, & with the expectation of thus starting a general slave insurrection. . . . Such a practical exercise of abolition principles is needed to stir the sluggish blood of the south."[3] Stir the South it did, as nothing before had done. If it was not the event that set in motion the region's rush to secession, it left it teetering on the edge, needing but one other earth-shaking event to bring the fear and paranoia about abolitionists that had been building for thirty years to a climax and plunge the South into the vortex of conflict with once-fellow Americans.

All of this drama is missing in the correspondence of the Lynches caught up in responding to the all-but-consuming demands of the business, medical, ecclesiastical, and academic worlds. Although slaveholders, their letters convey little awareness of the distant forces on a collision course that would all too soon radically change the Lynches and their world.

❧

Baptista Lynch, Ursuline Convent, Columbia, to Patrick Lynch, July Friday 8th[4]

. . . I am sorry I did not know before how inconvenient it would be to come on Saturday—since we have already told, & written the 16th & our pupils are diminishing weekly on account of the heat—I suppose it will now be better, to have it on the 19th, that is the Tuesday following. It will begin at nine o clock in the morning, while the day is cool & I trust be over before the heat of the day sets in.

We hope that by twelve o clock, the visitors will all have left, & we will have the house clear— . . .

Dr. Fair[5] wants us to take his place again & has reduced his price a little—but when you come & our Distribution is over we will talk about those things & do what you think A.M.D.G. I only beg that you will not give yourself any anxiety about us, for somehow or other I cannot, poor as we are—feel any distrust of our success. Not that I mean to say we shall ever become rich—The Sister Postulants are jealously asking when will they go begging—? I tell them you have not as yet given us the permission—. I wrote a few lines to the Ardent Miss Weed & told her we would receive her into our noviciate, but of course could not say how she would like it, or we would like her—but the trial we were willing to grant her, on account of your opinion of her, & that which we had formed from her letters—But that she must let me know before coming that I might procure a hard bed for her—since in our poverty we had not an extra one to spare—I told her I would not tempt her to our terrestrial paradise, by creature comforts.

❧

Baptista Lynch, Ursuline Convent, Columbia S.C. to Patrick Lynch, July 14th[6]

John, Hugh, Anna & myself are having a nice time of it here, and are expecting you on next Monday, to complete the quintette—But I am afraid you are not well? I thank you very much for those circulars which [we] received & intend sending them around very soon. Several persons have evinced some curiosity to be present at our "Distribution" I understand & should we receive the cards in time, I will send them about, but if you should find it inconvenient to send them, I will only regard it as providential—John is better than when you saw him—Hugh looks a little delicate—Anna is improving very much, she is learning the guitar & aiding us in the drawing lessons for the children—We are all as busy & anxious about our Distribution as if we expected a large

John Hugh Lynch, the second oldest child of Conlaw Peter and Eleanor Neison Lynch, practiced medicine, first in Cheraw and then Columbia. Courtesy of Ancestry.com.

attendance—I am sorry to say, that Revd Lawrence O Connell is quite indisposed. Father Joseph would have left for Sumter today had his brothers state of health allowed him—Father O Connell[7] is at Jewell [?] Hill—& may he stay & enjoy his visit there.

Our Sisters & children are (TG) generally well, with the exception of colds —We will rest awhile after the "distribution," I hope you will spend several days with us during which Mr Bollin[8] says he will drive you around town, & show you a place which he has selected as suitable for us.

Our next care will be our "Annual Spiritual Exercises" which I trust we may enter upon August 7th—& come out on the Feast of the Assumption — with the profession of Sr Loretta & reception of Sr. Rose both exclusively private— Since we are disappointed in having a Jesuit Father from a distance—I think I would like Father Joseph, to conduct our retreat—It would be better—more prudent perhaps for *you* not to do it—& as for the priests of the Diocese, the one whose practice is most conformable to his words, is the one I would prefer—. Of course we are thankful to get the services of any—. Hugh will be kind enough to make up my accounts in proper form, for your inspection, if that is possible—but I am afraid they will "puzzle a rookery"—If I do not get the cards for admission to our Distribution our Sisters think I would do well to purchase some here in Columbia, & secure at least the attendance of a few, after all our trouble. We can accommodate sixty persons without difficulty.

JOHN LYNCH, COLUMBIA, TO PATRICK LYNCH, JULY 25TH[9]

... The American Hotel will soon be sold, and I expect at quite a sacrifice. I merely mention the fact, for your consideration. I do not know the amt of land. I suppose 1⅓ acres facing on or rather on the corner of Richardson & the street the Charlotte depot is on—being the north Side of the Square. I delivered your messages to Sister Ellen & Mr Reilly,[10] when I told him who was proposed as the outsider to buy he expressed himself pretty plainly, and from his remarks, would suppose, I was more than half right in having my suspicions that there was some self-interest in the case, but we will see, if you have any suggestions at any time let me know. I am at least in this case without self. ...

FRANCIS LYNCH, CHERAW, TO PATRICK LYNCH, 27 JULY[11]

As time & tide waits for no one, so my notes at Bank have fixed periods, when attention is directed to them. With this is several for 4000$ which please endorse & have at the Bk of Ch of S.C. I have $62—there on deposit which will cover the discts.

As I much feared, you have overworked yourself during the hot days of summer; I am glad you are now resting (if you know how to do such thing) from your labors, and hope soon you will feel quite recovered. Bro Hugh & family & Sister Anna reached home last night all well. For my own part I am in excellent health. Henrietta and the children too are quite well. So are Father & mother & Revd Mr Cullinan. ...

I am delighted at the termination of the war with the relations with the Holy See. The policy that would desire the deprivation of all temporal power has been thwarted (that's a hard word to write) ...[12]

BAPTISTA LYNCH, URSULINE CONVENT COLUMBIA S.C., TO PATRICK LYNCH, JULY 27TH[13]

I am very sorry to hear thro your letter to brother John, that indisposition prevented your travelling. I trust you are quite well now & have rested awhile —rest is my sovereign panacea—John is so busy that I have not seen him for two days, his little Anna was very ill, but is much better now—Anna & Hugh with Cornelia & Alice Reilly have returned to Cheraw. Ellen Spann & Eliza will go over before the commencement of school, to pay their respects to their

Grandparents—I think they expect you next Sunday—. I received a "Baltimore Mirror" with accounts of some distributions—I thought probably it would be well, to send them ours & the Subscription of the following years. What do you think? And so the "South Carolinian" did not publish ours! A very good index that they fear our power—It is delightful to make Satan & his emissaries tremble —I am sure it is all for the best. So it is no matter—I was told today that we would no doubt have a flourishing school next year—We will see—I have just paid Miss Cullen $100.00 for teaching painting & drawing for five months!! We will try & avoid that next year.

. . . Our Sisters have several times reminded me to write & beg you to send us the St. Louis, Cincinnati, Louisville & New York papers with the various accounts of their Exhibitions, Distributions &c, &c Hugh & Anna say that persons received their cards too late & some did not understand them when they got them. So much the better, they will think it more than it was. Mrs Bauskett paid us a long visit for the purpose of laying before us all the advantages of purchasing Col Beden's place—which I have since heard is sold—

Prudence forbids my writing something about somebody, & the purchase of our selected spot, which Mr R[eilly] thinks should be sold for two thousand five hundred—

Shall we continue praying for peace until you tell us to stop, *as the* Miscellany says—or shall we make our thanksgiving—? I hope our Holy Father will refuse to accept the donation of Napoleon.[14] A nun meddling in politics!! I had better say "good night" for it is pretty late— . . .

ᜃ

JOHN LYNCH, COLUMBIA, TO PATRICK LYNCH, JULY 28TH[15]

I mentioned to you when I sent you the MS that the American Hotel was for sale. I went today to look at it, was pleased, reported to Sister Ellen who approved. Equally pleased, I now wish you to pass your opinion (leaving out the views) which you can't do without taking an inside view of, but I will give you some idea beforehand. it is situated on Richardson, Blanding & Marion (I believe) St., on Richardson one Hundred and—ft., on Blanding the side of a square,—On Marion ½ square—a plot something like this [inserts drawing depicting Blanding St to Marion in the figuration of a half square on the left and an acre on the right] . . . *They say* it has seventy rooms, besides passages &c. My reason for writing this hurriedly is that you may not compromise yourself in the other case, before looking at this. I have tried to see Dr. Boatwright before writing but have failed.[16] I know the place can be bought—for Eighteen thousand but I intend trying to see what fifteen will do. I know they don't want the money, as it is an estate property, and by making them perfectly secure may be bought at eight or ten years time . . . practice is tolerably brisk, prospects fair, if I don't get along it is my own fault, pray that I may. . . .

༄

BAPTISTA LYNCH, URSULINE CONVENT, COLUMBIA, S.C., TO
PATRICK LYNCH, JULY 29TH[17]

Our sisters join with me in expressing some little of the gratitude we feel, for the trouble which you have given yourself in drawing those plans, you were so kind as to send us. They are really very nice, & altho we will all propose another idea about the chapel, we will talk over it with a great deal of pleasure—I sent your note to Mr. Bollin at once, but Sister Rose returned, saying, that he was absent from home & would be so for a week— . . .

I am happy to hear that you are again able to travel. I trust you may not get sick again—if you would take soda crackers with you & eat them slowly as you read in the cars, you would I think find them a prevention to that sickness from which you sometimes suffer—. I suppose you have received John's letter about the American Hotel, which contains seventy rooms, & which he thinks quite a desirable bargain—Sister Ursula seems to prefer it to the *Hill*, since we have been told that our day school would fail us there, & she dreads the debt in building.

Sr Augustine is keen for building, & would spend right & left, trusting to Providence to pay her debts—Mrs McAully[18] is still very desirous that we should purchase their place—she showed Sister Rose the various apartments &c. . . .

If the American Hotel is such a good building, so spacious, & central as Mr Keitt says "to suit exactly," I am equally content—or if notwithstanding the remarks of others you judge the Hill the best, I am very much pleased.

We would indeed be sorry to involve you in either debt or difficulties—tho' when I this morning was deploring my doing so—Sister Augustine told me, not to concern myself, it was not for me, but for the good of religion you would undertake such a labor—Still Sʳ Ursula & myself, both of whom know a little more about money matters than she does, would be very sorry to lead you beyond your depth—We will do the praying, & leave to you the calculations & exercise of judgment in this affair— . . .

Yesterday Ellen & I recd letters from Sister Mary, . . . —The Old Lady's Magazine is a failure. Judge Rice is the same—Caroline worn down—the old lady & Topsy coming out to S.C. Dr. Spann talks of sending one of his daughters to us—crops are promising—&c. . . .

ᴼ

Baptista Lynch, Ursuline Convent Columbia S.C., to Patrick Lynch, Aug 7th[19]

Father Joseph is very satisfactory & giving us an excellent retreat. It is really edifying to see our Sisters, how they have plunged into it. We have office in choir three times a day—Meditation three times a day—consideration once—Examen twice—& practice of mortification.[20] It was beautiful to see one going round the choir kissing the feet of all the Sisters—then kneeling at the foot of the great cross accusing herself, & begging the prayers of her sisters—Another kneeling to receive a public reprimand at the foot of the cross—Is it not delightful—I trust such may bring the blessing of God on us—enable us to do much good & to pay you for the *American Hotel*. I feel like getting into a *nut-shell* when I think of that awful debt—We all feel, & express our gratitude for your goodness & generosity towards us, when you see so little prospect of our being able to make the return we would wish—especially we feel grateful, for the manner in which you have the deed drawn up—as our Convent has already suffered so much from the want of attention to such points between friends—May our good God accept our poor service, & may we all be instruments for His greater glory—I would like immediately after our retreat is over, to know your wishes about our going to the new convent—& if you think it well we should open our school this next session &c &c John thinks, & so do our Sisters, that it will be necessary to pack some of the furniture—since we cannot have a large & empty house, and it will be cheaper & more suitable than any other. . . .

Did I tell you that Mr Semmes wrote to me from Georgia?[21] I would not be surprised any day to see his daughters—Col J. J. Ryan very politely wrote to me, offering to make any purchases while north that we might wish—Have you seen the notices in the Columbia paper of your purchase—? . . .

ᴼ

Baptista Lynch, Ursuline Convent Columbia S.C., to Patrick Lynch, Aug 10th[22]

. . . We would be glad to make a renovation of our vows at the close of [re-treat], but shall be unable to do so unless you come up on Monday morning & say (as our rule prescribes) a private Mass for us. Am I not presumptuous? Sr. Augustine is at my elbow, & says yes _____. . . .

Mr William Huckles of New York called yesterday to place his two daughters, or rather enquire our terms—which he said were moderate—he is an Episcopalian, & has them at "Mrs Winchester's Academy" *Frederick* [Maryland.] We came to no decision—I wonder who he is, & why he would place them here?

He heard Mr Comerford speak of our Institution, & wanted to know when *our new convent* would be ready for us—? It is the topic of conversation in town I suppose—at least to many.

BAPTISTA LYNCH, URSULINE CONVENT COLUMBIA S.C., TO PATRICK LYNCH, AUGUST 12TH[23]

Perhaps you already know a great deal more than I can tell you of the *commotion* which exists in this place on account of your recent purchase—but if not, I thought it well to mention it altho in retreat—& you can learn all about it from those who know—

Being in retreat I knew nothing of it, until this morning, when Father Joseph whom I saw for a few moments in the parlor, told me that a meeting had been held, & resolutions taken, to petition you to relinquish the design of establishing the Academy & convent in the late "American Hotel" but he hoped you would not listen to it—I said quite the contrary, if you could sell it at a good profit—& enable us to build, it would be much more desirable—so he said in that case, he wished you would put it up at auction & run it up to its *full value, & make those gentlemen pay for it*—since it was very evident, prejudices rather than pecuniary interest actuated them, tho' they pretend it is because the converting the Hotel into our Academy, would seriously injure the mercantile interest of the city—

Would it not be fine if you could sell it for forty thousand dollars, & begin our building on the Glaize property—? We will talk about it when we have the pleasure of seeing you—Can you come on Monday morning? & let us renew our vows—you do not know what a delightful retreat we have had! John called yesterday, but I thought it more according to the spirit of our retreat to excuse myself to him—We will pray hard that you may be enlightened what to do for the greater glory of Almighty God— . . .

BAPTISTA LYNCH, URSULINE CONVENT, COLUMBIA S.C., TO PATRICK LYNCH, FEAST OF THE ASSUMPTION [AUGUST 15][24]

Is not the "tempest in a tea-pot" ridiculous, that the people here are making about the Hotel? What do they fear in the power of a few weak women—? It reminds me of what our "annals" relate of the Nuns when first they went to Cork—The penals[25] were in force—they could not wear their costume—& a council was held, to insist, on their dispersing.

A "Gamaliel"[26] of the Council rose, & asked what was the use of disturbing a set of *women* who *drank their tea* in peace together?

❦

JOHN LYNCH, COLUMBIA, TO PATRICK LYNCH, AUGUST 28TH[27]

I wrote you two letters a few days ago, in the last which I requested to be forwarded I enclosed a measurement of the windows—and advised your being here at the time of trial, the Court & jury made a misstrial [*sic*] yesterday, the case will be tried again on Tuesday 30th. Mr Bellinger[28] thinks your presence would not advance your cause, therefore thinks it best for you to remain away till after the trial. I have no doubt of the result of the trial on next Tuesday, the spirit evinced by Thompson, the crowd around him, and the jury making a miss trial [*sic*] after the evidence, has produced quite a sensation in the community, which I have no doubt will make the next jury take an impartial view of the case, and be of service to the School afterwards.

You had best get the blinds as soon as possible, as sister Ellen wishes to move in at once, after the blinds & doors are fixed, the other alterations she then could be present at, I have partially engaged a carpenter to do all the alterations

Sister Ellen received a letter from you postmarked Philadelphia Aug[t] 24th, please let me know as soon as you return to Charleston. It strikes me your interests have not been *pushed* if they have been looked to carefully. What will be the cost of the court and who will it fall on, is a question I have not asked Mr. Bellinger, if on Thompson he is not able to pay a cent, so the other party may have to pay. . . .

❦

JOHN LYNCH, [COLUMBIA], TO PATRICK LYNCH, THURSDAY, SEPT 1ST[29]

I don't know whether you have been advised of the termination of *the* suit that was pending. I expect *you* will have to pay costs, not meaning by that, you did not gain the suit, for I see by the Guardian that the other party was found *guilty*, of course you retain from Dr. Boatwright whatever you have to pay out; it makes no difference to *you* except as to time.

Eliza & myself took a survey of the house yesterday, her idea was to superintend the cleaning of it, but, after the survey, she backed out, nor would I have allowed her to have undertaken such a job. It is decidedly the dirtiest house *for the size* that I have ever seen. Sister Ellen is very anxious to get into it at once, but I cannot see any chance under three weeks, and if you send up the blinds at once, I don't wish to commence any alterations until I am advised by you. The sheriff gave me possession Tuesday Evening. I have exercised some little authority in granting some privileges which I have no doubt you will sanction when you come up. I will have to hire several hands to commence the cleaning process before we can think of whitewashing. This I shall commence today.

ട്ര

Baptista Lynch, Ursuline Convent, Columbia S.C. to Patrick Lynch, [September 1][30]

You will be glad to hear that we have three new boarders—Miss Virginia Semmes, Miss Jane Semmes & Miss Mary Warren of Augusta, Georgia. Misses Semmes are from "Miss. as you know, & Miss Warren is their cousin—We have received for them about $500.40 which I will either place in bank at your disposal or employ in the purchase of Harp & Globes for the academy—I would be very glad to purchase some articles of school furniture or apparatus as soon as our means will allow, from Brownville of N.Y., but will wait a little later on —Another piece of agreeable news I may tell you is that Sr Eliza as well as Sr. Margaret wishes not to leave—Sr Eliza begs me to let her remain until she gets a letter from her mother, says she cannot bear to go—& it may be that Providence will not require the sacrifice from her—. I am very much pleased to hear this, for she is very quiet reliable & good—and we are very much in want of teachers—Mrs Semmes asked me yesterday how many teachers we had—I said five, but my heart sunk, for I knew—& that her oldest daughter is eighteen years of age & has been a pupil at Nazareth & Georgetown, where she only left on account of her health, the climate being too cold—. Dr. Marks employs five gentlemen, & four lady teachers—the Female Wesleyan Academy about the same number, & we would require three efficient mistresses to aid in Music, Drawing & the higher classics. I am the best English & music teacher myself but am exhausted & unfit for other duties when I attend to those properly—Sr Augustine is the best for Painting Drawing & Languages & will have more than enough to do. Sr Ursula has entire charge of the conduct of children & teaches writing work &c &c— . . . —I have tried to teach the novices during vacation, but our wardrobe was in such disorder, on account of not having time during the year to attend to it, that they were obliged to sacrifice their time to it—I trust however we are training up a nice set of Nuns in our pupils, who will make more efficient mistresses in four or five years, than others educated elsewhere. I am so afraid that we cannot stand the perpetual strain until then—But after all "God is at the helm" & it is only His glory we seek so why need we be anxious— He will do His own work, if we are only faithful—

Tomorrow the carpenters will be here, so for now we have no place for our old boarders when they return—If we could only go into the Hotel by the 1st Oct. Yesterday Mrs Bauskett told me she thought if you would spend several days in Columbia & talk among the people, your presence would produce a good effect for religion & for us— . . .

☙

[Baptista Lynch, Columbia, to Patrick Lynch, August][31]

[Handwritten letterhead:] St Charles Institute For the education of young Ladies Under the Immediate Supervision / of the Religious of the Ursuline Convent / Columbia S.C.[32]

The Ladies of the Ursuline Community Columbia S.C. respectfully announce to their friends & to the public that the annual exercises of their Institute will commence at the usual period the 30th of September &c &c &c &c

My Dearest Brother,

I simply suggest the changes for your approval or non-approval. I think it is no longer necessary to conciliate either the Sisters or people by retaining a name which is but little known—so little that in a late work published here, "*The City Directory*" the name of "St. Mary's College" is omitted & "The Academy of the Imm. Con [Immaculate Conception]:" substituted, with Revd J. J. O Connell for President—Revd L O Connell vice president & Revd Joseph O Connell assistant—moreover, my letters from Booksellers, Music Stores & mail generally "Ursuline Academy"

I like our Chapel to be the "Church of the Imm. Con." but academy to be entitled as above, unless you think better not—I do not see any necessity for any longer making any allusion to the Sisters of Mercy, as I do not see that it has done any good—But all as you think best—[33]

I hope my dearest Brother that you are no longer suffering with the pain in your face, & that you have *rested yourself well*—you will then feel better—poor John is *tired out* nursing Eliza, who is still very sick he says—T.G. we are not married—John was here yesterday evening & I perceived had been drinking a little—not enough to cloud his intellect, but enough to make him bitter & misanthropic in his feelings—

He began it at home he said & had continued it here—I think so foolish, & wrong of him to trammel himself with promises to refrain totally from it for six months, as he has done for he cannot keep them & then he has a conscience that worries him when he fails, & makes him do worse—I do not feel so badly, since I am told it is not such a dreadful sin—but I tried to get him to ask permission to take it,[34] when necessary—not to be disheartened, & to approach Holy Communion on next Friday—I hope I may succeed— . . .

⤸

BAPTISTA LYNCH, URSULINE CONVENT COLUMBIA S.C. TO PATRICK LYNCH, SEPT 2ND[35]

I suppose you have received John's letters & communications from him about all the business of the Hotel—I am no judge in these matters of business, & therefore have been silent—I was a little annoyed both with Mr Bellinger for not carrying out your plans & with the people—but it is all settled most amiably now T G—& if you can only come up, we will move before the opening of our Academy I trust.

We have purchased the lumber for fixing this house, but will not go to any useless expense here, hoping to get in there in a fortnight. John says we can do so in perfect safety after you once come up & say what to have done—

I told you in my last of the arrival of the Misses Semmes of Miss—& their cousin Miss Warner of Augusta Georgia—I had to turn the Sisters out of the dormitory to give Miss W her bed, so now we have no room for another, even our old boarders, and Mary Ryan wrote word a day or two ago, that she would return before the opening of the Academy—also *Miss Frederick* of Augusta will be here soon. Will you not come as soon as possible?

I was so much gratified by your nice long letter from Philadelphia—the city of *brotherly love*.

And so Miss Weed[36] will come! It will be excellent when we move, to have a room for each of those new-comers who are perhaps fastidious—. I am very glad that Bishop Wood feels an interest in our convent & hope he may send us good & efficient postulants—What will Madame Hardy[37] say to you? Miss Aiken will be most welcome if she comes of her own free will. The good woman of whom you spoke would be very serviceable, especially since I fear Sr. Martha is going into decline (unless the cold weather reinstates her) . . .

John & Eliza called this morning, to ask about what was to be done at the Hotel, & to offer something about cleaning it out—It is very kind of them so I told them to give as to the poor of Christ, that they might have the merits of giving & we of being recipients—Eliza did not either like so or understand this very well—It would be my good fortune if the Ladies would charitably undertake that duty off of our hands— . . .

⤸

ANTONIA LYNCH, CARMELITE CONVENT, BALTIMORE, TO PATRICK LYNCH, [9] SEPT[38]

As we had not the pleasure of seeing you last week we concluded that you had returned home by the steamer as you first intended. My dear Brother your note of the 22nd to rev Mother was received. She returns many thanks for your kindness in anticipating the interest before due. Also for your donation. You may be sure of having secured the interest of the prayers of the Carmelites— your last sermon to us has won all our hearts. . . .

ॐ

BAPTISTA LYNCH, URSULINE CONVENT COLUMBIA S.C. TO PATRICK LYNCH, OCT 5TH[39]

I snatch a few minutes to tell you how peaceably & well all things are get- ting on.—Yesterday evening there was a meeting of the Engine Company near us, & I suppose they never assembled & dispersed so quickly[40]—Providence is taking good care of us, we have reason to be truly grateful—John has gone over to Cheraw with Conlaw & John, before leaving he spoke to the Mayor who very kindly said he would fill his place (a thing he could not do however hard he might try) John was disappointed in setting off, & came around at 10 o clock at night to see if all was quiet & who should he meet here, true to his word *doing sentinel* but the Mayor himself!

So at the meeting of the Engine Company he was there to prevent any annoyance. . . .

P.S. . . . We have another nice little day pupil, whose mother told me she had tried Protestant school, she told her friends, & would now try Catholic one. I hope she may become a convert.

I have promised Sister Ambrose to write & ask Mrs Thomas Taylor many of whose family reside in Montgomery, if she knew of any proper escort for a lady who would leave for that place in about a fortnight—She would like to go next Monday week—I need not say I have done & said every thing I could to prevent her re-entering the world, but, to no purpose—I have tried to persuade her to return to the Sisters,[41] which she would not hear of—Then I offered to write to any of the convents that I know of, for her, which offer she says she may accept at some future day—I think she is either a little deranged, under an illusion of Satan, or very imperfect—

"She enjoyed her retreat more than any she ever made since she entered re- ligion" & prays very much believing she is doing what is for the best! . . .

ॐ

BAPTISTA LYNCH, URSULINE CONVENT, COLUMBIA, TO PATRICK LYNCH, OCT 7TH[42]

This morning I received your letter enquiring about our receiving those Sis- ters of Mercy—At first, I thought it probably a means made use of by Almighty

God for sending us Sisters already well trained in religious life, a blessing which circumstances limit our enjoyment of here—then I reflected that probably they are disaffected fastidious members that superiors would be glad to get rid of— for in my opinion *no religious should travel for her health*, nor do I admire any one that would—again I see how much of Sister Maria's time is taken up by attending on S. Ambrose & what an inconvenience it is—

On the other hand, I liked their asking that charitable attention from us— & would like to show it without even requiring a remuneration, this however would be unjust to ourselves—After all my reflection, I consulted our Sisters who seem to agree in thinking it would be well to receive them cordially & entertain them the best we can, if they are willing to put up with what we can offer—It will not be as with Maria P— [Pinckney] they will be company for one another, & they can occupy some of those rooms designated for Ladies in retreat— . . .

This morning I recd a letter from Bishop Wood & will receive these sub- jects from Philadelphia soon for Lay Sisters, this will be enough for the present, I have answered Bp Wood, & while I thanked him, asked him to get us some *sensible pious choir novices with doweries*(!) Was it not clever?—I *must* stop. . . .

୶

JOHN LYNCH, COLUMBIA, TO PATRICK LYNCH, OCT 14TH[43]

. . . I am just from convent, all quite well—blinds not yet arrived. Watchman called last night and wanted to quit—Excuse—nothing to do, and lonesomeness —told him to wait till tomorrow night which would be ½ month, and to then call on me, think I will employ an old man Patrick Brennan, uncle of Sister DeSales who is anxious [for the post], will have to give him some place to warm by—the only fear is he may take in his *pocket* a companion; arouse his *pride* and he will not, but this after I hear from you—please hurry on the blinds, Wm McCants better, the old man very sore on the subject of the law suit

୶

BAPTISTA LYNCH, URSULINE CONVENT, TO PATRICK LYNCH, FEAST OF ST. TERESA [OCT 15][44]

I am very happy to hear that you have arrived safely & well . . . & that you have succeeded in renting the stores & rooms as it will give us some means to pay all these expenses—I can not bear the idea of draining your pocket-book by our wants— . . .

The lightening rod is being put up today— . . . I wish too that Mrs Pinckney would come to see Maria, who will remain until next Thursday—

∽

BAPTISTA LYNCH, URSULINE CONVENT, COLUMBIA, S.C., TO
PATRICK LYNCH, OCT 17TH[45]

Mrs Pinckney is here—& we are very glad of it—Maria says especially on
your account—They will both start for Montgomery on Wednesday morning at
5 oclock in the morning. I think Maria is very forthright in having her mother
to aid & accompany her—She sends her love to you, & says she is quite well
after travelling except that she knocked herself against the rail of the cars & hurt
her side a little. This is father's birth-day. I did not forget him at Mass.

John & myself have been *wondering* about the delay of the blinds—& the
workmen growing tired of waiting for them, have left—I wish very much they
were up, it would save us a good deal.

Our sisters are beginning to grow anxious to get into the chapel, away from
the noise of pianos, & children—& where we could have proper choir—How
soon do you think this can be—? Would you please either send or bring us a
lithograph of the Charleston cathedral, & *the portrait* that you had taken for
us? I am sending bills to every body that we have any claim on, so I hope we
shall not be obliged to call on you for money—Our class furniture has not yet
come—neither have I heard any thing, of the Sister from the North—. Mr Hal-
cott Green called here today to speak of taking Maria under his care—he asked
if the Mother Superior were *at home*. I went to the parlor & was much pleased
with his gentlemanly manner—I hope that he was equally pleased & will send
us some rich boarders from Alabama. Of course we said nothing of the kind.

... Mrs Pinckney has written to Thomas to meet her at Brantville & accompanying herself & Maria to Montgomery Ala. Maria told me that her mother at
first, like you & myself, wanted her to return to the Sisters, but that after she
told her all, she no longer wished it. —

M^rsPinckney & family would like Maria to join us, & it may be she is thinking of it. . . .

∽

BAPTISTA LYNCH, URSULINE CONVENT COLUMBIA S.C., TO PATRICK LYNCH,
OCT 20TH[46]

I hasten to tell you that our Sisters are desirous that I should have the altar
fixed in the centre of the house, just where the statue of the Blessed Lady stands,
& make a sanctuary of the place where we kneel –? This we can do, by simply
making a folding door at the arch which is partially closed, & erecting a sort
of grating outside of the folding doors of the class, which will be much cheaper
than making the fancy division for the large room we thought of making a

chapel of—and as they say—if our Lord's tabernacle were so removed from the sphere of our duties, it might be that he would not be visited so often, nor would we feel that he presided so immediately over our actions—

I have arranged with John to get the material & get the door at once, for we are heartily sick & tired of having the workmen thro' the house, but if it does not meet your approval, please say so, & we will stop our proceedings immediately—

The glaziers are going the rounds & will have probably two hundred panes of glass to put in—the kitchen range is being fixed & will soon be in operation—The stoves we want to get up this week, & also the coal hauled from the old convent—I asked John about it this morning—he is not very well, has a bad cold which he caught, I think, by going out to the depot with Mrs Pinckney without a shawl or cloak. Poor Maria, I hope you will write to her. I think she will either become M^rs N—as I thought before or apply to come here.

She seemed pleased & edified with her visit & expressed regret at her leaving.

Poor Mrs Pinckney told Eliza it was the greatest cross she ever had, but Maria thinks she does not feel it much or truly realize it— . . .

I paid Mr Lee \$56^00 for the lightening rod yesterday—he made a donation of \$7.25—which was kind. We received a bag of books from Anna & Sister Mary both complain that we are so silent. Sister Mary feels it very much I think. I have not written to Sr. Antonia either—but you can more readily excuse me than they can— . . .

Miss Weed can have Sr. Ambrose's room—it is ready.

ᴄ❧

Baptista Lynch, Ursuline Convent, Columbia S.C., to Patrick Lynch, Nov 16th[47]

Rev Father Lawrence sent a beautiful large wedding cake around to myself & his little God-daughter "Martha Gaffney" after which he came to hear our confessions. . . .

N.B. Father Lawrence says that no one can sell the house formerly occupied by us, of which the Sisters must relinquish the deed, until a mortgage is lifted which he (or the Sisters) hold, over it, for the Congregation.

I asked him if he thought that mortgage retarded the sale of the property— He answered certainly—it could not be sold until that was lifted—Had we not better conciliate those folks & get them to become generous hearted for religion's sake—. It is well we know that "God is at the helm, " or we might become misanthropic—Now let me tell you what a treasure we have in one of our new postulant Lay Sisters "Sr Mary Bridget" alias Mrs Kavanaugh she makes the most beautiful bread possible—Sr Mary says if it were exhibited at the fair it would take the prize—It is a pity we did not know her powers in that way before, it would have given such a good name to our Academy.

❧

JOHN LYNCH COLUMBIA, TO PATRICK LYNCH, NOV 23RD[48]

I intended writing you last Saturday but circumstances prevented. I was called on by Capt Wade, with a bill of $106.46 for work already done by him, and he appeared anxious for the balance of the blinds, (by the by what has become of them,) I paid him fifty dollars on his acct, putting him off, for the balance 'till the work was finished, for two reasons, first I thought the bill high and secondly, I knew that the whitewasher would call soon, and I have but fifty dollars more of Ellens money in my hands. She I know has not much if any to spare. She is also anxious that Mr Berry, the Butcher &c &c be paid, Mr Palmer of course I will leave in your hands. What I wish to know particularly is, whether you wish me to raise the money and pay the bills as presented, or whether you intend placing me in funds for that purpose. If you wish me to act I will commence at once, if not please inform me. . . .

❧

BAPTISTA LYNCH, URSULINE CONVENT, COLUMBIA S.C., TO PATRICK LYNCH, NOV 23RD[49]

. . . —I hear John's ring—I must go to him. You will be glad to hear that he has taken the pledge for a year. I trust he may have the strength to keep it, otherwise, his *dejection* arising from conscientiousness, will do him perhaps as much harm as any thing else—. I received a letter from the Mother Superior of the S^{rs} of Mercy a few days since, apprising me of their intended departure—we will endeavor to receive with religious hospitality, & make a merit of their visit, & not let them feel uncomfortable—Father Jeremiah O Connell has said Mass in our Convent twice lately! This morning (it being our Confession day) I sent Sister Catharine to ask if he would have the kindness to attend our confessional this after noon at 4 0 clock—He said that Father Lawrence was out of town, & he would hear our Confessions with pleasure. We understood very well the amiability intended, but we laughed at the expressions—Since we cannot have Father Joseph, it is immaterial which of the two Brothers I go to—or have for the novices— . . . We feel a little anxious to know if we got a prize at the fair or not—if you cannot get $50^{00} for the dress, I would prefer disposing of it in Columbia—

⌇

ROBERT LYNCH, COLLEGE OF CAMBREÉ, TO JOHN AND ELIZA LYNCH,
    12 DEC[50]

My dear Parents,

    . . . I cannot let the great feste [*sic*] of Christmas pass over without sending you a Christmas gift and I do not think that I could send you one that would please you better than a testimony of Application, Constancy, and above all of good behavior. . . . you cannot immagine [*sic*] how hard my heart beat when my name was called, not on my account but on yours for I knew that you would be very proud of your son because he had been rewarded in public on account of his good conduct. . . . I feel very sad whenever I think of home, as the great feast of Christmas approaches, . . . but I assure you that I am very well contented because I am one of the first of our class. I have the best notes for conduct. I go to confession every week, to Communion every two weeks I study hard having the view that one day I will be a Priest and that I will return back again to comfort my dear Parents in their old age and to save the souls of my countrymen. I. . . beg you to excuse the bad writing as the weather is very cold and the bad spelling in my head is full of the long french and latin lessons that I will have to say in an hour. . . .

⌇

BAPTISTA LYNCH, URSULINE CONVENT, TO PATRICK LYNCH, DEC 16TH[51]

    . . . we have arranged the new chapel very nicely so that you need not go to any expense to get a grating or division of any kind this year—This morning we had our first Mass & Father O' Connell blessed it with all the ceremonies &c &c giving a very pretty & complimentary address—He is *most attentive &c*
    A few days since Mrs Bauskett & Mrs Jones called on me & presented the bill for the carpet saying that Rev F O C had requested the Altar Society to pay for it—which it refused to do—saying we were able to do it ourselves with our school, but at least consented to pay one half—so I told Mrs. Jones who was far from possessing the generosity of Mrs Bauskett that I would send it to her in a few days—I asked our Sisters to pray about it—and judge of my surprise yesterday evening on opening my office book to find precisely the amt ($30°°) in gold left in it.
    Where it came from I have no idea—unless Father O Connell left it there during his Thanksgiving, while we were at breakfast!
    Was it not providential? It certainly was our Blessed Mother that sent it to us so today I have sent it to Mrs Jones. A.M. D.G.

1860 January–June

"I wish to turn everything to advantage."

In antebellum South Carolina, life was very precarious, a fever away from a person being in mortal danger during the summer and early fall of each year. Chronic diseases such as tuberculosis stalked individuals and families. The Lynch family had already lost two members of the second generation, Conlaw and Bernard, to consumption's maw. Others, among the youngest siblings, displayed disturbing signs of consumption's death march within them. Inside this highly unstable familial milieu, the older siblings vigorously pursued their callings. Patrick was particularly active in the real estate market, seizing opportunities to acquire facilities to meet the expanding needs of his diocese. Francis continued to import shoemakers from the North to augment his labor force of whites and slaves in order to steadily increase his production. John was ever attempting to build up his reputation—and practice—by seeking out difficult cases that eluded the diagnoses of other physicians and even by seizing on the opportunity of housing the most famous Catholic prelate in America. Meanwhile, his son Robert was bravely declaring his intention of becoming a missionary to China, even as he searched for heavenly signs confirming his priestly vocation.

Baptista had her own vision of mission. The mission country was her homeland, South Carolina. The convent and school she had founded in the heart of the state were her instruments for cultivating vocations to the religious life, the ultimate fruit in the proselytizing of South Carolina society. Acquiring and maintaining a sterling reputation were essential to reaching such an ambitious goal. With this in mind, Baptista struggled to calculate how best to cut short the academic year when yellow fever struck Columbia, lest the school be stigmatized within its halls with dead and stricken students. Meanwhile, she set her sights on finding the means to acquire or build a new facility that would be adequate for the academy she envisioned; for the present she made the most of their present quarters to build up a loyal base of supporters among the general public.

She exploited the curiosity that the convent as a cultural oddity incited by drawing learned speakers to give lectures and extending general invitations to the exhibitions that served as commencement ceremonies to bring the academic year to a close. In her search for funds, the possibility of substantial royalties from the sales of the Ursulines' Manual of Prayer *spurred her to find a publisher for a new edition, even though she did not yet hold the copyright nor was she sure that it was still in effect.*

Among the distinguished visitors to the Ursuline convent was the Belgian consul who confessed that he had come to Columbia to escape the "political turmoil" of Charleston. In late April the fractured Democratic Party held its convention in that city. As the epicenter of Southern secessionist forces, Charleston was probably the worst possible setting for the Democrats' slim chance of selecting a presidential candidate they could unite behind. Events quickly bore out the worst expectations. Southern radicals insisted that the party platform include the pledge of a slave code for the territories, thereby committing the party to the protection of the peculiar institution in that vast area. Northern Democrats proposed leaving the matter to the Supreme Court, which two and a half years before had declared in the Dred Scott *decision that slaves did not gain their freedom by being taken into a territory in which slavery was not codified by law. That was not sufficient for the fire-eaters from the Deep South, whose delegations bolted from the convention. When the remaining Southern delegations subsequently withdrew, the Northern Democrats voted to reconvene in Baltimore, a Southern city in a border state, in early June. Their Southern counterparts chose Richmond for their sectional convention. By their split, the last national political party handed the President's House to the Republican candidate. Like earlier transforming events, little of this seismic shift in the prospects of the major parties registered among most of the Lynches, who were still preoccupied with fund-raising, school facilities, and life-threatening diseases.*

JOHN LYNCH, COLUMBIA, TO PATRICK LYNCH, JAN 2ND[1]

I have at last seen Mr Green[2] he is to have the leases all fixed tomorrow. I have mentioned the fact to all but Shields.[3] I have also by Ellens consent rented the Barbershop for $200 to a Jew for a clothing store. I consider this the highest rent of all. If you had let me rent out the whole of the stores I would have made them pay $250, 250, & 200 = 700—Stables 300 = $1000 = which would be fifty dollars more than the interest on amt due = but it is now too late, and the fifty is on the other side—I have seen Nichols[4] & Huggins[5] they both very readily agreed to reduce their risk to 1 pr cent and filled out a notice which I enclose.

ROBERT LYNCH, CAMBREÉ, TO ELLEN LYNCH, 6TH JANY[6]

. . . My dear Aunt whenever I think of home I can hardly keep from crying although I tremble when I think of the danger I will run for the salvation of my soul if I return to America and I will tell you a secret. . . . I do not think that it is my vocation to return to America. Certainly every one will think that I am a very ungrateful boy towards my dear Parents, and my dear Uncle Patrick, but what harm will their thought do me if I save my soul. Certainly it will be a great trial for me and for my parents but they have seven others and certainly they can give me to Him Who has died for us and certainly . . . there is more want of Priests in China than in America where the poor pagans are dying of hunger and where they sell their children for a cent or bury them alive or throw them into the streets to die [of] hunger or to be eaten by the dogs. . . . And where is the man, woman, or child that has not a heart that will not throb with pity, that will not throb with ardear [*sic*] when he learns that there are thousands and thousands of souls saved in this country by a few zealous priests and where the heroes of the Church bend their heads to the . . . axes to receive the crown of diamonds for their works of this world. I am saving my money to take a visit in the Normandie next vacasion [*sic*] to make a pilgrimage to a celebrated statue of St. Joseph, maybe he will tell me something of my vocation.

JOHN LYNCH, COLUMBIA, TO PATRICK LYNCH, JANY 17TH[7]

I returned from Cheraw on Saturday evening. . . . Today also Stephens[8] will vacate his store. he has paid his rent to 1st Jany the balance he promises to pay as soon as he sells his remnant at auction, which will be tomorrow I expect. . . . I was glad to get the fifty dollars,
. . . as soon as he leaves, a much more desirable tenant will take his place (Mr Cox) a grocer, who neither uses or sells liquors, and will be prompt in paying his rents. He takes the store at the same price for the year with the privilege of keeping it four years. I took the precaution of not fixing the price further than this year, as I thought it would be well to see what next year may bring forth.
. . . every thing is getting on pretty fairly, but I think Ellen is not in as fine spirits about the school as she was. I am afraid she worries herself too much. Perhaps if she were to conform more to the ways of the world (as other *Catholic* schools do), she might get on as well herself, and the school increase also; until it get independent, it is not best to act *too independent* even in discipline, but this is not my business, of course I would not say so to her but merely make the

suggestion to yourself, who has a right to advise. I have picked up my ideas merely from Ellens own conversations with myself. I may be wrong in them, but feeling as much interest in the school as I do, I naturally am on the que vie for any and every influence both internally and externally that might in the least affect it; we will speak these things over when you next pay us a visit. You must tell me what you want me to do next, as I believe I am at the end of my row, the painter has finished, his bill was $90 for painting glazing &c. . . .

☙

BAPTISTA LYNCH, URSULINE CONVENT, COLUMBIA, S.C., TO
    PATRICK LYNCH, JAN 18TH[9]

. . . Sr. Johanna (Weed) is anxious to know, if you will visit Columbia before going to Baltimore & if you will have the kindness to take charge of her brother Ambler's trunk to Richmond? . . . —Sr A[ugustine] is mute again after a season of apparently exuberant joy—always in the extreme— . . . It will soon be time now, for us to receive our payments for the second session—I will be very happy if you accommodate yourself with the use of some of it, & I feel most grateful to you, for those cheques that you sent John—Our affairs are so mixed up now, that it will puzzle you—let alone me, to unravel them, for John has regarded it all our affair, which I am not willing to do—even tho' we are for the present mendicants, or if you will *"children of your bounty"*— Because, I know that so long as you & I live, it will all do very well, but the interest of the diocess, & the interest of the convent we also know, are to strangers, two distinct interests. Therefore I would like very much to know how much the convent is indebted to the Diocess—& all the arrangements about the purchase & payment for this house—John says in the eyes of the law we are but tenants, legally holding no right, receiving no rent—paying for no improvements—&c and unless it were willed to the Convent, should be liable to a *second turnout*[10] if Providence withdrew from us your support—which God forbid, I think, however we may manage it while we live, it is better to have our books straight—and yours & Johns are the only two leaves in my book that I looked upon with disquiet, not knowing what I ought to put down & afraid of cheating either the Convent or you, which latter would cost me most I believe—. Still I am very anxious for our convent, that it may give an asylum to many vocations.

I received a very satisfactory letter from Lizzie Condy this past week in which she said, that she no longer felt that duty required her at home, her mother's health being now reestablished, therefore she is preparing to join us after Easter immediately—she writes very sensibly & piously—I had a visit a few days since from that Miss Nora Weaver, of whom Revd J. Birmingham & Mrs DeLange spoke to me—she expresses great desire to come to our school—but

I expect has not the means—she has never made but one communion, therefore I advised her to come & make three days retreat, before going, as she proposes doing while here—She is at Dr Laborde's[11]—She seems a very interesting girl, & may have an incipient vocation—John is expecting you up to sign the leases, therefore does not write, to let you know that Mr. Shields has sold out & resigns the stables having paid up to the last—. John has promised the man who bought him out & who owns livery stables lower down in the city—to give him the first offer of them—but does not want them—only wishes to have no competitors—What is now to be done—are the stables to be rented or pulled down—? If you think it well, it seems to me better, to rent the other front room with cellar to some dry goods merchant—I mean Sr. DeNeri's school room (which we shall be unable to use during summer) & clean the yard—the rent of the school room would equal that of the stables perhaps—The reason why I support this is that both children & Nuns are loud in their complaints for fresh air—& a yard in which to exercise—Sr. A[ugustine] told the Srs of M[ercy] in my presence at full recreation—that she realized in *this house,* what was often said, that the convent was a prison, she never enjoyed the beauteous full light of day, or fresh air.—she would give anything almost to get out into the country, to see some green trees & enjoy the fresh air. . . .

I have received many humiliations from our Srs lately thank God—& hear continual complaints of the unsuitableness of this house both as to situation & construction for use—I feel these remarks much more sensibly than I appear to do, because I know that you have exceeded (not your generosity) but your Means, in purchasing it.

I acknowledge the truth of what they say, & saw it all the first time I ever visited the place—But it is no doubt an uncommonly fine Building for so new a convent to occupy—& the best way for us is to be truly grateful for the use of it—economize to prevent its being a sinking fund to you, & hope that Providen[ce] who has blessed us so far, may enable you to sell it at a good profit, & build in the course of eight or ten years, a convent for His greater glory—When our sisters mention to me its disadvantages, I tell them how grateful we ought to be for it, when we compare our condition with many infant convents, of which we read daily in our "Annals" at Lecture, for our instruction & encouragement—& to pray that you may get a good offer for it. They acknowledge their gratitude & go to prayer—I think when the spring comes, it will look more cheerful, or perhaps they will become so too.—I have at present $200.00 more or less in hand, so that when we receive our payments for the second session, I shall pay our debts here & be glad you used the rest—I would like to know how much H F Baker charges for the coal pr ton—Next year, please God— we will lay in our store in time— . . .

ᕗ

BAPTISTA LYNCH, URSULINE CONVENT, COLUMBIA, S.C., TO
PATRICK LYNCH, ASH WEDNESDAY[12]

Your letter from Florence was quite a relief to me as I had forgotten to ask
my permissions for Lent,[13] & was just going to write for them—Now I will do
as we did before—say every day the Miserere for our deficiencies in fasting &
let each one fast & abstain according to his strength—We have just rcd the box
of fish & thank you very much—Give my *sisterly love* to Sister Antonia & say
we are also well & beg a continuance of her daily prayers—

. . . Our *profound respects* to his Grace the Most Rev Abp—Kenrick—while
in Baltimore, I would feel very grateful, if you would attend to some business
for us—it is this I wrote to "Murphy & Co: offering to sell him the "copy right
of the latest & best edition of the Ursuline Manual—which *we alone* possess
& have not replicated, but a few days since I reced a letter from Messrs Kelly
Hedian & Piet,[14] saying that they had learned we wished to dispose of the
U[rsuline] Manual, & as they had been anxious since commencing business
to fix upon some important prayer book for publication, & had as yet none on
the list—they wished to ascertain if they could make arrangements with us for
ours—Having no other on their list they would give it undivided attention &c
&c Now I know but little of this sort of business—yet from the little I do know,
I should think it well to enter into some agreement with them, & I leave it to
you see about it or direct me as to what you think best—I should think its to
our advantage, but I have no idea what would be a good offer on their part, nor
what privileges we should claim—&c &c I also wanted to ask you when up
here, to allow us to erect in our noviciate the society & devotion to the Sacred
Hearts of Jesus & Mary—& will you ask the Jesuits to aggregate our members
to that of their Society of the Sacred Heart of Jesus. I thought of sending on
their names to the Revd Father Hempholder of Cincinnati who received me—
but thought after wards, it was better to belong to our own Archdiocese—I
would like too that we belonged to the Society among the *Jesuits* & others "for
the conversion of America," & that we had a number of the prayers of that
congregation— . . .

Anna wishes to make three days retreat at the Convent this week! . . .

ᕗ

BAPTISTA LYNCH, URSULINE CONVENT, COLUMBIA S.C., TO PATRICK LYNCH,
MARCH 2ND[15]

I am sorry to learn through your hurried letter that you were indisposed
& obliged to travel. I hope the Archbishop[16] will soon feel much better. It was

quite a relief to me when I found you did not contemplate bringing him up to Columbia.

I would of course feel complimented &c in forming the acquaintance of so great a man & one whom every one must admire yet I hate meeting dignitaries.

You will be glad to hear my dearest Brother that Mrs Gaffney is here, & has paid us in full—consequently we have in Bank $1400^00 for which we feel truly grateful, since I trust we will be able to manage without calling on you, & in the mean time, you know how happy we will be to accommodate you with the use of any—

... Today I received a letter from Murphy &c declining the purchase of the copyright of the Ursuline Manual which I had offered him hoping to pay in that way for some of our Books—therefore I will write to the editors of the Baltimore Mirror, & accept their proposal, if we can agree about the money arrangements, but I look to you for instruction.

I feel disposed to enclose Rose Wevers letter to you—she has been forced by her mother to attend the Protestant church since she went home & has I think her faith tampered with, & her desire to become a nun abused—I wrote to her, offering to receive her as a boarder for the sum of $100 per annum which inducement I offered for the preservation of her faith—I told her so—she thanks me for the offer but says her father is unable to give her more & she is unwilling to take it from her younger sisters & brothers—But wishes me to tell her who she must write to, & obtain permission to enter the Convent—she feels that she must incur her Brothers displeasure whenever she does that, & I think wishes to do so at once—*which I am not sorry for*. I will tell her to write to you—she told me her mother preferred you to any Catholic clergyman she had ever seen—. John & myself feel *most obliged* to you for the fish, but must beg you not to send us any more—*it is a losing business*—we never could consume such a quantity it spoils on our hands—we have tried to dispose of some of it—but without success—so between the freight, the quantity & last tho not least *your* part of the *trouble*—I think it just as well to get all that we want in Columbia, *unless* once in a while

MARY LYNCH SPANN, WASHINGTON COUNTY, TO PATRICK LYNCH, MARCH 6TH[17]

I have been promising myself to write to you for a good while in fact ever since we heard the joyful news that there was a prospect of your visiting Texas this spring—our own good Bishop was kind enough to send me word that you had promised him to extend your visit this far if it was possible as you expected to be in New Orleans after Easter & in reality my dear Brother it would be a little hard for us to know that you were so near twice as N. Orleans & for you not to come farther. Could you witness the delight that every one seemed to feel at the thought of seeing you here, I do not think you would fail to come. Of course in saying this I bear in mind if it is compatible with your important duties but I cannot help flattering myself that this little visit will not interfere as our Bishop takes such an interest in your coming. Try to imagine this wild country and what might be the fruits of a few soul-stirring sermons, would only a few souls be converted how well your time will have been spent. I have said nothing of the pleasure Mr Spann & myself would feel in seeing you, you can very well imagine it; I think it would make me at least twenty years younger, you may be sure that your name is often on our lips, & by the children also. I am sure I do not exaggerate when I say there is no one whose visit Mr Spann would enjoy & prize more than yours although you have seen so little of each other you would suit and understand one another well. . . . I am very glad to see through the Miscellany that you are preparing my dear Brother to have a "Male Orphan Asylum" in Charleston it must be greatly needed & it will be productive of much good. . . . —you will be glad to hear that Emily is nearly restored to health & Cara has been sent to the Convent[18] of Galveston. I must not write you any more of ourselves for we want you to come & see for yourself; it is delightful to look forward to hearing from yourself of our dear Father and Mother & all the different members of the family—I do not know when I shall have the happiness of making another visit home. I can only anticipate. I must not omit to say that our own little Pastor is anticipating your arrival with as much interest as anyone else & I would not be much surprised if he had a Te Deum sung on the occasion. I can only conclude my dear Brother by hoping to hear from you very soon & a favorable answer if practicable & if not try to make it so—if I were a St. Scholastica I might act as she did— . . .[19]

❧

BAPTISTA LYNCH, URSULINE CONVENT, COLUMBIA S.C., TO PATRICK LYNCH, MARCH 10TH[20]

. . . — Revd Father Birmingham[21] told me I might expect to see you very soon, as you were obliged to attend the Lancaster court soon.[22] We will pray for the success of your affair there—How is Archbp Hughes? We will give him a share in our novena to St. Joseph & a general communion (as far as I am concerned it is on your account)—but it would be amiable & expressive of charity to mention it to him—that is if you like. . . .

❧

BAPTISTA LYNCH, URSULINE CONVENT, COLUMBIA S.C., TO PATRICK LYNCH,
MARCH 14TH[23]

. . . 1st With your permission, we will receive a Postulant, whom Revd Father O Connell recommends as amiable, & accomplished lady, with a dower of $1000, who has been a governess in the first families in the state & is at present Principal of "Bay Springs Academy," Barnwell District. Her name is Miss Mary R Glen—is over forty years of age, but has been prevented heretofore from entering Religion by her duty to an aged parent whom she has recently lost—We answered in the affirmative presuming on your permission & wanting a good teacher—perhaps too it is all the better in a young house to have old hands—. She wishes to enter about Easter—.

2nd Your expression about copy right being out of date, leaves me at a non plus—It seems to me in reading it (I forgot to say *it* was sent to me recently from Black Rock Convent by Sr Angela Delany) that, altho dated 1841, it does not expire for us—& from the passage in the letter I sent you of Kelly H[edian] & P[iet], I see that Mr Lucas's copy rights of 1841 has expired—but I should have thought that meant he should purchase from the community of person who held the copy-right the liberty of purchasing a certain number of years again which it was optional to grant him or some other publisher—Is it also necessary that we should renew it—or is it of no value to us? I wish you could read it over—It seems to me it ought to be valuable—yet I am afraid I have ventured too much.

Please send me one or two of *Lucas's* Ursuline Manuals—I have none in the house. I hope I am not in *a fix*—but I was amused when in reperusing the letter which you returned, I saw the sentence—"Please send us by express your copy if you have it prepaid that we may examine it"

Lo! & behold! We have no copy—but only hold the copy right of Lucas's publication, which Mother Borgia[24] told me he never had the copy right of & therefore published it unsatisfactorily.

We want that edition published satisfactorily, & if possible to our profit—since we hold Mother Borgia's copy-right—But what if it is out of date—? Please advise me soon if you can & excuse my troubling you so much—I see by *clause the eighth* & section VIII of the Constitution of the United States, (which I find in Wilson's United States History) that a copy right may be secured for twenty-eight years, & renewed again for fourteen years—that formerly the term was fourteen years, but now it is twenty eight—. But the words of our copy right secure to *our community & successors forever*—so I do not understand it, & beg your instruction (you ought to see a dear little mouse that is playing all around me & even running on my habit as I write) This copy right is sealed with Mother

Borgia's seal, & witnessed by Peter Torre—3rd If Archbishop Hughes intends honoring Columbia with a visit please telegraph the day previous—We will expect you on the twenty sixth— ...

☙

John Lynch, Columbia, to Patrick Lynch, March 14th[25]

Ellen tells me Bishop Hughes will stop one night in Columbia, will it be possible for him to stop with us.[26] I would be more than pleased with the compliment. We can very well spare the room, viz the large bedroom for the Bishop, *your room* for the two clergymen, or if you prefer, we can give one of them the room upstairs that you sometimes occupy. We will still have the other garret room to spare, so if you can come up at the same time we can have a room for you also, please extend the invitation to the Bishop and his company to stop with me if it is only for the night, but if it will not interfere with his previous arrangements we will be gratified by his remaining longer with us, being close to the Convent and Church he will not be fatigued in visiting them, he can thus ride over the town and visit the Asylum cemetery, & State House, &c &c Tell him to direct the driver to take him to Dr. Lynches, or if you prefer I will meet him at the depot, (inter nos) this would be only half—the compliment to me. ... Practice is improving slightly, more in quality than quantity, but in both. I wish to turn *every thing* to advantage, but in a quiet way, and what better chance of an advertisement than, where did—– stop while in Columbia? Ans—I did not know &c!—you understand.—Excuse this lightness— ...

☙

Baptista Lynch, Ursuline Convent, Columbia S.C. to Patrick Lynch, Holy Thursday [April 5][27]

I would like to have written before & wished you a happy Easter, but owing to our academic examinations—(an abscess in the ear from which I have been suffering) & other pressing duties, I have been unable to do so before—Our examinations closed yesterday & today we have sent the children to attend the services in the church—John having very kindly arranged seats for them. Our altar is very handsome & was all arranged without my having to put a hand to it—the blessing of having numbers to share the labors—As it is, I am very *tired* as the children say & suppose you are too—after the "mandatum" & serving in the refectory "selon la regle"[28] (DG) Sr. Rose has been confined to her room with a swollen limb for a few days but is up just now—all the rest are quite well (TG) We had a visit from Miss Glen, in whom I am agreeably surprised—for I had pictured to myself a little hunchback, like Jeremy Maynard (if you recollect

him) She is very intelligent & may be of great service—Just think she was educated in the Ursuline Convent of New Orleans—! The Sisters[29] did not refuse
her, any more than she refused them; indeed she spoke as if it were only her own
inability to perform their duties, & disinclination to going out,[30] that caused
her to turn her thoughts elsewhere.

I received a "Holy Week" book from "Kelly Hedian & Piet" with compliments &c, asking about the manual—I answered that I had written to "Lucas &
Bros" but had recd no reply which I feared arose from my not knowing their
proper address which I could neither find in the "Mirror" or Almanac (by the
bye—where is the Almanac I asked you for—I am ashamed to ask Murphy for
one at this late day), and, if they would forward me the right address, it would
expedite the business—that it was, or is our intention to retain the copy rights
of our Manual, & ask from them 10[cts] for every copy sold—but could make no
arrangement before hearing from "Lucas & Bros"—

❧

BAPTISTA LYNCH, URSULINE CONVENT, COLUMBIA, S.C, TO PATRICK LYNCH,
   APRIL 14[31]

I suppose you have seen the Sisters of Mercy who left here on yesterday, in
the noon-day train, to meet the steamer Marion—according to the advice of
their Mother Superior.

We were most fortunate in seeing Mr Lafitte,[32] who offered most politely to
spare you all trouble & meet them at the cars—not only this, he said he would
see Capt Forester, or arrange everything for them—was not that kind, especially when he spoke as tho we conferred a favor on him, in allowing him to
serve us—Mrs E Bellinger came up yesterday evening, with her son Joseph, the
bride, & Miss G Bellinger—she seemed charmed at seeing her three daughters
so well & happy—& regrets she did not see Sr. Teresa's reception—(Why did
not the Miscellany publish it, & the pretty poetry?) I laughed heartily over Mrs
Bellinger's account of the wedding, & preceding difficulties— . . . We have a
little sickness at present. Sr Barbara (one of the Phila [Philadelphia] Srs) has
fever, but is not at all dangerous—Sr. Martha (a professed Sr) has also been sick
a little, & not yet fit for duty—but Sr. Rose is much better—. And the rest quite
well, thank God—I begin to feel quite anxious about our Distribution, but try to
remember that all is in the hands of Providence, & under the powerful protection of our Blessed Mother—. We enjoyed two interesting visits from Mr Baldwin[33] of Richmond V[a]—who is inquisitive about the doctrine of our Church—
he seemed very much pleased with his visit & Sr. Joanne is delighted that I went
down & treated him so friendly—He lectured with much applause here—John
was very much pleased & called on him. John proposed to me today our taking

stock in a "Building Committee" the shares of which, are almost all taken & soon will be—

His doing so arose from his presenting me a bill for the posts of the fence—I told him I thought he ought to keep accounts of all he paid out in that way for we thought it better, since we had evidence constantly of the unfitness of this place for a convent, that you should never give it to us, but let us rent it from you, at whatever you thought a reasonable price by the year, & sell it to the first good purchaser you could get—Instead of giving us a house you could if you chose give to us in the way of rents as much as you intended, which was $3,000 was it not, the value of the old house? John says now is the time for those who wish to build cheaply—that is, this Building Committee will facilitate—By taking stock now & paying the interest monthly $100 or if borrowing $200⁰⁰ monthly—we could look about quietly taking our time & choose a location, & slowly accomplish the building of our convent. By taking the hundred shares which John proposes we could borrow $20.000 to work upon—if I could only calculate with certainty to meet the payment of $200⁰⁰ every month—

I asked John if there were land adjoining the Church[34] that we could purchase & join our Convent on to it, so as [to] give our services as *sacristans* & choir to the church, for the benefit of religion, & as remuneration for the services of the Pastor—In this small & slowly growing place, it would be easy for us to do better than those who now fulfil [*sic*] those duties—& we do them for ourselves & might as well let others enjoy what we do—if it be AMDG—.

However, this is for after consideration—I would be very glad though if you would consider about the "building committee" & give me your advice as early as possible—John says he will attend to the business, if we will enter upon it, but there is no time to lose—.

I suppose Anna is again with our dear Parents—Are you thinking of going out to Texas—they are expecting you constantly—Mr Dr. Spann is preparing to be Baptized a Catholic— . . . How very fortunate you were in the purchase of the Presbyterian Church—it was *nuts* to Mr. Lafitte—I am happy to see such zeal for the advancement of religion in Charleston— . . .

෯

BAPTISTA LYNCH, URSULINE CONVENT, COLUMBIA S.C., TO PATRICK LYNCH, APRIL 16TH[35]

I am afraid our dear Parents will feel that Anna remains too long away from home. I hope she will enjoy herself at the fair.—the few trifles we have snatched the time to make, I will send to you by Mr Allemorige or some one whom John may give them in care of & I am very sorry we were not able to do a thousand times as much—. You will be glad to hear that our sick sisters are out of the

Doctor's hands, & will I hope soon be fit for duty—One of the Philadelphia sisters—the married woman—is going back & wishes to join the S^{rs} of Charity, she finds the labor of a lay sister too much for her—She has been very useful & industrious—but owing to her dispositions & circumstances we do not regret her leaving—

I have written to Bishop Wood at the same time with her—giving him an account of *his postulants* & asking for a *strong able-bodied washerwoman.*—& telling him how we are getting on in a general sort of a way—for I flatter myself he feels interested in our House.—We will be very glad to get the woman you propose as laysister with her $300^{oo} & think Providence is very good to us in sending us aid when we have so much to do. If she could come about the same time that Sr Bridget leaves I would be glad—I have been obliged to hire Uncle Cits' wife by the day, since our two Sisters were sick—for we not only lost their labors, but that of their attendants— . . .

I really feel indebted to Mr Lafitte for his kind attentions to the Srs Mercy I am glad they went to the Srs House,[36] but also pleased they were not heard—

They had an opportunity of seeing something of Southern hospitality & elegance at Mr Lafitte's[37]—yesterday I rced a letter from their Mother Superior, with a cheque from Bishop Loughlin[38] for $50^{oo} for myself—the last payment & more than I asked $20^{oo}. But it is very acceptable. Poor Lizzie Condy—I am truly sorry for her—Sr Teresa (Mary Clagett) says it is the family, her brother having committed suicide—& her mother having been frequently deranged— God is very good to us—in letting it manifest itself before she joined us—. May His holy name be praised—. John mentioned to me this morning that Mr W McGuinnes had shown him your letters, about selling the house to Mr. M Cooley for $4000 & he had made a suggestion; to transfer the note with good securities &c promised by Mr M. Cooley, to Mr Boatwright, in payment for this house—which suggestion pleased Mr McGuinnes very much—Don't you think it would be well if it could be accomplished?

Because the $4,000 (which seems to me very doubtful you would ever get) would be as so much cash in joining hands—so John says—. I am glad to learn that Francis is doing so well—I had not heard anything of his movements—.

[PS] Our Distribution has received a very high compliment from Mrs T Semmes[39] of Miss____ & we expect another young lady from the state. TG. . . .

Baptista Lynch, Ursuline Convent, Columbia, S.C., to
Patrick Lynch, April 21st[40]

What do you think of the Building Committee affair? When I wrote there remained one hundred shares, which John is saying we should take—now there is but seventy five, twenty five of which John took in his own name for us, there remain fifty-shares yet, which he hopes we will with your permission take— please write soon—How comes on the Fair? My love to Anna— . . . —. John is going down in a day or two perhaps. I am thinking of very quietly sending by him $300⁰⁰ to the Srs Mercy & getting a receipt, without making any allusion to their letter—shall I? I don't feel easy about them. . . .

&

BAPTISTA LYNCH, URSULINE CONVENT, COLUMBIA S.C., TO PATRICK LYNCH, APRIL 28TH[41]

I am happy to learn through John that you are quite well—I suppose Anna has returned home, & your busy season of "convention" is nearly over—

We had a visit or rather *visitation* from the *"Consul from Belgium"* who spoke of you, & entertained us in company with Rev Father Joseph with beautiful descriptions of the churches of St. Sophia & the Cathedral of Cologne— He begged me to present his compliments & say that he ran away from the turmoil of politics—I could understand very well what he said, but S^r. Augustine was my interpreter—he seemed much pleased with his visit, if we may judge by its length & his manner—

But that is nothing, for yesterday Sr Johanna (Weed) received the Richmond Dispatch, with an article on Columbia, written by Mr Baldwin, the lecturer, in which he mentions not a word of our Institution, which probably [is] the only one he visited—& which he seemed so much pleased with—So goes the popularity-seeking world! How happy a thing it is for us, that we seek our approbation & reward in so different a source! Thank God for all His blessings to us & they are immeasurable—John told you I suppose that Revd Father Murphy brought Miss Ferrall of Halifax as a boarder—her Father had written to you about her—he paid us $150⁰⁰—She is fifteen years of age & a very nice girl—

Mr Ambler Weed says that Bp McGill[42] has recd S^r M____ letters, & speaks with pleasure of officiating at her reception—but will not be able to leave until after or about the feast of the Ascension. Will you write to him also please— Some of the elite of Columbia have expressed a wish to witness such a ceremony —so I suppose it will be A.M.D.G. to have it as before, open to strangers—We will miss the black veils of the S^{rs} of Mercy in the procession—they wrote to me of their arrival home— . . .

៩

ANTONIA LYNCH, MOUNT CARMEL, [BALTIMORE], TO PATRICK LYNCH,
30TH APRIL[43]

My dear Brother, I hope our Blessed Lady will do a great deal for you, and
those under your charge. It is very refreshing to learn of the rapid progress you
are making, for I learn that lately . . . you have purchased two churches, but not
where they were—*one* I hear is for the Germans a very agreeable surprise to me
to think that in time, in all probability you will have the Redemptorist Fathers
in the Diocese.

៩

BAPTISTA LYNCH, URSULINE CONVENT, COLUMBIA S.C., TO PATRICK LYNCH,
MAY 22ND[44]

Although I am *tired out*, . . . I will not go to bed without writing a few
lines—as I am afraid tomorrow morning will find many calls on my time—
What would I do if I were a Bishop? I suppose I would love the *luxury of complaining* as Revd Father Faber says—!!

Drowsiness & Sr. Augustine force me to stop—(Wednesday morning)

We had the Board of health to visit us yesterday—Dr. Gibbs Dr. Rawles &
_____. I was just in the act of oiling the guitar strings & cleaning the instru-
ments so could not attend on them but sent Sister Teresa (Clagett) they were too
gentlemanly to ask much or examine, but went to John to learn particulars.

. . . —I believe I told you that Miss Rossipol has arrived—her father paid
$85.00 which I have almost paid out— . . .

What good sledge hammer will knock us into spiritual atoms this year?
In other words, who do you intend shall give us our annual retreat. Already,
we are consoling ourselves with the thoughts of it, after the bustle of preparing
for Distribution—. I hope it may be a perfect stranger & a Jesuit Father if
possible—.

. . . Yesterday a letter from Texas, where our family were only tolerably well,
Sister Mary had gone down to Galveston to try & break the chills & fevers she
has—they have had a great deal of sickness, & lost a good servant— . . .

૯৵

BAPTISTA LYNCH, URSULINE CONVENT, COLUMBIA S.C. FEAST OF
ST. ANGELA TO PATRICK LYNCH [MAY 31][45]

I was particularly gratified in getting your letter yesterday, as you write so
seldom of late, that I often feel at sea about little matters—which perhaps I
ought not to trouble you about— . . .

Col Ryan & Dr. Duncan called today. I hope Col Ryan will pay his bill since
he asked for it not long since—we have only about $300⁰⁰ in Bank now—so
that unless the few who owe us soon pay, I am afraid I will have to call on you
which I would indeed be sorry to do, & will if possible avoid—Our monthly
expenses I think average $300⁰⁰ & our Distribution expenses are always ultra,
or at least extra—But we will trust in the good Providence of God & the powerful mediation of our Blessed Mother—. Cannot Mr Joseph Murray send us
his oldest daughter for $200⁰⁰ per annum (which is I think as much of a reduc-
tion as we can afford) and leave his little daughter at the Sisters until she is
more grown & capable of appreciating the advantage offered in our Institution?
Sr. Teresa tells me that the oldest is only about thirteen years of age, the second
quite a *little thing*—. I do not like to make reductions for *little children* unless
totally deprived of religious instructions—which in this instance, is by no means
the case— . . .

. . . I have also heard of Miss Rossipol's cousins, whose father would not be
willing they should come to us, unless assured that we would not influence
them to become Catholics—Miss R ___ is very unprepossessing, but I hope will
improve. She expresses herself much pleased—(interruption no 3) I forgot to
note the others!! How I did laugh at yours— . . . I am so much interested in
preparing the children for the Distribution, that I forget my own feast-day—Sr.
Augustine is going to make a grand turn out of paintings &c at the exhibition
if I may judge by the list of frames &c.

The children are studying very hard, trying to be ready for the 28th June. I
would be glad if possibly we could have it that early, so they could be at home
for 4th of July—. But I am afraid we cannot—we will try— . . .

૯৵

BAPTISTA LYNCH, URSULINE CONVENT, COLUMBIA, TO PATRICK LYNCH,
JUNE 4TH[46]

Sr M Charles signed the deed for the sale of this house—at $9000—John &
I witnesses—Mr Baskin[47] notary.

Francis Lynch, Cheraw, to Patrick Lynch, 9 June[48]

Altho I am aware of your absence from the City just now, it is important that I write, that you may receive this in time to apprize you, and ask your acceptance of a draft I have this day drawn on you for eight hundred ($800) dollars through the Merch[an]ts Bank of this place, on six months time, I will count on providing for the payment of it on maturity.

You will oblige me much in accepting the Dr[a]ft on its being presented to you.—This is stepping rather fast, to draw without first asking you permission to do so, So much for your having such good credit. I have said nothing to my factors about drawing in advance of shipments, for I wish to avoid doing so— It will not be long, I hope, before I will be receiving orders from them, by the last stm^r [steamer] I recd about 800 ms. [?] from Georgetown besides having sent near 300 prs before—Mr Morison is looked for tonight. And next week my new recruits will I expect, be at work

Monday morning,

On Saturday night Mr Morison arrived with six disciples of St. Crispin,[49] while others would have been glad to have been with them.

If I can only steer aright this years business will be creditable.

Baptista Lynch, Ursuline Convent, Columbia, S.C., to Patrick Lynch, June 12th[50]

We are busy preparing to have our *Distribution* on June 28th . . . —There is so much debilitating sickness in Columbia & the children are complaining so much of heat weakness &c that we are anxious to liberate them from their studies with some credit to ourselves, & not have them getting sick on our hands or taken away by their parents—looking delicate as they are beginning to do— . . .

Baptista Lynch, Ursuline Convent, Columbia S.C., to Patrick Lynch, June 23rd[51]

Julie wrote to John that she will be here on Monday. She is coming to place herself under his care for some time. I am sorry to say she is suffering—.

Col Bauskett will be in Columbia the latter part of next week—I think you have perhaps made a mistake in sending me the enclosed letter as the woman seems to be well acquainted with the Srs of Mercy in Charleston & desires to enter them—Mere seamstresses are the most useless persons to us—yet if you think I am mistaken, I will write as she might be useful in other ways—we feel willing to give the *English Lady* with the *fancy name* a trial after proper preliminaries as we spoke the other evening—I would prefer writing to her myself first—

We *are* all opposed to receiving the other & would, to obviate anticipated trouble (should your influence alone procure admittance,) require a favorable account of her piety & good sense from the Super. & Sister Associates—as they are the only persons who really know how to estimate the members of their community—excuse me my very dearest Brother & Rt Revd Father, if I seem to speak very plainly, but, I feel it my duty to secure thus the peace & happiness of our own Community, than to gratify my own, or what is more your wishes—do not consider this an absolute refusal—but a necessary precaution—

I had a visit today from a Professor of Chapel Hill College with five ladies—all curiosity of course—they spoke [of] Abp Hughes & yourself & left apparently pleased.

☙

FRANCIS LYNCH, CHERAW, TO PATRICK LYNCH, 27 JUNE[52]

Thinking that very likely you would be at Columbia on tomorrow, I have sent to Mr Waring Cash Bk of the S. of S.C. a note for 3000$ covering one for two thousand at maturity on 29th inst—which you will please call for and endorse, thereby making it fully up to the mark.

Mother left for Columbia this morning. All are quite well except Bro. James, who is suffering from an attack of fever, I hope he will be well of it in a few days

☙

BAPTISTA, URSULINE CONVENT, TO PATRICK LYNCH, FRIDAY NIGHT
10 O'CLOCK, JUNE 27TH[53]

I have followed you in spirit all day, & I may say done nothing but make aspirations for our poor dear Brother—God grant they may serve him.

This evening John & I received Hugh's letter—it was kind of him to write so promptly—John fears poor James' case was mis-treated, since it was called apoplexy—

Has he the *last absolution* ever given him?

Tomorrow we will all go to holy communion for him—& the kind sympathy of our Sisters induce them to pray for him, I trust fervently & often—.

How I feel for our dear parents—Augusta & all—

Shortly after you left, I received a telegram from Revd P. O'Neill,[54] requesting me to send M Boyce down at once for her Mother had died at 7 A.M. She therefore must leave at 5 A.M. tomorrow—& John thinks it would be better for Eliza to go at the same time. I did wish to write to Sisters Mary, & Antonia to secure their prayers immediately for him, but did not feel able—.

1860 July–December

"Such a disruption could never be healed."

As the Lynches entered the second half of 1860, the repercussions of the Democratic schism more and more affected their lives. The uncertain times created by the political crisis put John Lynch back on a financial tightrope, as he struggled to meet his seemingly ever-increasing responsibilities and debts. The rates he had set for his moneylending before the current crisis could not compete with the much higher ones his competitors were forced to offer. To Mother Baptista the widening political split gave cause to wonder whether there was really a national currency anymore; specifically she questioned how acceptable the U.S. currency carried by a Southerner would be in the North, as though that section had already become a foreign land.

The fluid political situation played havoc with travel plans between the country's sections, even from a border area like Maryland to the Deep South, as Baptista discovered in August when the Jesuit coming from Frederick, Maryland, to Columbia, South Carolina, to give the Ursulines their annual retreat decided not to risk it, only to show up unannounced. The national crisis led some anxious parents to withdraw their daughters from the Ursuline Academy to bring them home. That loss was more than offset by a reverse pattern: the mass exodus of Southern students from the Northern institutions that Southern parents had favored in the antebellum era created a historic opportunity for a Southern female academy that Baptista was quick to recognize and exploit.

Lincoln's election was the final shock that set off a stampede toward secession in South Carolina, where the phobia about the designs of Black Republicans was most intense. John Lynch, ever the diagnostician, found himself examining the body politic and concluding that the fever of popular sentiment, if it continued to peak, would sweep along the state and region to independence, whatever the ultimate consequences proved to be. His brother Francis accepted an invitation to be an officer in the Cheraw home guard, but his main focus was on business:

consolidating his intersectional financial interests to best cope with the "turbulent times" that had rendered the future value of credit so uncertain. Preventive moves, however, were a sideline of Francis's economic activity. The secession crisis, he quickly grasped, had given rise to the extraordinary opportunity for his securing a major government contract. If South Carolina was creating an army, one of the first needs of that army would be shoes. And Francis Lynch intended to be a major supplier.

Patrick Lynch, like his diocesan newspaper, the United States Catholic Miscellany, *had remained on the political sidelines throughout the 1860 campaign. With Lincoln's victory, the paper's editor, James Corcoran, broke its silence by spelling out in an editorial the only honorable course that South Carolina and the South could take: "Long years of menace, insult, outrage and unconstitutional aggression have become at last, certain political as well as social evils which it is wiser to obviate beforehand, than to wait hopelessly in search of their remedy. . . . [T]hat evil day has come upon us, sooner than we would have wished, in order that with free counsel and untrammeled hands, we may deliberate upon and work out our future destiny."*

That destiny, Corcoran concluded, called them, with their sister "Sovereign States," to take up "a way that will leave untouched the honor and happiness of the South."[1] The "way" needed no explanation. Secession hung over South Carolina like a bright sun's promise of a fair future. Now a Catholic priest was urging the state to take that unprecedented step as the only course that honor would allow.

In New York Archbishop John Hughes expressed his shock that his friend and fellow Ulster émigré Patrick Lynch would have permitted such a radical piece in his diocesan paper. Lynch, in his response to Hughes, articulated for the first time his opinion about the crisis the nation was facing. Fear of what, under a Republican administration, the future held for the South's slave economy in which it had such a huge investment and the appeal of a free-trade Confederacy that would eliminate the heavy burden of inflated tariffs to prop up Northern industries—these, Lynch warned, were powerful incentives for the South to secede. Abetting those motives was the unspoken assumption that the joining together of a critical mass of seceding states would deter any attempt by those remaining in the Union to resort to force to preserve the present republic. In numbers there would be a very good likelihood of a peaceful separation.

Lynch himself hoped the Union would somehow hold together under the present crisis, but Union was not an end in itself. The South had to consider its own best interests. Not even the sacred Union enshrined in the Constitution could take precedence. The bottom line: region took precedence over country; or rather, region was the core of one's country. A few months earlier the bishop himself had acquired a major stake in the South's "peculiar institution." A South

Carolina court had awarded Lynch, as the legal body of the diocese, an estate that included a two-thousand-acre plantation and eighty-five slaves.

The special convention called to take up the question of secession convened in mid-December in Columbia, but an outbreak of smallpox quickly forced them to relocate to Charleston. There marching bands, fireworks, and parades of militia provided a carnival air to greet the new republic the delegates were birthing. They did not disappoint as they voted unanimously for secession. Less than a week later, South Carolina militia seized the lightly defended Castle Pinckney, one of several Federal forts surrounding Charleston harbor. On New Year's Day 1861, Patrick Lynch said Mass at the castle for the Meagher Guard, an Irish Catholic unit of the militia that had carried out this first action of the South's struggle for independence. Four days later, a new name appeared on the masthead of the diocesan paper: the Charleston Catholic Miscellany. *There was no longer a United States that Catholics in the Carolinas, as throughout the deep South, recognized.*

At the Pinckney plantation in Walterboro, where Julia Lynch Pinckney was slowly succumbing to consumption, an aborted slave uprising came in the immediate wake of the passing of the ordinance of secession, a shocking notice that the crisis was not just a political one. Disunion could as likely stir the fires of social revolution ever burning below the surface of Southern society as it could contain them.

☙

BAPTISTA LYNCH, URSULINE CONVENT, COLUMBIA S.C., TO PATRICK LYNCH, JULY 31ST[2]

We were quite disappointed in hearing that the case went against you, & our novena was not heard—But I suppose it must all be for the best. I am glad that the family & all expresses a willingness for a compromise, because it shows that their feelings are less bitter, & that your pressure effected some good!

I suppose if the money were your own you too would be glad to wind up the business by such a proceeding, but being only the protector, & agent for the Orphans to whom it is willed, you are bound to support the will to the last— John who spoke with Mr Allemorige says by a compromise you would render yourself liable, for as much as you should or would resign, by such compromise and that the orphans—their protecting society, or legal guardian could expect from you personally, or from your estate the payment of such amount—

But of course you know all these things better than I do— . . .[3]

Will you not be surprised to learn that we are going to take S[r] Rose's sister again—but this time as a Lay Sister, she has never taken her trunk away—strange to say—& she has been begging so earnestly & shown such good dispositions that we thought it better to give her another trial—. Today Aug 3rd I have recd a very satisfactory letter from the Pittsburg Lady—she is very candid & we are pleased with what she says—(all except that the $500⁰⁰ is not certain)—Presuming on your permission, I will give her a favorable reply—& tell her she may come on whenever she wishes—she has two sisters married in this country —one of whom occasionally acts—Mrs Darin—I will show you her letter—she making nothing of herself on requirements, but I am sorry she is with[out?] a certainty of means— . . . Ellen Spann wrote me a nice little letter a few days since & today Francis wrote—Julia is as usual subject to fevers (which John thinks Sister's on the beginning of consumption—The rest of the family T G are quite well— . . . I am sorry I did not give you $10⁰⁰ of Pittsburg money to use at the North. I suppose it would pass at par there—. Francis enclosed me $10⁰⁰ for the "poor of Christ" He is just as ever so kind & generous, but I hate to take it from him.

You ought to see how nicely John is clearing the grounds of all the rubbish &c. We feel as if we can breathe now. —

Sr Mary Glen & Sr. Elizabeth Jorby . . . so far . . . seem quite content, they express gratitude for being here—. The retreat is the all engrossing topic of conversation—at our recreations & we have all sorts of surmises about Revd Father Hitzelberger[4] whose presence some desire, others dread. . . .

I forget that you do not know John has another Son—he wrote to our dear Parents to get them to name it & they called it James—I cannot bear to call the name so soon but it was born on the eve of the Apostles day, & they like it to be called by that name—Eliza is up I think today & the infant is a very fine boy—

ᢖ

Baptista Lynch, Ursuline Convent, Columbia, S.C., to
Patrick Lynch, Aug 1st[5]

This morning Rev. Father McNeal sent me word that you would be up next Friday to give an "Annual Retreat"—We are very happy to hear of your good health & exceedingly obliged to you for taking the trouble to give us our Retreat & for making such efforts to procure a Jesuit Father to give it—. I suppose John & Eliza, as well as myself will feel much relieved of the embarrassment attendant on a stranger's visit—but I hope we may be able to render you comfortable & that you may not find it fatiguing or confining—. Of course your mind is not as free, as it was when you gave us our retreat in Brown County, & I am afraid you will feel anxious about home duties, while devoting your time to us—. We, or perhaps I should say *I*, as I am the greatest *miser* should be glad to be spared the travelling expenses of the J. [Jesuit] Father.

We are all very much pleased at the prospect of going into Retreat, altho' we have been *very regular* & applied ourselves closely this vacation—The Laysisters giving a thorough housecleaning & arranging childrens apartments &c &c— the Novices studying—drawing, & painting & practicing music, . . . —. All use- fully employed, I trust both for this world & the next—

Have no school duties to interfere, we have said the entire office of the day in Choir-Hours at 8 A.M.—Vespers & compline at 2½ PM & Matins & Lauds at ¼ to 8 PM which together with our examen & meditation filled out the days most agreeably—

Sr Josephine & I but *she principally* have arranged our accounts of the year —& I am happy to say I think we stand better than we did last year.

We have a prospect of three young ladies from Virginia & I hope we may have a full school notwithstanding the difficulties of the times—.

We are very happy to learn that the Northerners are evincing a better dis- position for peace—It is time for them— . . .

🙟

JULIA LYNCH PINCKNEY, WALTERBORO, TO PATRICK LYNCH, AUGUST 1[6]

I am sorry that I have caused you any unnecessary uneasiness with regards to my health. It is true that I have had a bad cold & cough for the last two months but now I am thankful to be able to say that it has nearly left me, at times I pass a whole day & night without coughing at all. Almost all of the family here have had as bad colds as mine was.

Your little God Son is the finest-looking, the prettiest & best child in Wal- terboro, although it is his mother that is saying it.

I am glad to hear that you were in Cheraw so lately. I hope you found all well. Anna mentioned that she was suffering a great deal from her teeth. My dear Brother I was a little disappointed when I saw accounts of your being at "White House," & did not come here to see us. I hope you will soon find time enough to come to the jumping off place as I heard a gentleman call Walterboro, some short-time since. I spent a most delightful day at Mr Bellinger's Planta- tion yesterday & never saw so many watermelons in my life at one time before. There were at least five hundred in his dwelling house. Eustace is quite well & I hope he may escape fever this summer. Hoping to hear from you soon I will conclude dear Brother, by begging your prayers For *Eustace, Conlaw & myself*

Your affectionate Sister

Mrs Pinckney has been quite sick, but is better. . . .

Julie

BAPTISTA LYNCH, URSULINE CONVENT, COLUMBIA, S.C., TO
   PATRICK LYNCH, AUG 5TH[7]

I recd a letter from Revd P O'Neill who had the politeness to tell me that
you were in New York—I hope however, that now you are at home, & that we
may expect the pleasure of seeing you in Columbia—during our retreat. Revd
Father Hitzelberger arrived quite unexpectedly on Monday morning & said
Mass for us—I am much pleased with him. . . . —Poor Father Hitzelberger
received a letter, which he opened almost at our door this evening, as he was
coming to open our retreat & it contained the announcement of his Brother's
death—A younger brother, who resided in N. Orleans & who intended to meet
him in Charleston, after he had finished our retreat—He was married but had
no children—R.I. P.

Would you have the kindness my dear Brother to correct our "Prospectus"
on the "Miscellany" & say our academic exercises will be resumed on the *first
Monday in Sep.* instead of the 26th & charges to $10⁰⁰ *for Drawing* crayons— . . .

BAPTISTA LYNCH, URSULINE CONVENT, COLUMBIA S.C., TO PATRICK LYNCH,
   AUG 10TH[8]

You would be edified with the earnest piety of our sisters if you saw them—
even the new-comers seem to be rapt up in their devotions & pious practices—
every night two at least make their accusations at the foot of the cross—& all
seem impressed by Rev Father Hitzelberger—solid, truthful lessons. . . .

Did you get my last letter? Please answer it, or what would be better, come
up on Sunday night train & see us—we shall have made such progress in the
"*via illuminata*"[9] by that time that you may mistake us for so many *Moseses*.

I am almost disposed to *levity*, I feel so *light*, since making my review of
seven years!

BAPTISTA LYNCH, URSULINE CONVENT, COLUMBIA, TO PATRICK LYNCH,
   SEPT 3RD[10]

We have opened our school with twenty-two pupils T.G. for so many—&
we expect an addition of several this evening—I received a letter from Miss
Adelaide Lowe last evening, she wrote from Phila [Philadelphia]—having left
Pittsburg & started last Saturday in steamer for Charleston from N.Y.—will be
here in a few days— . . .

❧

HENRIETTA LYNCH, CHERAW, TO PATRICK LYNCH, 4TH SEPT[ll]

My Dear D[r] Lynch,

. . . We find it impossible to learn any thing from you. Ma answered your letter and hopes that you received it. We also hope you are in good health. Your family are all well. We hear that Julia is much better and has a very good appetite.

We all regret much to hear that the fever is in Town. Ma speaks of leaving . . . about the end of this month but if possible I would be so happy to have her all October. I trust the fever will not keep you from paying the visit we have been looking forward to so much.

Dear Dr. Lynch, I have long wished to write you but I find so little time to write or read. The sad occasion of your Brother James' death gave me the desire. I wanted to tell you that his death made a very great impression on me, so deep was it that when I prepared for Confession two days after I can with safety say I felt happy in the piety that stole over me. I was able at the time to make a long and satisfactory examination, and what made me feel surer of myself was that I had an earnest desire of making a general Confession again, rather than be in the least uncertainty as to my eternal welfare.

A great dread was upon me as if the finger of God was upon us all, and the thought then came to my mind how I would speak to you and beg you to preach such sermons ever after, as would come to the hearts of your hearers. Short but sweet—even on the importance of living a life forever mindful of their salvation and how God may call them away in the midst of *health and life*. I consider no apology necessary in writing to you Dear Dr. Lynch because you have often told me to speak out to you my thoughts. God makes use of the weak to confound the strong. Oh, how I do wish I could always feel myself impressed with the fear of offending God as I did at that time. You know I have said I once became very pious from the example of Mrs. Bellinger. This goes to shew what example can do. Poor D[r] Bellinger! Truly has it been said of him his example was greater than a sermon. Oh I hope, I trust, that my soul may be saved. I always have such veneration for goodness though I know so well that I cannot approach it. I rely on your prayers and I earnestly entreat of you to take good care of your health and not to overtask your strength. Take this advice from me. Call me to mind in every Mass as well as my dear family and pray that piety and conversion may be given me as an earthly Blessing. Adieu my dear Father Brother friend & Bishop. Your affec. Henrietta

Baptista Lynch, Ursuline Convent, Columbia, S.C, to Patrick Lynch, Sept 21st[12]

Well, Messrs Kelly Hedian & Piet wrote to me yesterday, meeting our pro-posal half well, at the same time, saying if we did not accept their proposal after reasons which they alleged they would accept ours—we have thought it best to accept theirs—& accordingly wrote to them today saying so, & as they mentioned their interview with you &c—we said when we had learnd from you what alterations it would be requisite for us to make, & we would send our revision. I drew up with them the agreement they had expressed a readiness to enter upon—We also wrote by the aid of John an order on "Lucas Brothers" for the plates which we sent to Kelly Hedian & Piet—and in answering Lucas & Bros. sent a draft on K, H & P — payable 18 mos' after sight, for plates of Ursulan Manual—which closes for us, the business of the plates—

Miss Addie Lowe arrived the day after you left, I think—she is a remarkably fine looking & prepossessing person. I trust she may *wear* well, & always have as good dispositions as *she now* evinces—she unfortunately lost her portfolio of drawings in Columbia, which she has not yet recovered—[13]

This morning I received an offer of a lay sister postulant, from Rev. P. O'Neill of Charleston—I wrote him how we would not refuse any one recommended by him, yet at present did not need any—enquired [about] her age, strength &c could she wash, & iron &c &c.

Anna Lynch, Cheraw, to Patrick Lynch, Sept 28th[14]

I write to beg that you will let me know, by return mail, whether it will be perfectly safe for me, to go through Charleston on my way to see Julia next week. If there is any danger & I get your answer on Sunday, I will have Eustace to meet me [at] "George's Station" which he has offered to do, if I let him know in time. Julie is writing repeatedly for me to go down. She was not so well, when we heard a few days since & her baby & Lily were both quite sick. . . .

John Lynch, Columbia, to Patrick Lynch, 14 Oct[15]

I drop you a few lines to say that I am not sure I can get off tomorrow as you arranged; if I do not I hope it will not create a disappointment I have two or three cases I am afraid to leave in the hands of others without they are considerably better tonight. I will go down through Charleston as soon as possible. I recd a letter from Anna mentioning that Julia was not considered in immediate danger, but that there appeard to be a rising forming in her side, which the Dr appeard uneasy about and was trying to dissipate. I doubt if he will be able—if it points externally and is opened, if she has strength, to bear the drain, I think it will be the means of her cure, I would therefore advise poulticing to bring it to a head, and give tonics and rigorous diet, this of course, is prescribing without knowing exactly the state of the case, but supposing it from Annas description, and from having seen similar ones as I suppose hers to be; if you go down before I do you can judge if I am correct. . . .

ᠬᠥ

ANNA LYNCH, WALTERBORO, TO PATRICK LYNCH, OCT 23RD[16]

I think Julia has improved a little since you were here, in strength anyhow, but one day she seems a great deal better & the next not so well. So I cannot say, as I would wish, that she is really better. Brother John advises a plaster for her back which she put on on Sunday, & thinks has benefitted her hickey. She has been sitting up a good deal for the last week & sews a little occasionally. She is looking forward to your promising visit next week with *almost* as much pleasure as I am. I am quite well again, but have not heard from home for so long that I feel anxious Eustace is down the Country & the family here are well, except Mʳˢ Pinckney who is in bed today— . . .

ᠬᠥ

BAPTISTA LYNCH, URSULINE CONVENT, COLUMBIA, S.C., TO
PATRICK LYNCH, OCT 26TH[17]

We were gratified to learn through Anna's letter that Julie appears no worse, which John says is as much as to say, she is better—Cornelia was here yesterday afternoon & told me all at the dear home were quite well—she has left for Cheraw today—

Neither John or I feel very well owing to some fatigue & anxiety—we have had some sickness among both Sisters & pupils—With the Sisters it was not serious—but among the Children Lucia Bellinger has been quite sick with typhoid fever, which still lasts, though she appears better than she was—Mary Dehaigle, Minnie Clark & Alice Conaugton have had Dyptheria: & others have sore-throat of a less alarming nature—we have written to all their parents, but hope it will not be necessary to remove them from the school, & that with good care & nursing they may all get well—Columbia is at present very sickly & this

"Dyptheria" seems to baffle the skill of physicians & has proved very fatal to many—. Some of our Sisters are very much fatigued by nursing the sick & watching—Yet we would rather be so, than have the children to leave.

I was sorry to hear through Mrs Cunningham, who called this morning with Mrs Northrup, that the Yellow fever still exists in your city. . . .

Baptista Lynch, Ursuline Convent, Columbia, S.C., to Patrick Lynch, Nov 13[18]

You will be glad to hear that although Columbia is crowded, we are in perfect peace, & the political excitement seems to cast us quite in the shade. Another piece of good news is, that between the payments made by T Semmes esquire Col^n J J. Ryan & Mr J. Enright we have received within the two last days about $450^{00} which as you may suppose is very acceptable. God is indeed very good to us—never do we feel anxious to meet our bills, that he does not send us means to do so & our poor prayers seem to be always heard—He never gives us enough to make us feel proud or independent but just enough to strengthen our hopes & confidence in Him.

Col Ryan speaks of going to Georgetown[19] for Ida & placing her with us—I wonder if he will & if others will follow his example?

Poor John, I do admire him so much—he is in such a dilemma for money at present being called on at once to meet Louisa's wants & the payment of the "Boyden case" & with so small an income & large a family—! I really pity, but he is as calm gentlemanly & *well behaved* as we could wish. He is kept busy waiting on Eliza, Mrs Henderson &c during these *Fair & Session* times. They took Mrs Bellinger out today, & she seemed to enjoy herself very much. Lucie will go down with her mother to Charleston in a few days to recruit her strength—Our other invalids are, thank God, almost well—Our embroidery looks quite respectable at the Fair, & hope will get the prize.

John Lynch, Columbia, to Patrick Lynch, 16 Nov[20]

Enclosed I send you checks for twenty five hundred dollars ($2500) for Louisa, as I promised. I have advised Francis to send to your order the amt of his indebtedness to Louisa Six hundred dollars and interest amounting to about seven hundred dollars—if he sends his, there will be a surplus which I will need, as you well understand when I explain to you how I raised mine.

I was put to as close a strait as I have ever been in, but as Mother and Francis says, something always appears to turn up in my favour. I am afraid I trust too much to it (McCauley fashion) In doing what I have, I have placed myself in quite a crampt position, if things & times do not alter by the first of Jany—as I have taken everything at 7 percent till then. 10 & 12 is offerd freely, not only by the president of the Exchange Bank, but by the Prest [President] of the South Carolina R.R. and others, including merchants from Charleston &c as I have been credibly informed.

I see by your letter that you still have a doubtful opinion of Columbia, as regards the Convent; throw that aside, for I flatter myself, [that] respect for my feelings, after they have been tried, will controll. I expect things here after to go on quite smoothly, I sent you seventy five dollars for Louisa the other day but have not heard whether you received it. I recd quite a smart letter from Louisa yesterday. "I tell you, it hurried me up considerable," as you say, it will be best for me to *see* the papers all fixed right, so I will try and be down on Monday night, although Eliza is now complaining. Regarding Francis's part, I hope there may be no misunderstanding, as I wrote to him in time, if there should be, you must try and remedy it till I get down. I hope there will not be any necessity for your having any trouble.

In a letter from Cheraw today we hear that Anna reports Julia as some better. I hope it is so.

Political excitement is at its highest, if *they* can keep it at what it is till after the Convention, then the Union will be dissolved, otherwise it is very doubtful. We have large meetings every night and speeches—but to me it appears the excitement is not so great as it was a week ago.

The Convent was *fairly* represented in the *Fair*. I expect they will get some prizes, whether Miss Whiting is there or not; their work will show for itself. They have been visited with some sickness since I saw you, but thank God they are all getting well *again*.

֍

FRANCIS LYNCH, CHERAW, TO PATRICK LYNCH, 9TH DEC[21]

I am glad to learn through Henrietta letters of your good health, and was pleased that your visit north was postponed—It must be too cold for comfort there now, in more senses than one.

Sister Anna is a good correspondent and keeps us apprized of the changes with Sister Julia, whom I much fear will hardly recover.

It is extremely kind in Revd Mr Carr[22] to visit her so often. Sister Anna will remain for sometime yet. . . .

Just think of it, I have accepted the 3rd lieutenancy in the Fire Military home protection Company—this is a compliment in these turbulent times. . . .

⚜

BAPTISTA LYNCH, URSULINE CONVENT, COLUMBIA, S.C., TO
PATRICK LYNCH, DEC 18TH[23]

I wrote day before yesterday—or rather had Sr. Josephine to write to Dr.
L Northrop as well as all who owe us for the session ending Feb 1st requesting
payment at their earliest convenience. I was prompted to do this, because we
are obliged to pay $125 in a few days, besides our cursory expenses of provi-
sions, & have in hand only about $75. When Dr. Northrop places the payment
—partial or whole, will you please pay to F. Baker & Co. $100. in amt, & send
me the rest—I trust we may get favorable replies to our letters, otherwise we
shall be at a stand still for a short time—& would dislike so much to have to ask
any one to wait for payment, as we propose to pay cash on all bills presented
—. *You must not send me any of your money*—I really would not like it if you
did—Perhaps tomorrow's mail may bring us more than we actually need—and
already we are too much in your debt—. I only tell you this about Dr. Northrop
that you may not let the money lie there until you could bring it thinking it was
all the same to us— . . .

Our examination—Manual & Banner are in progress—& we are all T.G.
quite well. I have advertised the parents, with John's advice that the small-pox
has become an epidemic, tho' of a mild form—I suppose however all have left
who will, unless Mr Ferrall takes his daughter home. I have enjoyed your letter
to Abp Hughes, & the complimentary preface—I have just written to Bp Wood
of Phila [Philadelphia] to tell him of his postulants. John has small-pox among
his negroes & is "down in the cellar" about money—but there is a silver lining
to every cloud.

⚜

ANNA LYNCH, WALTERBORO, TO PATRICK LYNCH, DEC. 27TH[24]

. . . Julia is, or appears to be, much better—than when you were here, but
Eustace is not willing for her to leave home, *in these times,* but that is only an
excuse. Julia herself has given up the idea of travelling for the present since she
cannot go to Columbia.

If mother comes down I suppose you will bring her to us. It affords me no
pleasure in the world, to hear anything said about Julia's going home, because I
know the good will be taken out of the visit in the end, as usual & that would
certainly injure Julia, when she is as weak as she is—

Eustace cannot be away from home now, & that is the reason why he does
not wish Julia to go—& Julia is much better satisfied for him to be with her. He
is kind in his own way but hard hearted too. The negroes were to rise in the

holidays, & [in] this place, but the plot was discovered a few days beforehand & the leaders taken up. Nine were tried & four in jail to be hung, so it is not safe for Eustace to be away & every body is armed. He spoke of going to Charleston to buy a pair of pistols soon. . . .

FRANCIS LYNCH, CHERAW, TO PATRICK LYNCH, 27 DEC[25]

You will please endorse the enclosed note and place it in Bank, I will advise Mr. Waring of my having sent it to you, sending to him at same time, a draft covering 1000$ on the maturing note & the discount. Sales have been far better than usual with me the past season, nearly up to your anticipations—. The disturbed state of things may delay collections while a proper regard to the interests of my business would induce its vigourous prosecution.

If the Gov[mt] should need supplies I must try for the supply, and to this end, think to write to His Excellency next week.

It was with sorrow we read your account of the state of sister Julia's health.

Mother is undecided about going to Charleston, and says if Julia is coming home, she thinks it better to have the most comfortable arrangements made for her arrival—If Julia goes to Columbia mother will go there—Hoping every thing for the best for our dear sister. It is a great satisfaction to us all Sister Anna has been able to render her attentive care. . . .

Since writing the foregoing, I have been over at Father's—a letter was recd today from sister Anna—saying Julia is no worse. Mother would like to avoid travelling and will wait the receipt of another letter before determining what to do. Hoping for the best . . .

PATRICK LYNCH, CHARLESTON, TO JOHN HUGHES, JANUARY 6, 1861 (COPY)[26]

Dr. Corcoran writes as he pleases, I cannot say that his Editorials are not sometimes not to my taste—But he must write without restraints if he would write well. I certainly do not like the two last references he has made to political matters—But he has said nothing "contra fidem et mores." If we are not now in a state of war we are very like it and very near it. In the convention which passed the Secession ordinance, there was a larger proportion of thinking men who wished so to direct things that a conflict would be avoided, and all matters be settled by negotiation. All the officers of the Federal courts having resigned that point of contact was removed. There remained three others on which the Presidents declaration that he would enforce the laws, and protect United States property, might bring difficulty; the Post office, the Custom House, and the

James Corcoran, editor of the *United States Catholic Miscellany* and outspoken promoter of the Confederacy. Courtesy of the Roman Catholic Diocese of Charleston Archives.

Forts. It was proposed that secession should be considered as the dissolution of a partnership, and that the name of the old firm might be used for a reasonable time to be, until five or six other states should secede, and the movement have such proportions as to forbid any attempt at coercion. The matter was not so expressed, but I think that was the real idea. Some perhaps had a lingering hope that "something would turn up" to save the Union.

As to the Post Office, there was no difficulty. It cost us nothing, or rather its outlay in the state exceeded its income by perhaps $100,000 a year. We had nothing to put in its place—and to stop it, would throw the people of the state into too great a ferment. So the convention authorized the Postmasters to continue in the discharge of their duties. It was further said that the Postal service was by contracts not yet terminated, made in good faith, and to which S. Carolina in the Union, was a party, and it would be breach of faith to violate them now. The Custom House was the next point. Here the same policy was proposed. But the same interests were not at stake, and the further reason was urged that the Collection of duties is an act of sovereignty, which after the Act of Secession, could not properly be allowed to be done by the Federal authorities. The result was something of a compromise. The Collector and all his

View of Charleston circa 1862. Courtesy of the Library of Congress.

officials resigned their federal offices and were reappointed by state authority and were charged to act precisely as before, except that duties may be paid in bank bills, and must be deposited in the state bank. . . . The third point was left untouched in pursuance of an understanding with the President.—and three commissioners were sent to Washington. . . . They returned on the 4th inst. And on the 5th the Convention adjourned having appointed Commissioners to the several states expected to secede, empowered to offer the formation of a Southern Union. . . . Such a disruption could never be healed.

It would be based on strong motives. 1st a deep dislike, I might say, a very general intense hatred of the northern States, on account of their abolition speeches, sentiments, legislation, and course of action. 2nd on a sense of wrong done us, by such legislation in violation of the letter & spirit of the compact of the Constitution—by the systematized underground Railroads, and by the not unfrequent tampering with negroes here in the South. 3d on a feeling of the insecurity of slave property for the future,—a feeling aroused by the speeches of Senators Wilson,[27] Chase,[28] Sumner,[29] of Lovejoy,[30] Julian,[31] Campbell[32]—to say nothing of the use of Helper's Book[33] as a textbook for the Presidential canvass. 4th on a calculation that by seceding from the Union, and establishing a southern confederacy the five above named states would save over $50,000,000 a year,[34] which they pay to the North now, under the working of the Union, more than they would have to pay for the same articles, were they free to purchase in the cheapest market of the world, and to import, without duties, or with duties to be spent entirely at home. . . . Let this Union be broken. We at the

South will suffer to some extent. But the North will have to drain the Cup, of which they have but taken a sip as yet.

For the last year, especially since it was deemed probable that the Republicans would obtain controul of the forces of Government, documents have been industriously circulated all thro' the South, to spread and establish the positions I have indicated. Hence the rapid development of Disunion sentiments all through the Southern States, especially in the Cotton States, where the fourth ground has strongest application and weight. A movement based on such convictions and appealing to a sense of right—to a feeling of unjustice done—of wrongs threatened,—when once it has taken full hold of the popular heart, cannot well be stayed. In this state it has swept everything. I know only *two* southerners in this city of all my acquaintance, who may be set down as true Union men. There are doubtless others who would rejoice "quieta non movere,"[35] but would go with an United South. In Georgia, as I said, a fight for the Union will be made. Your legislative action will have some, perhaps much weight, for or against the secession, in that canvass.

I do not claim to be a Union man myself—Yet I would regret to see this Government, after a glorious, though brief ascent, burst like a rocket, and leave only burnt & noisesome fragments. I fear too, future civil wars strifes, and miseries. Could I be guaranteed from them, a Southern Confederacy would bring us far greater prosperity than we have enjoyed under the Union, at least of late years.—and if the spirit so inimical to the South, which has obtained the reins of power is now to act out, what it spoke, why the sooner we of the South are out of its clutches, the better. I hope the truth is, that the Constitution will be sacred and that the infractions of it will be redressed.

Here . . . I am not unfrequently thrown into connexion w members of our Legislature. I presume such must be the case with you too, and it may be that the plain statement of facts which I make may have some influence, where men will not trust to *tell-lie-graphic* reports, and [tales] of partisan newspapers—If you think proper to make any use of it, you are free to do so. (not using my name unless strictly confidentially) . . .

1861 January–June

"Pro Deo et pro Patria."

As Patrick Lynch had intimated to John Hughes, the cotton-producing states
were primed to seek justice for themselves outside the Union. Once South Carolina formally seceded in late December, in a whirlwind of withdrawals over a
three-week period the six other states in the Deep South followed. On February
1, in Montgomery, Alabama, the seven organized "the Confederate States of
America," whose constitution established slavery as a cornerstone of the new
republic by guaranteeing to its citizens the right to hold slaves and transport
them freely to any portion of the Confederacy.

As the Confederacy took shape in the lower South in the winter of 1860–61,
secessionists seized federal facilities within its borders. The garrisons of two
forts, in Florida and South Carolina respectively, refused to surrender them to
representatives of the newly created nation. Fort Sumter, in Charleston harbor,
as the chief symbol of federal resistance, came under siege from Confederate
forces on the surrounding promontories and islands. Capturing the fort, either
peacefully or by force, became the grand test for the infant nation. To meet it,
South Carolina society went on a war footing that caught up people, lands, and
industries. A minuteman atmosphere, reminiscent of the American Revolution,
was a constant reminder and assurance to white Southerners that they were
reliving their ancestors' heroic quest for independence. As military units descended upon Charleston to protect and advance the honor of the Confederacy,
the Lynches converged upon Walterboro, where Julia Lynch Pinckney was the
latest Lynch, the fourth in less than five years, to be struck fatally by the disease
that haunted the family.

When the war finally came to South Carolina in mid-April with the predawn firing on Fort Sumter, it had an immediate impact on the Lynches. The
very use of "we" by Patrick and other siblings in alluding to the Confederacy
revealed sharply enough their budding nationalism. John, who had hitherto
paid little attention to politics, now felt the need for political literacy to survive

in the rapidly changing conditions of a society at war. Francis finally had the incentive to make a quantum leap in his shoe production to meet the inevitable increased demand, which proved to be even better than he anticipated. Hugh was the one Lynch male to respond to the call to arms by enlisting. Baptista and her Ursuline community contributed to the nurturing of patriotism by sewing banners and flags for the organizing military volunteers. If it was a patriotic act, it was also, by design, a fund-raiser, whose price was determined by the ability of the receiving military unit to pay.

For his part, Bishop Lynch gave notice of his commitment to the Confederate cause by ordering a solemn Te Deum *to celebrate the fall of Fort Sumter. Several days after Robert Anderson's surrender, Patrick Lynch was likely among a group of dignitaries who toured the site on which the first battle of the long-coming war had taken place (see figure page 135). Though habitually the most reticent of public figures about political affairs, Patrick Lynch had long since established his credentials for civic-mindedness, most notably in his work on the city's water supply. To the bishop, participating in such a victory inspection was a power-fully visible demonstration of the patriotism of all the Catholics in the Carolinas whom he represented.[1] Five months later he publicly blessed a flag for the Irish Volunteers, a historic militia company of Charleston. Let that flag "teach you," the bishop instructed the soldiers, "of God—of Erin—of Carolina."[2] The emblems that adorned the banner—the harp, shamrock, palmetto, and stars—should be constant reminders to them of their intertwined commitment to their maker, homeland, and country that had given them a new start.*

On the very eve of the war, Patrick Lynch, in effect, became a large slave-holder, with far more slaves than the rest of his family combined. William McKenna, the wealthiest Catholic in the diocese, had, upon his death in 1859, left most of his estate, worth more than $250,000, to the diocese. When McKenna's family successfully challenged the will in court, Bishop Lynch and the surviving McKennas reached an agreement about dividing the estate. In the settlement the bishop legally acquired eighty-five slaves as well as a two-thousand-acre plantation.[3] Together with the slaves he had come to control through the legacies of other Catholics to his predecessors, Patrick Lynch counted nearly a hundred individuals whom he habitually referred to as his "servants" or "people" on two plantations in the upcountry, at Lancaster and at Lexington, the latter just outside Columbia. Patrick by necessity was an absentee owner. To manage the plantations the bishop depended upon his brother John in Lexington, and in Lancaster on his attorney, Claudian Bird Northrop, a convert from one of the first families of the state.

If the country had divided into two, the Roman Catholic Church in America had not. No changes were made to the church's structure of governance to reflect the new geopolitical realities, which made it difficult for church officials to communicate and administer across military lines and blockades. Prelates, like Patrick Lynch, coped as best they could with the challenges, although, as the war went on, far longer than most people had possibly imagined it might, pressures grew for developing lines of organization and authority which would match the sectional division of the American Catholic community.

BAPTISTA LYNCH, URSULINE CONVENT, COLUMBIA, TO PATRICK LYNCH, 8 JANUARY[4]

You will be glad to hear that we are all quite well—have finished embroidering the Banner, & received for it $65.00—! It is certainly a splendid piece of work & is especially admired, being hung up in Mr. Radcliffes[5] store for admiration. We hope it may do our Academy some good. A.M.D.G. We were called on by Mrs Passon &—to draw a design for their flag, & furnish some materials, for which we have today re^{c}d 11^{oo} & may get 15^{oo}. Is it not queer, for Nuns to be engaged preparing flags for war ____! I have not used your note, nor will I if I can avoid doing so. Providence has placed in our hands $300^{oo} by the above means & other payments, so that I hope to meet our expenses until next session without using your note. D.G.

Poor John has been very much pushed about his money matters, . . . I felt so much like lending him, as long as we had any—but I know our Rule prohibited me, & that already I had overstepped my principles in that way, since he is in our debt—. So I contented myself with praying for him, & remember too that if the drop in the bucket that I could lend might force us to call on you—so it would be robbing Peter to pay Paul—.

How is poor Julia—has she left Walterboro yet? When she does I hope it is home she will go, & not here—I would not think John's home any place for an invalid—however really disposed he & Eliza might be—. I suppose you remember this is John's birth day—the Joy-bells rang during the whole of Mass, & I thought it was a big fire—& sent a sister to look where it was—. I wish the other States would hurry & come out of the Union—that people might set about their business again—. We are told the people— soldiers, companies or whatever they are, are suffering greatly in Charleston—& on allowance—! . . . *We have been expecting you every day*—none of our pupils have yet returned, but studies are as usual. . . .[6]

PATRICK LYNCH TO [MAJ. ROBERT] ANDERSON, CHARLESTON, 10 JAN[7]

I take the liberty of sending to Fort Sumter, Rev. P. Ryan, DD [Doctor of Divinity], a Catholic Clergyman of this city in order that the Catholics at F. Sumter may be able to perform those Religious duties which are obligatory on them and which some will feel consolation in fulfilling.[8]

As his mission is purely religious and in no wise civil or military, I trust it will meet your earnest cooperation. He goes down under a pledge to act only as a clergyman acting in his ministerial capacity. . . .

ANNA LYNCH, WALTERBORO, TO PATRICK LYNCH, JAN 13TH[9]

Julia was quite sick on Friday night, from indigestion. Vomited a good deal & is very much weakened in consequence. So much so, that she slept all day, & could not be roused sufficiently to eat anything until five o'clock this afternoon. She appears very much prostrated but comparatively easy. I feel quite anxious about her although I believe she is considered in no immediate danger, but very sick. I would feel much relieved if you could send up Mr Carr[10] again, if convenient, because she looks so very badly. Miss Sarah & Charlie think she will live some weeks, if not months yet, as she generally improves after her sick spells, a good deal, but this one was particularly severe. . . .

Sunday morning—Julia looks very badly but appears a little stronger. I can't say she is any better.

BAPTISTA LYNCH, URSULINE CONVENT COLUMBIA, S.C., TO
PATRICK LYNCH, JAN 19TH[11]

We expected to see you this morning, on account of what you said in John's last letter—But altho a visit from [you] is always one of my greatest enjoyments, I was not sorry this morning that you did not come for I am suffering with one of my sick & nervous headaches—& am very poor company for any one & as you may perceive can scarcely write either—John was here this morning & the effects of night patrol tell on him somewhat in the same way— he asked to say to you that Mr W^m McGuinnes[12] told him yesterday to tell you he had collected our qrs rent for the old Convent which is at your disposal—I suppose you will be up here yourself to render it on Monday or Tuesday, & that would give a much better impression than to have him pay it to John or us I think—You will be glad to hear that most of our pupils have returned quite well

& happy, & their parents were highly pleased—My hand trembles too much to continue. I will only say that Providence blesses us with means to meet our bills & we hope to get on very well

ANNA LYNCH, WALTERBORO, TO PATRICK LYNCH, SATURDAY MORNING, 5 O'CLOCK 21ST [JANUARY][13]

Julia had another chill & attack of sick stomach last night, like what she had on Friday night at two o'clock four hours earlier, which weakened her so much that Miss Sarah herself thought she would [not] live through the night. I have been sitting up with her, & find her breathing a little easier now, but don't know what moment she may become worse & die. She is so weak. Eustace sends this letter to Green Pond by a boy, who will wait there until tomorrow with the buggy for yourself or Mr Carr. I hope Julia may live until a Priest reaches here, but her chill will probably return as many hours earlier on Tuesday & I have no sense she will live through another. These two have [brought] such a change she cannot raise her head off of the pillow without assistance to take water. . . . Eustace & Miss Sarah asked me yesterday evening to write for Mother & Father. You can do what you think best. I have no hope of Julia's living for them to reach here & I fear the consequences of the long travel for them, however it may be their pleasure to come. . . .

PATRICK LYNCH CHARLESTON, S.C. TO ABP. FRANCIS KENRICK, 9 FEB[14]

Most Rev. Dear Sir

In reply to your letter, I must express the hope that the Council will be held. While everything else is shaking or falling to pieces, it seems well to me that the church should be seen to stand firm and in no wise disturbed. As to making any declaration on the subject of slavery, touching its lawfulness, I do not think it necessary, or expedient, for the question has never been put in doubt here.— At Rome they are unwilling, or formerly were, to say anything on the subject. The reply to a case proposed by or through Rev. Ben Spalding[15] in my time, was "Consulat probatos auctores."[16] As to the duties of Catholic owners to slaves, especially Catholic ones, that is a very important point, and one really coming home to us here. Where the difficulties are so great as to make many feel melius homini foret,[17] if he never owned one. On that point I may try to draw up some questions. . . .

In the Political World, we are all agog here, and things look warlike as they have for five weeks past. Six Batteries of Columbiads and heavy cannon are planted around Fort Sumter, and are ready to open fire, whenever the word is given. The plan here I believe is to have all things ready in such force that when the attack commences, four days will end the business—too quickly for troops to be sent on to take part in it. Still if we can get the fort without a fight, or see any hopes of doing so, our authorities will patiently wait.

P.S. Dr. Corcoran is indeed very belligerent—much more so than any of us. So much so as nearly to cause the Miscellany to *blow up*. But I hope we will all be in peace soon.

Anna Lynch, Walterboro, to Patrick Lynch, Feb 14th[18]

Julie has not been quite so sick in the last two days, and Mother says, she will feel much better satisfied, if you can accept Eustace's offer & come up next Monday. So you can give your opinion about her. Her side is very painful & Julia imagines it is an internal boil which may break outside, that causes it to hurt her so much. I hardly think so. If you come up, please ask Daughter to send up my black shawl that I may see its size, and "Marion Elwood" by you. . . . Julia's appetite is better but I don't think she is improving materially. Mother is not as hopeful about her recovery, as she was— . . . I always write the best news I can about Julia home because I don't wish to distress Father's spirits too much in mother's absence. Mother has just told me that she no longer entertains any hope of Julia's recovery.

Anna Lynch, Walterboro, to Patrick Lynch, Sunday [Feb 24?][19]

Julia seems better, Eustace got your letter last evening, & has made arrangements to meet Brother John & yourself as you desired. I don't feel very well today & only wish to let you know your letter has been received. Julia joins in love to you. She seems very glad that Brother John & yourself are coming. Augusta is well. . . .

John Lynch, Columbia, to Patrick Lynch, March 9th[20]

Mr Burns called to see you last night. He says he will be ready to take the trip for you any time after the 15th as the work at Quarry & State house will stop for want of funds. I told him I did not know whether you still intended sending the negroes over, on account of Dr Burt's illness, but would write and let you know his disposition, and if you needed his services you could let me know.

We heard yesterday that a gun was accidentally discharged from Cummins point battery and the ball struck the door of Fort Sumter, that Anderson bristled for fight, till an explanation was made. Such carelessness or tricks might lead to serious results, although it may show with what accuracy the guns can be worked.

If you have heard any thing from Julia please let me know at once. . . .

FRANCIS LYNCH, CHERAW, TO PATRICK LYNCH, 9 MAR[21]

In order to provide payment for bill sold leather from Miss Ballardette, *just in time*, There being *no checks on N York to be had here*,—I have drawn on you (please accept) a draft for 1000$ at 30% which I will provide for. And sent a check for 900$ to Mr Thos. A Waring Cash, in my letter to him of this date, and also a check for blank amount, presuming the $1714 5/100 from Col[n] L M. Hatch . . . had been paid over to you & deposited to my credit, or that such would be the case, in time on Monday morning—That uniting both, he could mail on Monday noon's train a chk on N. Y. for 2500$ to Messrs Bullard & Co and thus secure the shipment of the leather prior to the 18th of this inst., after when duties will be lowered on imports. . . .

ANNA LYNCH, WALTERBORO, TO PATRICK LYNCH, M[ARCH] 20[22]

. . . Julia is still alive, but that is all, any hour may be her last. Do ask Brother come up immediately, when [he] gets back to Charleston, as she may possibly linger a day or so longer but her mind is wandering so much today, that I don't expect it; we are keeping her alive on brandy since Tuesday.

Eustace will take her home to be buried. She was looking anxiously for Mr Carr yesterday, & I cannot express my disappointment when the boy returned alone. I told her the cause & that Brother had been telegraphed for. Begging your prayers for her. . . .

Julia suffers very little & says she is better, but is not.

ANNA LYNCH, CHERAW, TO PATRICK LYNCH, MARCH 28[23]

We received your kind letter this morning & were glad to hear that you were well, & of your safe return in Charleston.

I am sure you do not regret your absence, at the time of Julia's illness & death less than we did, and of her being deprived of the presence of a Priest, at her last moments, a blessing she earnestly desired to the last. We kept her until Wednesday morning for you to come—and I cannot help regretting that the telegraph did not reach you in time for you to see her before she died. I hope you may be able to come up next week—it will be a pleasure to us all, & a great comfort to Father & Mother to see you who seem to feel Julia's death very much—The fatigue of mother's long travel was a great deal for her—She just arrived in Walterboro in time to see Julia before the coffin was closed—Sunday night.

JOHN LYNCH, COLUMBIA, TO PATRICK LYNCH, APRIL 12TH[24]

I was called on a few days ago by the Tax Collector, to know who would pay the taxes on the Convent & old House. I told him I did not know whether they were liable to tax but if they were I would pay them. I got him to wait till you would come up next Monday or Tuesday, but as I fear from the stopping of the telegraph today that the war has commenced, it may be uncertain whether you can come I would like you to let me know as soon as possible whether I have to pay the tax. I would also be pleased if you could keep me posted a little on political affairs. Although I do not mix much in them, I like to be up to what is going on, especially as the telegraph is stopped, we are thinned out very much both in the city & district five companies from Columbia, & two from the district. I understand also that the College company will go down today. We will have to be on the alert here to guard ourselves. I keep my mouth shut, but keep both eyes & ears open. I also call at the convent once or twice a day. Keep them in spirits, all are well & join in affectionate love.

JOHN LYNCH, COLUMBIA, TO PATRICK LYNCH, 12 APRIL[25]

I write tonight at the request of Sister Ellen. She has been making a flag for the Emmett Guards, Capt Keitts[26] Company, it is just finished and is no doubt the finest flag in the state. She heard this evening that the company had or were about disbanding, if they do, of course they will not want the flag. She wishes me to find out from Capt. Keitt, if it is so, I learn that he and Brennan, 1st lieutenant went down on the 2 oclock train. Will you be kind enough to contrive the enclosed note to Mr. Keitt for me, and if you have an opportunity speak to him on the subject. If he does not still want the flag, Sister Ellen wishes to offer it (for sale) to some of your Irish Companies, it is the Common Infantry size, on one side Blue, with Palmetto tree, with an Irish Harp (entwined with Shamrock) leaning against the trunk, worked in Silver, and brilliants, and a crescent in the corner also of silver, the other side is white with large Cross capped with

Bishop Lynch and other dignitaries inspecting Fort Sumter, 1861.
Courtesy of the Library of Congress.

seven stars above and motto below (+) in Gold & Brilliants—Pro deo et pro patria. Heavy gold fringe and gold cord and tassel, it is a splendid affair. On account of the poverty of the company and who it was made for I think they intended only asking one hundred and twenty five dollars for it, but if you could get one of your companies to take it, it ought to bring about three hundred dollars, so Ellen thinks but if Mr Keitt still wishes it of course he will have to have it, please let us know if you have seen Mr Keitt, or if you think in these military times it can be disposed of in Charleston.

We hear all kind of reports here about the Bombardment, since eleven o'clock, the telegraph has been working and we get the news oftener than you do perhaps, but not so correctly I expect. We heard this morning that a breach had been made in the south side of fort Sumter, that the Harriet Lane had attempted to enter was fired into, and put back, and that up to five o'clock none of ours were killed or wounded, this last seems improbable.

All are well at the Convent and at home. One or two new boarders this evening. I wrote this morning, hope you recd my letter, a large company cavalry, or mounted riflemen went down today, carrying the flag worked by the nuns.

෫

FRANCIS LYNCH, CHERAW, TO PATRICK LYNCH, 3RD MAY[27]

You were perhaps surprized that any special notice was taken of Mr. D. F. Murphy.

It was only to inquire of his business here, in these unsettled times—Hailing from where he did. All was quite satisfactory, and it was at the suggestion of himself that M^rPowell gave publicity to the matter.

I have agreed with Murphy at a salary of 100$ pmt and 10 p^ct on the yearly net gains of the business. On his part to invest 1000$ (much of it machinery) and with his attention & direction to make up 200 prs daily, and if leather can be supplied abundantly, a larger quantity employing some more hands—I trust he will return with the machinery soon, and that he will prove himself competent. I think it is highly important to push the production of shoes now.

I thank you for the Bank notice after my remissness before, protected by your kindness, I have been more mindful and will send to Mr Waring a draft on Col Manigault in time, that will cover the note.

Soon after, I hope a lively production business will warrant my further applications for means. We will soon expect your promised visit and wish Mr Murphy will be here, to show 'how things can be done.' He expected to be back by 12th of this month. Disturbances may delay him.

෫

FRANCIS LYNCH, CHERAW, TO PATRICK LYNCH, MAY 5[28]

While at the old Homestead, this afternoon, Father & Mother were speaking of your guest Revd Dr Cummings, and it was suggested that I would write, inviting yourself and the Revd Doctor, to favor us with a visit. It would be a high gratification to all, especially to our parents who treasure the kindnesses extended them while in New York[29]—if convenient and agreeable to grant us such a boon.

Father is about as usual. Mother is quite well and so the other members of the family DG. Bro Hugh does not appear in strong health. Col Hatch has given me a further order.

❧

JOHN LYNCH, COLUMBIA, TO PATRICK LYNCH, MAY 14TH[30]

I called on Mr. Nunnemaker as you requested about the corn. He had none to sell now, but recommended me to Mr. Butler the nearest neighbour to the plantation. I went over this morning and saw him, found him very pleasant, and disposed to be neighboroughly he agrees to let you have about one hundred bushels of corn, *shelled* at his barn for one dollar. I closed with him at once, as corn is scarce, and since the blockade is likely to run it up much higher, he can also supply you with fodder, his corn is in shuck but he will not sell it so, as he says it is small corn, or nubbin, and the only fair way of selling or buying it, is after it is shelled, he did not recommend me to buy it, but I had tried the market before starting over. Corn is selling in the streets at 1:[15] he also promised me to plough the corn, the first wet day. He also recommended to me a man as overseer, now living at Gibbs factory, formerly overseer for Mr Gingnard, he was raised in the neighbourhood, and in Dr. Wallaces[31] time owned the house across the road from the plantation, where he taught school. Mr Beekler recommends him as an honest, industrious and sober man, is about 45 or 50 years old, has a family (wife & three children) with him. I went by the factory and saw him, was pleased with his appearance, told him my business and by whom sent, made him an offer (which as yet, I don't exactly understand) which he accepted for the first year, of course subject to your approval. It is this, you to furnish himself & family with: *meal, meat, flour, sugar & coffee*, and pay him *One hundred dollars* a year cash the amount of each of the articles you are to agree on afterwards. I told him you would of course give what was usual in such cases—he is ready to commence anytime after this week, and will be over to see me on Saturday. You will therefore please write me at once, whether you have made any other arrangements, where to look for the negroes, what articles to buy here, and what you intend buying in Charleston. I am willing to do what I can in the business, but will do nothing definite without orders. . . . by the by Capt Keitt *paid* for his flag yesterday, and says if he could find out when you will be up he would have you to bless it in the Church, and have the presentation at the same time, what would be the effect "grand, gloomy or peculiar?"—but he says that is what he calculated on from the first—now, it might look a little pointed. This is inter nos.

❧

JOHN LYNCH, COLUMBIA, TO PATRICK LYNCH, 24TH MAY[32]

I am sorry to say your negroes have not yet arrived, neither have I heard anything of them. I have made arrangements for everything you mentioned, the Overseer's wages commenced last Monday, he has been waiting on the waggon to move his family, till today I hear he will get Mr Mecklers waggon to move him. I had the corn ploughed, by not having the waggon here, I fear we have lost some of the corn I bargained for, as the old man tells me he has had it shelled and it turns out so badly, he don't think he can spare more than fifty bushels. I fear the price may have some effect. Corn is $1.^{30} here now. I have engaged 500# fodder, and ten bushel of peas for planting, but if the hands do not hurry on there will be little use of planting this year, if you have not heard from them lately you had best hurry them on. . . .

Will not the two Congress' be convenient for sending over messages for adjustment of all the difficulties. Wonder if the line is marked out, or if it would be expedient to let the *Army* know what is in contemplation. Davis is a wise politician and understands human nature well, or he has good advisers.

John Lynch, Columbia, to Patrick Lynch, June 8th[33]

I started the waggon off on Saturday last, the negroes passed here Thursday evening late, the man sent me word he would call & see me yesterday, has not been here yet. I suppose there was no purchase of mules or waggon in Lancaster, on reflection, it is best for you to purchase such mules as those of Claffy, with them you can haul wood to market and pay well, for I expect wood to be higher this winter on account of scarcity of coal. You can also at any time get your money back for such mules if you wish to sell them, while with poor stock, you will be obliged to keep or sacrifice them. Claffy is not anxious to sell, but says I can do as I wish, either send them home or keep them, if you wish them you can have the mules at $200 each and the waggon & harness for $65— . . . I have not as yet purchased a cow, as the man I had been speaking to, has [raised the] price, I declined taking, I sent over the meat & molasses, &c on last Tuesday.

11 o clock

Mr Buff has just called. Some of the negroes have come over to get some things. . . . I like them, and have no doubt you will do well with them.

Enclosed I send the letter brought by Mr Buff. He did not take the R.R. as suggested, but came on with the waggon he handed me the ten dollars given him by Mr Quigley, his expenses were only six dollars—and five that I gave himself making eleven—he would have been satisfied with four dollars but I thought five little enough. Write me if I must buy the mules & waggon, I think it the best, if you can spare the money.

I will push them on in putting in what crop we can first, and fix the houses afterwards, we need rain, but must put in corn & peas any way. Potatoes we will have to wait for a season for.

۶⊱

FRANCIS LYNCH, CHERAW, TO PATRICK LYNCH, 28TH JUNE[34]

Your letter was received with enclosures, I thank you much for the same. Prior to the rct of it I had a blank note endorsed by my sureties & beg that you will add your name and lodge the note in Bank. I have filled the amount for 3000$ with the view of so making a place for the bonds, should I receive an order for shoes payable with them as yet I have no order, and would be glad to make more progress with my enggnts [engagements] before receiving one. On fixing 1^{50} pr as the price for Brogans I have orders already for about 2000 prs— Business if well managed will be good with me for some months. . . .

1861 July–December

"The separation of the Southern States is un fait accompli.*"*

With the South at war with what used to be its country, the old order of things no longer held. The mail system, which had always been such a reliable and safe medium of communication, now was severely disrupted, at best dependable only in those areas outside the theaters of war. Even within that zone of supposed security, Baptista did not trust her correspondence to it but resorted to using train conductors or acquaintances as letter carriers within and beyond the borders of the Confederacy.

Compensating for the disruptions of war was the lingering assumption that the war would be a brief one. In the late spring and early summer of 1861, the Confederacy seemed to have all the momentum. The border states appeared to be moving inevitably toward aligning themselves with the new republic that now called Richmond its capital. Then came the first major battle, which a great many persons in both sections thought would decide the matter of independence or preservation of union. The headlong flight of the Union forces back to Washington at the end of the day-long fighting on the plains of Manassas gave rise to a sense of invincibility to the Confederates and greatly reinforced the expectations that peace and independence were near. These developments emboldened Patrick Lynch, in a second letter to John Hughes, to make his case for the South's quest for independence.

Lynch probably assumed Hughes would publish it, as its intended audience would seem to be the Northern public much more than the Archbishop of New York. The Charleston prelate pointed out the tragedy that civil war constituted for the nation. War had destroyed the union of the sections, by whose complementary specialization the country had grown and prospered in unprecedented fashion. And those ultimately responsible for the war, according to the bishop, were the abolitionists who had inflicted their misguided religious dogmatism upon the North's policy-making. In this context secession was a prophylactic act to defend the South's special interests and institutions. Being unable to turn to any branch of government or to the people in general, Southerners had to defend themselves. War, Lynch owned, would widen, not seal, the chasm splitting the country. The North lacked the tactical military skills to fight battles at the scale modern conflict has attained. For all its wealth and industrialization, the North also lacked the economic weapons to impose its will upon the South. For the South, in contrast, the war was a golden opportunity for the region to become self-sufficient, not only in agriculture but in manufacturing as well, as home industries would provide unprecedented possibilities for advancement to poor whites throughout the South. An embargo upon the shipment of cotton to England and France would have a devastating impact upon those countries' manufacturing sector, so heavily dependent for their supplies upon Southern raw goods. Economic interests, not ethics nor ideology, would drive the geopolitical decisions of the European powers. For Bishop Lynch all this meant that separation was "un fait accompli" and the North should at last let the South go in peace. He knew better, of course. Indeed, in August he was already taking the initiative in providing Catholic chaplains for the Confederate armies and urging the bishop of Richmond to coordinate the planning and staffing of a Catholic chaplaincy.

If Patrick Lynch's ultimate audience was the Northern public, John Hughes accommodated his intention by publishing the Charleston bishop's letter, as well as his own response, in his diocesan paper, the New York Metropolitan Record. *Subsequently the New York* Daily Tribune *gave the letters even wider circulation by publishing both, introduced by an editorial that applauded this rare plunge into politics by Roman Catholic bishops. Hughes's rejoinder revealed a far different vantage point toward the war than his fellow Irish prelate had been led to believe he had.*

Civil War, John Lynch discovered, had its positive effects: one was a breakdown of the prejudice Catholics had traditionally faced in the upcountry of the Carolinas. This improved atmosphere enkindled hope that he would attract more patients as a consequence. The establishment of a hospital in Columbia provided a new opportunity for securing an institutional position that would anchor his practice of medicine in the community.

When peace did not materialize over the next months, frustration over the war's overall effects mounted on the home front. Francis, who had opened in North Carolina a second tanyard to provide additional leather for his greatly expanded shoe production, began to experience, if only lightly, the consequences of the economic sanctions of civil war. Inflation had a serious impact on the operations of the Ursulines' academy. "When will the war cease?" became a mantra for Baptista. In this economic climate, the recruitment of novices as a source of revenue as well as the lifeline of the community became even more pressing. With the loss of the episcopal network in the North as a reliable source of lay-sister postulants, the securing of candidates for choir sister became Baptista's chief focus. Meanwhile, Ellen Spann's entrance into the Ursuline community touched off a private civil war within the convent in which Baptista unexpectedly found herself front and center.

In November the war came to South Carolina with the seizure of Port Royal and the neighboring sea islands. Planters frantically abandoned their coastal plantations. Fear of further invasions ignited a panic in Charleston that set off a large-scale flight to the deep interior of the upcountry. Columbia became one of the favorite relocation sites for the refugees.

In mid-December disaster did strike Charleston—not from the sea but from a tornado of fire that roared through the center of the city, leaving behind a skeletal landscape. Among the fire's casualties were the core structures of the Diocese of Charleston: its cathedral, bishop's residence, seminary, free school, newspaper offices, and orphanage.

⚓

BAPTISTA LYNCH, URSULINE CONVENT, COLUMBIA, S.C. TO PATRICK LYNCH, JULY 6TH[1]

. . . I am anxious to forward letters to Europe for Miss Vassas, how shall I get them to you? I [do] not want to send them through mail—. And will it be convenient for you, to forward them immediately—I sent you by the conductor the list of premiums awarded at the Distribution for publication in the Miscellany. We have also published in the Columbia papers "puffs" on the same, which I would be glad the Miscellany would copy, if you think it well?

You ought to have seen Father on my feast-day. He seemed to be delighted—it was very pleasing to all. You will get a full description of it when you come to see us which *we all* hope you will do during the vacation—have you heard anything of our retreat? I hope some good *old* Jesuit Father—*very spiritual & very experienced* will come!!! Such as Revd Father Ardia[2]—the Master of Novices—Sr Addie is *breaking stones* but Sr Glen's departure has done some good. Sr. Augustine talks of going to the South of France, so be prepared for her Hygira [departure] at any time, but equally prepared that she should remain—, if pleased & honored sufficiently—You will be glad to hear that in the letters which we have received either from our pupils or their parents all seem *much* pleased with the past year & express themselves so & very grateful to us—this is very gratifying to us, especially when such letters are accompanied with full remittances, as has been the case with some, but I fear that few will be able to return if the War continues—What do you think of Ellen Spann joining our Noviciate in two or three months—? You know we spoke of her spending a year in Cheraw unless some opportunity should offer for her return to Texas—but before her departure she expressed a desire to enter our noviciate in preference not only to going to Cheraw, which she does not like at all—but even to going home—When I heard that, I spoke to her seriously about her vocation, & she seemed quite delighted at the prospect of returning to us soon.

I promised her a hard time in the noviciate, but she said laughingly she would not mind that—. When I spoke to Ellen, I was under the impression that a certain lay sister, of whom she is very fond would leave this summer for France or Cincinnati—so I felt quite free to speak to Ellen of her entrance. But now I do not know how far it would be prudent to expose Ellen to such influence, which gives me trouble so often with others & has recently—. Should she propose leaving please treat her as Miss Glen—. If not I suppose it is our duty to be as amiable as possible (St. Augustine has just stepped in & begs you to send a bundle of *Irish* & English Newspapers for vacation for she hears rumors of war, famine & plagues & she is not quite dead to the world yet.— . . .

JOHN LYNCH TO LOUISA [MACNAMARA], COLUMBIA, JULY 16TH[3]

Columbia is very healthy except colds amongst the children, it is also very dull, we hear nothing but rumours of the war, one day contradicting what another had as fact, so much so, that I have lost all confidence in newspapers & telegraphic accounts. I still hope to see the war ended without a general battle, but no matter how it ends we will have very hard times for a while to come, if the present state of affairs continue for twelve months the whole country, north and south, will be so far crippled that it will take years to regain the same state of prosperity it enjoyed before the war, that is in a monied point of view, of course speaking in a political sense, we are now in the enjoyment of such liberty as we have not had in years. I feel anxious to learn correctly what they are doing in Washington now, but as everything is done in secret session we can only surmise. I pray God they may be directed to act with a spirit of wisdom and justice, different from that of Lincoln and his advisers.

FRANCIS LYNCH, CHERAW, TO PATRICK LYNCH, 29 JULY[4]

I have written to Col. S. Hatch saying you would call & make settlement for me. The bill is rendd [rendered] for 1400 pair, the price to be fixed by him, at 2^{25} or 2 15/100 as agreed on, as the Col may determine—The 3 last boxes will [be] sent tomorrow—I have so advised him.

So confident I hope am I as to the ready payment—I have promised a chk for 1000$ on Wednesday next of the proceeds of this bill—Reserve the one doll advanced me here and also thirty doll for Mrs Enstor. . . .

✧

LETTER OF THE RT. REV. BISHOP OF CHARLESTON, CHARLESTON, S.C., TO RT. REV. ARCHBISHOP OF NEW YORK, AUG. 4[5]

. . . A paragraph, which has gone the rounds of the Southern papers, states that your grace has spoken strongly against the war policy of the Government of the United States, as fraught with much present suffering, and not calculated to attain any real advantage. What a change has come over these States since I wrote you a long letter last November, and even since I had the pleasure of seeing you last March. All that I anticipated in that letter has come to pass, and more than I looked for. All the hopes cherished last Spring of a peaceful solution have vanished before the dread realities of war. What is still before us? Missouri, Maryland, and Kentucky are nearer Secession now than Virginia, North Carolina, and Tennessee were four months ago. Missouri is a battle-field. I think that President Davis, after the victory at Stonebridge,[6] will probably, as his next move, throw a column into Maryland. Kentucky will, ere long be drawn into the struggle, and the United States will, in less than ten months, be divided into two not unequal parts, marshaling hundreds of thousands of men against each other.

The war is generally dated from the bombardment of Fort Sumter. There we fired the first gun, and the responsibility is charged on us. But, in reality, that responsibility should fall, on those who rendered the conflict unavoidable. The South, years ago, and a hundred times, declared that the triumph of the Abolition or Anti-Slavery policy would break up the Union. They were in earnest. When that party, appealing to the people on the Chicago platform,[7] elected their candidate by every Free State vote, (excepting New Jersey, which was divided), South Carolina seceded, and other states were preparing to do so. They were in earnest. Yet, as the people disbelieved it, or heeded it not at the ballot boxes, so Congress heeded it not at Washington, and stood doggedly on the Chicago platform, indorsed by the people. This consummated Secession. The Confederate Government was formed. The dogged obstinacy of the Black Republicans at Washington last Winter, made all the South Secessionists. Still there was peace. The new Administration professed the intention to preserve it. Peace gave time, and time can work wonders. . . . Commissioners were at Washington to arrange a peaceful separation. Favorable intimations were privately given them, and they had hopes of success. Nine Governors, however, it is said, put the screws on the Cabinet, which resolved on a policy, and as silently as they could, made warlike naval preparations. Then, after a month, the Commissioners were refused admission or dismissed, and it was plainly announced that there would be no negotiation. . . . When time rolled by . . . the mails were stopped to and from Fort Sumter. Among the letters seized was one from Major Anderson to President Lincoln, discussing the details of the plan of re-enforcement. . . . Then came the special messenger of the President, announcing that he intended revictualing the fort, quietly, if permitted, forcibly, if resisted; then the account of the sailing of the fleet from New York. The fort was at once attacked, and taken without awaiting their arrival. The attack was not made until the offer of negotiation and peaceful arrangement had been rejected, and until the United States Government was in the act of sending an armed force.[8] But it is of little use now to inquire on whom the responsibility properly rests, we have the war on us, with all its loss of life, and long train of evils of every kind. It is the latest, perhaps the strongest, instance history gives us, *quam parva sapientia regitur mundus.*[9] Here was a country, vast, populous, prosperous, and blessed in its material interest, if any country was. The South producing cotton, tobacco, sugar, rice, and naval stores for the supply, as far as needed, of the North and the North-west, to the value of perhaps $50,000,000 a year, and exporting to foreign countries over $220,000,000; the North-west producing chiefly grain and supplying the North and the South, and when the European crops failed, having, as last Winter, a large European market; the North manufacturing and supplying the South and the North-west, and struggling to compete with foreign goods abroad, and doing the trading and commerce of the South and the North-west.

Could the material interests of all the sections be more harmoniously and advantageously combined than in this union, where each was free to develop to the fullest extent, those branches of industry in which it could excel, and could draw from the others those products which it needed, but could not produce as well as they could. Even a child could see the vast benefits to all from this mutual cooperation. No wonder that in all material interests the country was prospering to an extent that intoxicated us and astonished the world. . . . Taking up Anti-Slavery, making it a religious dogma, and carrying it into politics, [the Yankees] have broken up the Union. While it was a mere intellectual opinion they might discuss it as they pleased. . . . They might even carry it into religion, and split their associations, and churches on it. . . . But when they carried it into politics, gaining one State Government after another, and defining their special policy by unconstitutional laws[10] and every mode of annoying and hostile action, and finally, . . . carrying the Presidential election in triumph, and grasping the power of the Federal Government, what could the South do but consult its own safety by withdrawing from the Union? . . . The alternative was thus forced on the South either of tame submission or of resistance. They did not hesitate. They desired to withdraw in peace. This war has been forced upon them.

It was unnecessary in the beginning. It brings ruin to thousands in its prosecution. It will be fruitless of any good. At its conclusion the parties will stand apart, exhausted and embittered by it; for every battle, however won or lost, will have served but to widen the chasm between the North and South, and to render more difficult, if not impossible, any future reconstruction. Will it be a long war, or a short and mighty one? The Cabinet and the Northern press has pronounced for the last. Yet this is little more than an idle dream. What could 400,000 men do? I do not think there is a general on either side able to fight 50,000. And the North would need eight or ten such Generals. Certainly the 40,000 under McDowell, after five hours fighting, fought on mechanically without any general-ship. The higher officers had completely lost the guiding reins. On our side the Southern troops ought to have been in Washington within forty-eight hours. But the 40,000 on the Confederate side were, I apprehend, too unwieldy a body for our generals. . . .

But without generals, what could 400,000 men do against the South? By force of numbers, and at great loss, they might take city after city. But unless they left large permanent garrisons, their authority would die out with the sound of their drums. Such an army marching through a country covered with forest and thickets, and occupied by a population hostile to a man, . . . would be decimated every hundred miles of its progress by a guerrilla warfare, against which it could find no protection. . . .

But it is probable that circumstances would again, as they have done, over-rule the designs of the Washington Cabinet, and make the war slow, long, and expensive-one to be decided, less by battles than by the resources and endurance of the combatants.

That portion of the former United States will suffer most in such a contest, and must finally succumb, which is least able to dispense with the support it received from the other two sections. How the North can do without our Southern trade I presume it can judge after three or four months' trial. But it would seem that the failure to sell to the South one hundred and twenty millions of our foreign exports and the return importations, and in our internal coasting trade, together with the loss of the profits and commissions on so vast a business, must have a very serious effect, one that I see no way of escaping. Truly, the North has to pay dearly for its whistle of Black Republicanism. . . .

How will it fare with the South should the war be long and so powerfully waged as to require the Southern Confederation to keep, say 100,000 men in arms, and if the ports are strictly blockaded? . . . Our needs will be provisions, clothing, money for the governmental and war expenses, and for the purchase from abroad of what we absolutely require, and are not already supplied with. As for provisions, . . . we are gathering enough for two years' abundant supply. Everyone is raising corn, wheat, and stock. . . . Again, Manufactures of every kind are springing up on all sides. . . . The supply of tea and coffee will, I presume, in time run out. This will put us to some trouble, but otherwise, neither for provisions nor for clothes, will the South be seriously inconvenienced. The blacks (by-the-by, more quiet and orderly now, if possible, than before) will remain devoted to agriculture, while the rapidly increasing demand for home productions of every kind gives ready employment to the poorer classes of the whites. What amount of gold and silver there is within the Confederate States I can only guess at—I suppose about $25,000,000. But as the greater part of our expenses is at home, any currency we are satisfied to use will do—whether bank bills, Confederate Bonds, or Treasury Notes. When we go abroad, it must be with gold or with cotton. This last is the spinal column of our financial system. . . . Two million, or two and a half, of bales will be conveyed to the Confederate Government, to be paid for in bonds or Treasury Notes. This cotton will be worth, at ordinary prices, $100,000,000. If it can be exported at once, it is so much gold. If it is retained, it will form the security for a loan that may be required abroad. The other third of the cotton will be sold by the planters as best they can on their own account. The chief difficulty is the blockade, which may prevent the export and sale abroad of the cotton. A loan on it as security, while it is still unshipped, and scattered in the interior in numberless small warehouses, could not easily be affected.

. . . the blockade, so far from doing any serious injury, has, on the contrary, benefited, and will continue to benefit, the South, forcing us to be active, and to do for ourselves much that we preferred formerly to pay others to do for us. I presume that next January, with a crop of 3,500,000 or 4,000,000 bales on hand, the South would become very restive under a strict blockade. Should it continue twelve months longer, property at the South would go down, as they say it has in New York.

But before that time comes, another very serious complication arises—how England and France will stand the cutting off of the supply of an article on which depend two-thirds of the manufacturing interests of the one and one-third of those of the other? They cannot, try as they never so much, supply the deficiency.[11] . . . [B]oth nations are decidedly and bitterly Anti-Slavery; but neither will be guilty of the mistake of the North, and utterly sacrifice vast interests for the sake of a speculative idea. If they find that they cannot do without Southern cotton, they will interfere, first probably to make peace, and if that effort fails, then in such other manner as will secure for them what will be a necessity. . . . Is the Federal Government strong enough for a war with England and France, in addition to that with the South?

One other warlike course remains—to capture and hold all the southern ports, and thus seek to control commerce independent of Secession, leaving the interior of the South to fret and fume as it pleases. This is the problem of belling the cat. The Northern forces would have to capture Norfolk; Charleston, Savanna, Wilmington, N.C.; Pensacola, Mobile, New-Orleans, and Galveston, besides some fifteen other similar points. At each of them they would find a Stone Bridge; and even if they should succeed, they could only hold military possession. . . . Peace could never be established by any such course. It . . . would never subjugate [the South].

The separation of the Southern States is *un fait accompli.* The Federal Government has no power to reverse it. Sooner or later it must be recognized. Why preface the recognition by a war equally needless and bloody? . . . If there is to be fighting, let those who voted the Black Republican ticket shoulder their muskets and bear the responsibility. Let them not send Irishmen to fight in their stead, and then stand looking on at the conflict, when, in their heart of hearts, they care little about which of the combatants destroys the other.[12]

. . . Nothing seems now to span the chasm but that bridge of Catholic union and charity of which your Grace spoke so eloquently last Patrick's Day.[13]

⟡

PATRICK LYNCH, CHARLESTON, TO JOHN MCGILL, 23 AUG[14]

Rev. Joseph Prachensky, S.J. of Mobile has just left us on his way to Virginia. Col. Lomax and Captain Sand and other officers & men of the Mobile Regiment, have sought him—and his Superiors have consented. He will be in Richmond next week—and will present himself to you—

The application I made for Rev. L. J. O'Connell was not for any special regiment. He is best known in our upcountry S.C. Regiments, but there are very few Catholics among them. He has not been sought for by any special corps and I proposed him simply because I thought a priest might be useful somewhere that you and Col. Northrop[15] might designate. I am not prepared to point out any special place, even now. But it would be well to have one or two priests to each large division—Norfolk has one, will have two or three—Has Magruder[16] any[?] Beauregard[17] has Teeling[18]— (By the by did B. really go to communion as the papers say?) Johnston[19] needs one, and you will have to send one with the army in Western Virginia. They will of course have faculties from you for our troops.

Here all things are quiet. But about six or eight weeks hence we look for smoking times when the flotilla of gunboats which some people think are abuilding somewhere in the north, will make descents on our coast and perhaps attack Charleston.

Baptista Lynch, Ursuline Convent, Columbia S.C., to Patrick Lynch, Aug. 24th[20]

If I had time I could write *ever so much*, but I have not. We are very busy embroidering the flag for the "Kirkwood Rangers" of Camden of which Miss M. Brownfield—wrote—& are getting on nicely (Window bell rings—Mrs Keitt has paid a long visit—& got some Books for her Protestant friends)—We are going to have such a nice vegetable garden this fall & winter—the seeds are coming up beautifully—we pay a man 75 [cts] per day for working & fixing it—I am anxious to get the leaks in the house remedied by having gutters overlooked & mended, & one low chimney on choir covered—but John thinks it useless expense & what cannot be remedied—what do you think? He, poor dear fellow, is so terribly harassed by his better half, that at present he may not be the best judge.

Bishop McGill speaks of another pupil Carrie (Miss Vassas) She has been at Georgetown[21] for four years—a Jewess—she asks for a Prospectus—

We recd a letter from Mother Superior Brown County Ohio—on yesterday —who sent it by some friend to N Orleans—All there much as usual—they had no Distribution but published premiums merited in the paper—they do not expect much of a school this coming session—fourteen thousand poor people in Cinc. [Cincinnati] live on the soup given only to them daily!!! When will the war cease?

Baptista Lynch, Ursuline Convent, Columbia, to Patrick Lynch, Aug 27th[22]

I enclose as you request, a half dozen of our circulars, that you may be able to use them to our advantage A.M.D.G. —You see we have been obliged to raise the price of our board this year on account of the high price of provisions that we cannot deduct from— . . . I suppose the expenses would be about $250⁰⁰ not including books stationary &c drawing materials—all of which are included under the head of *cursory expenses.*

We have rather a poor prospect for a school at present but we do not feel dejected on account of it, putting our trust in the powerful mediation of our Blessed Mother & in Him who has already shown us so many favors. . . .

With us—I am sorry that the retreat has produced so little change—& change I fear is hopeless in that case—I pity a miserable self-made miserable person.[23]

I was surprised to hear that you intended so soon going up to Cheraw. We are expecting Ellen over about the 5th Sept with Hugh & Conlaw.

I hope you will be able to forward on the letters to their proper destinations—you must have thought me quite a scribe to have penned as many but I only wrote to Sister Antonia & addressed the others—.

I hope success will attend Rev Father Prachensky's labors in Va. I am told that there are 15000 of our troops sick of typhoid fever in the hospitals—is not that melancholy—how much nurses must be needed! I heard the Srs of Charity were not permitted to come from Emmitsburg to aid their Srs—that they came as far as the Potomac & were refused a passage by Lincoln's men. . . .[24]

Our flag will be finished by Saturday I think & hope & is very pretty.

JOHN LYNCH, COLUMBIA, TO PATRICK LYNCH, AUGUST 27TH[25]

I had an application yesterday for the Overseers place, from a man who will suit you in some respects, if not in all, his name is Michael Bresnahan, an Irishman, and good Catholic, sober, industrious and appears to have a full share of common sense, but may be a little too quiet, he is about 45 years old, has a wife & 3 or 4 children in Baltimore, is now working for Mr Dougherty[26]—at the State house as polisher, appears to be anxious to get the situation, offers to give you any reference as to character, and for wages is willing to leave the fixing of them to you at whatever you think is right, he was raised to farming in the old country, and was on a farm in Virginia for two years, the only fear I would have of him, would be that he might not take a sufficient control over the negroes if it became necessary to use harsh means, give me your instructions and will try and carry them out for you.

FRANCIS LYNCH, CHERAW, TO PATRICK LYNCH, 7 SEPT[27]

. . . I have completed the first 1000 pr shoes for the Con. Gov^mt and sent on, some on the other contract, besides furnishing to Col L. M. Hatch, two cases per week for the past three weeks—And occasionally sending down some accoutrements. Since devoting so much attention to the shoes, the accoutrements are delayed more than I like, however I will soon complete my present contract and be ready for another if wanted.

My work would be greatly benefited by my having an additional *Carrier* and I have been trying to employ Mr. Ferguson (now clerking for Messrs H. Calhoun & Co.) . . .

Mother & E. Spann went to Columbia on Thursday last & write home all are well.

[PS] On yesterday was returned to me, a letter I had mailed 31st May to Sr. Antonia.

ॐ

BAPTISTA LYNCH, URSULINE CONVENT, COLUMBIA, TO PATRICK LYNCH, SUNDAY EVENING, SEPT 8TH[28]

Today three years ago we received Sr. Rose into our Noviciate—she was only in her nineteenth or twentieth year—& today we have received Sr Ellen (Spann) into our noviciate, who was the first boarder we received & offered to our Blessed Mother after our arrival in Columbia—I feel so deeply grateful to Almighty God for giving her a religious vocation—

She looks so sweet & innocent in the cap, & resembles Mother as much as you do—Mother has just left with John after sitting the afternoon with me & talking over home & its affairs.

What a model she is! My love & admiration for her are always on the increase—John begs me to say to you that he is *very anxious* that you should *see your farm*—& begs you to come up from Charleston on Tuesday night that you may go out there with him on Wednesday morning—I told him you would be busy here on Wednesday afternoon & all day on Thursday—

We have the children learning the music, but I am afraid they will not know it very well.—Ellen will be quite an acquisition in that branch, & I trust in many ways

Both Sisters & children seem delighted at her entrance—except Sr. A[ugustine] who has been acting worse & worse—& to whom I told Sister Ursula to say, that I wished her to leave, & go somewhere that she may be happier than she is here, & where she will give less trouble & disedification to the community—. I could not begin to describe the pride & haughtiness of her words & manner to me—her touchiness & suspicious disposition—& my imagination could never be as fertile as hers to discover things meant for offenses—her double dealing & apparent untruthfulness, deprives me of a shade even of reliance on her words or actions—so that I wish her to leave, & the sooner the better—.

She told me the other day that she would take off her habit if she acted according to her feelings, she doubted her perseverance—I pitied her self-torture, & proposed to Sr. Ursula to pay her board in the Visitation Convent Mobile, or S^rs. Mercy St. Augustine for the winter, under the pretext of delicate health—alas her soul is sick enough—But the next day when Mother came, I made it my business to see her & say that Mother had enquired for her, & would be pleased to see her when next she called. Instead of a polite acknowledgment of Mother's kind inquiry—she turned away most rudely saying—she can see her daughter that's enough for her—& sure enough while every other Sister has endeavored to manifest respect & attention to Mother, she has done the very opposite—I am not willing, that she should remain any longer in our house—[29]

[PS] Sr. A has not spoken to me except to give me a cup at recreation since retreat—at least I do not remember her doing so. She is like a porcupine to me, but in my absence all amiability to others.

FRANCIS LYNCH, CHERAW, TO PATRICK LYNCH, 19 SEPT[30]

Soon after my last, I wrote to Col. L. M. Hatch Q M Gen[l] to pay over $1500 the sum of bill recd on your calling for same but omitted to ask you to do so. At your convenience you will please receive the amt and place the same to my credit in Bank of the State of So Carolina in Chston.

Mr Waring apprizes me the Board does not assent to my paying in Con. Bonds, so I must use the cash for it. Business is pretty fair, that is the execution of work for orders would exceed my productions. . . .

Mother returned home on Tuesday night accompanied by John & Conlaw. We are all quite well. Mrs. Blain & Daughter appear to enjoy country life. Father is busy harvesting his crops which is good.

FRANCIS LYNCH, CHERAW, TO PATRICK LYNCH, 21 SEPT[31]

I am getting on tolerably monthly and my sole leather will last sometime yet. My debts north do not reach 800$ so I will not be any inconvenienced by the Sequestration Act.[32]

Wont it be folly for you to go to Baltimore . . . I fear after the publication of your very excellent letter to Archbishop [Hughes], no plea would save you in the land of Lincoln.[33] This is the opinion of Father and all of us—and we would regret the exposure on your part.

PATRICK LYNCH, NASHVILLE, TO FRANCIS KENRICK, 29 SEPTEMBER[34]

The opportunities of communication are so rare now that one feels tempted to seize any one that may present itself. I came here a few days ago to bring some sick religious to whom the Drs enjoined a change of air. As a clergyman is running the hostile lines into Ohio, I write to say that Bishop Verot[35] reached Charleston safely the Saturday after leaving Baltimore. Staid with us two days and then went to Savannah, and took possession the Sunday afterwards. He intended after staying there a few days to go to St. Augustine.

Bp. Verot said you had received some instruction from Rome on the Subject of Chaplains to the effect that they brought faculties for Sixty days from their own Bishop—which *if possible* are to be renewed by the Bp of the diocese in which he may be, if impossible, they are to continue in force—Is this correct?— Would not communication b/t a northern chaplain and a Southern Bishop, or vice versa, fall under the category of "impossible" whenever it is forbidden by the commanding generals.

The best chance for our getting letters from you, is I think for you to send them enclosed to Bp Spalding or his V Rev Brother.[36] It would not be difficult to get them as far as this.

Please let my Sister know that all the family are well. . . .

JOHN LYNCH, COLUMBIA, TO PATRICK LYNCH, OCT 16TH[37]

I recd yours of 12th making inquiry about board for M[rs]Lowe & family. I have inquired, and find M[rs] McMahon next [to] M[rs] Montague asks one dollar a day for all full boarders and four dollars pr week for those who go to the second table. M[rs] Rawls whose card I enclose will take them at twenty four dollars per month, and small children half price, no charge for infants, in both cases exclusive of wood or lights. M[rs] Jones has just mentioned that perhaps Mr Pierce would take them. I have not time to see before the mail closes, and M[rs] Rawls would like to know soon as two families from St. Mary's has written to her about board (M[rs] Simons boards with her, the same house we saw her in) I was speaking to M[c]Donald about his house & furniture next [to] the church (the parsonage) he cant give an answer till his wife returns, which will be next week, rents & Board are high here, so are provisions, but the family if economical had best rent as they will have to buy wood & light and have their washing done any way. I will write you . . . if I can find out anything further but all want to know the ages of the children, are they girls or boys, &c—Holmes has finished the house and is commencing about the cabins. I have not been able to go over for some time, practice is a little better, and I have a houseful of company. Yesterday I had Maj Beard, his daughter, Mr Fairfax of Tennessee, Hugh's wife & sister besides Mr. Haughton & family at dinner. I hope I can make it ultimately pay. Bishop Gregg[38] is to be in town, of course I must pay him some attention.[39]

All things appear to be getting on very smoothly at the convent & at home. Tell Francis if with you that I sent him up a small lot of leather and expect to send some more tomorrow, but Mr F says leather has gone up out of all reason. . . .

[PS] Maj Beard of course knew we were of an old family of the state, the Creek named after a branch of the family, a Protestant branch of course, consequently not *much* recognised.

BAPTISTA LYNCH, URSULINE CONVENT, COLUMBIA, S.C., TO
PATRICK LYNCH, OCT 17TH[40]

You will be glad to hear that I received a nice long letter from the *authoress* M[rs] McCord[41] about her little Rosa, who is doing very well. I do not know when I have ever seen a child with finer feelings, & more grateful heart than she possesses—in her letter to her mother, she details with so much gratitude your kindness to her when travelling, & ours since she came—poor little thing—John considers her quite diseased, he pencils her throat every day.

We have today finished our flag for Mrs McCord here, & will charge $100[00] for it. I wish you could see it, the scroll is very graceful & well done. . . .

Maj Beard had brought his daughter (M[rs] Anderson's granddaughter) to the convent—& we are very much pleased both with father & daughter he is a perfect gentleman of the old style—she, a plain but intelligent frank & simple convent child. . . .

I am told the soldiers here in the hospital are very sick & many dying—it occurred to me, that if three of the Sisters of Mercy could come up & nurse them, they might lead many of them to repentance & at least a desire of Baptism —if you thought well of it & their services were accepted—I think we could spare rooms for that number & for a while at least—John has never been called on, nor do I hear of a single Catholic among them.

John & Eliza had quite a dinner party the other night consisting of Revd Mr & Mrs Haughton (M[rs] Lord Parker-Haughton) M[r]Haughton is brother to Mr. Judge Heath, N.C. & half a Catholic, although attending Episcopal Convention —they had Maj. Beard & daughter—& would you believe it, Cornelia & Alice! All passed very pleasantly & satisfactorily.

BAPTISTA LYNCH, URSULINE CONVENT, COLUMBIA, S.C., TO
PATRICK LYNCH, OCT 25TH[42]

It was quite a relief both to John & myself to receive your letter. We began to feel anxious as to where or how you were—We were sorry to hear you had been indisposed & hope you are now quite well —. . . .

We will be very happy to receive the daughters of Mrs Huchet,[43] who have frequently edified us by their demeanor in our chapel—How old or advanced are they? We could not make any deduction in the *board* but would teach drawing & embroidery to *one* free of charge, or to *two* if their circumstances are limited—When we had four sisters Johnson, all paid the full—same for three Jebbatts & two Tylers &c &c—Here the Bellingers pay the full too—but if we suit ourselves to circumstances for one, I think we should prudently for more— If you are going to Nashville perhaps you would do well to take little McCord back with you—John thinks her a bad case—she has been able to study but two days since she has been here, she takes up a great deal of the Sr Infirmarian's time—suffers a good deal—must have a fire in the infirmary &c Poor child, she is not at all fit for school, & yet I don't like to send her home—Her mother has never sent her trunk, & she has a very scanty summer wardrobe. I do not like to buy for everything is so expensive, & I expect the trunk every day—. Moreover the little child in her simplicity tells all about her mother & home, & it seems they are *very poor*—but her step father is generous & a money making man—her mother is very extravagant & forgetful (poetess-like) so I am afraid we will have a great deal of trouble & expense without any profit—. John thinks if she does not get better she ought to go home for she should not be allowed to study.

I am sorry for you on account of Sr Gonzaga—but I think her coming here would perhaps be productive of evil—at least I fear it—We have two dangerous persons, who seem perfectly devoid of the proper religious spirit, & who might give her a handle either by misrepresentation, or their own unhappy disposition —on the other hand, she might be a trial of vocation to our sisters who are yet so inexperienced & have so few examples—. If she were sensible & pious but discontented, I might not think it so very dangerous for it might then be, she was not in her right sphere, but the letter from the Dominican Convent speaks volumes.

Our Lay sisters too have their hands full with the washing, cooking, & making fires through the house—more than they have strength to accomplish well, & I would be very sorry to increase their labor—Yet for all this, I do not say *no to you* because I would be glad to oblige you if possible & you are Sup.

I spoke to John, who seems to think that the best plan would be for the S^rs to pay her board in the asylum here, where the greater number of nurses are good Catholics—. This would be *good for others too*, as we know by experience —Perhaps Sr. G. would be glad to return after a few mos in the Asylum here— where I am sure she would meet with every kindness.

FRANCIS LYNCH, CHERAW, TO PATRICK LYNCH, 26 OCTR[44]

I was glad to learn through a letter recd by Henrietta, that you were quite well. We are all enjoying the same blessing D.G. On learning that probably you may again go to Memphis I will apprize you that. . . I wrote to Doct Parke enclosing a Bk Chk on Charleston for 500 in payment for the . . . right of his patent and ask the privilege of the use of it in our yard in N.C^a. I presume I will hear from him in 6 or 8 days more. It was I thought important to have the start in procuring the chemicals. . . .

PATRICK LYNCH, CHARLESTON, TO FRANCIS LYNCH, 13 NOV (COPY)[45]

In these troublesome times, so rife with panics, a great many as you may suppose are thinking of going to Cheraw as a very safe place, and yet with ready communication with Charleston and a good many wishing to go there ask me about it—especially Catholics.

Mrs Purcell[46] of Summerville, with her aged and rather invalid sister Miss Ryan, and her daughter Miss Purcell, wish to go. Could they get board with Cornelia, or with any one else. They would I presume have one or two servants. I believe they have a few negroes, but they could arrange otherwise for them.

Dr. White's wife, with Mrs. Posi, wish if possible to get a house to rent, with of course some out houses for servants. Can such a thing be got,—say for a year, and at what rates.

Is Augusta coming up-or is their house to rent—It would I think be jumped at, now. If any of your friends can take boarders,—now is their time to let it be.

Mrs Blain and Daughter will soon be forced to come up. Say, in a few weeks, for as yet no attack is threatened, but I advise them to send their trunk ahead. Mrs Carmand and her daughter are now stopping with them But they, together with Mrs Rasted, will probably be with Mrs Stinemetz on Friday night, unless they learn to-morrow that her terms are entirely too high—They expect she will not charge over $20 a month. If pleased they will stay a good long time— Perhaps Mrs Chartrand and Mrs Lebleux (both) and Mrs Macomb may follow, but not until the enemy is in sight.

If Henrietta gave Mrs Posi half an opening *she* would come to board with you,—or with any of the family—of course paying her way.

Tell father not to mind the thousand exaggerated lies and reports that are circulating through the country. The truth is this. The Yankees coming with an overwhelming force have taken Port Royal Harbour, the best in the South— and are busy fixing themselves firmly there. This will take five or six weeks at least, what they will do then we do not know. Perhaps they will if they think themselves strong enough, try to take Charleston. So far, they have behaved themselves decently, have I believe kept themselves to the islands at the Harbour, —and have troubled none of the residents (all ran away except one man, —who I believe has joined them), have burned nothing and as yet taken no negroes. But there are upwards of 2000 within their reach—many of whom they will seduce. It is said, how truly I know not, 50 cents a night for work on the entrenchments and batteries they are making—but the truth is, none of our people go within ten miles of the place to learn how things are going. Here people were wild with consternation for two or three days, just as I presume they were at Washington, after the battle of Manassas and the most absurd rumors are credited. But today we are comparatively quiet, and feel foolish after our fright. I hope we will have some sense, for it is very necessary in our position.

I saw a lady who visited Catherine a fortnight or so ago, and found her quite well She sends love, to all, and is praying hard for us but says I must not go there.

Mrs. Blain and Daughter are quite well. My love to Henrietta and the children, to Father Mother and Anna and John and to Cornelia, also to the warriors Hugh & Conlaw. Are they in the same company. Who is captain? . . .

Dr. Hume[47] spoke to me again today about the Fennel, has tried it over again with the same results—failure— . . . he can swear that you tried it, years ago—he gave me the enclosed items from the best Botanist in the state. Do you know the plants—I scarcely think they grow with you in the up country. However I send it.

JOHN LYNCH, COLUMBIA, S.C. TO PATRICK LYNCH, NOV 13TH[48]

I saw a letter from yourself to Sister Ellen this morning in which you inquire if I recd a letter from you, containing a check for three hundred dollars, and making some inquiries about the negro man Emmett. The reason of not answering your letter containing the check, was your mentioning you were leaving the city, and about the boy, the jailer told Mr Buff he would write to you at once about him, I recd a check of $300 from you, which I have you credited for on 29th Oct, but the payments for carpenters, brick, bricklayers, corn, &c &c has swallowed it up. You remember the check for $350 sent me in Sept I returned to you, it being on the wrong Bank. I gave Mr Buff some fifty dollars to go over to Edgefield for the boy. The jailor told him that not more than a quarter of an hour before his arrival Emmet with another negro had made their escape from the jail, and that he would write to you at once about it. Mr Buff's son returned me the fifty dollars and I paid him for his trouble and the hire of a horse five dollars (the mules being engaged hauling brick). The carpenters have nearly finished the two houses. I told Daniel if Emmett should come around the plantation to tell him to come in and go to work, as I did not blame him for trying to escape from prison, it was natural, he promises to do so. The bill for lumber has not come in yet neither have I yet paid for the nails, as I wish to have the whole amt at once.

There are other expences necessary, but I have told Mr Buff, we will have to do without them, for it really worries me to see so much money spending, where there is so little prospect of a return. I have had to take home my man Anderson (for a while anyway) since old Cits sickness I fear he will be of little or no use to me again, he has a paralytic stroke. Mr Buff thinks he could employ two or three more good hands profitably just now, and if the times were better he would like one or two more mules he appears bent on trying to make the places do something next year. I have been so much engaged at home that I have not been able to go over since the houses were commenced. I hear the place bears quite a different appearance. I hope you will be satisfied at the manner of the expenditures. There has been but little complaint amongst the negroes.

I think my prospects begin to brighten although there is a tremendous pressure against them. I was not aware until lately of the extent, and from quarters, where I did not expect it. This pressure has been so strong that it has over done itself, the consequence will be to my advantage, if bigotry does not override everything else I am getting into some families, if I could only get into one or two influential families, I think I would be established, but we will see.

᧦

Francis Lynch, Cheraw, to Patrick Lynch, 16 Nov[49]

Much concern was felt here at the taking of Port Royal by the enemies' forces. Still on second thought, it would appear too imaginative to expect the Defenders there to withstand so forcible an attack.—Bro. Hugh has been elected 2nd Lieut of Cheraw Guards-Conlaw remains at school.

In the moving of the Guards I think that Conlaw will go to Columbia, altho his arm has knitted the Doctor now finds that his shoulder is still dislocated, not having apprehended this it passed his observation—I cannot yet say what Bro Hugh will do with his dwelling. With everything so new, he does not like to risk the abuse attendant on renting.

Augusta was written to a few days ago to know if she will need her house, . . . —If not wanted by her, I think with the expenditure of a few hundred dollars it would rent so as to repay its outlay and would perhaps suit Mrs Purcell or Mrs. White.

Henrietta has written to her mother, I think, signifying her assent to Mrs Posi's wishes. I am glad to hear from Sister Catherine. . . .

My shipments of shoes to day for Col Glover QM Genl completed another 1000 pr. I will send him bill, and request that you call on him next week and receive the payment 2500$ for me—When the stir of last week took place I sent down 300 sets of accoutrements finishing my contract for them. And now am devoting my energies on the shoes.

My pegging machine so far has been a Silent investment but I hope better things of it when the Lasts & pegs etc. are all conformable to requirements.

As regards the movements of the Fleet, while it is well to be prepared for the offensive operations of it, I do not apprehend an early attack on your City. . . .

It will afford us much pleasure to have Mrs Blain & Daughter with us again.

ఆ

BAPTISTA LYNCH, URSULINE CONVENT, COLUMBIA, S.C., TO
PATRICK LYNCH, NOV 17TH[50]

It was very kind of you to write so often to me of late & your last letter inspired with a great confidence—. I wrote to Mrs Lowe[51] immediately & hope they may be able to send their daughters. We made every favorable offer that we could, & charged them only $416°° from now until next July—. The very high price of provisions will not allow us who have every thing to buy, even the milk we use—to lessen the terms for board—We charge less now for tuition, board bedding washing, mending, fuel & lights, than any hotel charges for board alone, without washing &c fuel & lighting—. We are most fortunate in having John & good Mr Comerford to purchase for us—Mr Comerford has been almost a regular caterer for us lately.

Did I tell you that Miss Clarke had been sent for by her father, & returned with Mrs Bauskett to Winesboro in the hope of getting permission to come soon to the Convent. Her great friend Nannie Ferrall is very convent-sick too.

Dr. Clark called on John to attend his wife who gave birth to a son today at her mother's—Mrs Bauskett's—All well & doing well—. I received a *queer* letter from Revd Wm Dundas Seale of Penn[sylvania], now resident of Florida, formerly of Arkansas who is of the same family of the Biddles of Phila—&c &c &c And we will accept his daughter, who I think wishes to be a nun! I will answer little McCord's letter soon & am very glad that she is not to return—

My reply to Mrs Carey was not I suppose altogether satisfactory but it would be *utterly impossible* for us to take parlor boarders—. Nor can I say that we feel called on, to make any extra concessions to those who only use us as a convenience—I am anxious to get the Huchets & am sorry they have not arrived, as I said all I could to induce them to.

I was very much pleased with a lady who called here the other day—when I entered the parlor she said so naively—"I am anxious to become a member of your church. Would you please tell me how"—I instructed her for two hours, found her intelligent, interesting & apparently much interested. She told me she was M[rs] George B. Lamb of Charleston, that her husband is in the insane asylum here, where she often visits him—she has one little son about two years of age—her own age is about 23 I presume, & that of her husband about 38 she says—Her father is Lieut. Col[n] Hamilton of Grey's regiment, VA & Col Ripley is her Uncle by marriage. The Haywoods & Middletons are her family—her mother I think she said was a Middleton—I appointed next Tuesday 4 P.M. for her next visit—Judge of my surprise & sadness when I heard this: the reports of her servant in Columbia that she is disreputable! —I cannot credit it—she may be very imprudent, but I am unwilling to believe her, what her *Catholic tattling servant* nurse rumours about. Did you ever hear of her & of her being turned out of two hotels in Charleston for misconduct. I think the Charleston hotel, & the Mills House—? If she is what she seems to me, an unhappy vain young lady, whose imprudences & perhaps flirtation have exposed her to censure, she might by instruction & the grace of God be converted—but if she is what her servant reports, I must let her know that I cannot instruct her—She is anxious to see you, she wishes she says [to] become a Catholic as soon as possible, & to be confirmed, for she does not know how long she may stay here—She spoke of seeing the priest, but I thought it better she should see you (not having heard these rumors at the time) I told her you would call on her when you came, she is boarding at Café Matthis near the Arsenal—a very respectable place.

FRANCIS LYNCH, CHERAW, TO PATRICK LYNCH, 25TH NOVEMBER[52]

I recd your most welcome letter last week. Thinking that the services of Conlaw (a lad of sixteen) were not desirable in the military I have put the notion of volunteering out of his head.

The Cheraw Guards of which Bro Hugh is 2nd Lieut is headd by Genl Hauber and may be called in two weeks—On Monday last I forwarded to Col Glenn Q M the remainder of 1000 pr army boots, and advised him you would call and receipt for me on the paymt of the amt say 2500$.

Your friend Mr J. L. Petigrew[53] has favoured me with a letter. I will reply to him tomorrow. Dr. Irvings letter was rcd and answered. It grieves me to be behind hand in shoes and our making all effort to extricate the difficulty in my pegging machines not adapted for heavy work and has in a measure helped to upset my calculations. As yet only the first bill for 1000 pr shoes has been paid me in Richmond. I expect further payments soon and with pleasure will comply in the Bonds. . . .

ᷟ

BAPTISTA LYNCH, URSULINE CONVENT, COLUMBIA, S.C., TO
PATRICK LYNCH, DEC 10TH[54]

I snatch a few minutes before retiring to rest, to ask how you are after your *very hurried* visit—? Did you find your umbrella in the cars, as I suppose it was there you left it?

Sr Ursula & Sr. Augustine regretted not seeing you before you left—the latter had not been summoned to the parlor, nor was Sr Loretta—. The next time I hope you will stay longer with us, & afford *all* the sisters the pleasure & consolation of seeing you as well as myself . . .

Minnie Clarke entered the noviciate today & is capped. Poor little thing, I had no idea she would appear so young & delicate as she does in the Postulants dress—Ellen told her it was the rule, to sit at the piano & pray for the M. Sup. immediately on her entrance into the noviciate & to do so without being asked—she was very obedient, never dreaming that she was the amusement of all, until I told her—Sr Charles laughed till the tears rolled down her cheeks at Ellen's composure & Minnie's obedience. Such a trick to play the poor child—!

I told the washerwoman that we had had, that her month would be up to-morrow, & we should not want her any more, or rather were not able to hire anyone—She felt badly & said "Your reverence, I never was wid any body I liked so much as a mistress & I likes that I can say my prayers here—"

I promised among other things that I would try to get a place for her—but the first thing I heard was that she was crying out loud in the kitchen like a big baby, nor would she be pacified, until I sent her word that I would see her & speak to her again & that she must take her supper now, so I suppose I will have to let her stay another week—

I am truly sorry to see by today's paper of the troops landing at Beaufort—May God & our Blessed Mother protect us—! . . .

ᷟ

FRANCIS LYNCH, CHERAW, TO PATRICK LYNCH, 14 DEC[55]

It was with profound grief that we heard of the awful fire in your city, spreading so much destruction in its way, heightened by the calamitous destruction of your premises and our grand Cathedral.

And we feel to sympathize with you. Mrs Blain & Daughter too are among the sufferers.

In this regard the pleasure of having them with us in a measure repays the loss, and Marie says the ground is not burnt—and perhaps if Insur offices can pay, it will be as well as if the city was bombarded.

Today I have wrote [*sic*] to Mr TR Waring paying my last note in the Bank there—I enclose you chk for twenty dolls to be used as you may see fit in these times of distress. . . . When a new Cathedral is to rise from the pile, I will hope to contribute one thousand dolls towards the desirable object.

⚐

BAPTISTA LYNCH, URSULINE CONVENT, COLUMBIA, S.C., TO PATRICK LYNCH, DEC. 14TH[56]

I did not think that *you* required so stern a lesson in "holy indifference"—
Well! You are the very one to say "Fiat voluntas Dei"[57] in all things—& although I am afraid you will experience many anxieties in consequence of this dreadful fire, I am sure it is for some good to[o] as . . . I see you are among the committee of relief & I suppose you have many coming to you for aid—I pity the poor who suffer—.

John thinks of going down this week if he can get off but that is uncertain. . . .

enclosed I send $500⁰⁰ which please place to our credit

⚐

ANNA LYNCH, CHERAW, TO PATRICK LYNCH, DEC 14TH[58]

Father & mother desire me to write and say that they are very sorry to hear of your heavy losses, by the late fire and of the destruction of the beautiful Cathedral, which is certainly, to be regretted very much, and that they would be glad if you would come up, & spend some time, as soon as you can conveniently leave the City. I hope you were able to save at least some of your things from the fire, which appears, to have been so dreadful, in its effects. We were quite relieved to hear of M�rˢ Blain & Daughter's safety on yesterday and hope they will come up, as soon as possible before something else happens.

I was very sorry too, to see the name of M�rˢ McNeal among the sufferers. The "Sisters" were very fortunate in escaping but I suppose they lost a great deal. It was a sad calamity, and perhaps a subject of great rejoicement to the Yankees, who may soon try and put a finish to the work. I am glad they did not burn the Cathedral. We heard from Columbia & Walterboro recently. All were well. Augusta intends coming up before Christmas, if she gets an opportunity. . . .

The remains of the interior of the Charleston Cathedral of St. Thomas and St. Finbar, following the devastating fire of December 1861. Courtesy of the Library of Congress.

BAPTISTA LYNCH, URSULINE CONVENT, COLUMBIA, S.C., TO
    PATRICK LYNCH, DEC 22ND[59]

Every body seem to sympathise with you in the loss of the Cathedral—& I have [*sic*] wondering how you will be able to meet the payments on the Convent, & thinking that I cannot be one to live in your house, & you have none for yourself—

Is any of the McKenna estate of advantage to you just now—? Even if this dreadful war were not in existence, it would not be so trying to you, but how will you now meet your debts—?

I received a letter today from Rosa McCord, who is still quite sick in Wilmington, N.C. but has not been baptized—Shall I send the small amount which we should return to her—? I imagined that you had somehow aided Mrs Vernon & that perhaps, it was more yours than hers—please let me know, as I ought to send it at once, if not—. I suppose you know that Hugh is here, he came over, with John. . . .

Our sisters are busy preparing for Christmas & for the Profession & reception on 3rd Jan —. Dr. Clarke has paid me by note, for amt due for last year's tuition &c of Minnie & they seem rather pleased at Minnie's choice—she herself is very satisfactory & apparently happy—. We expect the Florida lady today or tomorrow—& Mr Jos Murray asked us to take his second daughter on the same terms as we offered his eldest, which we will do— . . . This morning I received two letters from Brigadier General Blanchard[60]—one for Madam Blanchard & one for myself, saying that they would place their daughter Victoria in our Institution—I suppose they will arrive in this evening's train—Deo gratias for all blessings.

I am going to give into Col Bausketts hands the bill against Mr Engelke—as John & Hugh advise— . . .

Engelke will neither work for us nor pay any rent, nor behave himself as he promised, so the best way is to put the bill in the hands of Col. Bauskett who will manage it properly for John can do nothing with him.

৶

JOHN LYNCH, COLUMBIA, TO PATRICK LYNCH, DEC 25TH[61]

I notice in today's Mercury that a state hospital is to be established here, in the house next to Dr. O Connell's. Of course there is to be a physician to the hospital, if one has not been appointed, what is to hinder me from getting the appointment, who makes the appointment, if Genl Jones has any thing to say in the matter I might count on his influence. Your influence with Genl Jameson, and my acquaintance with Col Wilson, might fix the matter, if they are the body who have the appointment, but if the Governor, of course it will be Dr. Gibbs. I merely write for information, and to be in time if anything can be done. I have not mentioned this to any one, even the family, as the idea has just suggested itself. Christmas has passed off quietly. There were at least two hundred communicants this morning. Hugh & his wife amongst the number. Hugh is looking very well, and will leave tomorrow for immediate service I believe, his wife's arm is doing as well as I could expect. Two new boards at the Convent, go in in the morning from N. Orleans, Daughters of Genl Blanchard I believe now at Norfolk. . . .

☞

BAPTISTA LYNCH, URSULINE CONVENT, COLUMBIA, S.C., TO
PATRICK LYNCH, DEC 29TH[62]

I saw Mr Ewd Lafitte yesterday, who told me that you were too busy to
write, but were quite well & would be up at the appointed time, which we were
very glad to hear—How busy you must be—! We have been besieged by so
many Protestants wishing to see the convent—Miss Stone of some of the upper
Districts—The Misses Heywood, Mrs Peloh & Mrs Pendleton—&c I suppose we
shall have plenty at the reception, as a good many have asked to come. Stella
Clark wishes to receive Holy Communion for the first time at your hands—&
is trying I think to prepare well for it—

John says you ought to make up your mind to stay in Columbia & preach
on the following Sunday, as the Convention will most probably still be in session & the *best heads* of the State are assembled—thinks it would do some good
if you would prepare your sermon, announce it beforehand, & preach here on
the first Sunday in January. ____

Mrs Lamb continues to come for instructions constantly & hopes to be Baptized by you when next you come. I hear so much against her & a little for her,
but see nothing that I can absolutely disapprove of—that I do not know what
to say—She appears to be sincere & well-intentioned—Mrs General Blanchard
arrived here on Christmas day with her daughters, & the daughter of a friend a
Miss Beaumiller of N.O. She had for me a letter of introduction from Mr Den-
nis, the Editor of the N.O. Catholic Standard—.

I wrote to him together with many others last summer & sent our circulars,
& found him exceedingly kind & generous. . . .

My jaw is paining me so very much, that I can scarcely write—Do you know
Mademoiselle LePrince—? Governess in the family of Nathaniel Heywood?—

1862 January–June

"Is not the country in an awful state?"

During the first months of 1862 the tide of war turned very much against the Confederacy: from the loss of key fortresses on the Cumberland and Tennessee Rivers, which opened up the West for Federal inroads, to the horrors of Shiloh in early April with its unprecedented casualties and loss of Tennessee. Later that month, New Orleans, the South's largest city and port, capitulated to a Federal fleet, sealing off the mouth of the Mississippi. Worst of all, George McClellan landed a vast army of over 100,000 men on the peninsula between the James and York Rivers and began a slow but seemingly unstoppable march toward Richmond against the far fewer Confederates who stood in his way. When McClellan threw up siege lines around Richmond, speculation arose that Columbia might become the third capital of the Confederacy. But by June reports of Federal incursions in the lowcountry north of Charleston stirred fears that Columbia itself might be in danger of falling to the Yankees.

The Federal occupation of off-shore islands and other enclaves of the low-country, together with the prospect of an imminent naval attack on Charleston, led to the dispatching of slaves to the more secure uplands. Claudian Northrop,[1] Patrick Lynch's attorney and manager of his Lancaster plantation, had difficulty finding an upcountry planter willing to take on his urban slaves unaccustomed to agrarian labor. The war was not only producing mass transfers of slaves, but it was also eroding discipline within the slave quarters. John Lynch encountered this in attempting to hire out and then to sell one of his slave families. Even when discipline was not an issue, the caring for others' slaves amid the disruptions of war created a special burden, as Francis Lynch and Northrop quickly discovered.

The blockade of Charleston harbor began to affect the access of South Carolinians to goods and to generate the need to find homegrown substitutes for basics in their diet (for example, coffee). In this economy of scarcity, inflation steadily worsened and led some to have second thoughts about the war they had rushed into with such joy. Ruptures in the community's support of the war began to appear, the most dramatic evidence of which was the failure of many soldiers in the Charleston area to reenlist.

In coping with the uncharted territory war had put them in, the Lynch siblings (even Baptista in her deferentially commanding way) turned to their oldest brother for advice and decisions. They particularly looked to Patrick for evaluations of the political state of things, assuming he was in the best position, living in Charleston, to read the signs of the times. Amid the rising pessimism that all his siblings shared to some extent, Bishop Lynch was characteristically optimistic about the South's prospects. Even with Federal forces at the gates of Richmond and Charleston, and Federal armies seemingly everywhere closing in on the Confederacy, Patrick Lynch expected a peace settlement by the fall. In the early spring, he escorted the Sisters of Our Lady of Mercy, who had been administering the military hospital in Greenbrier, Virginia, to Montgomery White Sulphur Springs in the westernmost part of the state, to escape the maneuverings of several Federal armies in the Shenandoah Valley futilely attempting to corner and bag the elusive foot cavalry of Stonewall Jackson.

As virtually the only Catholic academy for females between the District of Columbia and New Orleans, the Ursuline school in Columbia, serendipitously founded at the very time Southern parents began to withdraw their children from the Northern educational institutions they had traditionally patronized, was excellently situated to offer a welcome alternative for the offspring of the wealthy. With the outbreak of war cutting off Northern institutions, the Ursuline Academy, in its upcountry setting far from the early theaters of the conflict, became even more of a magnet not only for Catholics but for Protestants, especially those Episcopalians who were to a greater or lesser extent moved by the residual currents of the Oxford Movement toward Catholicism. For more than a few Protestant teenagers, the Ursuline Academy became their road to Rome.

The dislocation of so many lowcountry residents created a transient population in Columbia and other upcountry towns. Many, both Catholic and Protestant, sought out the cloister-bound Mother Baptista for advice and assistance in finding new homes. The nuns' parlor became a place for providing migrant assistance as well as promoting conversions among dislocated Protestants, some by way of traditional retreat exercises, which Baptista began to lead. She also published a new edition of the Ursuline book of prayers, in part to meet the public spiritual need that was bringing strangers and acquaintances to their parlor. Such religious inquirers brought themselves not only to the convent but to St. Peter's Church, where Baptista regarded the O'Connell brothers and the *resident clergy under their sway to be serious deterrents to those considering Catholicism. She scorned their shanty-Irish, heavy-handed, money-grubbing ways, epitomized by Jeremiah O'Connell nailing shut the pews in the church whose habitual occupants had not paid their annual rent. That kind of money-obsessed, uncharitable behavior was sure to offend Episcopalians who were the most likely Protestants to be exploring Catholicism by experiencing its signature liturgy at the local church, behavior that contrasted so badly with the treatment visitors received in Episcopal churches, where ushers readily seated visitors in whatever available pew space there was. Ultimately, she faulted her bishop brother for suffering them to do as they pleased, no matter the consequences, and did not hesitate to tell him so in her own inimitable manner.*

In the makeshift dispositions of property that war occasioned, an opportunity suddenly arose for the Ursulines to acquire property for a future home in peacetime, a site that matched perfectly the ideal one that Baptista had long had in mind to fulfill the mission to which she felt deeply called. It reinforced the spiritual satisfaction that Baptista took, even amid the trials and disturbances of wartime, in the work they had accomplished in South Carolina of establishing a convent and academy as another beachhead for the Catholic faith in her native land.

❧

John Lynch, Columbia, S.C., to Patrick Lynch, January 6th[2]

I got the negroes home safely and sent them over to the plantation on Saturday, they are all stowed away pretty comfortably.[3] I sent word to Mr. Buff to get out the timbers and order the lumber for two more houses, have engaged the carpenter and bricklayer to go to work as soon as the material is ready. I also today purchased a very good mule for $74 at auction. You will need one or two more, but I will put off the evil day as long as possible, for the expenses are more than you are aware. . . .

Ellen is suffering with jaw ache, I extracted two teeth for her yesterday. . . .

❧

Baptista Lynch, Ursuline Convent, Columbia S.C., to Patrick Lynch, Jan 7th[4]

Our school is increasing since the arrival of Misses Huchet & Miss Kate Seule, our Boarders number 30—& we expect Miss Avilla of Charleston & a granddaughter of Madame Filette,[5] Miss Gyles, next week—. Mr Hinton mentioned in a letter to his daughter that the Misses Lowe would he expected soon be here. Deo Gratias for all things—we cannot get a strong black wooden chair in Columbia, nor a single bedstead—but we can manage for the present, & I prefer not paying the high prices now asked, so long as we can do without anything—

I was called down to the parlor to see "Chancellor Inglis"[6] who wanted a prospectus for a *Mrs* Semmes of Virginia, whom he had met at the Springs. I spoke of having a pupil of the same name & a relative—he asked to see her & I was right well pleased to hear her tell him of her sister & self having been here so long &c

You must know that I have not common patience with his narrow-minded bigotry against Catholics, & his shame of his Catholic aunt who is a nun—Madam St. Angela of N. Orleans—He did not mention her & of course I did not either, but was all civility—he was the same—

Miss Preston & Miss Heywood called to see us a few days since & seemed delighted with the ceremony of the "reception" & Miss Preston described some of those ceremonies she had witnessed in Rome—She assured me she was by no means one of those narrow-minded bigoted Protestants—I have heard that she & her sister wish to be Catholic and are only prevented by family ties—the same of one of the Misses Heywood—they asked particularly for Mrs Lamb—who I am sorry to say has been ill ever since you were here—Our Sisters I am happy to say continue to enjoy their usual good health, & are doing very well I trust in every way—We want a good Lay sister to help in the work since that servant woman has another place, but they all are cheerfully willing to do all they can—what are we to do for salt—soap & candles—what prices—! Do not buy for us—because I asked that—. We are not out yet—.

⟨✦⟩

JOHN LYNCH, COLUMBIA, TO PATRICK LYNCH, JANUARY 18[7]

. . . About the plantation, I fear you have allowd other business to engross your time, to the detriment of its interests. I was obliged on Wednesday in addition to my purchase of corn &c to purchase gallons of molasses at 60^c. I find that there is not over one hundred pounds of bacon left. Corn is selling at \$1.00 with an upwards tendency. I have been thinking of sending Mr Buff ten or fifteen miles above the plantation to see if he could not buy some cheaper. I cant see why the price keeps up so, there is plenty in the country. I understand that they are certainly dependent on what I buy for not only the food for the negroes but corn for the mules also. I would be glad to be able to go over, but the same cause which prevented my going to see father, prevents me leaving town just now. I begin to fear that Mr. B is taking advantage of his liberty and should have a little more check which I am unable to give just now. I have the lumber ready for building one house more. The workmen will commence on Monday, so they say. What can you get nails at; they ask 8 & 10^c here, 10¢ for the kind we need.

⤸

JOHN LYNCH, COLUMBIA, TO PATRICK LYNCH, 22 JANUARY[8]

I recd yours by Mr Mullin, sent him over to the plantation in the Buggy, he found one of Emmett's children with the measles, and as the weather was so bad did not move them, nor tell them he had bought them, he proposes paying the expenses of someone taking them over or coming for them himself as soon as I think they can be moved without danger, now if there are no new cases in the family, they can go the first good weather, but I fear there will be. I am to see Emmett and tell him Mr. M has bought himself & family, and get him willing to go quietly, as I understand he refuses to be hired quietly. Mr M, said he might go down and see you. I hope he will, as he made rather a sorry report to me of the place, which I asked him to repeat to you. I have since learned from Anderson who drove him over, that he was mistaken in part, as some of the men were out at work, still I fear things are not pushed forward. I have been so busy for a little while back that I have not had time to go over, except when sent for the other day, to see after matters & things. . . . Excuse haste & bad writing have been up & busy since 2 o'clock last night. . . .

⤸

BAPTISTA LYNCH, URSULINE CHAPEL COLUMBIA, TO PATRICK LYNCH,
    JAN 23RD[9]

We have another little boarder in the person of Miss Lyles of Richmond Va—the little girl about whom her parents wrote some time since, & about whose coming I threw cold water upon—well, she is here—a nice little thing, a Protestant—Her father is quarter-master in the Army of the Potomac[10]—We frequently hear from Mrs Blanchard & even the Gen^{rl} whose daughter has had the measles but is now quite well—Several of our pupils are sniffling from colds & other effects, which gives Sr Angela something to do—& yesterday we had three sick Sisters. but although inconvenient, it was nothing serious. What do you think of the present state of the country, & how should [it] effect the arrangements of our school. Shall I begin as usual to arrange things with a view to the Distribution? This is the time we generally begin to do so, & I would be glad to know what you would think it best to do. If we have a distribution, the children must devote their time & the Sisters too, to studying Duets &c &c. But if not it would be better for them, & more satisfactory to their Parents, to make a different arrangement of their studies.

At present we have more boarders than we have had since we came to Columbus. I would like to do whatever will make the Institution most popular—A.M.D.G.

John & Family are quite well. He has lost several patients with Diphtheria &c they were young children I think.

Good night—it is just ten o clock—I wish you a comfortable night's rest—I wonder how poor Hugh is getting on down the coast? It takes some of the comfort out of the fire & bed, when I think of his exposure. I do hope he may not get sick while down there. . . .

JOHN LYNCH, COLUMBIA, TO PATRICK LYNCH, JANY 25TH[11]

M^r or rather Capt Aveilhé left your letter at the house this morning while I was out. I will try and see him, I recd your letter with the $25 enclosed for Lieut Hamlin, and gave it to Capt Schiver who said there would be no difficulty about it. I told him to say, it came from an old college mate. I recd the two barrells molasses and sent over two gallons today. Also had to buy 12 bushels corn at $1.10 a bushel. I have sent for Emmett to come over tomorrow and will write to Mr. Mullen at once after speaking with him. It was not John's wife that died, but Isaacs. She was a sickly woman they say.

The carpenters are working at the house, but I am afraid I will be troubled a little about the brick, as the man is about selling the whole to another party, but if the worst comes to the worst, I can get them here and haul them by the other road. I have been quite engaged lately with some profitable & some unprofitable cases, have lost three cases amongst children, one measles one dyptheria & one convulsions. It is uncomfortable, but when you do your best, have to be satisfied. Could not have lost them if I had not them to attend to, have some others very sick. . . .

[P.S.] what do you think of the times politically

BAPTISTA LYNCH, URSULINE CONVENT, COLUMBIA, S.C., TO
PATRICK LYNCH, JAN 26TH[12]

Your introductory letter was handed to me by Capt & Mrs Aveilhé with whom I am much pleased—Their little daughter makes our thirtieth boarder, Deo gratias. This is doing well for us—Madame Togno[13] has only ten boarders & the Methodist College only fifty.

Miss Graham (sister-in-law, to Professor Le Compte[14]) was here yesterday afternoon, & says the College is most satisfactory to the Professors this year, the war having claimed all the wild & idle young men, & left to it, only the steady & studious, who number there about sixty or seventy—.

Mrs Lamb has not been here often of late, owing to the inclement weather, & partly to her own indisposition—The last time she came I was unable to see her, & so sent Sr. Charles a convert *to a convert*—She mentioned how much her feelings had been hurt by Rev Father O Connell's manner—it seems he has been a real Yankee about money lately & lowering his dignity by constant & plain speeches about the people not paying for their pews &c &c

She told me some time ago that she felt badly in consequence, & wished to know in what way she could remunerate for the seat which she occupied—as she did not wish to rent a pew, being only a transient visitor in Columbia—I told her to contribute something every Sunday, & that would suffice—she said she was accustomed to do so—It seems that on two Sundays ago he went down the aisles himself, & sent some one else on the other to get contributions to pay the insurance which was due that week—As each one contributed, he would call out at the top of his voice—"put down $5" "What only $2^{oo}"&c &c—Now this was anything but edifying or dignified—On the following, that is last Sunday when persons went to church, every pew was not only locked but had a board nailed across the door, except those which were rented & I suppose paid for—consequently, some came in went from pew to pew, & finding all shut against them—left the church—Mrs L—went also from pew to pew, until some old mean looking woman (probably Miss Cary at the Church) had the charity to offer her a seat—when presently another of the same cast came in & those three heard Mass in the same pew—She was grateful for the offer, & did not show any little near pride in mentioning this, on the contrary—but she felt very badly at the whole proceeding, which I am sure is strikingly in contrast with the genteel manner in episcopal churches, where as I know from experience, a stranger no sooner is seen in the aisle looking for a seat, that pew after pew is thrown open invitingly & some gentleman *warden* steps forward, to relieve your embarrassment.

Why have they not wardens here?

John asks the question, is this church God's House, or is it Mr O'Connell's that he should be allowed to act in it in this manner? I wish you were as independent of your priests as Abp Purcell is, or B Lamy, both of whom present a very different course from yours of letting each one be his own master.

But of course you know your own business best—I was very much pleased to hear Capt Aveilhé say that the Spanish consul had written to Havana with a view of raising funds for the reconstruction of your Cathedral—he seems to think that you will be able to build, & on a much larger plan before very long.

Are you "on to Richmond"? If so, will you come by this way? Sr Charles & S^r St Etienne are both quite sick & should you come by this way, would I suppose have many messages to send.

Our sick sisters are better except Sr. DeNeri & two children are indisposed—I recd a long letter from Mrs Farley, begging to come back—but of course we will not take her—Mrs Glen too, occasionally sends us a reminder such as a picture returned &—poor things—What do you think of Mrs Lafitte joining us (a Barbot that was)—? She did not write to me, but sent a message to Sr Theresa— . . .

⋘

HENRIETTA LYNCH, CHERAW, TO PATRICK LYNCH, 29TH JANUARY[15]

. . . The weather for two weeks has been very rainy so much so as to keep every one at home. We now have a few clear days. We have all been tolerably well. Every one in the kitchen has been down with measles. It has been the same at your mother's but her cases have been less favorable. Your Brother James' little boy took them & they turned to pneumonia, the child is said to be very low, so also is Boykin, with the same disease. You appear to have little hope of the Blockade being broken for which we are all quite sorry. . . . We have only heard news of Mr George McInis being made Major & Hugh 1st Lieutenant. They have heard through him that Hugh is well. Mr Lynch will try to send you the rye in a short time. He expects it from the country. Mrs. Posi[16] is writing to you today. I hope dear Dr. Lynch you will keep from colds & sickness and hope that we will hear from you often before you go to Virginia. . . .

⋘

ANTONIA LYNCH, [BALTIMORE], TO PATRICK LYNCH, 13TH FEB[17]

I was so happy to hear from you through Sr M. Charles. It has been many months since I last heard from any of the family. I cannot tell you my dear Brother how much I suffered with you when I heard the news of the great fire and of your great loss. I cannot but think our Lord will reward you some other way most bountifully. I almost began doubting the care of St. Joseph for at that very time I was in the midst of a Novena in his Honour—for you. I now tell him he must not let you suffer in your temporal affairs. It must be a great consolation to dear Father Mother and all that you are so resigned and cheerful under your trials. Yesterday Mrs Meede from Va called upon us and very kindly offered to deliver a letter to you. I was much relieved to think I might be sure of your getting it.

My dear Brother when Mr. Murphy came he told us that as their [*sic*] was not any name specified upon the Bond, should it be lost, or anything happen to it on the way it would never be recovered, and he felt sure that even should at some future time there . . . be some difficulty about money matters he felt certain that Maryland would not suffer from the South; but that there would be a general compromise in that line. Rev. Mother returns you many thanks for your offer of kind assistance but as transportation is so very uncertain, will now leave it in the hand of a kind Providence.

We have had a great deal of sickness the last six weeks; it came on with a severe cold but affected the nuns differently. Only three escaped and I was one of that number. On last Saturday morning Sr. Mary of the Incarnation a lay-Sister died. Will you please pray for her. She had a very happy death, we all loved her very much. Sr. Ambrosia has been very ill but is thought out of danger. She asks you to pray for her. We have also another in the last stage of consumption. I was very happy to learn so much good news of the Nuns in Columbia, that Sr. M. Charles told me. I would rather Ellen Spann would be devoted to St. Gertrude next after St. Joseph and St. Teresa. It seems too, like the name will suit her. . . . I hope Conlaw Lynch is a good boy, will you ask him to wear this scapular and Agnus Dei which has a Gospel and Pallet within it, and tell him that every day I will ask our Lady to take care of him, but he must do so *too*. I will be glad when Sr. Mary Charles calls again that I may ask about Hugh. I did not hear how his health was. It must be a great comfort to Father & Mother for them both to be at home.

ᘒ

BAPTISTA LYNCH, URSULINE CONVENT, COLUMBIA, TO PATRICK LYNCH, MARCH 2ND[18]

I know you have a great deal to do. After your absence, I think though you might run up here for a short time—Please let me know two days beforehand that we may prepare Stella Clark & Mrs. Lamb for the Sacraments, should you judge fit to administer them.

We have been trying to do the agreeable to Bp McGill, who I like well enough—he is a second edition of Bp Reynolds only more talented—but I will be glad when he leaves.

The first evening, he asked for those of our pupils who were from Va. Also for Misses Blanchard & Semmes, whose friends he knows. A few days after, we took [him] up to the Second Class room, where the children were assembled, & he paid them quite a visit, seemingly much pleased.

. . . The Bishop gave us a very pleasing instruction on the sacraments. . . .

Mr. A. Weed wrote to his sister, that you were in Richmond & proposed an exchange of Bishops—. But there would be more voices than one on that subject.

Do you fear or rather anticipate an early attack on Charleston from the dreadful Northern fleet? If the Northerners should reach Columbia, we intend to *stay at home*, but don't you think if we erected a large cross it would be for our safety, in as much as it would indicate that we were a religious Institution? Mr Bollin[19] tells me that the citizens will destroy the town on the approach of the enemy rather than let it fall into their hands. What should we then do?

I would feel like refusing to move until the city authorities would provide a place for us, but if all the adjoining places were burned we could not hope to be saved. We are not of the world, nor do we take part in its strife, save by prayers, therefore I do not think it necessary to destroy our property to testify to our loyalty. But it is easy to talk[;] in the event of the Columbians setting fire to the city where shall we go &c?

Old Mrs Anderson asks me this question.

You have heard of course of the death of Alice Reilly[20] & little Nancy Stern RIP—Poor Mr & Mrs Reilly I pity them sincerely—Cornelia & Mrs McCabe are both here—All were well at home when last we heard—Has Mad^elle [Mademoiselle] *Marnier* written to you since her visit here—She is a very singular lady, though pleasing. Ellen Spann is much better now, but was quite indisposed. M DeNeri is sinking—little Enright has the measles—Srs Hedrian & Huchet out still— . . .

ऒ

HUGH LYNCH, CAMP MANIGAULT, TO PATRICK LYNCH, 2ND MARCH[21]

I heard yesterday that you had passed down the NERR on your way to Charleston and as I have a particular favor to ask of you I have concluded to write you at once. As I would like to get it as soon as possible. While in your City some 10 days since, I called to see you but learned that you had not yet returned from Va—the favor I wish of you is to write an obituary for Alice Reilly—Cornelia is anxious that I should write it in preference to any one else. And I do not feel myself competent to do so. And will be very much obliged if you will write a short notice for me and send it to me by return mail. "Alice Julia born 26th Oct 1844 died 8th Feby 1862"

I am getting on very well down here—fattening up Considerable and in better health than I have been in for 7 or 8 years. I hope you are enjoying your usual good health. We are encamped about 6 miles from Georgetown and about One mile from Black River—from preparations that are going on—it looks like we are preparing for a brush—but whether they will attack us or not, I can't say—if they do—we Can't give much of a fight, as we have very little ammunition. . . .

Francis Lynch, Cheraw, to Patrick Lynch, 4 March[22]

Your most welcome letter reached me on Sunday morning—I was glad you are well and again safely in Charleston.

Mrs Reilly arrived here on Saturday night having come for Cornelia. I was happy with the aid of your letter, to ease her mind, in reference to her daughter.[23] Father & mother and the rest of us are all well D.G. Daughter has been a little indisposed but is well again. Mrs. Posi seems quite at home. I intend making arrangements as quickly as possible for the reception of Col[n] Northrop's negroes.[24] Possibly I may be able to write you tomorrow for them. Be assured I will not delay in the matter. I have rented to the Revd J. C. Coit[25] . . . Bro James' place for two hundred dolls for the year. . . .

I was the more willing to rent to Mr Coit as very likely he may become the purchaser of the property.

Francis Lynch, Cheraw, to Patrick Lynch, 6 Mar[26]

Your favour of the 4th inst was recd and yesterday and the day before, I have been endeavoring to make arrangement about these negroes without success. On Saturday I hope to hear from another party, residing in Richmond County—who would have taken them in Jany. I will lose no time in advising you—For my own part, to undertake to keep them now would be folly—The only land procurable within reach would require so much clearing, ditching & preparation, that a crop the present year would be out of the question—beginning at this late period, to say nothing of the risk of health from exposed work, so different from the usual employment of them—the best suitable lands have been already leased. Appreciating greatly the kind consideration of Col[n] Northrop, I would regret that the result of such a generous transaction on his part would be unsatisfactory to him as well as myself, in my hands. However should I succeed in persuading the party in Richmond to take them, of which I will know on Saturday or Monday next I have good reason to believe the Negros will be well cared for, and in a healthy location. On conferring with Doct Guerin[27] sometime ago, I was anxious for an early reply, because of the consequent necessary arrangements, now too late to effect. I wrote at once that other arrangements as to the disposition of the forces, may be entertained by you.

❧

Henrietta Lynch, Cheraw, to Patrick Lynch, March 8th[28]

We were very happy indeed to learn of your safe arrival home in good health. Daughter has had a serious bilious spell. She is better now. The remainder have been well, but I have had a very disagreeable time with a negro child who is still so low it may not live. We had to bring it into the house. These things are not pleasant & less so because of Mrs. P[osi]. who is not backward in remarks.

In writing I will take the opportunity of telling you I hope Mr. Lynch will not have to take Mr. Northrop's negroes for I think it would kill, kill, him, he is so hard upon himself in sickness & has so much to do for others as well as for himself. If you would see how little he cares for his meals. The weather is very severe indeed yesterday it snowed. There has been rain all the winter. The rye was not sent to you while you were away, but will be sent right off. The preparation is this—wash some of it & dry in the sun or an oven then parch like coffee but do coffee & rye separately, mix equal quantities of these articles, or you may use more rye than coffee. Some prefer it thinking it stronger. Another way is to boil the rye but not allow it to burst then dry as before. In this way a large quantity can be kept a long time.

How sad it is dear Dr Lynch to think there is no probability of peace. The war has brought on so many disasters. I know you must have your hands full. I trust & pray the committee of relief will give ma a great deal on the house. She is indeed to be pitied. Do you think the Yankees will take C—they are so averse to reenlist there. The Muellers must have left because he is exempt from duty.

. . . Dear Dr Lynch do pay attention to what I say of Mr. Northrops negroes. Mr Lynch is much worried by all he has. He cannot give attention to any thing he needs for his servants comforts &c &c I have been very unwell Or I would write more. . . .

❧

Baptista Lynch, Ursuline Convent, Columbia, S.C., to
Patrick Lynch, March 14th[29]

This is the second day this week that I have gone to Holy Communion for you—on your birth-day the 10th & today the anniversary of your consecration.

Well, what is your experience of having worn the mitre four years—Do you say, like good Bishop Wood, that is no easy thing—? How much has transpired since your consecration! And now you are almost like one beginning, except that you have before you in eternity, treasures I trust stored up—

For myself, who am nearly as long Superior—while I sometimes grow weary, very weary & almost tired with, I arouse myself & renew my first beginnings & fervor, with the thought of God's great goodness to me, in placing me in a position where I can labor more for Him, & for my own sanctification, than so many others can—and as one of our Lay Sisters said, when the body is tired, the soul is not, because it is for God we work—It seems to me, I realize more and more every day the greater & inestimable blessings of Faith & religious vocation, especially when I have heard in the parlor the trials of persons in all conditions, highest as much as lowest, who seem to seek comfort in the peaceful influence of the convent.

As Mrs Lowe has not arrived, I suppose we may expect you on the 26th. Stella will I hope be ready, & Mrs. Lamb seems earnestly preparing—. She brought her little boy—a fine little fellow, with her on last Sunday, to see us— ought she not to have it baptized at the same time with herself—?

You will be sorry to hear that we have a case of scarletina[30] in our house— little Mary English of Atlanta first had measles, & now has scarletina—she is very sick & John has written to her father—

(Saturday morning) Mary will go to confession tomorrow after Mass & make her first communion—for we would not forgive ourselves if she died without the sacraments. But she may get well—.

Sister De Neri says she is a *child* of *obedience* (which she really is) "for she is going to be much better as you told her to do—"

The rest are as you left, & happy to see such beautiful spring weather.

Our children seem to partake of the disturbing influence outside—they are more unruly than we have ever before known them to be—but it is better to have them high-spirited than sick— I have this morning received a letter from a Mrs George G. McWharten of Augusta Georgia who wishes to send a Miss Eliza Hungerford to us—It seems the young lady is *a case*—

Did you write to Miss Jones? I hope she will not come until I can get up some bedsteads & make a few house arrangements—I have a second-hand Harp offered me with stand for $300.—shall I buy it—? What about your papers in the event of an attack on Charleston which I see the Yankees intend to make within 30 days—? Shall we subscribe to *The gunboat*—?[31] The *Va* [*Virginia*][32] did such good work—didn't it—? . . .

John is dejected about his sick children who have scarlet fever, & two of whom, give him very little rest at night—Eliza—Anna, Louisa, & James are all sick—sometimes better & sometimes worse—. All were well at home when Anna wrote day before yesterday—

Mother sent a nice dressing gown both to Srs Ursula & Sr. A_____. It was a real act of virtue for me to give the latter—a strong act of obedience & self-denial—We expect the Huchets to reenter on Monday. They have been very polite sending us bouquets of flowers & other little presents thus removing any unpleasant feeling that may have arisen about their remarks concerning their sickness. . . .

JOHN LYNCH, COLUMBIA, TO PATRICK LYNCH, MARCH 17TH[33]

Knowing you have enough to bother you, independent of your negroes, I have tried to keep from you complaints made by them, but today I had a complaint from the other side, which I said I would refer to you, as I thought the complaint just, and that proper reperation [*sic*] should be made, still, as I understood you to say you intended making a different disposition of one of the parties, I thought it best to consult you first. Mr Buffs complaint is, first that he has some very lazy & idle negroes to deal with, that he has indulged them as far as he thought he could in justice to you, that he has noticed in particular a son of Johns, half grown, who has on several occasions, as soon as his back is turned quit the work he had given him to do, and idled his time. On last Saturday he gave him a piece of work to do, and went off, but kept his Eye on him, he soon slipped on his coat and was idling about, he returned and called him up, gave him a strapping, when the boys Mother hearing the fuss came running up, and made fight for the boy, saying Mr B was not put there to whip them &c, undertook to strike with a hoe-plank &c—You can imagine the Scene. Now Mr B calls for her punishment, but waits Your say so, that she should be punished is evident, but as I told Mr B—if you intended selling her, a whipping such as she would be obliged to receive, would not increase her value. Mr B says justly if this goes unpunished and the woman remains it will be the ruining of all the young negroes, for when he undertakes to correct any of them their mothers will take this as a precedent. If you see any chance of parting with Johns family to the man you spoke of in Augusta, my advice is, do it, as soon as possible, for I consider him a good fellow, but slow, and all his family, require some one to look close after them to make them earn their bread, in fact I am sorry to say they are all a lazy set, even Mr B—sees it, and I don't think he is able to remedy it. He asked me today if you wished him for another year, as his time would be out in about two months, and it was necessary for him to look out in time. he mentioned that he had had an offer, but did not say what. If you wish to make a change now would be a good time, but without you know of some one, who will answer better, I cant say that I do. It might be as well *now* (that is, since the neighbours know you & I) for you to put a stranger on the place, but if you make a change, be sure and put one who knows how to make the negroes work, without that qualification I expect Mr B—will answer your purpose as well as any one. I told him I had not heard you express yourself at all about keeping him, but would write you what he said, so it is all fair sailing. You will be a better judge of how things are going on, when you pay your promised visit. For my part I must be one of Jobs comforters to you, for I think the concern will be an expence to you as long as you keep it up. The only question seems to me, how to make the expence as light as possible.

Baptista Lynch, Ursuline Convent, Columbia S.C., to Patrick Lynch, Feast of St. Joseph [March 19][34]

Today I asked John to enquire what premium we should pay for species as I wanted to get some, but he suggested my asking you, if you had any on deposit, as the premium would be probably very high.

If *perfectly convenient* I would be glad if you would bring me *in gold* \$500[00] & if that is the *slightest trouble* don't mind it.

We are all pretty well now except the children who have scarletina but are doing well—.

We will be ready for Miss Jones, whenever she may honor us with her company.

John's children are better also T.G. Poor old Mrs. McGinnis—*Billy's wife* died of a fit, very suddenly & was interred today—

Your tenants in the old convent are sending to know when you are expected —they want to get off from paying the rent I suppose as "old Billy" is going to sell them out—I don't pity them because Mr Fry is not sober—We teach their daughters gratuitously & that is enough—John's kind heart is sorry for them, but of course will not interfere with the old man's proceedings— . . .

John Lynch, Columbia, S.C., to Patrick Lynch, April 1st[35]

Allow me to introduce to you Capt George from Charlotte N.C. who has taken with him to Charleston, at the invitation of Maj Stephens I believe, his breech loading cannon, if you are only half as much pleased with the action of it as I am, I am sure you will use what influence you have, in trying to have a battery of them made immediately. I look on it as both Arms and men, two articles we are much in need of at once. The Captain will explain the cannon to you much better than I can. I took ex-Governor Gist to see it last Friday. He appears much pleased with it, the captain does not claim that the *particular gun he* is *exhibiting* would do to go safely into the battlefield, as it was built under many inconveniences, but a gun built on the same principal [*sic*] in any good workshop he contends is the thing needed. The specimen exhibited is to show the action, principal & rapidity of firing. I would be glad if it meets your views, that you take the same interest that I have here, from Capt George, who is a worthy, industrious mechanic of Charlotte.

<hr/>

PATRICK LYNCH, CHARLESTON, S.C. TO BAPTISTA LYNCH, 2 APRIL 1862 (COPY)[36]

I enclose to you a letter from Mr. M Ferrall of Halifax N.C. about Nannie.[37] It is easy to see he is in very low spirits. I am afraid too his long continued illness has made him very exacting and easily dissatisfied.

My own health is pretty good now. Some cough remains, and I am still weak. But I am going about my business. I thought I would be up before this, but I do not now see that I can well be with you before Monday morning and on Sunday I may shrink from night travel.

I think you would do well to lay up a large stock of flour and rice, and provisions, for it is pretty clear that they will get much dearer before long.

Things are all very quiet here just now. And every day increases my confidence that now we will be let alone until autumn. Perhaps by that time we may have peace.

<hr/>

HENRIETTA LYNCH, CHERAW, TO PATRICK LYNCH, 2D APRIL[38]

. . . I have written to you twice at least. I think as no answer came you are displeased that Mr. L did not like to take those negroes. Mrs Posi said they would not be willing to plow as they are city negroes nor to eat corn bread as they do here. So what would he do with them. In this case they would torment him to death. . . .

<hr/>

FRANCIS LYNCH, CHERAW, TO PATRICK LYNCH, 17 APRIL[39]

It gives me much pleasure to learn your health is better and hope you will be able to visit us after Easter— . . . If you are passing Col[n] Glove's Headquarters, you will please [get] receipt for 1000 prs shoes deliv[r] the price was 2⁵⁰/100 pr pair. The Col[n] may make some deduction on the first 200 pr as he wrote me a portion of them were inferior—Though I think the better quality of the remainder more than compensates for the deficiency of the two first cases, I am willing to abide the Col[s] decision in the matter.

In regard to Co^n Northrops negroes I am making further trial for their disposition—Should I not find a planter who will take the whole, I suppose I could hire them at Bennettsville on the first Monday in May until the 1st of Jany next, if this would be satisfactory. They would very likely have comfortable homes in this way.

I will try & find a place for the whole & write you by Monday's mail. I cannot employ them in my business. . . .

BAPTISTA LYNCH, URSULINE CONVENT, COLUMBIA, S.C.. TO
PATRICK LYNCH, HOLY SATURDAY [APRIL 19][40]

(Easter Sunday) . . . This morning we had for the first time a whole Mass sung through—Stella played Peter's Mass which was sung by Victoria Blanchard Lucia Bellinger & Sr. Gertrude. I assure it was really good music & very sweet—nearly all of our pupils approached Holy Communion—& could not help feeling how grateful you & I should be, for being instruments in the hands of God in providing S.C. with a convent & academy, which is doing so much I trust & believe for our Holy Faith, here, where it is so much needed.

This is the *utopia* of my youth fully realized—It was to me always as a charming fancy, that I never expected to see fulfilled & looked upon without anxiety & enjoy.

I thought this morning when I heard the universal expression of admiration from the children for our church services & even the long offices, which they sat & listened to in such respectful silence, that you had, like Cardinal Himenes,[41] made your first work the establishment of such an institution as he founded as his first ecclesiastical work & I prayed that you might enjoy the reward of this good work— . . .

(another interruption) evening —

Poor S^r De Neri I think will not last much longer & Sister Agnes & Sr. Theresa are nearly tired out—. She is perfectly helpless—. (interrupted)

Mrs Lamb has just called to say "good bye" she is leaving for Charleston & speaks of being baptized there—her health does not appear good, she has a severe cough which looks consumptive—. I have offered to make her the bearer of this letter. I pity her very much & wish she had some support from the Sisters or others who could lead her to virtue & the practice of our holy Faith. . . .

When do you start for Va? Things look pretty dark in that quarter, do they not—Miss Heywood told us that Columbia was to be the Capitol of the Confederate states & already some things had been brought here from Richmond. Is this so?

FRANCIS LYNCH, CHERAW, TO PATRICK LYNCH, 21ST APR[42]

As yet I have no answer from M^r McDaniel in reference to the negroes,—If however you determine that it is best to send them at any rate, I will suggest that you so apprize me, and I will advertize them for hire on the 1st Monday of next month at Bennettsville. Or it may be as well to have them continue their earnings in the City a while longer—As when work is commenced on the coal-fields road, Col^n Macfarlan may be willing to take them. . . .

ANNA LYNCH, CHERAW, TO PATRICK LYNCH, 21 APRIL[43]

We have had Brother Hugh at home, for the last two weeks, on a sick furlough, which has been extended, for some weeks longer, as he is not well enough to return, although much better than when he came up. Dr. Kollack does not consider that he can stand camp life but he has no notion of resigning without trying it again. Father Mother & the rest of the family are quite well. Augusta returns to Walterboro this week, or the first of next. We will miss the children & herself, a good deal. . . .

BAPTISTA LYNCH, URSULINE CONVENT, COLUMBIA, S.C., TO
PATRICK LYNCH, APRIL 23RD[44]

. . . —Sr. Addie alias Miss Lowe left this morning for Savannah via Charleston —She will present herself to Bishop Verot, who is you know Superior of the Srs of Mercy St. Augustine, & perhaps stay awhile at the Sisters of Mercy in Sav [Savannah]—. I gave her $50^{00} & wrote two notes which she may use either to get pupils in drawing, or help to get her into some House of Mercy—I was thankful when Our Lord sent away Mrs Farley & Miss Glenn because of their unsuitableness, but now, I thank for more than that—they are good, & I have no doubt always will be so.

Poor Sister DeNeri[45] had an awful paroxysm on yesterday morning, & we thought she could not live an hour, but she was able to receive Viaticum this morning, & still lives— . . . I am so laconic this morning for I am much fatigued & did not take off my clothes all night— . . .

❧

Baptista Lynch, Ursuline Convent, Columbia, S.C., to
Patrick Lynch, May 1st[46]

I was very much gratified on receiving your letter, for your silence had begun to create some uneasiness—& you would scarcely believe how lonesome & sad I sometimes feel since poor Sr De Neri's death R.I.P. But I also feel very happy, knowing she must be so—& grateful to Almighty [God] for permitting me to be instrumental to that happiness & His glory—.

Today I received a letter from Bishop Verot making inquiries about Miss Lowe, to whom the Sisters had shown hospitality, which I tried to answer truthfully & kindly—. He at the same time proposed a lady to us—"Madam de Bertheville, who has been with the Ladies of the Sacred Heart in France & also in St. Augustine. She is gifted with high talents in language, sciences, music &c &c, but her imagination towers above all her accomplishments" He adds—"Perhaps you could manage her more successfully than others. She could at once teach a graduating class in Latin Geometry Botany & Philosophy—& she is very pious (in her way)"

I like Bp Verots letter very much & am disposed to give the lady a trial, unless you disapprove. We need & we shall need good teachers—She is French. I am partial to them when they are good—She is not a convert I presume as Sr Addie was—&—but Sr Ursula laughs at my readiness to receive her after Miss Lowe.

What do you say? I wrote to the Bp that we felt timid about receiving her, as experience had taught that the scourges of communities are precisely those persons of fine talents & fertile imaginations, however our desire to have efficient teachers caused me not to refuse her, but ask her to wait until I could get your advice & permission to act. In the meantime we would, by prayer, ask our Blessed Mother to direct us what is for the best. Talents, I said, were very desirable in our order, but a *good spirit much more so.*

Have you seen Miss Jones? Sr Etienne (Miss Vassas)[47] received a very pleasing reply to her letter & will write again. She hopes you will tell her about the wonderful conversion of her father since her entrance into Religion & his even becoming a religious—.

I would not be at all surprised to see that Mr Ambler Weed came to stay in your diocese from what I see in the letter.

He has left Bp McGill—has been sick—feels himself obliged to help to support his sister who has been deprived by the war of her income—but still continues his studies under Dr Teeling[48] & had acted with advice of Father Andrews—.[49]

Seeing that Sr Charles' sister[50] was in such circumstances with her little son to educate, I proposed that Sr C—would give her dower to her, we will not miss it (as mother says what we never had, we never lost) & it will be of much use to her—

Before the war it amounted to about three thousand dollars, but now it is only eighteen hundred. Moreover S^r C attaches so much importance to *mine*, & *thine* that it will be for the spiritual profit to have no dower, & perhaps for the peace of community too.

She is charmed with what she is pleased to term my generosity—& wrote immediately to that effect, saying how like the early Christians religious were ___. She thinks it will do so much good with her sister & brother who are not Catholics.

We trust it may—They have always been very genteel with us about money matters—

Of course I did not take all this on myself, but consulted Sr Ursula who agreed perfectly with me, & thought you would too—otherwise I would not have done so. Revd P O'Neil of the Neck—asked particularly after this lay sister postulant, that we have . I was obliged to give him a very poor acct of her we all think her— "demented!"

I wish you could get a good strong German lay-sister in Richmond. Father Meyers or Father Andrews might know somebody that would suit—. We hire a woman to wash every week—

We wrote today for Rice to Mr Huchet who offered to supply us & attend to our wants in that way. I ordered 3 tierce [barrels], one for us & two for your plantation—was that right or wrong? John was so fortunate as to get quantity of bacon at 37^{cts} which he bought for you & we will buy from the same lot to-morrow D.V.—We will also buy in a store of flour & sugar—our molasses is nearly out, but I think we will not get any more it is so high—

I am sorry now we did not take Mr Bollins' advice given some three months ago to lay in a supply of all sorts of provisions, however as yet, we have no reason to complain—.

Nannie Ferrall arrived today, under the protection of Mr P. Ferrall of Raleigh & seems delighted to get back—If the Porquegroms come we will have close to 40 boarders—

How much reason we have to be grateful. . . .

BAPTISTA LYNCH, URSULINE CONVENT, COLUMBIA, TO PATRICK LYNCH, 26 MAY[51]

Your long & exceedingly interesting letter was such a relief to us—! We had received your telegram, but calculated that you were on your way home, & feared some accident had befallen you. We had telegraphed to Richmond & to

Lynchburg—got an unsatisfactory answer from Richmond & none from Lynchburg. We had heard of your narrow escape with the sisters, but that was all—indeed we had almost concluded that you must have been overtaken by the Yankees.

I wish you would hurry home or I fear you shall be. The war news tonight is bad for us—but of course you know it. Our boarders are increasing, & but few of the old ones will go home this summer so that we shall want some efficient co-laborers, both in choir sisters department & lay sisters department. I have heard nothing from madam de Bertheville. I suppose she has seen Miss Lowe—but I am sure all is for the best You will probably see Miss Jones, & a woman in Richmond named Louisa whom Sister Etienne knows—.

Our pupils are deep in their annual Retreat these three Rogation Days[52] & will go to H. Communion on Ascension Day & Revd Mr McNeal is conducting it & they are in excellent dispositions.

Even Miss Seule Miss Davis & Miss Warren asked to go in it, & have done so.

Poor Sr Charles is terribly disappointed, & would I believe have preferred that Revd Mr McNeal had performed the ceremony, rather than wait—or in any way postpone the time of her profession—. All her family positively, politely, & proudly refuse to accept her dower—they compliment me highly on my generosity, which was nothing much after all—in them it might have been something, but in me it was nothing—

How much those good Srs of Mercy have done in VA! It was delightful to read of the number of confessions communions & confirmed. —

Baptista Lynch, Ursuline Convent, Columbia, to Patrick Lynch, May 27th[53]

. . . But the papers had nothing of your "hegira" in them that I saw. Among the many mysteries & inconveniences of . . . [your being in Virginia was,] John felt[,] that of having no one to call on for money to meet the plantation wants—who is your *factor* in Charleston? He said he should call on Francis, who I suppose owes you. I suppose however his business is a losing one just now, for the want of material.

We hope you will enjoy the fine climate & delightful waters of the white sulphur springs as long as you feel them beneficial, our only anxiety will be lest the enemy should take you prisoner. I heard a lady say yesterday that as she was coming to Columbia from Richmond, a gentleman in the car said, "you will be running from Columbia faster than you are running to it, in about a fortnight." I hope he is a false prophet—but I am glad that you are not in Charleston at the approach of the enemy—

The Sisters' orphans have not left yet, neither have the city orphans & many others—Mr Huchet is up preparing a house for his family—Mrs Daforte from the Neck is here & many others—A Mrs Keating with two other ladies from Petersburg called to see us.

The Misses Pizzini will be here this week—daughters of Andrew Pizzini. . . .[54]

🦎

JOHN LYNCH, COLUMBIA, S.C., TO PATRICK LYNCH, MAY 29TH[55]

. . . I was called on last night by a Mr T. A. Jackson, C.S. Navy & friend who are in the service of the Confederacy who wish to erect a powder mill on the side of the hill near the river, and want to get a lease during the continuance of the war of that portion marked on the sketch I sent you as no 1 & 2. They were very particular in stating it was for Government purposes solely and not for private enterprise. They were connected with the powder works in Petersburg, but had to abandon them, they have been working through NC & this state for a suitable place to erect a mill, where they could have water power, and they say this is the best place they have found. . . . I told them at first I did not know what disposition you intended making of it, and wished to put them off till you returned, but they appeared in such a hurry and wished even to telegraph you about it that I took the liberty of saying to them they might go ahead at the work, leaving whatever bargain was to be made to be settled by you on your return, as I knew you would assist in an enterprise of the kind as soon as any one. I learned from them that they made the powder that was used on the Merrimac, and that they are both Catholicks [sic], this of course was an inducement to me. Thirdly Mr Keitt has been anxious to see you for the last two weeks and this morning told me the reason (I suppose you are aware of the death of Wm. Keitt, childbed fever) since his death Mr. K. Is resolved to sell his place, it is now in market but he wished to see you first to give you the preference, if you wished it for a college, school or convent; I told him I thought you intended the plantation over the river for something of the kind, he then said if you had an idea of the kind, his place was the very one, and he would not sell until he heard from you, although he expected a man from the Low Country today, who expected to buy it. He says he wishes to make a donation, and will do it in the sale. he wants a school for his boys, therefore his anxiety, since, I have learned from Wm Bauskett, that he says he will sell to you as long as you wish to pay for it, also that his price is twelve thousand dollars.

If the Congress moves here I think you had better look out for another place for the Convent. I am trying to get a vacant *square* in the city for them. I have Col Bauskett & Mr Phillips on the track for it. I only wonder I never noticed it before so you see I am keeping both eyes open to business! for you & Ellen, but must say the plantation worries me to think of. It is a sinking fund, and always will be. I thought I had found a lead mine on it, but for fear it might prove more dead weight have touched it lightly. Practice is pretty fair, I get a little of the Charleston practice, enough that I should not complain. Eliza still up, but expects to be down any day, her health is not good, I recommend her to your prayers. . . .

ฉันเหนึ่

Baptista Lynch, Ursuline Convent, Columbia, S.C., to
Patrick Lynch, June 1st[56]

John has had quite an accident to befall him on Saturday afternoon. The kitchen chimney caught fire & set fire to the whole roof of his dwelling giving a great fright to us all, but fortunately every thing was saved, & the engines were so well worked that John says the water did more harm than the fire. The roof was entirely burned off the dwelling & the furniture injured in its hasty removal but they were most fortunate in not having it to occur in the night—at present they are at the house of some M^rs McDonald but will move down to the old convent until John can have his house repaired. He thinks his loss will be covered by the insurance, except that of his furniture.

Should the Orphans have to leave Charleston, John says there will be room for them too, as he will only occupy two or three rooms— . . .

How will you get back if Richmond is taken by the enemy? I would be sorry to hasten your return so long as you find the springs to serve you so much, but I am greatly afraid the R.R. may be taken before you get back.

. . . the Yankees . . . have passed Georgetown on their way up the river—precautions have been taken to prevent their reaching Cheraw which on account of the cotton & government stores there, is an object to them—.

They are also approaching Charleston slowly, I do hope you may not be in Charleston when they reach it. . . . The Va children will remain during vacation but the Georgians leave. At present we have thirty-six boarders & expect more. It is on account of this increase that I am so anxious to get Laysisters to do their work. If all fails, I told John I would have to call on you or himself for a woman, & you know I hate to have negroes in the yard—

Did you get John's letter about Mr Keitt's offer—M^rsBauskett came to see me about the same.—I am quite charmed with it & it is so strange that the getting of that place has been a sort of utopia for the future with me—If you will get Sr Charles's (Miss Vassas') dower from Mr Borden, we will be perfectly willing to invest it in that property—John's purchase of real estate seems to be a prudential mania at present—the refugees from the coast are investing their money in

Romanticized sketch of a Sister of Our Lady of Mercy ministering
on a battlefield in Virginia. This drawing originally appeared in a
local newspaper in observing the Golden anniversary of the Civil War.
Courtesy of the Roman Catholic Diocese of Charleston Archives.

that way, as the surest from confiscation or loss, would it not be well to accept
Mr K's offer—It will perhaps be long before we get such another.

It may after a while be considered a military necessity to take this house, &
we will be then doubly pleased to have a plan in reserve

Mr Bauskett told me that Mr Keitt thought there was land enough for two
seminaries for education—one convent & Acad and a Jesuits college for Boys
and that he would build some place near—send his girls to us, & boys to them

Apropos to the Jesuits, I entirely forgot when writing, to mention what is so
often on my mind *our Retreat* Will you write to the Jesuits of Mobile or shall I?
I would much prefer that you would, if you have no objections, & it is perfectly
convenient or perhaps you could get Revd Father Gache, who is now in the
Army in Va—to come, as he has a great ettrait for conducting retreats.[57]

I am told the Yankees have taken the Jesuits house or college in N.O for a
hospital.

So many strangers are constantly calling that I could repeat a great deal of news to you, but I cannot write it all—

Dr Marx[58] has just called, to beg us to give hospitality to Mademoiselle Le Pierre, his French teacher for a short time—I suppose we cannot well refuse the act of Charity, but I dislike it very much—however she is a perfect & a most exemplary Catholic—. He said "she is a systematically & well educated lady & her peculiar characteristic is a scrupulous fulfillment of duty & exactitude of conscience—" I told him such praise did honor alike to himself & to her. (This is the fourth time I have left this letter to go to the parlor)

Mrs. J. R. Dowell[59] who had visited us before, & is from Richmond Va called to say she had received a telegram from her husband, saying that Richmond would be safe by Thursday & she could return. God grant it may be so. But she says our army is dreadfully cut up. She had intended placing her daughter here, but now cannot.

The Misses Pizzini, daughters of Andrew Pizzini, are in Columbia & may come to board with us, though at present they are with Madam de Reguiere at the hotel—Bishop McGill asked us to take them for two months—M[rs] Blanchard has just returned—

We are making another flag!

... John expected his boys home, but now that his house has been burned, I suppose they will stay in Cheraw—Hugh is better, but declined the office of aid or adjutant. Francis & Family as usual—Poor Mary is cut off from us & Sr. Antonia is the same. Fiat voluntas Dei.

BAPTISTA LYNCH, URSULINE CONVENT, COLUMBIA, S.C., TO
PATRICK LYNCH, JUNE 4TH[60]

We are delighted to hear that your health is quite reinstated, & anxious as we are to see you, would much prefer that you would remain a week or two longer, especially as they are fighting below Charleston—Yesterday & today the booming of the cannon is heard in the City & I am told even shakes the houses. The Yankees are trying to take James Island from which they may shell the city without any exposure of their cowardly set.

I am so glad you are not there, I am a very strong secessionist, but only generous with *other peoples brothers.* ...

Have you given your answer about the erection of the government powder mills & about the purchase of M[r] Keitts place, both of which John is [inclined] to answer *positively* & is pressed to do so.

He says of course you will be glad to have the powder mills on your grounds —as for the purchase of M[r] Keitts, if the present mania of purchasing country places is political &c &c & as they say, you could not have a more desirable offer—I wish we could talk the pros & cons . . . Madame de Reguiere was here this morning & wished you would purchase it [Mr Keitts place] & rent it to her during this summer. She is a refugee whose husband is on Gen Magruder's staff—wishes a country residence near him.

We are all charmed at Stonewall Jackson's bravery, & hope that Maryland will as the song says "arise in majesty." I do hope the Washingtonians & Philadelphians may feel a little of what we have suffered from their aggression. Some suppose the attack below Charleston by Burnside, is not real, but only a feint to prevent our men from going to Richmond. Of course you know all about the battle there. Is not the country in an awful state? Mrs Blanchard, who I told you was *fit* to be a *generals* wife, has just returned from N. Orleans after hairbreadth escapes, having entered under an assumed name—her maiden name, secured her papers, saw that her daughter was safe &c & is now all anxiety to be with the general. ___

. . . I do wonder if the Yankees will be able to pass Marrs Bluff & reach Cheraw. I do pray for confusion to our enemies. I hope you will send the sisters & orphans up here before it is too late. I would be glad they were safe here—& John says the house is large enough for all.—

༄

BAPTISTA, COLUMBIA, SC. URSULINE CONVENT, TO PATRICK LYNCH, FEAST OF CORPUS CHRISTI [19 JUNE][61]

What in the world has become of you—Don't you intend to honor us with your *Lordship's* presence on Friday 27 inst—the day of our exhibition—? *We* expect you, the *pupils* expect & the *parents* who will be here expect you—!

. . . John & Eliza are quite in love with your house, & are comfortably located there until theirs shall be roofed & finished—I am very glad you think of bringing the Orphans and Sisters up to Columbia for safety. Will you not do so soon? . . .

I was told that Charleston never was in such imminent danger—Of course you have seen the newspaper accounts of the battles on James Island,[62] with our success but considerable loss of life. I wish the Sisters had a Hospital in Charleston[63] & the Clergy could go freely among the Soldiers—Poor fellows I pity & pray for them—We heard of the death of Mr Jones of Orangeburg, Brother to one of our Boarders—was shot on James' Island—only seventeen years of age, & had never made his first Communion.

The Sisters & children are preparing to keep my feast day 24th St. John Baptists' day with convivial celebration, but it is saddened to me, by the constant remembrance of poor Sr De Neri's active kindness last year—our circle seems less, though in reality it is not, for Ellen & Minnie[64] more than supply the place of herself & Miss Lowe. . . .

We have been very fortunate in hiring by the day a good washerwoman—a low country negro who is more satisfactory than the Charleston postulant or most low white persons—The latter [the postulant] is crazy we think & will have to leave—We have also been fortunate [in] provisions—even butter at a moderate price for these times—our great trouble now is coal or coke which [we] shall soon need— . . . I see that Edgefield Dist[rict] can furnish salt enough for the whole Confederacy . . .

As we have heard of no recent engagements in Western Va, I suppose the S[rs] have but few in their hospital—We pray they may convert them all, with God's grace— . . .

Did I tell you that Col Lucas Northrop deposited some valuable papers in our convent?

FRANCIS LYNCH, CHERAW, TO PATRICK LYNCH, 30 JUN[65]

. . . —On the anniversary of our marriage and about the same hour— Henrietta gave birth to a fine son—and now we are joyful. . . . The news from the great Battle near Richmond, is very cheering, and altogether, I begin to hope the clouds of War are being dispelled, and the glad tidings of peace will soon be proclaimed. Time will tell. . . .

1862 July–December

"What glorious news of late!"

From late June to August's end, the fortunes of war shifted dramatically for the Confederacy. The theater of war in the East moved from the outskirts of the Confederate capital to those of the Federal, from Union forces laying siege at the gates of Richmond to a Washington panic-stricken in its anticipation of an imminent rebel attack. In the West, at Shiloh, Union forces in April had paid an unprecedented toll in casualties to drive the Confederates out of Tennessee; three months later rebel armies were once more on the march northward. As summer approached its end, the Confederates launched two campaigns into the key border states of Maryland and Kentucky, following overwhelming victories at Manassas and Richmond, Kentucky, respectively. It seemed a miraculous floodtide that could penetrate deep into the North and produce the autumn peace that Patrick Lynch had predicted.

The expanding reach of the war into the perimeter of the Confederacy, from Louisiana to Virginia, made Columbia even more attractive as a safe place for parents to send their daughters from areas under enemy occupation or the threat of it. To complement word-of-mouth advertising, Baptista turned to the widespread distribution of circulars to promote the Ursuline Academy. The steady increase in enrollment at the school put more pressure on Baptista to expand the faculty, which meant securing choir sisters, either among students, current and alumnae, or outsiders expressing an interest in the religious life. The pressure could lead, on occasion, to some unseemly competition with other religious communities for a particularly promising prospect, a business to which Patrick Lynch was not above lending his formidable powers of persuasion. In one protracted effort to recruit a young woman from Richmond, Baptista was all too ready to regard the barriers the war had thrown up for Southern women to enter a Northern or even border religious community as a sign of God's will for an individual to join the Ursulines in Columbia. Closer to home, the war had not dissolved the perennial tensions between Catholics and Protestants. In

Augusta, Georgia, it manifested itself in the local priest's refusal to participate in the burial of a Confederate general who had converted to Catholicism but was being laid to rest in the plot of his Protestant family. Baptista herself, seeing Protestant relief efforts as merely a way for Protestants to use money as a form of power to assert their privileged status in Southern society, would have no part with supporting them. Instead she scrupulously channeled her fiscal charity to Catholic institutions and agencies.

Antonia, cut off from family and news of home in Baltimore, keenly felt the isolation. Like her Carmelite community, with its deep southern roots, Antonia was decidedly Southern in her sympathies but did not share the sectional nationalism of her siblings. Antonia could never say, with her Ursuline sister, "I am a strong secessionist." For Antonia there was still but one country, a sentiment she maintained even after Lee invaded Maryland, partly in the hope of touching off a popular movement for the Confederacy. Ironically, the Carmelites, lacking the regular income the Ursulines were enjoying from tuition and other fees, suffered more from the inflationary economy the war had brought, Patrick's frustrated attempts to help by mailing money notwithstanding.

In the late winter of 1862, when the fate of the Confederacy hung on the ability of its armies both east and west to turn back the Federal invaders, the Confederate Congress had passed a conscription law to provide the manpower that voluntary enlistments no longer could. Hugh Lynch, who had already resigned from the army because of his deteriorating health, now figured that his medical condition would not exempt him from the draft. Like his siblings, he turned to his brother Patrick, with an appeal that the latter use his influence to secure Hugh a position on General Beauregard's staff. Not only would the administrative work be less taxing, but having that experience on his war record would also strengthen his profile in the community, a big asset in the commercial world he hoped to be part of once peace returned. When the invitation subsequently came, he accepted despite his unimproved condition, but after a few days his worsening health forced his return home.

Francis realized extraordinary profits from the armies' persistent demand for shoes, despite an inflationary economy that made it difficult for him to fulfill his government contracts. In Columbia, John's practice improved, largely from the influx of refugees, but he still struggled to make ends meet; the refugees' need for housing provided an opportunity to supplement his income by taking in boarders.

ANTONIA LYNCH, [BALTIMORE], TO PATRICK LYNCH, 8TH JULY[1]

You must pray for us. Since January three of our number have died, and several others are in a very weak state, although not dangerous I think it must be partly from sympathy for the country. I am in better health than usual only suffering from weakness. We have had cold weather until the past week during which time it is very oppressive. . . .

BAPTISTA LYNCH, URSULINE CONVENT, COLUMBIA, S.C., TO
PATRICK LYNCH, JULY 11TH[2]

We have been expecting a letter from you ever since your return from Halifax [North Carolina] but are disappointed. We are all as well as usual—John & family with Anna the same, Hugh & Cornelia passed thro on their way [to] the Springs in N. Carolina.

John told me today that Mr Boatright says we can buy the $3000 mortgage, so he will meet him today to speak about it— . . .

What about our retreat & Revd Father Bixio?[3] The time is very near.

I have heard nothing of our Coal from Chattanooga, & wood sells here at seven & eight dollars a load—! Is there any hope of the ports being open, so that we can get Coal from England before winter—?

We have one of your negroes "*Isaac*" working here who is so good a gardener & industrious a fellow, that I would be glad to have him all the time about the yard. We could hire him by the year & he would give us a fine garden & keep every place in such good order, without requiring to be constantly looked after—We could save too, by buying a cow which he could attend to, for, our milk bill, is not less than $450 this year, & perhaps more—Sr. Josephine & I have not yet fully calculated our income & expenditures this year, but will try & let you know before you come.

Anna & Miss Mary Pizzini are making a sort of a retreat of three days but I have been called off so much today that I suppose they think themselves neglected, so, I will hurriedly say good-bye for a while.

BAPTISTA LYNCH, URSULINE CONVENT, COLUMBIA, S.C., TO
PATRICK LYNCH, JULY 11TH[4]

Our children, fifteen in number, are very cheerful & good, & those who have left write most satisfactorily & gratefully—.

Mrs Ferebee—wife of Col Ferebee N.C. or rather of Norfolk, called to see our academy, & see about placing her daughter here. Mrs Blanchard stayed at her house in Norfolk, & spoke of our Institute—It was for this lady (Protestant) that Miss Heartz wanted our circular—. I hope we may have a good school next year & be able to get *coal* & provisions.

Why does not McFarland hasten the R.R. & coal mine? I got Sarah Beard to write to M Fairbanks (her brother in law) & I wrote myself to get him to send me some Tenn[essee] coal from Chattanooga, but I'm afraid the enemy will prevent.

Wood is awfully high-priced—& it will break us to get it—

Mr. Boatwright would not sell us the bond—said he could have sold it often if he had wished. . . but did not—only $1,800 will be due in Aug—! How is that?

Anna & Hugh are both here and looking first rate.

I hope your Halifax[5] business is all satisfactory—N. Ferrall is the most annoying child in the house. I am told, & says she was told by her "cousin Pat" who visited this week, that the *"will"* said she must stay in the Convent until she was twenty-one, therefore she had plenty of time before her, for study & self-improvement. Is that stated in her father's will?

᪣

Baptista Lynch, Ursuline Convent, Columbia, S.C., to Patrick Lynch, July 22nd[6]

I have written you two letters to which I received no reply—& you know postage is *something* now—but as Rev A. McNeal is going down I will cheat *Uncle Sam* (?) & trouble you—And so you have bought Capt Keitts place, I suppose every body knows it by this time, for Miss Preston & her cousin Miss Carty called here yesterday & spoke of it. Some say it is for a Jesuits college & some say for us when you sell this place to all of which I listen, & feel glad in my heart that it should be for either—John told me that Mr Reilly, Cornelia's father, asked about the purchase of this house, saying that some man in Columbia, who had gone to California & made a fortune, wished to invest it in real estate & would purchase this property & let the occupants have the privilege of renting it as long as desirable—? I do not tell you this to induce you to sell it, for I have no desire that you should for some years, yet on the other hand I should be sorry you lost a good opportunity on our account, as it will constantly become less valuable I suppose—. We have the $3000 bond & debenture [voucher] which as you said gives us a mortgage of 7000 on the house, and we have in Bank free of claims on debt $4,719.65—and $1,800 in a cotton investment. In that I include Miss Vassas' dower $4,122.70 which you will perceive makes our clear profit of the year only about $2000—

Next year I fear will be worse unless we can get coal, for wood is selling at $7.00 a load—. I thank God that we are doing even as well as that, but that is slow payment for property.

BAPTISTA LYNCH, URSULINE CONVENT, COLUMBIA, S.C. JULY 28TH[7]

I send you these few hasty lines, to tell you that yesterday M[r] Polk[8] (uncle of Gov Lowe's[9] daughters whose business is in the office of the Provost marshal Richmond, Va.) called to see his nieces; in the course of conversation he spoke so highly of Revd Fath[er] Hubert, S.J[10] who is the chaplain of the regiment to which he belongs, that I asked where he now was, & he told me of the recent change in their movements—I explained my reasons for inquiring, as I thought, he not being a Catholic, might give a wrong interpretation to it.

So he very politely offered to be the bearer of a letter & see it delivered—I accepted the offer & wrote a few lines, which I hope will secure his services for our retreat & spare you that fatigue & trouble. I had just thought of your asking Bishop Verot to give it, since he likes giving retreats, but this is much better.

HENRIETTA LYNCH, CHERAW, TO PATRICK LYNCH, 15TH AUG[11]

The day before you left for N.C. Ma received a letter from you with a check she wrote back immediately to let you get it before you would leave. Do write & say if it got safe. How thankful we all feel for this addition to the first, cannot thank God sufficiently, or tell you how much we owe you. . . . How sad about poor Mr Reeves.[12] To think he was here singing this day week; as they say—his song had not died on our ear when we hear of his death which I am sure was connected with his travelling here & back in the insupportable heat. A concert was given here on the second night by which he made about 65$. He was rather dull on that night. He was invited here by the Williams to aid in a concert for the soldiers.

. . . I dreamed of you for two nights that you had deserted us. I was so very unhappy in my sleep. I wish this war would come to an end. . . . There is no news here, everything goes on the same from day to day. The people of Cheraw find fault with all the Charlestonians because they say they cannot find any thing to eat. . . .

Francis Lynch, Cheraw, to Patrick Lynch, 21 August[13]

While in Richmond I engaged to furnish to Gov^{mt}. at 4^{50}/100—I could not buy lea [yarn] at present rates & do so to advantage—At the time of my agreeing I thought the Commissary Dept wd sell me a large quantity of Hides—Since my return home I am advised the Ordnance Dept takes them all for the present. I think I may go on next week to Richmond—and *propose* to the *War Department* direct, that if the Gov^{mt} will deliver to me here a given quantity of hides at fair rates, I will obligate to furnish army shoes at the rate of 100 pr per day, in accordance with the quantity of hides furnished. In the present need for shoes, perhaps this might be done by that department. . . .

While speaking of hides, may I request you to see Capt Guerin and suggest that if he will have the butchers do their work for a given fair price, that I will be very glad to buy the Hides & tallow. And should my efforts fail to procure hides in Richmond, my necessities for them would induce me to employ Butchers and do the slaughtering on the same terms he is paying for it, or less.

Unless some arrangement can be effected so as to evade the speculators, prices of leather & shoes must be necessarily too high. I am paying 36 cents per lb for hides now and hardly dry at that. This state of things should be corrected.

With this I enclose you a hand bill as I have had disseminated showing on my part a willingness to furnish brogans at 1^{50} /100 per pr *in exchange* for hides at *nine cts pr lb* and tanned hide at comparative prices. I have sent one to Messrs Ingraham & Webb— . . . The upper yard is now yielding me leather, tanned in less than 40 days—and If I can keep both my yards at full work—altogether will accomplish a good deal, notwithstanding the many little inconveniences.

Antonia Lynch, [Baltimore], to Patrick Lynch, 25th August[14]

I received your kind letter on last Saturday evening. It gave me much pleasure to hear from you all at home—although I know we are in the hands of a kind Providence,—still these times one is apt to have some fears, for those we feel interested in.

. . . I am sure could we in the Convent or your friends in Baltimore by our sympathy have lightened your burden this year past,—you would not have felt the weights of them long. I can easily imagine how you feel when looking on the ruins of the beautiful Cathedral. As it took place during the Octave of the Immaculate Conception (to which you are so devoted) I think our Blessed

Chapel, on Aisquith Street, Baltimore, contiguous to the Monastery of the Carmelite Community of which Catherine Antonia Lynch became Superior in 1863. Courtesy of the Archives of the Carmelite Monastery, Baltimore.

Lady will in that case bring good out of evil—although we cannot see it at present. I am happy to hear that our dear Parents are in good health. . . . I hope Hugh will not recover his strength until after the war is over. I am sure Cornelia is willing to nurse him.

. . . My dear Brother in regard to the interest you asked about,—we did not receive it. Rev Mother wishes me to write you, that unless you know it would *reach us safely* she thinks it would be better to wait until such times would come. We are much pressed but still it is useless for you to attempt to send what in all probability would never reach us. Every day we can thank our Lord for drawing us out of the busy world where there is so much sorrow, and since I trust in his mercy he will soon withdraw His scourge, I will be very glad when the times will so change that you can come on again to Baltimore. . . . I hope the Community in Columbia will continue to prosper. My only consolation during this trouble in the country is the hope that religion may prosper especially in the South. . . .

BAPTISTA LYNCH, URSULINE CONVENT, COLUMBIA, S.C., TO PATRICK LYNCH, AUG 29TH[15]

Mrs Aveilhé very kindly offers to be the bearer of my letter which I will take advantage of, to tell you all the news (Don't you admire this blockade paper? I have just laid in a supply & can give you some when you come up)

To begin with our school,—we cannot be sufficiently grateful, for the success which attended our religious instructions of last year, & the effects of it on our pupils, when at home—consequently we have a good many new applications from others for circulars, & seemingly, may expect a full school, though not at the opening—

We have also had more applications of day scholars, among whom are the daughters of Z.B. Baker of Charleston & of Mr. Bardell of the Bank, to whom you recommended our school. J. S. Ryan Broker, will send his daughter as a boarder. We expect two more from Richmond—one is Miss Dooley.[16] What do you think[?] Anna Davis has been baptized since her return home by Bishop McGill! Most of our old boarders write most gratefully & affectionately, & are anxious to return & those in the house are "as happy as larks."

So far for the Academy, now for the teachers, of which we want more. We are generally thank God very well & strengthened by our retreat to renew our labors A.M.D.G.

I wrote to Francis a few days since, requesting him to call on Revd Father Mulvey,[17] when on his way to Richmond, & let him know the time of his return & that he would take Miss Jones under his protection to Columbia—I told him he would oblige both you & myself, by so doing if not inconvenient—I hope my letter was in time. . . .

Today, Sr Charles got a letter from her brother who mentioned a "Miss Fannie Fennell" who is from Florida, & whose father is in the Navy department, saying, she is an earnest practical Catholic, & very anxious to know her vocation for the religious life. He seems very much taken with her.

I told Sr. C___ to write to her & invite her to spend a few days of retreat in our Convent. Have you any objection? . . .

We have just concluded our arrangements of Mistresses for the different classes, and hours. I do not know how we shall manage for books, although we did not allow any of our pupils to carry theirs away at the close of last session. If you could lend us a "Gazeteer"—"Encyclopedia" or any other reference books for teachers, we would be most grateful. "Fellers Dictionary" is another work I covet. We would be very much obliged also, if you could lend us some travels, such as "Laird Pattersons travels to the Holy Land" "Hue's Travels in India" "Taylor's voyage around the world" &c &c or others that you may have—this sort of reading is very necessary for days or hours of recreation, as well as during sewing classes on Saturday, when one reads aloud for all who are engaged in needle-work.

Are we not fortunate to be able to get as much coke as we want, & to expect a carload this week for which I have received a bill of lading. It will cost us about .48 or 50 cts per bushel I think & John tells me this evening that Mr. Glaze says he gets it cheaper than that, direct from Chattanooga & will let us have it at first cost here. Ought we not to be very grateful?

Sister informed me, much to my surprise that we have anthracite coal enough in our cellar, to do in our kitchen range for the whole year! We will use it for that alone, & use the coke for the grates. . . .

We were so sorry to hear from Capt Aveilhé,[18] of the painful duty you had to perform recently in attending that deserter. I hope he did not wish to throw his own opprobrium on the Catholic Church. Miss Preston told me that he belonged to her brother's company. She is reading Catholic Doctrine & borrowed my "Ursuline Manual." We have been working at our new edition & I am getting very anxious to see it out—especially as there is such a call for prayer-books here both among our pupils & the families of refugees many of whom have given theirs away to the soldiers. Will you not write an approbatory page in front? . . . We have undertaken the instruction of your man "Isaac" who is very apt & anxious to learn our religion he says. When Mr Quigley[19] had the negroes all together he used to do a great deal of good with them but, since then they have forgotten a great deal. Isaac has four children & wishes they were here that they too might learn religion. Shall I consider that we hire him at $10 per month, that is what John gets for Nelson from Col Duncan. Unless I can get a washerwoman in town, I will ask you to let me have a woman from the plantation for two or three days in the week, unless inconvenient. I was glad to hear today that a Boy's School would be opened this week for the children of the congregation—to be taught by Revd Mr. McNeal. I hope it will be the means of keeping them off the streets & preparing them for all the sacraments.

HUGH LYNCH, CHERAW, SC, TO PATRICK LYNCH, 8TH SEP[20]

On a running visit to your city on Saturday last I called to see you but as you had gone down towards the Bay failed to do so and as I had only come down on the morning train to attend some business and wanted to come out on the one o'clock train I had not much time to spare. Dear Brother by my recent trip into the country I find my health greatly restored and I expect (being within the conscript age) will have to go into service again this winter. . . . I have determined to ask your advice in the following case and also to ask your aid if you approve of the same. Genl Beauregard will be in your city shortly and will want aid in many or some of his staff departments and I think by getting you to apply to him for me that I may possibly get an appointment. I am confident that many will urge their claims to get their sons or relatives into some of the vacancies but perhaps if you will try early you may get me a shewing. My claims can be urged very well as: my rank at present is 1st Lieut and had to resign on account of bad health. 2nd I can bring testimonials from Col Graham, Col. Dargans & Major McIver all of 21st Regt as to my competency as an officer. 3rd I am "counted" a good accountant and write a tolerable fair hand and 4th[ly] it is due to this section of the state and especially to the command at Charleston that there should be some appointment from this section of the state as the 21st Regt the 20th Regt Smiths Battalion and several other companies also the 4th Squadron of Cavalry are all from this portion of the state and in courtesy to them the Genl commanding should make some of his appointments from the section that these commands are from.

. . . All are quite well at home. Br. Francis has taken a trip to Richmond—

BAPTISTA LYNCH, URSULINE CONVENT, COLUMBIA, SC, TO PATRICK LYNCH, SEPT 10TH[21]

I was quite surprised to hear that you were in Savannah & hope you made a pleasant visit. Aggie Dillon made us laugh about *your Monitoring* Revd Father O Neill[22] Ser. We hope he & Revd Father Whelan[23] are both quite well—I was very glad to learn that Bishop Verot had escaped detention in St Augustine. Have you met Madame de Bertheville? The lady of sublime imagination! How did poor Sister Addie meet you—? I am expecting Miss Jones to arrive with Francis this afternoon, she wrote me a very interesting letter which I answered & hope she will come soon as our music pupils are numerous—. We have about twenty eight boarders & I suppose about the same number of day scholars—more than we have ever had at so early a session before in Columbia.

We also expect the return of several old pupils next week. The Va children will wait until about the 1st of Oct. I am sorry to say that we have been deprived of the Holy Sacrifice of Mass frequently of late. It seems that Rev. Mr. O'Connell has more to do on the mission, than he can accomplish, & leaves Revd McNeal to do his duty at the church, & since he will not allow the congregation of the Parish church to attend Mass in our chapel, our chaplain (quasi) comes & gives us holy communion, & goes off to the church to celebrate mass for a half dozen or less. The refugees from Charleston do not seem to take to "the O'Connells" as they call them, & if ever you wished for a favorable moment to break up this nest of _____ now seems to be your time— . . . I sometimes pity them for the disrespect they meet with from the refugees, but it is just according to our maxim in religion, "an obedient humble religious ensures respect without seeking it" & those who are the opposite, our Lord punishes, as they treat others. I received a letter from Mother Theresa saying she would take the $300 that I had offered her as settlement of that affair about the furniture—I was surprised to hear from Capt. Aveilhé that the Sisters had a good sum of money in the Savings Bank—I was very glad to hear it—but at the same time, I thought it was not so necessary that such a poor mouth should be made & a subscription made from house to house in Columbia for them— . . .

Am I not in an irritable mood—I have a very bad cold but I ought not to be governed by indisposition—We are receiving our car load of coke—are we not fortunate—? 237 bushels! . . .

I had a letter from Anna today where all were quite well at home. Hugh had returned from Charleston without seeing you—& said Yellow fever is there, is it? I sincerely trust not for the sake of the army—what glorious news of late! . . .

[PS] We have plenty of money now if you would like to have some [you] are most welcome.

໑ঙ

Baptista Lynch, Ursuline Convent, Columbia, S.C., to Patrick Lynch, Sept 14th[24]

We have reason to be very grateful that our academy is prospering—we have now thirty-one boarders, & the best day school we have ever had in Columbia. We also expect several more boarders and have applications frequently from Catholic & Protestant.

I was quite disappointed the other day, when Francis arrived without Miss Jones, & with Miss Pizzini, for I had set my heart on getting some one to teach my music pupils & leave me free for other duties. However, I received a letter last night from Miss Jones, who had not received my letter dated the 5th until after Francis reached Columbia. She seemed delighted with me! And said were she her own director, it would not require pen & ink to express her many & sincere thanks for my kind . . . letter. She also begged me when I wrote, to present her most kindly & gratefully to you & said she would let us know a day beforehand, when she would be in Columbia, which she hopes would be soon.

Francis is here still having been too late for the cars yesterday, he looks exceedingly well & like myself is increasing in flesh. He is learning to take things easy John says, since he is a rich man. We have deposited $800 this week in the "Palmetto Savings Institute" Capt Aveilhé advising us—

Mr Huchet is up in Columbia & again sick, poor man. I am afraid he is not long for this world, though his family seem to apprehend no danger—

. . . Mr. Bollin has placed Celia to board with us again, at the suggestion of his sister—he & a great many others wish you would establish the Jesuits at Capt Keitt's place. John, who has been attending . . . out at Mad[am] Togno's, says he sees the inconveniences under which we would labor, situated as they are—But you know he was always averse to our being out of town . . . & very naturally—on the other hand, it would be our duty to go to a more retired & appropriate place for a female academy, as soon as Providence may give us means, for our surroundings are often inconvenient, & were our pupils numerous, might be more than that. So far, our children are too good, & have too much self respect to countenance any liberty taken with them, but even I have had the light reflected from a mirror into my room recently, which of course it was my policy not to see or feel ___. I think I told you in my last letter that we have anthracite coal enough to last us for our Kitchen range for the winter. I have never seen coke before, & hope this may give us warm fires. As yet we have not opened the last bag of coffee we got, but use half rice & half coffee, which is very nice—we have a barrel & a half of sugar & about six barrels of flour. Will have to supply ourselves with every thing in November. I do hope our late prosperity in war may continue & our ports soon may be open. Do you expect the Yankees to attack Charleston this winter? I do hope they may be put to confusion & peace soon restored. We received long letters from Sister Mary yesterday—all were quite well in Texas & she sent her love to you. . . .

[PS] I hope Sister Antonia is quite safe in Baltimore. How I would enjoy seeing Mr. E[dward]. Purcell when Cin was demanded![25]

HUGH LYNCH, CHERAW S.C., TO PATRICK LYNCH, 16TH SEPT[26]

. . . The cause of my writing you about the position I was wishing to try and get in the recent orders of Genl Cooper[27] calling for the exempt all to be enrolled and those that were not strong enough to go into the field to be placed in Hospitals, commissary departments or quartermaster departments as adjutants and by so doing relieve the able bodied men therein and let them take the field. Although I might be able to keep out, if I could get a position of Genl. B it would be something of credit in after life. And there is not much exposure attending it. If after trying it I found that it did not agree with me I could easily resign and still have due credit of having had the Position. . . .

᭑

JOHN LYNCH, COLUMBIA, S.C., TO PATRICK LYNCH, SEPT 17[28]

Your man I suppose told you all about Keitts place; on his suggestion I have bought you some cows with heifer calves. I have five costing three hundred dollars—this has run me out of funds. I will also want to buy you some sows, so that you may commence raising stock at once, if you can get a good man for Lexington by next year, I expect you had better engage him in time, perhaps you may find one that can do something there, as soon as Keitt settles, you had better let him take the negroes home, and stop that much of the expense. I do not know what we will do for clothing, none to be had here now. The war tax will have to be paid during next month. . . .

᭑

JOHN LYNCH, COLUMBIA, S.C., TO PATRICK LYNCH, SEPT 26TH[29]

. . . You said nothing about keeping Mr Buff, he has said nothing to me as yet, but would like to be able to answer him, if he should.

Practice has been tolerably brisk since I have seen you. I think I have as much if not more to do now than either of the other physicians in the place. If it could always remain just as it is I would be satisfied (I think). Cases all progressing finely—new ones coming in. Every one satisfied now, how it will be when the bills come in can't say. I have not a single case that is not able to pay. The family all well & join in affectionate love to yourself & Louisa, who I learn is going to Virginia. . . .

[P.S.] Will you travel this road, or by Wilmington, where the Yellow fever is prevailing. . . .

᭑

BAPTISTA LYNCH, URSULINE CONVENT, COLUMBIA S.C., TO PATRICK LYNCH, FEAST OF ST. FRANCIS BORGIA [OCTOBER 10][30]

I wrote to you very recently, but as I hear that Revd Father Lawrence[31] is in town & to remain some weeks, during which time you are to remain at the Hospital,[32] I concluded to write & tell you how we are getting on—our Academy gets on first rate, T.G. Our pupils in general enjoy good health. Poor Mary Frederick was obliged to return home however, after only one month's stay with us—she left very reluctantly poor child & with the fear that she should never see us again. She coughs dreadfully. We have thirty-nine boarders & expect a few more. The Misses Crenshaw of Richmond were to have followed Sr. Etienne (Miss Vassas) but yesterday she received a letter from one of them, saying please to inform her if it were true, that the convent was an old tavern or hospital, very dirty, & situated in the center of the city, instead of being a large cleanly & commodious house situated in the country, or where they would have healthy country air? So, I suppose they will not come. If they do[,] well & good, if not—the same. In all things "fiat voluntas Dei." John had told me about a week ago that we ought to get Mr. Tierney to draw the plans of a Convent now, when he had nothing to do, so when you come back, I think I'll ask you to ask him to do so, that when the war ceases & we get able we may be ready to begin, if such objections are raised—may they never have a worse home than this to live in. _____.

I suppose you have heard of the death of the Genl Smith[33] whom you attended, he was interred in Augusta, where his family (all Presbyterians & Baptists) reside—at his own request he was buried without military honors.

The service was read over him in the Catholic Church, & then a Protestant minister officiated at the grave to which the Priest did not go! Mrs Gov Lowe is greatly disappointed & surprised at the coldness of the Georgia Catholics—which she attributed to the absence of Religious orders—she says "would that the Jesuits were established through this country & how differently w[oul]d things be _____.

. . . There is great sympathy here for the sufferers of Wilmington N.C. The Protestants of course held a meeting to see . . . what good they could do, so they determined to make a collection & I determined not to put into their hands & those of their nurses my subscription, so I enclosed $10 to the S^{rs} of Mercy, & when they called, I very politely sent word I had already sent aid to the S^{rs} of Mercy there—The same was done for the soldiers in Va & sent $10 to Revd Father Hubert. Money is power in the world, & Protestants have too much of that any way. You will be glad to hear that we placed $600—six hundred dollars in the Savings Bank last week.

John has been very busy, but is not very well, he complains a good deal of his chest pains between his shoulders. This morning he seemed to feel threatened with pneumonia, but I hope it is only cold which will pass off. The weather is very chilly & damp; I scarcely think of what I feel it to be, but think of our poor soldiers who are so destitute & suffering in Va, where the frost I suppose is common—here we have had until today, very warm weather, there, I suppose you find it bracingly cold. I hope you are well provided with necessary clothing & were able to get that shawl . . . before you left.

You gave John no instructions about the Keitt place, hands, &c and I think he has been a little bothered in consequence. Your boy from Charleston has not made his appearance, & John did not know who to write to concerning him, at last hearing from home, that, Hugh was in Charleston where you had procured him the honorable post of Aid to Beauregard, he wrote to Hugh about your boy, & learned that he had been started up here a week ago. Whether he has gone to the Yankees or to Lancaster is the question.

Murphy, finding himself, as he said forgotten, without helpers talked about returning to the city. John sent to Mr Buff for a couple of hands, he said this was his busiest time, that if John said so he could send them but it would be greatly to his disadvantage—so John took only one hand from the plantation of Buff & sent Isaac from us, which I did not at all like, for we need him. John said nothing to me about it, but we found ourselves minus Isaac, & when I sent to John to ask for Anderson to cut some wood &c until Isaac's child whom he had been nursing out at the farm would get better, he told him Isaac was not there at all now, but out at the Keitt place where it was necessary two hands should assist Mr. Murphy, & that he saw Mr Buff could not well spare two ____.

John would have been better pleased had you written him word exactly what you wanted him to do, he does not like to act without your directions with Mr Buff & Mr Murphy. I understand that Revd Father L O'Connell is going to take up a collection for the Hospital while here. I hope he will soon go back again & leave you free to return—though perhaps it is just as well, if the Yankees are to attack Charleston that you were where you are if the climate is not too cold for you—I hope you took your flannels with you— . . .

Miss Jones would have come over with Anna Davis had she known when she was coming. I am sorry she did not (Our best prospect!!!)

HUGH LYNCH, CHERAW, TO PATRICK LYNCH, 14TH OCT[34]

I received your kind letter some two weeks ago and would have written you sooner but did not know you intended to remain so long in Va. I last week recd a note from Capt [*sic*] Beauregard telling me that the Adjt [Adjutant] Genl could give me a situation in his office and though I was not very well at the time concluded I would go down and make a beginning. On Monday last Genl Jordan[35] put me at work in his office but said that it was not necessary for me to be at it as he would not be exactly ready for me for some 6 or 8 days. But as there was a lot of copying to be done—put me at it—I remained in the office till Friday and finding I was not getting any better in fact was quite unwell for Thursday and Friday. On Saturday morning I asked Genl Jordan to let me come in the country for a few days which he readily granted so I came up home on the same day. I will remain here till Thursday and if strong enough will go down and try it again—as the weather has turned right cool—I think I can stand it much better than I could last week.

᳇

Baptista Lynch, Ursuline Convent, Columbia, S.C., to Patrick Lynch
Oct 23rd[36]

. . . We are very happy to hear of your good health, & that of the sisters whose labors are so arduous, & who must effect much good A.M.D.G. Revd Father Lawrence took up a subscription while here, & of course we were happy to contribute our share to so good a work, & gave to Eliza for him $10. & some old linen for lint &c. I suppose you will return soon, but I would much prefer that you were in safety where you are, than to be exposed in Charleston where they are expecting an attack from the enemy.

Mrs. Aveilhé & her daughter Mrs. OConnor were here yesterday & said that they had just received a letter from Augustus Aveilhé saying it was rumoured that in thirty-eight hours all the women & children should be ordered to leave Charleston. They had come up to the wedding of Miss Trumbo & Mr. O'Connor, which took place in the Church on the evening of St. Ursula's feast, both having approached the Holy Communion at Mass that morning. . . .

The rumor today is, that the Yankees are attacking Pocotaligo & RR. _____ I hope this very cold change of weather will put a stop to the yellow fever in Wilmington where I heard that Dr. Corcoran had it for the first time. I hope ere this he is quite well again.

John & family have moved back to their own house, where I am told every thing looks better than ever. The insurance company gave him $800 for damages by fire, which was very good, though he estimated his loss at $1200. We received specimens of sweet potatoes from your Malta farm & butter from your Keitt place, both of which were very good. John is highly pleased with Mr. Murphy.

You will be pleased to hear that we have now forty-one boarding pupils & more expected—we have recently from Va. Miss Harrison who is grandniece to Genl Lee & to President Harrison, whose nephew was her father. Next to her is Mary Hogan daughter of John Hogan the cow-driver of Charleston!!

I am thankful that we are all blessed with our usual health, for each sister's services are needed; as Sister Etienne says, if we had more to do, we should be teachers only, & not religious, since she hardly finds time to say her office &

prayers of Rule, not to speak of prayers &c of devotion—so it is with us all, excepting Sr. Ursula & myself who have to sacrifice often our duty for another of obligation making choice of that which will contribute most A.M.D.G.

You will be sorry to hear that Sr. Etienne received a letter from Miss Jones yesterday saying that the Superior & Mistress of Novices Mt. de Sales had both written saying she must not join any other community, but come to them by flag of truce— . . .

I had written her a very cordial letter a few days previous to this coming to hand & will leave all in the Hands of that good Providence who has so signally favored our little colony—. Miss Jones herself writes to Sr. Etienne that she would have answered her sooner, had she not been suffering from a violent attack of neuralgia, & did not the cherished hope of seeing Bishop Lynch, by whom she could send all the news of herself, cause her to defer doing so &c &c (She says) "One month since, I felt that very soon I should enjoy the full observance of holy rules & recreations at Columbia, yet Almighty God in His goodness & mercy sees fit to delay still longer the anticipated pleasure & further to prove my fidelity—When Bishop Lynch first asked me to consider the step of joining the Ursuline Convent (which was in Feb last) I assured him that such a thing was impossible, as I had been received at Mt DeSales & doubted the expediency of entering another Order without some little explanation or release— still he persisted, & fearing lest I might place some obstacle in that path marked out for me by Almighty God I yielded to his importunities & gladly accepted his kind solicitation—in the interval of a few months some friend has written to Mt. DeSales, informing the Nuns of my intention to join the convent at Columbia & forthwith comes a letter from Mother Regina of the Visitation, begging me not to think of such a thing, that the way would soon be opened, & if it was not, to attempt the truce Boat.

. . . Father Mulvey says I have not finished my contract with the cross &c &c."

Now I like Miss Jones letter very much, but I wrote again that since Abp of Baltimore, who is the Superior of the *Spr* of Mt de Sales, considered that circumstances prevented her entrance in their convent, they should consider it so too, & take it as the will of God. And as you are both her Bishop & our Superior your voice should be to us the will of God ___ . . . I think that like Sr. Carrie, she will be thankful that circumstances led her into our order, when once she knows its superior object.

If she admires the Jesuits, she must admire our beautiful & noble order for the Instruction of youth—the Constitutions of which were drawn up by the Fathers of the Society of Jesus, & are as much like their own, as was possible to conform a society of Ladies to that of Gentlemen.

Revd Father Hitzelberger when conducting our retreat was surprised to read even pages of our Constitution verbatim with that of the Jesuits—By the bye he is the first person who ever mentioned Miss Mary Jones to me, he received at that time a letter from her written while in Baltimore where she had gone to enter a Convent I think. He spoke to me of her at some length & then added: She ought to have come here—she certainly could not have known your convent? . . .

P.S. The yankees had torn up a portion of the RR near Pocotaligo but were driven back & our men mended it again—if reliable.

⤸

JOHN LYNCH, COLUMBIA, S.C., TO PATRICK LYNCH, NOV 20TH[37]

. . . Francis has just left. He has completed a contract with Mr Kerrisson Prest of Central Association for four thousand pr shoes to be delivered within 6 weeks, the association getting some seven or eight hands detailed which he named, furnishing him 16000 dry hides at Cheraw at 80 ¢#—and paying him $7.50 a pair for the balance. Francis is pleased with the arrangement, he also purchased a negro boy (Shoemaker) 16 years old for thirteen hundred dollars, and a lathe to turn lasts from Mr Glazer for two hundred dollars. All this kept him very busy—it is a great pleasure to me to see him getting on so well in the world, but it makes me scratch my head to see those around me coining money, when I am merely striving to get along. Eliza has taken two other boarders, who will be here this evening A Mr Middleton and wife, I know nothing of them further than, he has a plantation on the coast which is in the possession of the yankees, he is an elderly man a little deaf, and has a young wife, without family, they are Episcopalians, if they give no more trouble than the others we can get on very well, they pay also twelve dollars per week each.

⤸

HUGH LYNCH, CHERAW, TO PATRICK LYNCH, 24TH NOV[38]

I arrived home safe last week, and have been keeping pretty close ever since Dr. Kollack examined me and says by careful treatments and keeping warm he thinks I will get on very well—as he considers this the turning point with me. He thinks the cause of the hemorrhage has been in my system ever since my attack of last spring & says it is the best thing for me. I am now using Croton Oil Externally on my chest and taking Cod Liver Oil regularly during the day. . . . Bro Francis had to leave yesterday for Raleigh NC to see the Gov'nor[39] of the state as he has placed an embargo on any thing coming out of the State, and this stops his getting anything from his NC yard. I am at present attending to the yard for him but keep close by the fire or well wrapped up when I go out.

Baptista Lynch, Ursuline Convent Columbia, S.C., to
Patrick Lynch, Nov 25th[40]

... —I have been obliged to advertise in the papers for a washerwoman, the labor of 72 doz clothes per week being too heavy for our lay sisters, who are so cheerful & willing to do it all but I could not in conscience allow them. ...

Mary Burns has not made her appearance yet, neither have those two young ladies from Ala—Miss Bowman from Charleston entered since you were here making the forty-fourth boarder—

As you advised, I bought six bbls flour at $39.00 per bbl, & John is getting more for us. Mrs. James Rose (we are great friends!) has offered me a recipe for making soap out of rosin & lye which is very cheap. Mrs. DeLaigh of Augusta sent me a bag of large sweet potatoes—We are getting cow food from your plantations.

The bell rings –...

Baptista Lynch, Ursuline Convent, Columbia, S.C., to Patrick
Lynch, Dec 15th[41]

I hope you feel quite well now & that when you return I will not see you feeling your pulse— ...

We received yesterday little Julia Semmes who was brought by her uncle, Hon. Thos. J. Semmes,[42] the senator—he paid for the entire year $505.00 and asked if his niece Miss Payson had yet arrived? Saying that she would be soon if not—so we may expect more &c &c—Is it not strange that Mary Burns from Mobile [has not arrived]? Maybe she has stopped with the Srs of Mercy at Columbus as no doubt her escort, Rev Mr Hamilton of that place, brought her there to rest—I now write to ask your permission to receive among our Lay Srs the woman whom we have hired as a washwoman who seems a good creature & hard working? Her name is Catherine Lawler—has been a servant for five years in the family of Mrs Procter, an acquaintance of Sr. Theresa—has relatives up King Street who keep a fowl yard she says—knows Rev. P. O'Neill—She would like to enter soon, as she is out of a situation—Is it not strange that we have not heard from Mde de Bertheville? I saw in a letter to M Hinton that Miss Jones & Sister were at Goldsboro, N.C.

I received a long letter from Jane Semmes through her cousin Senator Semmes, who calls her "the little abbess"—She says that every day confirms her in her vocation to be an Ursuline Religious & begs our prayers that her mother may soon relent & allow her to join us. ...

❧

FRANCIS LYNCH, CHERAW, TO PATRICK LYNCH, 15 DEC[43]

I have made a further purchase of land, and the next consideration is the tilling of it. If the opptty [opportunity] offd me last spring of Mr Northrops hands should be repeated I could now take them myself, or some other batch of them—If however you would desire to sell me a portion of yours, I would be willing to purchase a few families—Still its desirable with me to move early as the matter for the time of hiring is the 1st of Jan[ry] and until determining I am rather at sea, as to the arrangements I sought to make in reference to planting —Business with me is rather crowded, but going on tolerably fairly. . . .

❧

FRANCIS LYNCH, CHERAW, TO PATRICK LYNCH, 16 DEC 1862[44]

I had the pleasure of writing you on yesterday. Today the bearer Mr Casey came from my upper yard and is on his way to Charleston, thinking to make avail of the protection of the British Consul—and asks of me a letter to you, that you may direct him to the proper office—hence my thus troubling you in the matter—Mr Casey seems to have no love for fighting, as a common labourer. I have no right to apply for his exemption nor do I believe it would be accorded him. He looks like too good a specimen of the material for a good soldier. . . .

1863 January–June

"Do you expect peace . . . as soon as everybody else?"

The "glorious news" about the triumphs of the Army of Northern Virginia that had so elated Baptista in early September 1862 gave way, just a week after she wrote, to chilling casualty lists of unprecedented length. Around Antietam Creek in western Maryland, the bloodiest day of the war produced a tactical victory for the Confederacy but a strategic defeat, as Robert E. Lee, with less than half the men George McClellan had in his Army of the Potomac, managed to hold his ground along the five-mile stretch of fighting, yet had no recourse in the aftermath but to order a retreat across the Potomac River to Virginia. Thus ended the Maryland Campaign, with its unrealized goals of giving another slave state the opportunity to join the Confederacy and producing a decisive victory on Northern soil that would stir the public to force the Lincoln administration to seek a peaceful settlement of the conflict. Three weeks later, on the hills outside the village of Perryville in Central Kentucky, the western Confederate thrust into the North stalled in a grim replication of the horrific fighting at Sharpsburg: a tactical victory for outnumbered Confederate forces but a subsequent retreat back into Tennessee that spelled their strategic defeat.

Despite these setbacks, peace sentiment remained strong in the South. In part, Southern optimism fed on the negative response in much of the North to Lincoln's bold measure, announced just days after the bloodbath at Antietam, that changed the nature of the war: the Emancipation Proclamation. The feeling that Northern public opinion was turning against the war and becoming an unstoppable force for a peaceful resolution was clearly strengthened in November by Republican losses in the off-year elections and the following month by the horrendous defeat the Federals suffered at Fredericksburg, the latest demoralizing failure to take Richmond. Add the persistent rumors of the impending intervention of the chief European powers to protect their economic interests, and it was little wonder that prospects for peace seemed far brighter for the South at the beginning of 1863 than they had a year earlier. And for most

Southerners, including the Lynches, peace meant independence, not reunion even of the most nominal kind.

By February the news had taken a turn for the worse in South Carolina. The threat of an imminent attack upon Charleston became constant; in late April threat became reality as the first bombs fell on the city. The British consulate pulled out of Columbia. The situation was dire enough for John Lynch to give his consent to his seventeen-year-old son, Conlaw, to join the army. Baptista found herself replacing her trust in political and military developments as a road to peace with a reliance on prayer alone.

Groping with the havoc that war plays with a society's economy required more than prayer, as Baptista struggled to find the safest investments for their modest financial assets. Another ill effect of the war, Baptista recognized, was its aggravation of the precarious existence of the slaves on her own family's plantations and beyond. At least this Lynch had conflicted feelings about slavery, which led her, in part, to appreciate the compulsion that drove abolitionists to shape the war's ends.

For all the evils it brought in its wake, the war itself continued to be the Ursuline academy's best recruiter, "blessings" Baptista was happy to exploit to the fullest extent regarding students and candidates for the religious order. The apocalyptic atmosphere of wartime, casting in bold shadows the utterly contingent nature of life, spurred vocations in women. Indeed, the Ursulines in Columbia experienced a glut of women seeking to enter. Baptista tried to keep a balance between exercising prudent judgment about the suitability and qualifications of candidates and the academy's need for faculty and staff to meet the swelling enrollment.

Perennial diseases take no sabbatical during wars: smallpox, yellow fever, measles, and malaria still showed themselves regularly, now on a greater scale than before the war, given the much greater concentration of people in armies and in cities overflowing with refugees. And then there were the chronic diseases such as tuberculosis (or consumption), which continued to claim victims among the Lynches, Hugh succumbing at age thirty in late March. John's chest ailment boded poorly for his future, one that was further jeopardized by overwork. And Anna, now the youngest and the last sibling at home, saw signs of advancing consumption in her own declining health. Prodded by her siblings, she reluctantly accepted the Mercy Sisters' invitation to spend the summer at Montgomery White Sulphur Springs.

꿿

Baptista Lynch, Ursuline Convent & Academy, Columbia, S.C., to Patrick Lynch, Jan 2nd[1]

We had a visit on the same evening you left from a Mrs Cohen, whose husband is a son of Mr Jacob Cohen & was educated with or rather by you—the purport of her visit I do not know, but she seemed *very* anxious to see you, & asked for your address which I gave her for her husband. He was taken prisoner, & recently has returned home on parole. I suspect he wants your interest in some affair of business.

Mrs Cohen is cousin to Mad^m Gertrude in the Ursuline Convent in N. Orleans, whom I know very well—was herself baptised a Catholic, but was withdrawn from the Convent by protestant relations before being confirmed, or making her first Communion—we hope to serve her—

I had a visit from Mr & M^rs O'Hara who were introduced by M^rs McCants—they will place M^r O'H's little daughter, about nine years of age to board with us—His first wife was Miss Antonia Alverez of St. Augustine, this his second, Miss Byrne formerly of Baltimore—more latterly of St. Augustine—the little girl has been at the school of the S^rs of Mercy there—I was much pleased with the Lady & recommended John to take her to board—Have you noticed our *triple advertisement*? I hope it may be to our advantage. M^r O'Hara says he thinks our school will stand a poor chance when peace is proclaimed & I am disposed to think so myself—However, we will be thankful for present blessings.

If you have not already written to Sister DeSales concerning that Hotel furniture, Sister tells me that we would do well to get fifty pair of sheet & one hundred pillow cases, if sold reasonably unless we have a speedy prospect of peace. . . . I see by the paper that some of Beauregard's family have arrived at Mobile so I presume we may soon expect Madame Hardee.

I almost dread her coming. . . .

꿿

Baptista Lynch, Ursuline Convent, Columbia, SC., to Patrick Lynch, Jan 13th[2]

I . . . ask you to say to M. Theresa—to whom we did the civil to our fullest extent—that she forgot her *watch*, which we *will send* to her by the first good opportunity—Please ask her also will she take as half orphans Sr Rose's three little Sisters, & at what charge—? I ask this, supposing Charleston will not be attacked—

We have now forty-seven boarders, having recd "Signoretta Montaneu & Miss Riddick within the last few days—

Do you not see by my writing how little command I have of my pen? The result of the conduct of our scourge or rather my scourge—(Sr [Augustine]__)

Did Mother Teresa tell you how much she enjoyed her visit to C[olumbia] & admired your property, the Keitt place—? Now that we have some more money in hand, I thought of you, especially as I have the $100. bill— ...

What do you think of Nannie Ferrall going home? Please answer this question when you write, & soon—My reason for asking is, that her conduct since spending out the Christmas vacation has merited expulsion—but she is doing better now, & promises fairly.

But as she has spoken very freely of her dissatisfaction, & desire to go home, Sr Ursula & I both thought it might be as well, for her to go at the close of this session—& give her bed & bedding to some of the new-comers who would pay better—be more satisfactory in conduct & profit more of the advantages offered—But we would be slow to act without your advice, & if it were better to keep her, of course we would do so very readily—Madame Hardee has not yet arrived— ...

❧

Henrietta Lynch, [Cheraw], to Patrick Lynch, Jan 14th[3]

I have been sick in bed and have no time to write more than a few words. It is reported up here that Mr. Posi is in prison and we fear she will hear it without our knowing what to tell her. Mrs. Walker of Charleston brought up the news. It is generally know[n] now but they say Garibaldi put him in.[4] Will you visit and tell us what to tell her. ...

❧

Baptista Lynch, Ursuline Convent, Columbia, S.C., to
Patrick Lynch, Jan 26th[5]

It would seem that by mutual consent we are silent, but I have heard that you were very busy, & we have been anxious & occupied about Minnie Ryan—daughter of J. S. Ryan of Charleston—who has had pneumonia so severe that we had fears that she could not recover. However John has given us another proof of his skill, & between his attentions & Sr Theresa's nursing, she is now D.G. Convalescent—I believe you know we have now 48 boarding pupils & yesterday Mr Hinton of Petersburg came to see his daughter, & mentioned to me that Maj Payne, brother-in-law to Senator Semmes[6] had sent to George-town for his daughter, that he might place her here with her little cousin Julia Semmes—The Yankees refused to let her come but he will apply again— ...

Do you expect peace & open ports as soon as every body else? The visitors of our Pupils—Gov Lowe—Mr. Carroll & Dr. Semmes[7] together with Mr. Hinton speak as if our prospects were very bright—I do hope Charleston may never be attacked—Have the Srs chosen any other place of resort, as I think they would prefer not coming to Columbia. Mother Theresa has written to me in a most grateful style-I am very glad they came, since it will promote charity.

ↄ⊷

BAPTISTA LYNCH, URSULINE CONVENT, COLUMBIA S.C., TO PATRICK LYNCH, JAN 28TH[8]

... We are much obliged for your kind thoughtfulness concerning the piano, & if you could get us one such as you bought before or one of "Nunns & Clarks" make, I will suppose it would be . . . well. . . . Unless you learn of such . . . I would like to purchase Miss Fowler's Harp, if you have no objection, as we need one. . . . It is one of Erardo's best . . ..

When shall we have peace? Why is not this secret session to discuss the proposals of the West?![9] Is not Napoleon[10] mediating now? Or as soon as the South will accept his terms?! Am I not sanguine? Dr. Semmes said that the various "Banks, Pope, &c &c had been before the war, violent *Know-nothings*, as *was Lincoln*—such being the case I hope Providence will frustrate their designs, & never permit even a nominal union.[11] It may be that with states as with some people, quarrels but increase their friendship & union, but I could never understand that principle, therefore I am totally opposed to a reunion & hear no one speak of such an idea here. (What folly for a cloistered nun to offer an opinion on politics!). Mrs O'Hara is at John's, he mentioned that she arrived day before yesterday—Beauregard's protege [Madam Hardee]has not come yet—I hope we shall have peace before we have to lay in a supply of flour again—we are using now, what you sent us from Charleston & whoever sold you that, *cheated you awfully*—it is rye-flour & darker than any seconds we ever had—it is as dark brown as oat meal cakes—it was that, caused some of the trouble with the children but the molasses compensates for it if you bought it from the same person, for John opened a barrell the other day, which is beautiful syrup, such as we would prize in the best of times.

Daniel has returned from Lancaster with one man & woman & children (I think that is what John said). He says the Negroes up there are in a wretched condition & very anxious to come down here. John asked him if they got on worse there, than they did with Mr Buff—he said, oh yes, they (at the Wallace farm) were well off, compared with their fellow servants in Lancaster—that they were so destitute & neglected, that the overseer threatens to leave, unless some provision is made for them—This I represent as John told me, that you may judge as you think fit—Your only notion in buying these negroes was to secure to them religion, but under protestant overseers in the Country, they are as badly off as they could be if you sold them, & they must be a great deal of trouble & anxiety to you.

I pity the poor half-starved & half clothed creatures with no religion, no means of acquiring it, to sustain them—I know something of change of superiors, & therefore know how to compassionate them in their helpless condition—

I never have patience with the Yankees, except when I think of the abolition of slavery—(here I was happily interrupted by Johns ring). . . . —If Charleston is to be attacked, would it not be well to get a quantity of salt beforehand, as the works must then be destroyed? . . . We have a little snow this morning & it is very rainy, disagreeable weather—

. . . We had the children all vaccinated—the small-pox seems to be spreading over the whole country, but I trust we shall not get it in our large family—there is one case of malaria in town the papers say—John was most fortunate with his patients when it was here before, not losing a single one—He adopted Mother's treatment.

The bell has rung, so I must go to my music lesson—Mdm de Bertheville turns out to be a great musician & was organist & principal singer in the choir at Aix le Chapelle for several years—consequently, is perfectly familiar with all the church service music &c &c.

You ought to see some bigoted letters sent to Miss Harrison by her aunts & the way in which I returned them with a "billet doux" [love letter]: which will disturb their reposeful equilibrium for awhile I think. I was amused at myself & Sr Charles & Sr Etienne who know them very well, enjoyed my polite spicy note, & said they would give a good deal to see them when they open the letters returned—

Sr. Charles' brother Ambler [Weed] made her a present of $20 this week, they are a devoted family & remind me of my own— . . .

John Lynch, Columbia, S.C., to Patrick Lynch, Feby 2nd[12]

I find by the enclosed note from Mr. Buff, that the expenses at the Lexington farm is about commencing again in the old style. I am sorry for it, but of course it cannot now be helped. I suppose I must give Mr B. an order to buy corn, it is selling in the neighborhood of $1.80 or $2.00 pr bushel. Mr Murphy went to Lancaster and brought down one negro man two women & children. I learn that two of the children are sick & I have to go out and see them this evening. Mr M brings bad accounts from Lancaster, and Daniel who went with him says the negroes all want to come down here. Mr Murphy has a message for you from the overseer. I fear you will find the negroes a great annoyance and expense, if you can find the proper purchasers for them, you might sell them at a profit. I saw some sold here today at pretty good prices, but they were bought principally by speculators, this looks like they will be much higher as soon as the war ends. . . . I have been pretty busy for the last month, I find I cannot do as much work as I formerly could and am much more easily fatigued, still I manage to get on pretty well. We have not only Mr. & Mrs Middleton with us, but also Mrs O'Hara, but we keep your room always ready for you. . . .

BAPTISTA LYNCH, URSULINE CONVENT, COLUMBIA S.C., TO PATRICK LYNCH, FEB 5TH[13]

We have been thrown into some excitement by the intended departure of the British Consul, which looks very ominous & as if the war were coming home to us. Still we pray that our Blessed Mother may intercede on our behalf—& frustrate the designs of the enemy. What saint & Bishop was it that when called on in a time of war to curse the enemy refused to do so, but went up on an eminence, & lifted up his hands towards heaven & over towards the enemy, & prayed that our Lord would send such a quantity of gnats as would put them into confusion. When immediately his prayer was heard, & gnats filled the nostrils of horses & elephants to such a degree, that they became restive, throwing their riders & defeating the enemy! Can you not do something like that for Charleston?[14] What will become of the Sisters & orphans? Will they go to Sumter, Summerville or here? . . .

I begin to feel now that our payments for the new session are coming in, that we have too much money doing nothing, & it would be better to fund it in some way that you would advise. Shall we buy another mortgage on this house or buy Isaac(!) Or put it in the Savings Bank? Should this currency ever become worthless (which God forbid) would not all in Bank be useless to us, & as if we had none? If so, it would be better to purchase property. If you like we will buy a mortgage on the Keitt place—? Or whatever you advise. I have not seen John today—he suffers a good deal from his chest. . . .

ANNA LYNCH, CHERAW, TO PATRICK LYNCH, FEB 12TH[15]

Mr Laughlin, who has been fortunate enough to escape camp life by procuring work in the Arsenal, goes to Charleston this afternoon. Mother avails herself of the opportunity to send you a pair of socks she has just finished knitting together with the pair you left up here. I did not write myself but I suppose you heard through others of Father's sickness. Since you were up he contracted a severe cold which confined him to his room for several weeks. He is much better again, however, I am sure, a visit from you, could you make it convenient to come up would serve him very much & be a pleasure to us all. The changes of weather this winter, have been so frequent & severe, that we have had a good deal of sickness, & many deaths in consequence among old persons especially, so we consider Father very fortunate in getting over his attack so easily. Mother, & the rest of the family are quite well, except Bro Hugh who had a slight hemorrage again last week—we are looking for Brother John, over to pay us a visit soon. Mr Blain has been sick ever since he came up from camp, but is better, I believe. The others of the family are well. . . . I believe I am getting the mumps this morning. My throat & neck is swollen & painful and I have never had them. . . .

෨

BAPTISTA LYNCH, URSULINE CONVENT, COLUMBIA, S.C., TO
  PATRICK LYNCH, FEB 14TH[16]

I was so anxious to write to you last night & tell you we had fifty boarders! But today we have one less since M. DeLaigh left this morning for good. We expect however another in a few days. We received *the* Miss Robinson of Montgomery Ala this week, who comes to perfect herself in French & music—she also brought with her a Miss Martin from Tuscaloosa who wishes to pursue the same course of study.

Besides this, Miss Herndon a "bas bleux"[17] of Columbia takes private lessons in French & German preparatory to making a tour on the continent. Deo Gratias for all this temporal prosperity—may it all tend A.M.D.G.

Poor Mademoiselle Marnier has just interrupted me. She has lost her Mother & thinks of entering our Noviciate! . . .

Poor dear John looks so badly at times that my heart aches to see him so, but I would not like him to know it or think so, on the contrary, I seem cheerful & even unsympathising when he complains of his chest.

Mrs. O'Hara has given birth to a little daughter & is very well—her husband has gone for his little daughter to place her in our Academy.

Did you get my letter with all its questions, & about the disposal of our funds—I have placed in the "Saving Banks" with Mr. Aveilhé $1,608.69/100 this past week, & will receive more I suppose soon.—I have kept in my possession $100 bills, five in number, for you because you said they brought a premium in Charleston. When Isaac heard that you were coming, he asked us to ask you if his children might come from the Wallace place to the Keitts place, as it would be the same to you perhaps, & be for him much easier to go & see them on Sundays & he could return earlier on Mondays—Moreover he said he could then bring them in to receive such instructions as we gave him—that he taught them the best he knew how on Sunday, what he had learned during the week, but he could not teach them well.

. . . please write me our Lent regulations—although there is so much indisposition among the sisters & difficulty in accomplishing the necessary duties now, that I do not know how they will do on Lenten diet—especially as there is no such thing as fish to be had now.

Jane Semmes has not come yet, nor is her mother less opposed than before. Still Jennie wrote to Sr Ursula that she would leave home for our convent in a few days, so we are expecting her until we hear to the contrary. . . .

Hugh is suffering a good deal still. . . .

BAPTISTA LYNCH, URSULINE CONVENT S.C., TO PATRICK LYNCH, FEB 19TH[18]

I have just heard of the intended attack on Charleston, which is, they say, to be on Sunday 22nd inst—We are all anxiety, & especially about you, who will of course be exposed in aiding the wounded & dying—May our Blessed lady protect you. I need not assure you of the continued prayers & aspirations of our Sisters who love & respect you so much. May God preserve all our friends & put our enemies to confusion.

Where will the Sisters of Mercy go with their orphans? As they seem to prefer Sumter or some location nearer to Charleston than this, I will not expect them here but should they come, we will try & do for them, all that you would wish.

You will be glad to hear that we have received $3,500 more or less tuition money since the beginning of this session. Of course we have heavy expenses in buying provisions, which continue to rise, but we feel very grateful that we are doing as well as we are. I have ordered one dozen bed-stands, but we have not rooms in which we could put up more than six I think.—John told me this morning that Mr O'Hara arrived with his little daughter—our pupil.

What shocking conduct on the part of the people of St. Augustine, or rather the Yankees toward them—to turn out in the snow defenseless women, little children & even Mothers with young infants, exposing them alike to the inclemencies of the weather & the insults of the rabble![19] What mercy have Charlestonians to expect! I sent a letter a few days since to sister Antonia and I was glad to have a good opportunity for doing so. . . . If you should get even a scratch, you may expect to see me with John down beside you.

But of course I respect too much our rule of cloister to think of going without necessity & a sister or two accompanying me.—In this you must leave me free to act, with the advice of John though I sincerely trust Charleston will triumph & with safety to all, especially to all whom I value or esteem. We will pray particularly for Beauregard the head & leader, from whom so much is expected & upon whom so much depends. If he is a good Catholic our Blessed Mother will protect him—Mrs Hardee never came. Please write & telegraph me from time to time. . . . [P.S.] John has not heard this of Sunday being appointed as the day of attack on Charleston . . .

I forgot to tell you we have a new & singular application to enter our novicitate —a Miss Amelia Lancaster[20] who was educated at Georgetown—young—talented —rather fast—but now awakened to a sense of her duty. . . . I answered her kindly but cautiously.

ᗧ

BAPTISTA LYNCH, URSULINE CONVENT & ACADEMY COLUMBIA, S.C., TO PATRICK LYNCH, MARCH 6TH[21]

We were quite disappointed by your non-arrival on yesterday morning—it is the third time we have arranged our altars, made the parlor fires, & prepared breakfast for you, & been disappointed so we almost lost our patience. John says however that you are really so occupied as to deserve our compassion.—I am sorry those deserters claim your attention, excepting for their souls' sake— poor fellows—are they Irish Catholics? I've lost all sympathy for the soldier of late, since some of them have visited our convent & were such low vulgar fellows. I wished more than ever for our grating—which I suppose will become a necessity after the disbanding of the army— . . . And now, I write on important business to us & to which I will beg a reply by return mail if possible—as I have delayed for some time already in the hope of speaking with you. Three ladies have offered as choir postulants, to whom I am anxious to give immediate replies. One is "Miss Amelia Lancaster" of Washington city, where her father was chief clerk in the Fiscal Bureau, until he became a warm secessionist & left. She is now with him in Richmond—a penniless refugee—her Mother & eight younger children still residing in Washington. She was educated at Georgetown where she graduated with honor—was called there the "little Aloysius." . . .[22]

Since leaving Georgetown her course has been by no means pious—just the contrary, she abandoned her religion—read infidel works—was worldly in the extreme &c &c—and now has awakened to a sense of all this evil course & writes a passionate appeal for mercy & kindness and to be received into our noviciate. She is about 20 years of age. This is a bad case, but perhaps the best of the three. The second lady is as old as I am myself or older—is remarkably well informed—a good linguist, musician, &c &c has been brought up with great care & piously—was educated in a convent, & since has always been a very pious & regular communicant—she has no means & has supported herself by teaching. She had always thought herself an orphan until about 22 years of age, when her relations made known to her the sad truth that her mother still lived & was a woman of ill fame— . . .

Now for the third & worst case. . . . She is a Lady mingling with the first class of society—talented, accomplished &c &c about thirty-five years of age, fashionable. . . . —When she was a young girl . . . she fell in love with a wicked man with whom she had by stealth & from time to time criminal intercourse— . . . Afterward having repented she asked her confessor . . . if she could be a religious—he answered yes—

. . . According to our Constitutions illegitimate birth is an *impediment* to membership in our order—also having ever borne a bad reputation— . . . I must confess, much as I desire subjects, I do not feel attracted to either [*sic*] of them. I would to Miss Lancaster were she less passionate & romantic. . . .

᭼

BAPTISTA LYNCH, URSULINE CONVENT, TO PATRICK LYNCH, MARCH 7TH[23]

I am going to treat you to another sheet of my beautiful chirography & this blue lined paper. Mr Ambler Weed who is always so kindly interested for us, & posts us up about provisions &c wrote to Sister Charles last evening advising that you would write to Col^n Northrop & obtain permission to get flour for us from Richmond where it is selling at \$22^{oo} per barrel, while I paid today 60. He thinks in so good a cause the permission would be granted through your interest & Col Northrops—I like the idea very much—& have before tried to get Mr Bollin to get me some, but to no effect.

. . . —Mr Weed, although generally so sanguine about the war—seems to have some gloomy forebodings, & recommends our laying in a large supply of provisions—but does not wish his ideas made known.

Well, what do you think of the three candidates?

I almost feel like taking them all this morning, when Sr Etienne & Sr Charles were both worn down—If we had a room off from all communication with the Academy, where they could have real noviciate life & training, they might do very well—at least two of them. . . .

Excuse great haste—please let me know about the flour—every day the prices rise—

ᥫ

JOHN LYNCH, COLUMBIA, TO PATRICK LYNCH, MARCH 19TH[24]

I have concluded to let Conlaw go down to camp today, and as his horse goes by the freight train he will have to wait in the city a little while for his arrival[.] I have taken the liberty of sending him to your house to wait for him. I have no doubt Conlaw will get on very well in the position I have secured for him, he proved to me the other day that he had the requisite qualifications for a soldier viz coolness & judgment, in an emergency—a horse running away with a lady on his back passed him in the street, he called out to her to hold on firm and not be frightened, instead of running his horse after her, he went around a few squares and heard her horse, rode close enough and caught her bridle stopping both his own & her horse at once, enabling her to alight without further injury than a severe fright. After that I thought it wrong to keep him from camp as he seemed anxious to go down. I expect him to remain about Mt. Pleasant. I have therefore allowed him to take down a small trunk which he can with our permission leave at your house, and occasionally go over and get a change. . . . I am called off & have not time to write more and I fear will not be able to see Conlaw off, give him some good advice, and try and keep an eye over him. . . .

ᥫ

BAPTISTA LYNCH, URSULINE CONVENT, COLUMBIA S.C, TO PATRICK LYNCH,
    APRIL 9TH[25]

Yesterday afternoon Mr Frazier called with your *heavy box,* which he placed with all proper formality in my own hands, for safe keeping. I have put [it] in our cell[ar], & hope you will be able to call for it in all security soon—until which time I am very happy to take the best possible care of it.—If all the current reports are true, one would suppose that the iron-clads are far from proving either invulnerable or even very advantageous—or that our men & guns achieved wonders. We trust & pray that the enemy may be put to confusion, & that notwithstanding the clouds which now overhang us, we shall soon have peace granted[26]—This is my hope trusting in the powerful mediation of our Blessed Mother—I heard that Beauregard was at Mass on Easter Sunday— & that you officiated in St. Joseph's Church— . . . —Our Holy Week services offices—Mandatum—repository &c &c all went off in the usual manner & very satisfactory. Many even Protestants visited our Chapel on Holy Thursday & Good Friday, & admired very much the tasteful & beautiful decorations. I think it will do as much good as the Convent did in Charleston. . . .

... I have not heard from Miss Lancaster since—Mr A Weed says that Bp McGill thinks we might as well give her a trial—it seems her family is remarkable for giving to the Church Priests & nuns. I suppose Rev. Mr. Lancaster of Kentucky, who was in the Propaganda with you, is a relative of hers. Miss Marnier wrote a few days since, & still entertains the idea of joining us.

FRANCIS LYNCH, CHERAW, TO PATRICK LYNCH, 9 APR[27]

The accounts this morning from the city are cheering. Mr Ingraham writes me one of the Iron Clads is reported sunk—Do if you can request my friend Prof Hume, test the turning properties of Pyroligneous acid, my test of it is quite favorable, but it would require a heavy out lay in the preparation. I would like much his opinion of it. Mr Trott Druggist on King & Broad Sts. had of the acid, I am told. . . .

BAPTISTA LYNCH, URSULINE CONVENT COLUMBIA, S. CAROLINA, TO PATRICK LYNCH, MAY 19TH[28]

Bishop McGill has just left this morning after spending Sunday & Monday here. Of course we did the civil, & I think pleased him & his Richmond friends here—Yesterday afternoon he saw the children (you know he has great talent for small talk & pleasing ladies) & he did remind me so much of poor Bishop Reynolds.

We were much obliged to him for saying Mass & giving us Benediction & a delightful sermon on Sunday—we also admired his simplicity & humility—

... —On the whole he was I think quite pleased with this visit to Columbia & seemed to enjoy better health & spirits than when here before—We interested him in poor Miss Lancaster, hoping he could do her some good—& he spoke in the highest terms of Miss Fenwick, who will I hope come on with you—You have no idea how anxious I am feeling about you, as you have not written me a line since your departure & I have written to you such long letters, which I hope you will destroy—.

... —I do hope your trip to the mountains may be both agreeable & beneficial do not forget that our Distribution will take place June 24 Feast of our Patronal saint, DV, & allow for delays on your return—remember last year that the room was crowded & waiting, before the Cars arrived, so you had better come this time the day before, & meet Bp of Mobile[29] at John's beforehand— . . .

❧

ANNA LYNCH, CHERAW, TO PATRICK LYNCH, MAY 29TH[30]

I received your kind letter with Sister DeSales' about a week since, and would have replied earlier, but had not made up my mind about going. I feel so averse to leaving Father & Mother, so much alone, & at this time particularly, when duty, as well as inclination, almost requires me to stay with them, but as they, with the rest of the family agree with you, in advising the change, I have concluded to accept Sister De Sales' kind invitation and if nothing happens to prevent, will go on with Mother Teresa, who telegraphed me this morning, that she would leave on Tuesday next.

I have not been quite so well or strong this spring as usual, but my health is very good. I hope I will derive all of the benefit from the change I expect, and that nothing will happen at home, while I am away.

I am much obliged to you my dear brother, for your kind offer in my regard but I expect what money Brother Francis generously furnishes, will be quite enough to defray my expenses. . . .

1863 July–September

"We are storming heaven for Charleston now."

Once campaigning resumed in the Virginia theater in May, the skies brightened for the Confederacy as Robert E. Lee, in a brilliantly orchestrated flanking maneuver, deployed a critical mass of his army, outnumbered by more than two to one, to rout the right wing of the Army of the Potomac in the thickly wooded terrain west of Fredericksburg. The reunited corps of the Army of Northern Virginia then pressed an offensive over several days that forced the Federal troops to retreat across the Rappahannock. It marked the latest disaster of the war in the East for the Union, and morale in the North plummeted. Meanwhile Southern hopes for an early peace soared, particularly when news broke in early June that General Lee, for a second time within the year, was heading north. This time the Army of Northern Virginia's target was not a border state but the heart of the Union: Pennsylvania, the second most important state of the North.

The eyes and minds of the Lynches were not on Pennsylvania, however, but on Charleston, whose outer lines of defense—Fort Sumter and Fort Wagner (on Morris Island)—had been under assault since April. On July 10 a Union force landed on Morris Island and occupied most of the three-mile barrier south of Wagner. Two attempts a week apart to storm the fort in mid-July failed with decimating casualties (the 54th Massachusetts suffering the worst of them). Five weeks later, on August 22, in a morally challenged retaliation for General P. G. T. Beauregard's refusal to surrender Charleston, Union guns on Morris Island began their bombardment of the city itself. Charleston thus became the first major city in the Confederacy to experience a direct bombardment, with the Federals employing guns twice as large as those used in previous sieges. Over the next eighteen months, the on-again-off-again rain of shells and mortars left the lower city a wasteland of battered and burnt-out structures.

Amid the shifting fortunes of war, the sudden death in July of the archbishop of Baltimore, Francis Kenrick, presented a challenge in observing the normal process for selecting a successor for the premier see of the Roman Catholic

Church in America. When Civil War had come, neither Rome nor the Ameri-can bishops as a body made any attempt to reorganize the dioceses or religious communities to reflect the new political divisions. The basic structure of the Catholic Church in the United States was the province, consisting of an arch-diocese (the metropolitan see) with several suffragan dioceses. The Baltimore Province, for instance, comprised Baltimore, Charleston, Erie, Philadelphia, Pittsburgh, Richmond, Savannah, and Wheeling. Beginning in 1861, three of the eight were squarely in the Confederacy; a fourth, Wheeling, was in a contested area, a breakaway from Virginia. How to involve the prelates of both sections in the selection process? The answer: As best as one could, despite the isolating and disrupting tendencies of war, by maintaining the status quo that recognized but one Catholic community in two de facto nations. The Holy See, in so doing, was implicitly agreeing with the Lincoln administration that there were not now two sovereign nations but rather a portion of the states in rebel-lion against the duly constituted U.S. government. Despite this implication, Lynch had no illusions that Rome would appoint a Southerner to head up the premier see. Many might have found him the ideal candidate to succeed Kenrick; Lynch knew better.

The disheartening outcomes at Gettysburg and Vicksburg in high summer sapped Southern confidence in the Confederacy's ability to sustain its revolt. Even a sure-footed optimist such as Patrick Lynch found himself shaken at the turn of events. The home front increasingly felt the war's impact. The South's ever-rising casualty toll forced it to increase the pool of the draft-eligible by extending the age limit and eliminating exemptions. The widened draft brought the first Lynch of the third generation, Conlaw, John's second oldest son at seventeen, into the Confederate army. Even his uncle Francis had to plead the importance of his shoe business to the war economy to retain his civilian status. As the mili-tary situation grew more critical, the Confederate government asserted itself more and more into everyday life: impressment of slaves, property, and crops to meet war's needs; an income tax; government-issued passes to control civilian traffic. Worsening military prospects spelled disaster for Confederate currency and bonds. The Lynches scrambled, like other entrepreneurs in the region, to find the most secure form of investment—property, cotton, other staples—to protect assets. Cotton shipped to Nassau, a plantation acquired outside of Columbia: all became means of coping with a fluid economy marked by runaway inflation.

For Baptista the war continued to generate applications for the academy, driven by parents in more exposed areas of the Confederacy; this put the nuns in the sorry position of being unable to accommodate them all. Her private war with Sr. Augustine escalated to the point that Baptista appealed to her brother to exercise his authority as their superior and remove her poisonous influence from the community. Then there was the alarmingly declining health of her

*niece Ellen (Sr. Gertrude). Her "delicate condition" seemed a sad reflection of
the country's state of health. But the wars, public and private, as well as her
family concerns, did not divert Baptista from her self-imposed mission of converting the daughters of prominent Protestants. Such opportunities seemed to
multiply as the new applications tended to be heavily Protestant in religious
affiliation.*

*The need for larger quarters in a healthier setting spurred the search for
a new rural site for the academy and convent. With Union forces closing in
by land and sea, there were no longer any sanctuaries in the South, even in
upcountry Carolina, as John Lynch slowly concluded. Fears revived about the
enemy reaching Columbia and stirred thoughts of how best to respond to such
a crisis. All in all, the long summer of 1863 produced a growing resignation in
more and more white Southerners to the bitter reality that the Union forces
would prevail; the only remaining question was not whether Charleston and
the rest of South Carolina would fall to the Yankees, but when. That the Yankees
were coming seemed inevitable.*

⤚

BAPTISTA LYNCH, URSULINE CONVENT, COLUMBIA, S.C., TO
PATRICK LYNCH, JULY 1ST[1]

Yesterday evening John brought me a package addressed to you—You know
I am not at all curious, but somehow I felt like opening that package, & asked
Johns advice—as it was mailed at Camden where there was no priest stationed,
I concluded it contained no secrets, & it might refer to us, & require immediate
attention, so I concluded to open it & did so It proved to be a copy of the *will*
of Capt Jas Connor, in which he leaves all his property to you or the Church—,
with a letter from the agt [agent] for W. Daly requesting you to visit Camden
at your earliest convenience where he will take pleasure in showing you the
real estate—& notifying you that he has collected & deposited in the Branch
Bank Camden $1,144.75/100 subject to your disposal—A godsend—is it not at
this time?

I received another letter this morning from Madame Togno, proposing to
lease Barhamville to us, & awaiting our Answer, before writing to the Numerous pupils engaged for her next session—My reply was necessarily indefinite—
told her of our intended visit on the 14th & 15th &c & proposed exchange of
residences & transfer of her pupils to us—M[rs] Englebrecht of Belle Haven Institute[2] called to rent this house in the event of our going to Barhamville— . . .

. . . I do not know how it is, but I am afraid we shall be this year as last but
indeed I hope not—for this year I have enjoyed less privileges than any since I
have entered religion i.e. seventeen years—We were without Mass several days

during the Octave of Easter—the same during the Oct of Pentecost—again Oct Corpus Christi & now during the Oct of St. J. Baptist tis the same Mr McNeal sent to say that some body was waiting for a month, to have him perform the marriage ceremony, & he wished to leave on Monday, of course I did not feel myself at liberty to say "stay at home & do your duty" and [what] do you think, already he has advised the two new postulants not to remain here if they are not perfectly satisfied, assuring them that they can do a great deal of good in the world—& asked them had they examined other orders, recommending the Sisters of Mercy—Just Joseph O'Connell over again— . . . Poor John has had a dreadful fall, his horse ran away here in town, & after rearing, pitching & running he suddenly turned & dashed John out of the buggy against a tree—giving his cheek & temple a violent blow— . . . his face is bruised scratched & he feels generally sore, but is attending his patients as usual— . . . —it was a very narrow escape.

❧

Anna Lynch, Mont. W. S. Springs, to Patrick Lynch, July 5th[3]

I was delighted to get your kind letter, by Mrs Crogan, on yesterday. The pleasure it afforded was especially enhanced as it was an unlooked for favor. I did not expect you to feel like writing, after the fatigue of travelling, and appreciated accordingly. . . . I am getting on very well. Today I am suffering a little, from my chest but am very well otherwise. I will try the merit of croton oil tonight, & expect to be effectually relieved in a day or two. The weather still precludes the possibility of our walking, as John advised, but I hope it will clear up some of these days. When, I am sure, we will be tired enough of the house, to need no persuasion to do so. I find it lately as warm here, in the middle of the day, & sometimes at night, as we generally have it at home, in this season. . . . I as well as the whole neighborhood, am getting the benefit of Mr Sipes afternoon sermon & choir, and am necessarily distracted by his appealing eloquence, and enlivening Psalms. . . .

P.S. . . . I must add that after a few more such Sundays, Mr Sipes cannot but effect the spiritual improvement which I conclude was implied in your expressive wish for my general improvement in every respect. If the cure will affect my chest instead of heart, I will not object.

❧

Baptista Lynch, Ursuline Convent, to Patrick Lynch [July][4]

We had our first Mass this week on Thursday Morning, when Rev. A. McNeal as usual chose his own time . . . he is disedifying our community very much by his neglect of duty & temper or humor, & it is the first time since I have been in religion that I have seen a Priest act as these Columbian Priests do—. I only consider Mr McN as the tool of the others.

I mentioned to you in my last about [how] Mr Mc.N. is tampering with the vocations of the two postulants whom you brought last from Va. Now Sr. Laura comes to me saying she had felt quite troubled since her last confession on account of something which the Priest said to her—. I asked what was the trouble—She said he spoke as if against *this house* by the impressions he made on her, that she asked his prayers as she was preparing to take the religious habit, & he asked her if she was satisfied in *this convent* & if she had thought on this—the Sisters of Mercy &c &c-pretty much as he spoke to the others— But it being the first time she ever heard a Priest speak or insinuate anything disparagingly of an convent, for she has when in the world been directed by the Jesuits principally, or by very pious clergymen, she feared there might be something wrong *in this house* though she could not see it herself, & has every confidence in me—That is just Rev Joseph O'Connell's work over again—They are too ignorant of their own duties as well as ours, to have anything to do with a convent. . . .

I have received two notes from Madam Togno about Barhamville, one I think I mentioned to you, in which she begged an answer without delay, as she was obliged to receive back her refugee pupils by the 15th July if at all—You being absent, & having no local Revd Superior, I was obliged to postpone a definite answer—but told her you would accompany us out to Barhamville on the 15th probably, when we would give her an answer, she wrote yesterday very kindly & politely, regretting her inability to await my time, but said, she thought it worth while to see Barhamville, as it was an admirable place for such an institution as ours she thought—& that it was with a heavy heart she resumed her duties, after the loss of her daughter.

I suppose you have left Nannie Ferrall & Sister quite well, & hope you have arranged the business satisfactorily—We are sending all our small bill of cursory expenses home to the parents, but we will present you a large one for her, educational as well as current. . . .

Francis Lynch, Cheraw, to Patrick Lynch, 11 July[5]

. . . I have subscribed to the Cotton Association[6] and will want to buy some cotton for my subscription; if not inconvenient you will please let me make use of the parcel you have here in store—I will either propose to pay for it 40 ct plus the Confed. tax (if it will class so, with the association), or replace the quantity of cotton to you when wanted—Do let me know early.

And now for another matter (I almost blush for it) Late in winter & early spring I had bot this cattle with the view of making disposition of them (when fit) in the City—In May last a Mr Jno Green from the City who was buying Beef cattle here, proposed to join me in the business. He was to sell in the City and return me the Hides and purchase other Hides for me. Mr Green referred me to D[r] Carey & Revd Father O'Neill—true I did not write to those gentlemen, as I was pleased with the reference—Since then I have sent between 30 & 40 head of cattle but have recd only a portion of the hides, and none of the money from the sales. Today I have written Mr Green to make a deposit in the Bank for me—Mr Green may be, and I trust is a very correct man, but in these unsettled times he may abuse the confidence I have placed in him, by want of promptness. . . . I am aware of having reposed large confidence in Mr Green—and if misplaced—I would like to avoid being chided for such want of business rule.

⚗

Baptista Lynch, Ursuline Convent, Columbia, S.C., to
Patrick Lynch, July 11th[7]

. . . As for Barhamville, Madame Togno has been obliged to keep it & has published her intentions to do so for one more year— . . . You say "if I were to be taken away, you would need some Clergyman to stand your friend"—Were you taken away my dearest Brother, which God forbid, I hope my exile would soon end also—if left after you, I should leave the labors care & responsibility —which I have borne for well nigh five years to one who would know better to adapt herself to the Manners of Clergymen than I do—& they would be too happy to get a foothold in the Convent—But I trust it is Gods holy will to spare you as He has done Mother, whom you are so much like, until a venerable old age—when you can look around on the large numbers of your priests, & religions communities—your Boys & girls Orphans Asylum, & your rebuilt Cathedral—the new temple far exceeding the beauty & magnitude of the old—. You would feel gratified in reading the letters which come to us from our absent Pupils & their Parents. The pupils are already tired & want to come back to the Convent— . . . Stella Clark . . . has written to ask her father's permission to enter the Noviciate, & begs to be allowed to do so in August—!

We have a nice set of children staying with us this vacation—only seven—& all grown, or nearly so—. Miss Scule is at their head—who seems to be thinking of being a Religious. I received a long & touching letter from M[rs] Bellinger's daughter concerning Julia's coming to us. I answered, & will tell you about it when you come. We are very much pleased with the two new postulants, Sr. Fannie (Miss Fennell) is remarkably sensible & prudent for her age, having been the companion of both Father & Mother in all their difficulties & trials.

She is desirous that two friends of hers should obtain a place in our Noviciate, & if they are like her, we would be glad to get them—Sr. Angela has been confined to her bed a great deal lately, & I suppose cannot last much longer. She is so good & useful when needed, that it will be *very hard* to fill her place— . . . .

. . . The rest of us are as usual D.G.—Sr Gertrude is I think some better tho delicate—We have school for the Noviciate now, & all are busy praying, studying or working—. They are storming heaven for Charleston now—

Anna Lynch, Mont W.S. Springs, to Patrick Lynch, July 14th[8]

. . . every day, [Sister DeSales] compliments me by saying how well I look. Though sometimes indisposed as I have been at home I am a great deal better, & stronger, & if I continue to improve will be well repaid for the length of my visit, which I am afraid will inconvenience Mother. . . . I hope very much that Charleston will not meet with the unfortunate fate of Vicksburg but since our late reverses, I would not be surprised at anything. Mr Crogan is disappointed at not getting the Courier which would give a detailed account of the fight, but here we only get telegraphs. . . .

Baptista Lynch, Ursuline Convent, Columbia S.C., to Patrick Lynch, July 15th[9]

I feel so anxious about you tonight—not having heard why you are not able to keep your appointment & fearing it is a continuance of your indisposition—.

If I only knew that you were charitably engaged in your ministerial duties in the Hospitals & elsewhere, I would feel not only content, but happy—for it is such a privilege to be instrumental in leading one soldier to know God, & serve Him through our holy Faith, but I am so afraid that this excitement in the City has been too much for your strength, & rendered you unfit alike for duty & for travel—I proposed a telegram to you this morning, but John dissuaded me from sending it and, now, I feel very much like starting down to see you I will hope for good news tomorrow morning under the protection of our Blessed Lady of Mt Carmel—.[10]

. . . —We are storming heaven in behalf of Charleston— . . .

[PS] . . . I am sorry to say Ellen has a bad cough & looks delicate . . .

۶۶

FRANCIS LYNCH, CHERAW, TO PATRICK LYNCH, 17 JULY[11]

It afforded me much pleasure to hear from you, and that you had recovered from the Bilious attack,—There is enough now to keep one above fever pitch, independent of such ailings and hope you may be free from them.

I would feel more anxiety as to the fate of the cherished old City, Charleston, did not the confidence I repose in the commanding Genl. and the determined resistance impress me with high hopes. . . .

I thank you much for your assistance in reference to the cotton. It is my opinion the Cotton association will not for the present year risk of running the Blockade. . . . If I learn that I can return safely from the City, perhaps I will go down next week—For my Stock of cattle would permit my sending more to the City, if I can do so safely. What I want, is the return of the Hides & tallows to me, and the mt price for the Beef, by quantity after it is butchered there, I wd prefer selling to this free market— . . .

۶۶

BAPTISTA LYNCH, URSULINE CONVENT & ACADEMY COLUMBIA S.C., TO PATRICK LYNCH, JULY 21ST 1863[12]

We are so much obliged to you for that excellent chart, & study it with each account in the paper.

I'm sorry to say, however exposed the enemy will be in erecting a battery on the North end of Morris Island, it seems there is a possibility, with their vast resources of their succeeding—This morning's papers gives us good news of the noble bravery of our men, & of their success. Since we can only aid them by our poor prayers, they certainly shall have them. How is Conlaw & where is he? We are perfectly sure of his bravery & courage, & wish to be equally so of his safety. Give our best love to him—I wrote about the black calico, which he & you were so kind as to look after, & send me word about. I think I told you I would like to get a piece of the pure black. You might send it (as I am anxious to have it for the Lay-Sisters Habits—as they are literally in rags) if you cannot leave Charleston soon.

We think it as well to let the old lady—Md^m de Bertheville wait a little longer for her veil & habit, as she made a demonstration of her nervousness, after she was disappointed at your not coming. Poor soul! She is very good but the *ditto* of poor Sr. DeNeri (R.I.P.)

Mrs Ambler Weed (who they say is going into consumption) advises Sr Charles to fund her money in the Barhamville property or some solid investment —of course reserving it to us for decision—We are beginning to be afraid of the enemy's raids, & think what we should do, if they came to Columbia. The letters of the children are written by panic stricken parents, & are calculated to make us ask ourselves this question—altho thank God, our hearts unlike theirs are not engaged with the things of this earth, & there would be a vast difference between us, & the parents of families, should such a disaster befall us. Neither loss of property or loss of life with us, could affect the happiness of others, & therefore the disengagement beforehand, brings peace now. But prudence again suggests the question, & I make it to you for guidance. What shall we do, in the event of the Yankees coming, or even approaching to Columbia from any direction?

Do you advise us to send our mattresses or instruments of music to Mr Buff or some out of the way place? Or take any prudential measures? It seems to me that our place is as safe as another—indeed many persons think a Convent the safest place. What would you think of our erecting a large cross just over the middle of the front & underneath it in large letters "Convent & Academy?" Or perhaps better over our entrance door in relief? I fear the rabble of Columbia who stoned us, as much as the Yankees, & if they came on a raid they would not look out for sign boards or respect persons or institutions—so it is hard to say what is best or most prudent. One thing seems to me prudent—& that is to invest the little that we have in real estate—so we may as well look at Barhamville. We are constantly hearing from Protestant applicants that our Academy is perhaps the best in the Confederacy & it promises to become a Protestant Institute this coming winter. We'll have to make a good retreat & get the grace to convert them all. Our present set of children is a very agreeable one—only six in number & all grown, they spend their time very agreeably in practicing music, reading history & other improving books, mutually assisting each other —they are Misses Kate Seale—Mary Mitchell—Mary Jane Robinson—Dora Martin—Florence Alden & Julia Semmes. The first & last are Catholics & the rest Protestants but three of them are studying our Catechism & I think all of them will become Catholics—I mentioned in my last letter about two young ladies, friends of Miss Fenwick, who wish to become religious—what do you think of our encouraging them?

Stella Clark sent me word, that she would not buy herself any more dresses, until she heard her Fathers reply to her letter, asking his permission to enter our noviciate on the 15th May—as she wanted to keep the money which I gave her for that purpose, to buy a black postulants dress. What do you think of her?

Judging from the present we ought as soon as possible to get a spacious airy place, for such a confined position tells & must tell more on ourselves & pupils. But perhaps the Yankees will give us fresh air enough before the winter is over?—God forbid. . . .

The Huchets' children have just left after a morning call. I hear they said Revd A. McNeal was to be pastor of German Church in Charleston. I'm very glad.

M[r] Ambler Weed writes "tell the M. Sup. that I have just sent Revd Gache his furlough for 21 days from Aug 1st," so we trust there will be no disappointment about our long looked for & much desired retreat. M[r] & M[rs] Debow (of the DeBows Review)[13] enter as boarders at John's today—& I'm glad of it, as I think they missed M[r] & M[rs] Middleton's *society & money too*—. Eliza is to be one of our *Boarders* next session—

Ellen's cough has left her, but she is still suffering from debility & looks pale—consequently is unable to study & practice as much as we would like & the harp is a very fatiguing instrument—John says he sent you an account of money matters in my last letter, but you have not noticed it—now is the time to pay all debts—can you make any copayment on this house? Or can we do it for you—? John is very much put out with M[r] Murphy's mismanagement— Our sick Sisters are better now & all usefully employed. . . .

[P S] Bishop McGill seems to feel the death of the Abp of Baltimore. I wonder who will fill his see. Sr Augustine says, & has always said, that you would. Strange to say, she used to tease me with that idea in Brown Co. when we talked of coming here, & even in N. Orleans. I wonder if she will prove a good prophetess.

⚜

John Lynch, Columbia S.C., to Patrick Lynch, July 23rd[14]

I recd a letter from Conlaw yesterday in which he says he can buy salt in Charleston at $12.00 a bushel, if you can purchase at that price and get transportation for it, you had better buy a supply for the two farms for some time, it is selling here for $20—per bushel & I had to buy some for the plantation yesterday. Conlaw wrote me he was not well, I hope it may be nothing serious the matter, from his own & your acc[t] of him, he has been conducting himself very properly & creditably, I hope he may continue in the same course, if he is spared I see the making of a business man in him.

There will be a great struggle for Charleston but I do not believe they will ever be able to take it, the gallant fighting at Wagner[15] is proof to them, if they cannot bring overwhelming numbers, they cannot take even the Island, and there is not room for an overwhelming force on the Island, I expect they will abandon this attack and try a third plan, what it may be is impossible to see, without it is to bring all their boats from the Mississippi and force their way by the fort by running the gauntlet, having previously landed forces on the main above Sullivans island, then they can attack Charleston in the rear, but what good would Charleston do them without the fort, could they land forces & provisions through the Stono? if they could do that, by getting possession of Charleston they could laugh at the forts, and make their raids through the country at pleasure. I will believe it when I see it[;] we have again taken a couple of boarders to help along: Mr DeBow & wife—I hope we will be mutually pleased. . . .

BAPTISTA LYNCH, URSULINE CONVENT, COLUMBIA, S.C., TO
PATRICK LYNCH, JULY 25TH 1863[16]

I write a few hasty lines to thank you for the hogshead of sugar which you have kindly & providently sent us. . . . But this has just come in good time—ours was getting low, & we expected to pay the market price for what we should get. We have to lay in a provision of flour & meat too I suppose. God grant it may not be for the Yankees. We learned last night, that Jane Semmes' mother & family were driven from their home which they burned to the ground. We have not heard from the Semmes family.

Today we have received three little girls—daughters of Col. B. Deshai Harman—formerly of Memphis, & Staunton Va—Protestants, like most of our other pupils—we have now seven Protestant pupils, & only two Catholics, but they are all very satisfactory.

. . . —Francis & John are both talking about this "Cotton Loan Association" —Have you any interest in it—? I wonder if Mr Bernard O'Neill has been called on by the firm of "W. Bee & Co." for the remaining two bales of cotton that we want to send to Nassau? I'm afraid we must say "good-bye" to the Books from N[assau]. Is it not astonishing how cooly persons talk about the attack of Charleston, on the possibility, even probability of its being taken by the enemy—

I have heard three different persons say that it could be a longer siege than that of Vicksburg but unless Beauregard supplied the Forts & Charleston with a *twelve months provision*, it too must succumb to the enemy. I cannot commit to paper the "QED" of the case—it would be too long, but sounded to me quite reasonable— & you know outsiders can see better sometimes than those who are deeply interested & incapable of looking dispassionately on the subject.

When may we expect you? Are you not allowed to leave the City—? Md^me de Bertheville has edified us by her humility & we are willing to give her the habit & I would be glad to see Barhamville during the vacation—even before our retreat if convenient. What would you think of our going out there with John, & to the Keitt place, if you cannot come? You know we have not much time to lose now.

Our retreat will soon be upon us, & when that is over, we always plunge into the management of our classes &c for the coming session—

ᘒ

PATRICK LYNCH, CHARLESTON, S.C., TO JOHN McGILL,[17] 26 JULY[18]

. . . I do not much like the principle of filling the Metropolitan Sees by a Translation.—[19] For myself, were such a translation offered me,—(I can speak of it as it is impossible under the circumstances—I would refuse; nothing short of a mandate from Rome would induce me to accept. It may in course of time lead to too much evil and ambition even among the Prelates. Circumstances may of course sometimes render it necessary. But as a general thing I would avoid it.

I somewhat jocosely proposed that some how application should be made to Seward for permission for the three Suffragans in the Confederacy to go on to Baltimore to see to the election of a Successor. He would probably refuse,— then we would be no worse off, than we are now, and the refusal might bring him such odium as would help to disgust, still more, the Catholic and Irish element at the North. It might be that he would grant it, for us to meet at Baltimore,—(not elsewhere)

I do not think our Government would make any objection. It would however be well to ascertain this informally at the beginning.

Now as to the succession itself. I do not think that there is the least probability that Maryland will ever belong to the Southern Confederacy—and we cannot look for a Southern man to succeed Abp. Kenrick. Among the Prelates, practically eligible, I presume Bp. Whelan[20] is the most eligible one of the province. If we could go out of the province Bp. Bailey of Newark would I think do admirably—Still there is the paper or list which I presume the good Abp has left and much deference is due to his selection.

As I write this fine Sunday evening I hear the cannon, one every three minutes. I fear before a week is over the enemy will have all Morris Island. Then will commence the struggle in earnest—they to put up batteries to destroy Fort Sumter, we to prevent them from putting up such works. We will have 80 or 100 guns and mortars to play on the space where the battery will have to be erected. Time will show. If the Yankees try long enough and hard enough, and spend lives enough, of course they can take Charleston. But we will fight hard. The possession of Morris Island has so far cost them over 2500 men.

On last Friday we exchanged wounded Prisoners. I went down on our Flag of truce boat, and had a near view of the Ironsides and the Monitors, one of them not 50 feet off part of the time,—The Yankees Surgeons, whom I saw, especially chief surgeon Dr. Craven were remarkably polite, and seemed moved by the attention which we had paid to their wounded and expressed themselves handsomely on the subject. We delivered 104 wounded, and received 40, which they had taken so much better care of than we of theirs, that we felt somewhat mortified.

Where are we drifting? To subjugation? Things really look dark. From Joe Johnston and from Bragg I look for very little. Here at Charleston we will do our best. But we hope Lee will strike some telling blow. I do not know which has disheartened us more the fall of Vicksburg and Port Hudson or the repulse of Lee in Pennsylvania. The 40000 prisoner lie of the latter's success but rendered the truth more discouraging. Deus providebit.

ख़

BAPTISTA LYNCH, URSULINE CONVENT, COLUMBIA, S.C., TO PATRICK LYNCH, JULY 31ST[21]

Both John & I have been wondering at your silence—he feels a little hurt at your not noticing his letters, & so neglecting him I believe—. Today he tells me of another hogshead of sugar being at the depot for us, & we are so much obliged to you for it.

Mr. Dempsey of Macon Georgia who has just left, offers to purchase sugar for us there too, at a cheaper rate than it sells here, & John advises me to get some as a safe investment—we also want coffee & rice—but if you don't send the *bills* along with the merchandise, I'll not be satisfied.

Please write soon, & tell us how you are & if you will visit us before or after our retreat. You know we enter into it on the feast of the "Transfiguration" & remain until the "Assumption."—Father Gache will I expect leave Lynchburg on tomorrow, as his furlough extends from Aug 1st to the 20th. I asked you in my last letter about our going out to see Barhamville with John, but I am afraid retreat time will come before I get your reply. We have almost concluded to try it & am anxious to do so—the interest of our Academy & the health of our Sisters both seem to require a country place & fresh air—Pupils are already coming in, & soon we shall have thousands of Confederate money on hand, besides what we already have in Bank & invested in cotton—we propose also selling our cotton rather than pay the present taxes, storage, & insurance on it, & turning that, in to Barhamville property also. . . .

Gen[l] Beauregard's sister called here a few days since—M[rs] Proctor, I think is her name, we had quite a pleasant conversation & she spoke of placing her little daughter with us. . . .

Sister Gertrude, I am sorry to say, is growing every day more like poor Bernard & is growing more inert—every thing fatigues her—Sr. Rose too looks very much like a consumptive—Sr. Maria St. Agnes is confined to her bed the greater part of her time, & today we have three sick Lay Sisters the last however I do not mind, it is only the warm weather & some little disarrangement of system—

. . . I will say nothing of the sign of the times, for I have not space—.

Baptista Lynch, Ursuline Convent & Academy, Columbia S.C., to Patrick Lynch, August 17th[22]

I write to you in haste because I want you to get this letter before Revd Fr. Gache leaves that you may consult him about the course to pursue with Sr. Augustine—He knows what she is, & has very little hope of her conversion & I think it much better to expel her, to save others from being injured by her— today, I was told in the parlor that for *several months* she has been speaking against me in the parlor—just as she had done in Cin. & in N. Orleans against her superiors there—moreover that she had spoken to the clergy in the same way.

I suspected as much before, as I told you, but was not positively certain—I have had much to contend with in her, during the past year, which I have never troubled you with, & even at present she is injuring Miss Scule very much— who is becoming under her influence . . . more bitter & sarcastic & less confiding every day—of course I am the butt of all their spleen—that is the M[other] Superior is the butt of her spleen always.

Now I pray that if it is A.M.D.G. she will take it into her head to go some where else before our school commences (unless our Lord sees fit to leave me this cross) for we are expecting a number of *very intelligent pretty & rich* young ladies who I fear she will play havoc among—& who, I feel are sent to us to be converted to the true faith—I do not feel like leaving such an opposition as she may give within, our Chaplain without, & the labor which is before me presents —Harassing contentions, weaken me more than hard work.

But I hope this is an exaggerated version, of what is before me still. I lay it before you—S[r] A has never staid five years in any convent before—& I think a change would be as agreeable to herself as to us. She has no idea that I have heard this intelligence this morning. Anyhow it is just the old story with her— Artful innuendoes sighs & rolling eyes with half finished sentences—an affected scrupulosity to say the whole, while the impression produced is worse than anything she could say plainly. Then the affected surprise when spoken to about it! I'm disgusted with her hypocrisy & falsehood. Still if it is God's will let her stay where she is—we'll endeavor to be silent & charitable. . . .

❧

JOHN LYNCH, COLUMBIA, TO PATRICK LYNCH, AUGUST 19TH[23]

I intended writing you a long letter by Father Gache, but perhaps it is as well not, as I have not time. I have been very busy for the last few days, attending the sick & collecting for the orphans in Charleston. The old doctor appointed four collectors last Sunday dividing the town so as to give a beat to each, Mr Montague in the first, myself in the second Mr Comerford in the third & Mr McGuinnis in the fourth, the rest have so far made but a poor collection, I have $900 so far, and will make it over the thousand before I am done. . . .

I inquired about D[r] Marks place he has concluded not to sell just now as he does not know what to do with the money, perhaps if he could get Confederate Bonds 7 pr cent he would sell, but I did not press the matter, as we can wait longer, having waited so long.

Francis tells me he is not so sure but he may have to go into the army, have you heard any thing of it. I hope he is mistaken, and if the officer has made a mistake that you will use your influence and keep him out.

❧

BAPTISTA LYNCH, URSULINE CONVENT & ACADEMY COLUMBIA, S.C. AUG 23RD[24]

John will tell you all about Barhamville more accurately than I can do—I hope it will be no inconvenience to you to invest $10,000 or $12,000 in it—I thought we had more in hand than we have—S[r] Charles wrote to her Brother Ambler to have her dower ready to hand over at any moment, & he wishes to purchase some 20 or 30 acres near & farm them—John proposes a cottage near which Dr. Marks offers for $3,500 with the desired quantity of land near—Sister Charles has written to her brother & invited him to come & see it. He says his sickness has been as good as a retreat & intimates that he will not long delay following his wish of becoming a priest—I think it is with you.—It would be particularly desirable to have his protection & interest with us at Barhamville should we arrange to go there next year, or even later—Yesterday Mr. Martin of Tuscaloosa, Ala called on his way to Richmond to see his sister—expressed himself highly gratified with her improvement—most grateful to us & said that his minister (a Presbyterian) had given him quite a lecture, for creating a mania among the young ladies for convent education—he is the cause of three other young ladies coming from that place.

We expect the daughter of Mayor Monroe[25] of N. Orleans who spoke so nobly & bravely to the people of that city, & was taken by the Yankees & imprisoned—

he has escaped & passed with his family to Winnesboro [*sic*], near which place he has an Uncle living— . . . I hope you will come soon to see us & when will you visit Cheraw & go for Annie. . . .

Mrs Michael O'Conner, who has recently lost a little girl, came up last night & so did Mrs Aveilhé whose little child is very ill—they were startled by a shell falling near their house—I suppose most of the women & children must leave —What about the Sisters & orphans—Would it not be grand if they could rent that "Orangeburg Institute" that Mr Lafitte spoke to us about buying? I feel very much for them & for you too, since they all look to you for guidance in an emergency.

John says we may as well keep quiet, for, it would be useless to seek a place of safety for anything—And you, I think, say the same. We are storming heaven for deliverance from the evils of war, famine & pestilence, & to obtain a speedy & honorable peace—What shall we do for eatables this winter when our house is full—? Yesterday we tried up & downtown for butter, & Isaac could not get any but many others were the same—Gov Lowe wrote to me about getting a house to rent in Columbia, but it was impossible. Two gentlemen called during our retreat to see about placing the daughter of Genl Hindman[26] here—Finding she was a Protestant, I recommended the other Institutes of Columbia but the gentleman said the Genl preferred a Catholic Institution, & the very high reputation of our Academy precluded the necessity of further inquiry—!

. . . Do you know anything of the cotton sent to Nassau—or if it was all sent? I wish if you see Mr Bernard O'Neill you would ask if the remaining 2 bales were shipped, or if he still has them stored—? If still on hand would it not be well to sell it—here John can sell what we have at 50^cts per lb. I am very anxious about our boxes of Books &c, from Nassau, & have written to Messrs Lafitte & B. O'Neill, but I suppose they are all so engaged with the war & self interest, that they forget my (to them minor) affairs—they are not minor to us though, & we must keep a steady eye on them.

(Excuse my abominable writing) I almost relinquish the hope of getting coal this year. Mr Dempsey sent me the bill of one Hhd [Hogshead] sugar & one bag coffee—such a bill—!! . . . Do write often & keep us posted on the state of affairs with you; so far the telegrams have been correct, & tally exactly with your letters—but the reports—! . . .

. . . I feel more than sad about our beloved home. I will not give up until it falls into the hands of the enemy. You did not say in your letter what you thought would be its fate if you have a moment to write do tell me what you think of it & if you intend remaining if the Yankees take it. I sincerely trust & pray that you have no such intention. We have all been looking forward with much pleasure to that promised visit but we have given up all hope of seeing you for a long time.

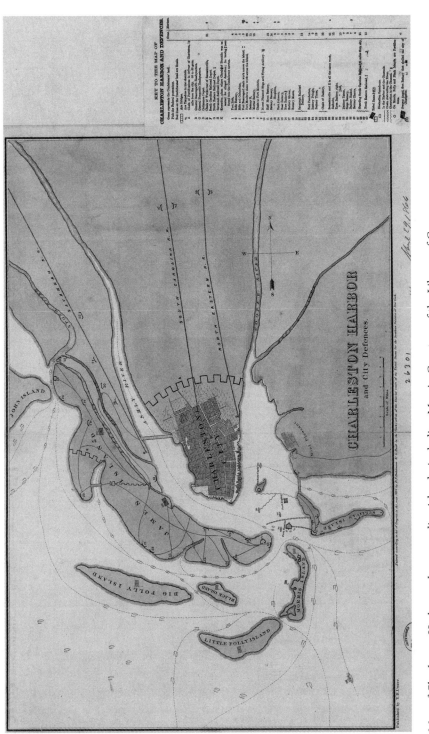

Map of Charleston Harbor and surrounding islands, including Morris. Courtesy of the Library of Congress.

◈

FRANCIS LYNCH, CHERAW, TO PATRICK LYNCH, AUG 24[27]

... In a day or two I will send a bundle of four pr of cav[alry] boots pr express to your care in compliance with request of Conlaw for Capt Keitt. We are all in excellent health (D.G.) And hope you are enjoying the same.

In reference to the conscription—The Exemption law covers Tanners—The enrolling off. does not consider me as classing with them, unless I were actually doing manual labor, but has referred the matter to Maj Melton Commd[r] of Conscripts. . . .

Should he coincide with the En Off [Enrolling Officer] then I will have to try to be detailed. Col[n] Northrop writes that he will do what he can for me (I sent to him a copy of my application as a Tanner). The Col advises my writing to Maj F. W. Dillard Q.M. C.S. With whom I have a contract, to apply for a detail for me.

◈

BAPTISTA LYNCH, URSULINE CONVENT & ACADEMY CHARLESTON, S.C., TO PATRICK LYNCH SEPT. 4TH[28]

You will be gratified to hear that our academy opened with a larger number of pupils this year than ever before, that is, since we came to Columbia. We have thirty Boarders already, & I fear we shall not be able to accommodate all in Convent style, all who have applied. . . .

Can you not say the Mass of the Holy Ghost for us on next Sunday. You know we always have that at the opening of school—& this year we have great need of His light & grace for ourselves & pupils, many of whom are Protestant.

I have not written before, because I have felt much worried, & even pained —which feeling I bore in silence—knowing it to be best. I wrote to you as the Revd Sup to remedy an evil which is beyond my power—& you seem to disregard it entirely—of course then, it is my duty to support it. But as I am far from being dead to self, it costs me many interior struggles known only to Almighty God—for I have no Counselor. Each Sister would be, & often is a sincere sympathiser, but that can scarcely be called a support. When Revd F G[ache] saw how that Sister was & he did not learn it from me, but from her protégé) he told me, had he known as much, he would have hesitated to expose one, in whom he felt so much influence, to such an influence for he knew well, what it was in their own Society—That it was *a diabolical spirit*, for which he might say there was *no* cure—Afterwards, he told me it was evident there was some flaw in the mind, but the most was a great spiritual pride—which rendered [her] very dangerous to others—& were he the Superior, he would send her right out—& feel it his duty to the others to take that step. When her conversion was spoken of, he smiled doubtingly & shook his head.

I had not then heard of the reports she had circulated in Columbia.

I knew that she had from the first here, done as she did in New Orleans & Cincinnati—viz—intriguingly insinuated herself into the favors of the pupils at the expense of those charged with their conduct—represented herself artfully as the most superior person in the house, & for this alone, an object of jealousy envy & dislike to all—that she had insinuated distrust into the minds of novices when under temptations, by her unfinished sentences, sighs & inuendoes. All this I have [had to?] endure—as I had seen it endured or admonished in N.O. & Cin—But I was not aware until the day I wrote to you, that she had in the parlor told a young lady—(I have reason to know) Miss McElhany, who spoke of entering our Noviciate that in another Convent, under different superiors, no doubt she could be happy, but not here where the M.S. was so tyrannical that the S^{rs} were not happy & moreover here in this Convent, the rule was not observed as in Europe where the M. superior is changed regularly &c &c.

This has been going on for several months & while it produced its influence, delicacy & a fear of wounding my feelings, made the parties concerned silent to me. At length Mademoiselle Marnier warmed up on the subject, & told it to me, after defending me—espousing my cause against those who had been influenced by these falsehoods—viz—the clergy—the young lady whom I take to be Miss McElhany & perhaps Miss Garnett—how many more I do not know, as this matter was a subject of conversation at Mrs. Kulps[?] But Miss Marnier who says that she was driven out of the convent in France, by just such a character, advises me strongly never to let her go to the parlor, or have any intercourse with either S^{rs} or pupils saying—"did you experience what I have done, you certainly would not—indeed I would not let her stay in a house the reputation of which she has injured so." She also told me to tell you, that this report also affected her at first, experienced as she was, & no doubt it would prevent many from entering.

I had expected a letter to myself or to S^r A___ on the subject which you know can be *perfectly private* & since you have made no proposal to remedy the evil—I will suggest that she would start off on her own house & be the head herself, she can take Sr Martha & Sr Vincent with two professed—which will make the foundation canonical as far as members are concerned. We will forward her $1000 & you locate her in Raleigh—Edgefield or wherever you think a school will prosper best & she can begin with a day school.

I would not hesitate to start tomorrow on such a plan, & would feel certain of success. We read in our annals, of many enterprises with less means, which were ultimately crowned with success. The blessing of God not being with her, I would not be surprised if she failed, but she would learn a salutary lesson &

we would have obtained at least a short respite from "Hooker-like" abuse—and our novices will be materially served— . . .

What a pity that Abp [Hughes] had any thing to say to those rioters[29]— Those abolitionists deserve them & so far as there is no offense to Almighty God I would be pleased that they felt them throughout the entire north & west, if it would only give us peace—did you see that the Catholics of Pittsburgh Pa. paid $10900 (I think) to save the Priests from the draft?

Is it so here too—? When did you see Conlaw last—? Poor dear Boy—he is faring rather badly, but he says better than many others, he has been sick, & is now half starved I hear, as are most of those on Mt Pleasant.

I have no fear of the Yankees reaching us via Charleston but, I look with increased anxiety towards Chattanooga & other points in Georgia.[30] But if Rosecrans comes, I will write to him & beg him by our mutual regard for Abp Purcell by the friendship existing between his brother & our community the Ursulines of B.C. & the prayers which were offered for his own recovery, when by a sad accident he was almost deprived of life in Cincinnati, to show mercy to our Convent & its inmates, & require the same of all his men.[31]

❧

JOHN LYNCH, COLUMBIA S.C., TO PATRICK LYNCH, SEPT 5TH[32]

. . . I am much broken of my rest by the little children with the whooping cough. I do not know whether to say I am sorry or glad to be able to say that Dr Marks, flew quite off the handle about the trade, he tried twice to tell me; the second time I drew it from him, Mr Bobo wrote to him the place was worth 60,000, I told him I was not trading with Mr Bobo but with Dr Marks, and wished to know if he held himself bound by his written agreement to me, he did not, without he could invest, the investing I told him lay with himself, he then refused to sell for less than 60,000$. I bow'd and told him I was not disappointed and still expected to buy the place of one half of what I had offer'd some day, thus ends the farce of trade with Dr Marks. . . .

If perfectly convenient let me hear about the big gun, and whether there is any truth about the ironclads coming over that we hear of through northern accounts.[33]

❧

BAPTISTA LYNCH, URSULINE CONVENT & ACADEMY COLUMBIA S.C., TO
　　PATRICK LYNCH, SEPT. 9TH[34]

Did you get John's telegram today about "Daniel."—He is very anxious that Daniel should be left at the farm, otherwise they cannot do much, & we are equally anxious on account of our wood—especially since we have not been able to get coal this year. You will be glad to hear that we have forty-four boarders already—more than we have ever had so early in the session since we came to Columbia. We celebrated our fifth anniversary here on Sept 1st, very quietly but busily. The greater number of our boarders are new & Protestant, & so many are applying that I fear we cannot accommodate all.

We are having the house in the yard—small wooden one—cleaned up & whitewashed & will put four of the Lay Sisters to sleep up there—they are very comfortable little rooms.

John is just looking around for our winter provision of flour &c. We have a good deal of money on hand, but expect our expenses this winter to be very great—Everything works like clock-work now, & the regularity & silence is delightful, how long it will continue I cannot say. All the troublesome ones of last year are gone, except Maria Lafitte, & she is doing very well from necessity— One young lady sixteen years of age, & daughter of Col^n Pickett of N. Orleans, said: "Mother I come as much to learn your religion as your Books, it has always had a fascination for me" & I trust we may be instrumental in leading many of these young hearts to God through a knowledge of our Holy Faith—

You must have laughed at my request to say the "Mass of the Holy Ghost" on the feast of the Nativity B.V.M. [Blessed Virgin Mary]. But you must know I did not look at the "Ordo" or even recollect the day of the month. When can you come and say it? I know you have stern duties to fulfill now, with the wounded & dying. All we can do is to perform the part of Moses, & I believe it was partly our prayers to the Blessed lady that obtained that repulse for Fort Sumter.

❧

JOHN LYNCH, COLUMBIA, TO PATRICK LYNCH, SEPT 9TH[35]

I wrote to you I believe a few days ago, I am induced to do so today, on account of a message Danl brought me, he says *they* [Confederate officials] have been after him to go to the coast to work. Mr Buff told *them,* he was the only road hand on the farm, and he could not spare him, he would pay the fine first, the answer was we don't want money but help, either send him or find a substitute, a substitute I don't think can be found, as he is ordered to have him here at the depot, on Friday morning. I wish your instructions, my interpretation of the law, would say he is not liable. Still he may be, this I leave you to decide. . . .

The report of the repulse from Fort Sumter today is excellent. There must have been Irishmen in it to have thought of the old way of fighting with Brickbats, if our report is true, it is the best thing of the fight, none of ours killed, three stand of arms taken, 15 commissioned officers, 102 privates taken prisoner and barges captured, how they were taken does not appear, it is well to have a streak of daylight now and then for things have been looking very dark for some time. I hope Charleston may hold out yet, if the fleet *we read about* comes, we are safe, hope on hope ever, they are still receiving new pupils or rather boarders at the Convent, it will soon be full, and overflowing, what about the Sisters & orphans.

I was fortunate enough to increase my subscription list to fourteen hundred and twenty one dollars. The others did not increase. I have been spoken to about your Keitt house for the refugees. I have always replied it was held in reserve for the Orphans when they left Charleston, am I right? . . . by the by what about Anna, should she not come home soon, is it not getting a little dangerous out there, if you cannot go yourself cannot you send a substitute. . . .

ᥲ

Francis Lynch, Cheraw, to Patrick Lynch, 10 Sepr[36]

Since my last I have not been favoured with any of yours. The incidents of war, with the [enemy] knocking on the portals of the city, are now so interesting I presume you have but little time to devote as bursar. Fortunately the shelling of the city is suspended, the repose of its inhabitants may for awhile be more calm.[37] Father is very uneasy about sister Anna, and wishes to know your purpose as to her return home. It may be too inconvenient for you to go for her; if so, some opportunity might be sought after to that goal.

I understand Miss Drake came on to Santee last week. You will have noticed I have offered for sale the Real Est [Estate] of Bro James—for the dwelling I have a bid of 8000$ from M[r] Ingraham, it may bring more. On Sunday last I had a letter from S[r] Augusta asking that the dwelling be bot in—and that she wrote by advice. Ordinarily the property would be considered a good investment but with the debts of Est [Estate] unpaid I think the sale advisable and so wrote to her, especially as it will bring full double the price of former times. . . .

ᥲ

Francis Lynch, Cheraw, to Patrick Lynch, 14 Sep[38]

I think the interest of the estate of Brother James will be better served in the sale of the dwelling, and that your investment will be more judiciously made in cotton, altho the price of it is about 60[cts] per lb, pardon my giving my opinion, I think I can also purchase for Mrs Posi.

The lot of cotton bot for you, has not been at all disturbed, I keep it insured. The note enclosed should have been sent by this morning's mail. A dispatch was recd from Sr Anna, that she expected to arrive on Saturday night with Father Sullivan they will be looked for tonight.

It is unfortunate that the large cannon burst, much was hoped from it. However it was but an accident in our defenses and more reliance must be placed on others.[39]

The glowing accounts given by Mr Woodward of the bulwark defenses of the city make me more hopeful. . . .

BAPTISTA LYNCH, URSULINE CONVENT & ACADEMY, COLUMBIA, S.C. TO PATRICK LYNCH, SEPT 14TH

We have now nearly fifty Boarders—Who do you think came with her Father & applied to enter here—Miss *Belle* Cohen! One of the gayest young ladies in Columbia—!

You know her Father who intends using his influence with you to get her in, on the condition that she may go to the synagogue every Saturday!

I told them thro' Sr Charles that I would let them know whether we had a vacancy or not in about a month, since if all who I expected come, I could receive no more on any condition. . . .

JOHN LYNCH, COLUMBIA, S.C., TO PATRICK LYNCH, SEPT 18TH[40]

I have been called on by Mr Thos. W. Keys who says you asked him about purchasing provisions for the Convent, in N.C. he proposes going up next week, and if you say so I will get him to buy six or eight hundred bushels of wheat, and run the risk of getting it down, the only trouble he says he apprehends is impressment, he thinks if you or I give him a certificate stating that he is purchasing for the use of the Academy, and not for speculation, and get the certificate endorsed by the proper officer in Charleston, that he can purchase, without the fear of the officers before his eyes, if you think so, and will send up such a paper, . . . I will furnish him with the means, and will think it a good speculation, if he succeeds in getting the wheat, we can have it ground here at any time, I recd your letter regarding Danl, from your telegraph I stopped him and told the overseer you had a substitute for him in Charleston, he told me he did not think he was liable this time, but had been, at a previous call. I don't think so, the name of the overseer who summoned Danl was Lorick, he says I may yet have to appear before the commissioners at Lexington C.H. If I am summoned I expect I will let them fine me for default.

I am glad the Sisters have moved their school to Sumter, for I fear getting provisions for them here. I suppose if the orphans come up I will have to cater for them also.

We hear nothing from the movements about Charleston, there has been quite a number of soldiers passing through today for Tennessee, the whole of Jenkins Brigade and some others, they appeared well clad and shod, except a few who I suppose were from the hospitals, and had not recd their clothes. I hear that Genl Lee and the President have planned a campaign against *Rosencrantz* [*sic*], which will tax his utmost skill, to extricate himself from, and they expect to rout or capture the whole army. I hope so! The number of troops passing here and what I hear are passing the western route to take him in the rear, seems to favour the report, the interest in and about Charleston seems to have died out. Everyone looking on it as safe I suppose. What were you all at that you did not take advantage of last night—and make a Raid on Battery Wagner & Gregg, when the boats could not participate, it would have been a beautiful night for a raid of picked men with Bowie Knives & Revolvers taking them by surprise, you might have done them a vast deal of injury, spiked their guns and demolished their works besides taken prisoners (if you wished them). I think such a raid would have as great an effect on them as their last surprise at Sumter.

The school is getting on first rate only Ellen is fretting because you cannot come up and see them. I tell her you have to stay at your post just now, by the by, what is the Legislature called for, is it to elect a Senator to Congress, or is it about Charleston. I suppose they will hold secret sessions, so we will know but little of what they do.

[PS] I paid insurance for $6000 premium $60 on the Convent yesterday, the other amts are not due yet a while. Have you insured the Keitt house or do you intend doing so.

Baptista Lynch, Ursuline Convent, to Patrick Lynch, Oct [Octave] holy name Mary, [Sept 19][41]

As I posted a letter to you so recently, I only write now about the enclosed letter[42]—which please *read* & if you think proper, deliver.

From what I saw of Sᴿ C—while at the Sisters I like her—I also desire her talent for our Institute, it is the very talent we want now, if Miss Jones comes—I will be very glad to get her talent too, the more the better—But of course *nothing* could compensate for a proper religious spirit.

I have a great dislike to this underhand work. I imagine M. Theresa has large views enough to second the views of God even when they are opposed to her individual interests—At least such is my opinion & esteem for her that I would dislike paining her in any way. She must have trouble & anxiety enough at this time—I am glad to hear they have located in Sumter & hope they will do well. . . .

I am much obliged to you for writing on the subject of my former letter—& think very much as you do.

Our poor crazy lay-sister is in a bad way too. There must be something in the atmosphere that induces restlessness & a belligerent spirit. I wonder if we are still passing through the "comet region" that we were said to be in some-time ago.

Baptista Lynch, Ursuline Convent & Academy Columbia, S.C., to Patrick Lynch, Sept 23rd[43]

As you were so successful, in procuring a *pass* for M[rs] Lafitte, formerly Miss Barbot—her sister in law M[rs] Barbot, formerly Miss Huchet begs me to interest you in doing the same favor for her as she is particularly anxious to visit her husband in town—If you could conveniently do this, I would feel very much gratified & obliged because the Huchets are such good & disinterested friends to our convent—M[r] Huchet got permission from Gen. Beauregard to send us two tierces of rice, when he refused to do the same for any one else—& as for M[rs] Huchet, she never sees butter, eggs, &c &c on the street, that she does not interest herself for us, just as John does—In the same way, whenever we want anything out of the stores, she is always ready to do the duty of an out sister, so that we call on her constantly, & she does it so amiably & agreeably, therefore I would be glad to do her this favor, if possible— . . . John told me that a few days ago when he went to market our twenty lbs of beef were put on one side for us—& that there was not that much more in the market, while a hundred people stood around calling for meat & could not get it—. M[rs] Horlbeck is very anxious too to get a pass to return to Charleston—the sea breeze seems essential to her health & besides her brother who has been absent in Virginia for a long time has just returned to Charleston, if it would be right & proper for you to get one for her & let me give it to her I would be glad to render her that service— . . . I tried to send by express a box of Altar Breads but Government had monopolized so entirely the R.R.—that I did not succeed—I'm afraid if John does not take the pledge again soon, he will regret it—

We have been expecting you with Miss Jones from Wilmington yesterday & today—Did you get a letter from Mr Cohen relative to his daughter coming here—? I saw him myself, said all I could politely, to dissuade him from sending her to us, & finally concluded to take her, without granting *any concessions*— He seemed much pleased complimented me on my striking resemblance to yourself in appearance, voice & manner.

Make up your mind to hear a bucketful on a "tempest in a tea-pot" when you come, & bring a stock of patience & discretion with you to share with me— . . .

❧

FRANCIS LYNCH, CHERAW, TO PATRICK LYNCH, 24 SEP[44]

It is so near mail time that I must control myself with a business letter to you this time, acknowledging the rct of yours with the checks summing 6806.38 Six thousand eight hundred and six 38/100 to be invested as you have directed. . . .

[P.S.] The 57 Bales of Cotton promised for you by our late Bro Hugh (R.I.P.) are in store and insured. I will send M[r] [ends]

1863 October–December

"I do not know what will become of us."

The shelling of Charleston and its forts continued intermittently for the remainder of the year. Despite the pleas of family and others, Patrick Lynch refused to move from his episcopal residence in the lower part of town, making his own small but brave gesture of defiance. Many other Charlestonians and tidal-area residents continued to seek the shelter of the upcountry. Columbia remained a major destination for these forced migrants, many of them Catholics. The Catholic newcomers so swelled the congregation of St. Peter's that the pastor, J. J. O'Connell, found this influx an extraordinary opportunity to raise funds by auctioning off the pews hitherto rented at a set price. Baptista Lynch, among others, was appalled at this latest affront of the O'Connells, thinking such clerical "moneychangers" had no place in the Catholic Church. As it was, they functioned like bishops, authorities unto themselves and lording it over all others in their parishes, both lay and religious. No bishop, she (once more) told her episcopal brother, should ever tolerate such insolence and suggested how he might end it.

Baptista's academy itself was flourishing, thanks to the stream of student refugees, who accounted for half of the enrollment, which exceeded 120 by the end of the year, with a waiting list to boot. The added revenue allowed the Ursulines to secure the necessary provisions for the school, even at the runaway prices in the marketplace, where flour was $70 a barrel and a cow cost $1,000. Her main worry was having sufficient faculty to meet the expanding student population. Her major lifeline for the faculty, a critical mass of novices capable of staffing the classrooms, was threatened by too high a dropout rate, which Baptista largely attributed to their chaplain, Laurence O'Connell, and Baptista's bête noire in the community, Augustine England. O'Connell, Baptista was convinced, had little respect for religious life and tended to discourage aspirants from pursuing it. In Augustine the priest had an inside ally whose negativity *nurtured departures from the novitiate. Both of these troublemakers the Ursuline superior tried to remove: O'Connell, by having her brother in effect trade his services for those of a Jesuit military chaplain in Virginia; Augustine, by getting a religious community in Florida to give her a home.*

Baptista's other concern was the health of her niece, Sr. Gertrude, who was clearly losing her struggle against tuberculosis. As 1863 neared its end, the superior was counting the days until Gertrude had fulfilled the minimum probation period of one day over two years that the Ursuline constitutions required before a novice could make her profession. For all her troubles, Baptista would be nowhere else. She cherished her vocation.

What to Baptista was an ongoing blessing was to her nephew, Robert Lynch, a nightmare that should long ago have ended. Mustering the will finally to assert himself and declare his feelings after five years abroad, Robert made an anguished plea to his parents to release him from the seminary. As far back as St. Charles's minor seminary in Maryland, there had been signs of his being in the wrong place, preparing for the wrong future. His family chose to overlook them; tradition prevailed and Robert sailed off to France. But changed skies brought no relief to Robert, more out of place in Cambrai than he had been in Maryland.

At the Baltimore Carmel, a bloc within the community, intent upon establishing a foundation in St. Louis, managed, through the apparent assistance of Francis and Richard Kenrick (archbishops of Baltimore and St. Louis respectively), to force the resignation of Mother Teresa Sewall as prioress. Having put one of their own into the position, the come-outer group subsequently received an invitation from Richard Kenrick to inaugurate a Carmel in his see. In the wake of their departure, the remaining Carmelites in October elected Antonia Lynch as the prioress of the decimated community.

November brought a renewal of the full-time shelling of Charleston by the Union fleet, whose guns now had a range of up to nine miles in spreading terror. When one of its missiles deposited itself in the backyard of the episcopal residence, Patrick Lynch finally acceded to the pleading of his family and others and moved his quarters out of the guns' reach, to the rectory of St. Joseph's parish, a half mile to the north. That same month he issued a pastoral in the form of a prayer for peace. They were in God's hands, he wrote. Only God could rescue them from the deluge of iron that day by day was leveling the city that launched their war for independence. The cumulative physical and spiritual evils unleashed by war left them reduced to petitioning God to save them from themselves by bringing about the peace that he alone could give. The key to the end of war and the dawning of peace, Patrick instructed his subjects, was prayer informed by pure hearts that had owned their sins and amended their lives.

Only by seeking peace through prayer and penance could they realize the more virtuous life and just society that peace brought.

To Henrietta Lynch in her darkest thoughts, which she would only commit to paper that she could count on being destroyed, their lives had taken on a runaway character that mocked their economy; they were being helplessly swept along by incomprehensible forces toward disaster. As Christmas approached, even her ever-resilient sister-in-law, Baptista Lynch, had to admit that there was no escaping "the gloom hanging over the country." When the local bank refused to honor the Confederate money she presented as a payment on their mortgage, it was a shocking sign of the precarious state of the nation. Baptista willed herself to find in the celebration of Christ's birth the peace that their arms and prayers had failed to deliver.

BAPTISTA LYNCH, URSULINE CONVENT & INSTITUTE, COLUMBIA, S.C. TO PATRICK LYNCH, OCT 5TH[1]

. . . John has brought us from Capt Keitt $900 worth of Sorghum Molasses —& Mr Keys will buy the wheat for which we are making bags—Capt Keitt will also let us have some wheat, so that with the blessing of God I trust we may be provided against the coming trials of the winter which I so much dread— . . .

(interrupted) Miss Belle Cohen has just come in, bringing with her quite a little Library, & so over-anxious to learn Spanish, for which we have no teacher—. I regret her coming, but may-be, it will be for the best—. Was it not kind in Mr Bernard O'Neill to manage our cotton so nicely? Bishop Verot has written to me saying he regretted that I had not written about a month ago, when he took on a sister for the same reason as I mentioned (the similarity is greater than he knows) & says there will be no difficulty in crossing the enemies lines on account of their willingness to return the kindness shown their wounded, by the Srs in Charleston[2]—but it would require the escort of a clergyman from Jacksonville to St Augustine.

He is very cordial, but says it would be well to consult the Sister Superior of Columbus Georgia. I suppose she is the Superioress of both Houses[;] therefore I will make the arrangements with her & see on what terms she will receive S^r A [Augustine]. . . . As for the Lay-Sister, since she has no influence, it would be better to try & bear with her infirmities than to pay board for her elsewhere, unless we are compelled to send her to an asylum—. There can be no doubt of her crazyness, though she is doing very well ever since you left—You have no idea how much "*interior satisfaction*" your last visit gave the sisters & how grateful I feel for it—

We have deposited $4000 in the Palmetto Savings Institute, but if you want it or any money that we have you are most welcome, I forgot to say so when you were here—. Did you know that we offered to make a payment on this house when due in Aug & they refused to receive Confederate money.

I hope we may be able to lay in a good supply of provisions this winter, or it will take all we got to live on— . . .

I forgot to say we are all delighted with Miss Jones—.

֍

BAPTISTA LYNCH, URSULINE CONVENT, COLUMBIA, S.C., TO
PATRICK LYNCH, OCT 16TH[3]

. . . I have not heard from the Sisters of Mercy yet, about this troublesome S[r] here. I felt today as if I could stand it no longer, & never forgive you for bringing her here, when you knew or at least were told, what she is—Our school continues prosperous, D.G. We have I believe fifty four Boarders & about the same number of day scholars—What a pity we have not a large Convent we could have as flourishing a school as at Georgetown.[4] But it is wise to creep before we attempt to walk, & I suppose it will come in God's own time—. When you bring some religious order here, the Jesuits, or Paulists, or something to train the Boys, then we will do more—It is a miracle of grace, how our novices are doing ever as well as they are, with such a Chaplain & this Sister Augustine in the house—They talk I suppose about everybody's business but their own & I may become the brunt of it all—if you have a good priest in your diocese—I believe Revd F Fillion is one—& so is Revd P O'Neill—could you not give us the former, or establish the Jesuits—Redemptorists—Paulists or somebody here, that has some religious & some gentlemanly principles—? The Jesuits you know will establish themselves, if you will give them the church, & For all the good its income is to you, or religion in your diocese, you may as well—. I have just been writing to your former friend the Commissary General [Lucius Bell-inger Northrop], about his pictures & a mirror that D[r] Guerin wrote to me was packed up with them—There is an old [Manet] among the paintings, which has been much injured, it is a splendid painting.

We have bought a piano from M[rs] Huchet at $2000. I ought to have written to you & asked your permission first, but it was a necessity & we had $2500. Offered in Charleston, so I thought it better to take it at once.

Tomorrow, D.V. Sister Etienne & Sister Gertrude make their first demand "selon la Regle,"[5] for their religious Profession, after which, will begin their dis-tant preparation for that holy & solemn exercise—. You know that two years in the white veil will terminate January 3rd.

They can be professed then, any day after the 4th, the Rule requiring "*two years & a day*," you will please appoint the day as most convenient.

It seems like looking ahead to talk so, but time flies so rapidly in the convent that we always anticipate it—We heard from Anna a few days since, they are very anxious for a visit from you, & complain that you forget even to write. I hope you have written ere this—What about Nannie Ferralls marriage—did you forget it—? And did you send a priest to perform the ceremony for them on the 15th the day appointed—? I suppose you have received Johns letter of questions, about the Keitt place being occupied by Gen Blanchard[6] & family &c &c—He is anxiously expecting a reply to *all* his questions—.

We expected you as Mr Barbot told us, but were disappointed—did he make a mistake or how was it—? . . .

᷎

BAPTISTA LYNCH, URSULINE CONVENT & ACADEMY COLUMBIA, S.C., TO PATRICK LYNCH, OCT 24TH[7]

We have received two new pupils as boarders & several day scholars since I wrote to you—Miss *May* from Lynchburg is among the former—& Miss Trezevant & Miss Taylor—daughter & grand-daughter of old Dr Trezevant[8] of this city—are among the latter—. We are now obliged to register the names of applicants, & promise the first vacancy—. I am much pleased with the arrangement we have made about the little Orphan girl who is satisfactory & we hope will be very useful. Miss Scule is anxious to get a situation as governess. . . .

Madame Togno & myself had a little confidential conversation in which she gave me some account of her life as a *Catholic*— told me her Mother Madame Guyar of Philadelphia of whom you knew—died a sainted member of St. John's Church—where Father Barbelin[9] knew & esteemed her—!

I pity poor Madam Togno from my heart—& trust & think she will return to our holy Mother Church, which she still loves & reveres—. We will pray for her Conversion—I received a letter from Jane Semmes a few days since—she is as anxious as ever to enter our Noviciate but is detained from month to month by her Mother which is a most fortunate thing for her, whose affections were so enlisted by our unfortunate Sister A––. If it be God's will, I trust she may be out of the house before Jane comes—, It would be a terrible trial of her vocation— Miss Jones who is no child & has been very much associated with Religious, like sister Laura sees through her at once, she has not ventured to speak to me of her, but did to Sr Etienne & wonders that such a one is retained in religion.

Do not think my dearest Brother that your last forcible but kind reproof has been unheeded, since I write the above—no, I have made it the subject of meditation—& you have brought forward nothing new to me, so often have I endeavored to analyse my sentiments on that subject; except the comparison with the traitor Judas— . . .

I wrote my few last letters as I feel when under the influence of some annoying act of hers—I do not *always* feel, as then, & I did that on purpose, that *you* might see the effects of her exasperating conduct. I have often been made to feel so, but when I do, I go to the chapel & if possible do not cease to pray until the feeling subsides—I trust no one knows it—But I wish you to do so. I may say I *never* encourage that unendurable feeling, which hushes every kind sentiment, & I have tried to discover its motives as if examining a third person but cannot persuade myself that it is either envy or jealousy—there are other sisters whose knowledge, acquirements &c are much more to be desired & much superior to hers—therefore I do not think it can be either—It is not the position of Superior, for I refused that in Cin—& am sick & tired of it here— were she a good religious, there is no sister in the house whom I would more cheerfully see in the post than herself, because she is the niece of Bishop England, who first brought the Ursulines to this diocese. I have thought it more prudent not to mention names, or commit ourselves in any way until certain of a passport to St Augustine—which is yet unsettled. . . .

I will now close this painful subject, both to you & to me, before which my *feelings* alter but my *judgment* always remains the same—I am glad that you do put yourself on the defensive against my representations—I wish you to do so, & would not write freely, if I thought you did not—I am reading "Mahoney's Six Years in the Monasteries of Italy"[10] as a warning, & have learnt a lesson very different to what he intended to convey—It may be that I will run myself crazy on this point if I am subject to a long continuance of trial, for my will is indomitable, & I hope both mind & body may give way, rather than that I should offend Almighty God—my greatest happiness having always consisted in His service—

Robert Lynch to Parents, Cambreé the 6th November[11]

In the letter which I addressed you by the Rev. Mr. Flynn . . . I spoke to you rightly and plainly on a subject on which depends not only my happiness on the earth but also my future life, my vocation. Perhaps you will be surprised, my dear parents, for you have always thought that I would certainly be a priest, but you counted too steadfastly on a resolution that had been formed in me, before I gained the age of reflection and of studying to see if really it was my vocation to be a priest or not. This age has come, and the moment itself has arrived. Placed in an ecclesiastical college since five years, kept by priests, I have

Robert Aloysius Lynch as a
seminarian. Courtesy of
Ancestry.com.

been able to study all the qualities necessary for this holy state, as also the thousand dangers for one who embraces it with out the qualities necessary for this
holy state. Perhaps if I would say to you all of a sudden "I do not want to be a
priest," you could ask me with justice why so, and if I could not give you creditable reasons perhaps you would be irritated justly, but when I tell you that,
arrived at an age where man commences to think for himself, and to reason
pro and against, when I tell you that I have weighed the qualities necessaries
[*sic*] to make a good priest and also my defaults, and that I find that I am not fit
to make a priest, you cannot, I think, my dear Parents, feel any ressentiment
[*sic*] and blame me for it, for although this news may hurt you and fully, yet I
am sure that you would be happier to hear [manuscript incomplete] than to
think that I had condemned myself to be unhappy in this life and likely in the
next and why? For fear of speaking plainly to you and telling you that if I am a
priest it is not because it is my vocation but because you wish it. And certainly
this would be the case with me, for I feel something in the bottom of my heart
that warns me that if I would wish to be a priest, I would fall in to the wrong
road. To speak to you plainly my dear Parents, I ought never to have come to
France; I am there five years, I have staid there five years too long.

    . . . Perhaps you will ask me what state of life I would wish to embrace then?
My dear parents, the question is not hard to answer. In finding myself in South
Carolina at the end of the war with a little money I could gain a good deal in
the cotton trade; but we will talk all this over when I will have the happinesse

of seeing you which will be soon I hope. As my classes are finished I would like to leave France as soon as possible; not later than the month of May if possible, if the war is not yet finished at this time I would like to leave any way, being able to go to Canada or Nassau where I would certainly find a place until the end of the war, especially in the first country, and once the war finished I would return immediately to Columbia. I hope you will not refuse to acceed to my desires my dear Parents, for every day my desire of seeing you increases and my dislike of the Frenchmen likewise, and it will be astonishing if we can keep well together until I receive a letter from you telling me to leave. I hope the letter will not be long coming for the quicker the better for me. I will look for an answer to my letter until the month of September next, if it is not then arrived I will gain America as best I can. . . . My dear parents, I do not know what Uncle Patrick will think, but you understand that he cannot be angry with me and that he would be perfectly wrong in trying to persuade me to act against my vocation which he will certainly do if he wished me still to be a priest. . . .

ANTONIA LYNCH, MOUNT CARMEL, TO PATRICK LYNCH, NOV 6TH[12]

It was with much pleasure that I read your very welcome letter of the 20 inst. I have been wishing to write you for some time past but will not now put it off any longer. I am happy to learn of the good health of our dear Parents, and other members of the family, it would have given me so much pleasure could Anna have come on to Baltimore this past summer. Our Community has had some changes the last few months from a Foundation of the Order being made in St. Louis. The Prioress of our Convent taking that charge upon herself. Our Community in electing another chose *unworthy me* to fill that place. . . .

BAPTISTA LYNCH, URSULINE CONVENT & ACADEMY COLUMBIA, S.C., NOV 8TH[13]

What a grand turn out you have had in Charleston—! No wonder you could not come to Columbia, when you had such grand doings down there with President Davis! How did you like him? My experience is that great people always diminish in proportion as I approach to them—the lens of my imagination no doubt being a much greater magnifier than that of my reason. Did I ever tell you that I once wrote to Mrs Jeff Davis, & she answered me very amiably & cordially—? . . . You must come & tell us all about your turn out— Our school has about 120 scholars counting externs [day students]—among whom Miss Singleton, Miss Trezevant, Miss Taylor, Miss Seibles & Beauregards niece, little Proctor—We expect as a boarder Miss Douglass of Va daughter of Senator D___ who I am told is one of the cleverest men of our time. She wishes to become a Catholic—Let me tell you something good—we have been trying to get a good cow, having disposed of one that was no account. . . . We saw an advertisement of a splendid cow, warranted to give 20 qts per diem, & wrote immediately to Mr. W. M. Rivers of Winnesboro [*sic*] S.C. to purchase it of him. . . . Mr Rivers warrants the cow to give 20 quarts a day & says with good feeding she will, he thinks give 30.

She is $600 delivered in Winnesboro. We should pay $1000 here for one much inferior.

. . . Miss Jones talks of writing to you. I'm afraid she has no religious vocation. I'm sorry—if not. . . .

Henrietta Lynch, Cheraw, to Patrick Lynch, Nov 17th[14]

. . . Do you think the Yankees will leave Charleston.[?] Mrs Feugas will not leave again till driven away. Did you hear of the dreadful accident that happened to Major Moore? He was standing on the track when the cars backed and his leg was crushed. They amputated it entire, they say, this was at Florence where he has remained at the Hospital. He had great fortitude Dr. Maloy is in a very bad way we do not think he will recover. Dear Dr. Lynch do not be offended if I remind you of the Alpaca for the dress. I am in dreadful distress about one especially as there is no hopes of things getting better. Two dresses would be 20 yds and if you have good opportunity I would beg with great humility for this quantity tho' we will be exceedingly grateful for one. I know Mr Lynch will be willing to give any price for them if they can only be obtained. I wished to be so saving that I would not buy when I could have had it at 3$ per yard. But now I do not know what will become of us. Do us this favor, dear Doctor Lynch and we will owe you an everlasting obligation for the millionth time. . . .

Baptista Lynch, Ursuline Convent & Academy, Columbia, to Patrick Lynch, Nov 19th[15]

Apropos to Beauregard—I received quite a compliment from him yesterday —or rather our Community did—You remember I told you of his sister's visit to us, when of course I expressed our earnest wishes for the safety of Charleston, & the prayers for its brave defenders &c &c Well, yesterday I receivd a very nice note from Mrs Proctor, one which was evidently intended for me—requesting her to *present* the enclosed photograph—his own—to the Mother Superior &c &c with his compliments & sincere thanks for her kind wishes & prayers &c with assurances that he would exert himself to the utmost to deserve success in our sacred cause—Of course I replied by a note to Mrs Proctor, thanking her for the photography of *her* honored Brother & *our* brave Genl Beauregard— begging her to express our thanks to him & prayers that he may ever rank first in the cause of God & our Country—That is all very *pretty* isn't it? Now let us see the *good* of it—if it works A.M.D.G.?

We are very much pleased with the cloth[16] you got from Nassau, it suits better as a substitute for flannel, than for man's clothes—John is having it priced—

Have you seen anything about this association for getting provisions at reasonable terms—? John has taken two shares for himself & five for us—$100 per share.

I wrote home yesterday a long letter—for me—We have a good deal of indisposition in the house just now arising I suppose from cold changes I expect & from they say fatigue—it is a singular fact that the more help we get, the more we want, I suppose the labor increases in proportion—Miss Jones suggests very strongly my writing to the Misses Heath, three of whom she says ought to be here, to be in their right sphere. I suggested her breaking the ice, but she prefers not & wishes me to do it myself as being more influential, which I interpret, that she does not wish to praise too highly a convent in which *she* does not intend to remain. However, I hope I am mistaken—But what do you think of opening a correspondence with those ladies—or of my doing it—If I did it, of course, it would be simply a friendly style & might not lead to anything but all three are teaching & admirably fitted for that duty. I'm afraid Madame de Bertheville is getting like she was in St. Augustine & Savannah. She has yielded very much to her nervous streaks within the last two months, but three days ago was worse than ever I saw her before. In fact she was crazy— uncontrollably so—should she continue to have such scenes as that one—it would be impossible to keep her I suppose, as she disturbs every one & exposes herself to any & every body, children as well as Sisters by her exhibition of feeling, complaints & cries—Moreover it is exceedingly fatiguing to me & whoever has the management of her—Poor Sr Etienne was perfectly annoyed with her.

Our friend Mrs Horlbeck called today to beg that we would let her little daughter be a day-Boarder with us—as she loses by her associations in the afternoon the good she learns here in the morning—We have several such—so I received her— . . .

She told me that Charleston is being again shelled & some injury done—I trust you will move out of the range of the cannons' shot & shell. I read that their range is now nine miles! I hear nothing from Mr. Keyes & the wheat, except that he cannot get it for $10 per Bushel! And is trying in another quarter.

In the meantime, we are buying flour at the rate of $70. per Barrell & we use two barrels per week, besides corn meal. We ought indeed to be thankful that our school affords us the means of subsistence at a time like this.

Shall I write to Mr Ewd Coningland[17] or did you do so? We had two more applicants yesterday, but of course give the preference to Catholics . . .

[P.S.]We're afraid that we lost our Habit stuff in that vessel taken by the Yankees—

ᔑ

BAPTISTA LYNCH, URSULINE CONVENT & ACADEMY COLUMBIA, S.C., TO
PATRICK LYNCH, NOV 24TH[18]

Mrs Allemorige has come to John's & says that you are imprudently staying within the range of the enemy's shells, although the Spanish Consul has offered you his house above George's Street. I trust this is not true.—We feel anxious that you should be in a place of safety, & avoid all dangers—It is time that all should look out, & avoid such reports as you so well & amusingly described, & which Dr. Hughes *did not relish*. Did the shells burst in the Sisters' yard, & another strike the Hibernian Hall—? Please remember that "prudence is the better part of valor"— . . .

I expect Miss *Marnier* here this week to negotiate about becoming a secular teacher in our academy—Perhaps you remember that I refused her offer to that effect about a month ago but now since Miss Jones is on the go, I consulted with Sisters Ursula & Etienne & concluded it will be a necessity on account of the number of our music pupils especially & if we have to get a secular teacher, we prefer Miss Marnier to any other—

I think Miss Marnier has a vocation but combats it—& Miss Jones has none, but *thinks* she would like to have one. She would & would not—I have a letter on my desk which she has just written to consult Father Gache S.J.—I gave her permission to seal it—& I will write tomorrow—(interrupted by Miss Jones) She certainly is a very interesting lady & I cannot help wishing she had a vocation—She has not told me so plainly but I concluded that her present confessor has unhinged her ideas on the subject a little—it certainly is very strange, to have a convent chaplain who has no esteem for religious vocations & throws cold water on every candidate's ideas—I have been deterred only from a fear of displeasing you or giving you some inconvenience in writing to Col. Northrop asking his interest in getting Revd F. Gache removed from Lynchburg to this place as Hospital Chaplain, which is a nominal thing, & by this exchange with Father Lawrence we could have him as our chaplain[19]—I now ask your permission to do so, if Rev. J.G. will consent to the removal—? It will be for the spiritual interest of our novices especially & also for our pupils & selves—.

And you would gain the services of one more priest, which seems greatly needed through the country when so many ask for the sacraments & cannot get them. Please give me your answer to this request?

Mary Ryan left for good today on account of ill health. This was her fifth year with us & she could not bear to go. She is devoted to the practice of our holy religion & in Barnwell will feel desolate.

Miss Scule has advertised for a situation as governess & has many offers, one of which she will accept on Jan. 1st 1864, D.V.— . . . —Please move into a safe locality & write often— . . .

[P.S] Braggs news is good— . . .[20]

ॐ

Patrick Lynch, Pastoral Prayers for Peace, Charleston, S.C., 26 November[21]

BELOVED BRETHREN: Deeply moved by the calamities of these times, and in agreement with our Venerable Brethren of the Episcopate, we invite you to join with the Faithful in other Dioceses in earnest and persevering prayers to the Father of Mercy and the Giver of every good gift, to obtain from Him, in whose hand are the hearts of men, a cessation of the war which at present afflicts our country, and the speedy establishment of a just and honorable peace.

War is a consequence and a punishment of the sins of man. However just in its origin any special war may be, however necessary for the protection of important rights unjustly assailed, it is unavoidably attended by many evils and much suffering. Even when the commanders who guide it endeavor strictly to conform to those rules which the civilizing influence of Christianity has introduced and established, to restrain the lawless outbreaks of savage passions, there will still remain a vast amount of deplorable horrors, essentially connected with the sanguinary conflicts of nations. . . .

We need not seek abroad or in the distant past for these consequences of war. They press heavily on us at home. Who shall count the thousands and tens of thousands already slain on the battle field, or who died of disease in the camp or the hospital, or who have returned home maimed or decrepit for life? Who shall tell of the aged parents, whose mourning for the untimely death of the sons God gave them, is intensified by the helplessness in which they must now linger on, the remainder of their days, deprived of the support on which their old age fondly hoped to lean? The moans of stricken widows and of weeping orphans ascend to Heaven from many a desolate home. They have now no hope save in Him who is the protector of the widow and the fatherless. . . .

Who can measure the pernicious influence of camp life on habits, morals, and character? And even outside the camp, do we not behold the spirit of greed, extortion, and injustice stalking over the land? And may we not fear, that should this war endure long, it will, at its close, return to their homes thousands whom it will have entirely unfitted for the calm and quiet routine of agricultural life, or the assiduous industry of the workshop, or for the paths of peaceful commerce?

And if we can withdraw our minds from these sensible effects to still more weighty ones, who can think without fear and shuddering, of the vast increase of sins against God, and of the vast numbers hurried, without preparation, before the Judgment Seat of their Maker?

Truly war, springing from the passions and injustices of men, is, in the hands of Divine Providence, a potent means whereby sinful nations become the instruments of their own signal chastisement.

While our rulers and our armies in their respective spheres are making every effort, and shrinking from no sacrifice, to bring this struggle to a happy termination, it is fitting, beloved brethren, that in the spirit of religion we should have recourse to Him, in whose power are all things. . . . Let us acknowledge our sinfulness. . . . Let us seek Him with all our heart, and we shall find Him, and His thoughts toward us shall be thoughts of peace and not of affliction, to give us an end, and peace. *(Jer. xxix)* . . .

We, therefore, enjoin on the Pastors of the several Churches of this Diocess to invite the faithful . . . to assemble . . . for a *Novena,* and other special devotions . . . on Sunday, December 6th, and that the exercises consist of such prayers and instructions as are suitable to lead the people to penance. . . . Beside this, let the Rosary be recited, or the Litany of Loretto, and appropriate prayers for peace. . . .

II. We further direct that, on the 12th of December, the several clergymen of this Diocess celebrate the Votive Mass *Pro Pace;* and that . . . they will in all Masses, where it is allowable according to the Rubrics, subjoin the Collect and Prayers *Pro Pace* to those of the day.

. . . God will hear the prayers of the just and pure. He delights to welcome and to forgive the repentant sinner, who, with earnest and sincere heart, returns to Him and throws himself on His mercy. Let us all raise our voices to Him. "Spare, O Lord, spare thy people. Be not angry with us forever."

≪

Baptista Lynch, Ursuline Convent & Academy Columbia, S.C., to Patrick Lynch, Feast St. Andrew [Nov 30][22]

I had a very pleasant visit from M[rs] Hayes, formerly Miss Proctor & a pupil at the Ursuline Convent N. Orleans. She seemed so delighted to speak again with a Religious, & told me, that she was taken out of the Institute because she was so fond of it, that her family feared her becoming a Catholic—I think she has tendencies still to Catholicism—her little daughter is a pupil of ours, a day scholar like her cousin—Beauregard's niece. . . .

. . . I expect Miss Mary Jones to leave soon—She has received a letter from her Father enclosing one from Sister de Chantel of Mt deSales which will serve as another impetus to her leaving.

Our work is very continuous but our strength is from above.—Our music lessons we feel the most especially vocal music—& have in all about 160 or 170 per week—Deo gratias for all things—Miss Marnier having already engaged herself for another year, I must only begin again & step into Miss Jones' shoes—certainly I am stronger now at 40, than I was at 21 years of age— . . .

We have every reason to feel grateful for the very high opinion which the grown young ladies express of our school & mode of government—their docility & agreeability in religious matters—

ᙟ

ANNA LYNCH, CHERAW, TO PATRICK LYNCH, DEC 1ST[23]

. . . I hope, you have moved out of reach of the shells, for I understand that on Friday last they came very near, if not in your premises. I can't imagine how you can sleep with any peace within range of them, not knowing as the Irishman would say, whether you will wake up alive, and as good people are scarce, this ought to be a consideration for you. . . . Sister Ellen wishes Father & [mother] to attend Ellen's profession, which they would like to do, if bad weather, & the risk incurred in travelling, does not prevent. I hope that we will hear from you soon again when you will have moved out of range—

ᙟ

BAPTISTA LYNCH, URSULINE CONVENT & ACADEMY COLUMBIA, S.C., TO PATRICK LYNCH, DEC 6TH[24]

I hope you are now comfortably located in the upper part of town, where none of the Yankees' shells can reach, that during your absence the *key* was found & everything moved & placed in order for you, by your return.

I wonder what house you will occupy when you come to Columbia to live—will you rent one near the Church or where—? What do you think the income of the church here is? John told me today, that they are going to rent the pews for which there are now many applicants, by auction to the highest bidders, that M[r] Comerford & M[r] McGinnis are appointed to do this—Neither he, M[rs] Bauskett, or M[r] Jones, are willing to pay higher than their present rent—viz[25] $45. & 50. but such speculators as Ingalls[26] & Flannigan,[27] &c will give they say as high as $1000, to secure their pews. Eliza expressed to J. J. O'C—her wish to keep the pew they always had rented, but unwillingness to pay more—he said, let the Dr. bid up & we can settle it afterwards. But John is not willing to sanction such cheating or extortion, & says he will come to the convent chapel as Mrs Huchet & others, if he cannot get his pew—.

Where is the vestry—? What [is] the salary of this clergyman here, & have they any superior—? I wish these money changers were turned out of the sanctuary, or their den broken up—I am at this moment indignant, at the cool impudence with which these O'Cs [O'Connells] manage the affairs of your diocese, & make themselves our superiors—Some time ago by their arrangement, I was called down to the parlor, to learn from M^r McNeal *their* tool, that he was to be our Confessor— . . . There is not one in the diocese unless yourself & Father Fillion fit to direct a convent—I am *thoroughly disgusted* with these Irish priests though I thought I could not be more so, than I was in the west—.[28] I never saw one yet, or a religious either, that I could esteem. You will say I do not understand them. It is strange I do not, when our dear Parents whom we are obliged to love & esteem in the most exalted way are Irish but how unlike them, any I have met—No, they do very well for making money & making merry—but not for religion—.

. . . The truth is, if you let this man here, go on making money, so as to enable him to keep open house for all these young priests, living high . . . he will win their hearts & just twist them around his fingers, leaving you the name, & no more of "father Bishop."

It is in your house, & at your Board they should love to assemble, & into your ear they should love to pour all their little trials & troubles—Come to Columbia, establish yourself in the Church, give these gentlemen a salary, & no more somewhere, & see what they will do—

. . . Miss Jones has heard from Father Gache who like myself thinks her vocation for the world.

ॐ

Baptista Lynch, Ursuline Convent & Academy Columbia, S.C., to Patrick Lynch, Dec 9th[29]

Your heart would have rejoiced yesterday—the feast of the Imm. Conc. to see so many communicants among our pupils & such happy faces—It was quite a day of devotion—At 12 o'clock we had the novena for peace—vespers in Choir at 3 P.M. At 2 ½ Benediction [of the] B. S. followed immediately by our usual Procession on that festival— . . . The statue & banners were carried by the children who all seem quite impressed by the ceremony. At the conclusion we received some children into the first grade of the "Children of Mary" & gave an appropriate instruction on the object & nature of procession in honor of Our Blessed Mother, which gratified & instructed both Protestants & Catholics— Our friend Mrs Horlbeck found her way in with her little daughter, & seemed perfectly absorbed by all that she saw & heard—. She must have a leaning towards Catholicity.

We have received another new boarder—quite a character & very clever. Her mother, Mrs Keeling & herself are both studying to become Catholics— & I have just answered an application from Capt Elliott of Pocotaligo & from J. E. Tobin Esqr[30] of Barnwell, S.C. & engaged to receive at Jan 1st a Miss Mann niece of Mr John Caldwell[31] of the R.R.—Presidency. These together with Miss Mulder, will fill up all our vacancies left by the departure of Misses Scule, Woodruff, &c—

And what do you think—? We have a new application—a postulant for our noviciate, to fill the vacancy left by Miss Jones—Oh! I believe I have not told you that she left on Monday morning bright & early under the protection of young Blanchard the Genl^s son—

I congratulate my self on the nice way I fixed for her departure—she having on Sunday received a letter from F. Gache, who decides with me but expresses what I would not, that her vocation is not for any religious order, but if her infirmity will permit, is for the married life—I thought the sooner the better she was out of the house, where she viewed everything thro' a distorted medium & so amiably got her off at once, much to my relief.—She appears *to my face* great affection & gratitude—. I think she & Stella Clarke very much alike in general character. Stella has the advantage in education & training—. But who do you think proposed herself to me—No other than Victoria Blanchard—what do you think of our receiving her? Her mother opposes the step as an ungrateful one to her, & says she is too fond of admiration ever to be a Nun—Her Father rejoices at the idea, & I have no doubt it is partly owing to his counsel that she offers herself, although she says not—It is true she often said when our pupil, that she found she could never save her soul in the world &c—But I attached no importance to it—thinking her so thoroughly worldly—Sister Charles her confidante says however, that she is not surprised—Do you remember the affair of Col Schaller? Of course that had died out entirely, & since then she has had another suitor, but she will not accept him—and will if her mother concurs with her father, wish to enter our noviciate at some not very distant day—In the mean time we will engage her to give singing lessons to some of our pupils—I would be delighted if she *really had a true vocation* for she is much superior to Miss Jones, who seems to fancy that the house would fall when she left—I will expect Annie Lowe to be our next offer—She is another highly gifted girl & would be very useful. . . .

❧

John Lynch, Columbia, S.C., to Patrick Lynch, Decr 15th[32]

. . . if you have the money idle, you can send me up a check for one thousand dolls. Christmas time I will have to give the negroes something, and I think a little money will suit them better, and be cheaper just now, than any thing else. I am sorry to have to tell you that the Nassau cloth is damaged, and that badly, was it insured? I let Ellen have a bolt and she first discovered it. I gave the men & women at the Keitt place clothes of it. I have taken a bolt for my children, but am afraid it will prove unprofitable. The balance I have on hand, I think it must have got wet with bilge water on the way from Nassau, which may account for the peculiar odour it has, if it was good it would bring a good price, but as it is, I am afraid it will not be a profitable investment, still it will be best to keep it, from all appearances we will be much worse off yet, and it will clothe the negroes.

Your friend Mr Mitchell[33] came up a day before your telegram. We were much pleased with him, he only stayed five days. He fixed the price himself, or rather with great delicacy he said he knew more about the prices than I did and insisted on my taking the amt he offered, on my demurring, he insisted that I take the difference between us for a Christmas present for the little Bishop, after that I could say no more, he appeard to have taken a fancy to little James all the children were quite at home with him, and he seemed to be perfectly at home himself. Such an one is never any trouble about a house, All are well, and practice brisk, although the town is healthy (so said) . . .

❧

Baptista Lynch, Ursuline Convent & Academy, Columbia S.C., to
   Patrick Lynch, Dec 17th[34]

As your boy Moses—brother to Isaac, has call[ed] on his way to Charleston & offers to be the bearer of any messages to you I will send a few lines, although I have written so often lately.—We still continue to have demands for circulars & have received another young lady from Richmond—but I expect we shall lose our Alabama pupils, now that they fear communication being cut off—Miss Woodruff left with her father a few days since & Dora Martin's friend from the same place, Tuscaloosa, wrote to tell her she should return with him, but Dora wrote & telegraphed also begging to remain until Jan^y.—She cried all night about having a dream that she had gone home & had fallen into—perdition, & was calling from the bottomless pit to one of the Nuns to save her, when lo! & behold I stretched out my hand & took [her] into the Convent which she thought was heaven—! Our pupils are better than when I last wrote but the

Lower Charleston after months of bombardment.
Courtesy of the Library of Congress.

colds & sickness is among the sisters now & Sister Agnes is right sick—Poor Sister Martha is as "mad as a march hen" again—I keep out of her way this time. But she is awful.

We also had a breakout with the French old lady, on last Sunday—to such an extent, that I told her if she had a house & means, we certainly would not keep her, but *in consideration of this* &c &c she might remain, but her conduct had annulled all the time of probation past & she could only count from next Sunday. She is very repentant—she is very good but that will not give her sense—and you know Daniel O'Connell used to say—"From pious fools—O Lord deliver us"—

We succeeded in getting some cow-feed, & heard today of our wheat coming too.

Baptista Lynch, Ursuline Convent & Academy, to Patrick Lynch, Dec 21st[35]

Having dispatched between twenty & thirty letters for the children & having my brains a little frazzled over them, & hands stiff from cold—I begin my letter to you, hoping you will excuse the chirography, &c &c. Notwithstanding the gloom which seems to hang over the country, I wish you my dearest Brother a happy Christmas & season—To us, who only look with a spirit of faith in the stable of Bethlehem—the gloom—the privations &c are like so many sources of merit, & being such our Christmas is a happy one in spite of them—for it recalls forcibly the nothingness of all that the world esteems & poor human nature loves.

We made the arrangement to have the Profession of Sisters Etienne & Gertrude, & the reception of Sr. Francis on the 5th Jan I believe, but it occurs to me, that if you would come on the 5th & examine those to be professed & then profess them on the 6th when we must suspend our school it would be a better arrangement.[36] Since you have no cathedral you may as well officiate in our chapel on that day & you know we must give holiday to our pupils on the profession day, so we may as well combine the two. . . .

. . . —The demands for circulars *"have an upward tendency"* & every body seems pleased with our Institute Thank God—May it all tend A.M.D.G. —.

This morning we had a visit from another party—(bridal) from Va . . . Col Washington was one of the party, his son is engaged to be married soon to Miss Laine, whose sister is with us—I humbugged them as I generally do, explained our chapel, usages in Church &c—so that they said they were charmed . . .

I am so glad to learn that you are delivering a delightful course of instructive lectures, which I have no doubt are well attended & will do much good. This war makes men wake up to the necessity of religion.

It is so dark I have to stop—& I have a racking tooth ache—I wonder what the soldiers do when they have tooth-ache, & sleep out in the cold—poor fellows—may our blessed Mother cover them with her mantle— . . .

[P.S.] got letters from Miss Jones & from Miss Lowe—Both satisfied to be as they are—.

❧

Anna Lynch, Cheraw, to Patrick Lynch, Dec 27th[37]

. . . I have just finished a letter to Uncle Hugh for Mother, which she will send by Mr Adderly, who leaves in the morning for Wilmington enroute to Nassau, and expects to get through safely.

Christmas passed very quietly, & was unusually still, but we had our enjoyment beforehand in the pleasure your visit afforded us, and hope you may be able to repeat it after your return from the springs. . . .

1864 January–March

"The whole is a matter of endurance."

To Baptista Lynch's surprise, Christmastide in the Confederacy proved to be not the bleak season she anticipated but a festive one, the war virtually forgotten amid celebrations both on the front lines in Georgia and Virginia, as well as on the home front. It was as though the entire Confederate nation was in denial of its grim condition.

Maintaining the cycle of religious life with its solemn moments of veil taking and profession was one way to dispel the gloom that declining military fortunes were producing. The Ursuline community concluded its Christmas festivities with the solemn vows of two members of the community, including Sr. Gertrude (Ellen Spann), and the reception of a third. The only damper on the daylong celebration was the failure of Patrick Lynch to show and preside over all the rites and events that accompanied these critical passages of religious life, a failing that annoyed Baptista greatly, as she made clear to her brother.

Patrick Lynch himself was not one to let emotion cloud his judgment. That determination applied to the war as well. As he observed to one of his priests, its outcome was still to be decided. The year 1864 would be a decisive year, he thought, but exactly how favorably or not it broke for either side depended on a number of interconnected factors: whether the South could maintain enough uncontested territory in which it could grow the staples to sustain both its military forces and its people as a whole; whether Northern morale would be good enough to generate the high reenlistment rates that were a prerequisite for the success of any new Union campaigns to divide and conquer the Confederacy; whether the Democratic Party, which was committed to making a peace settlement with the seceded states on liberal terms, would receive a popular mandate in the coming fall elections. All things considered, the bishop thought the South had two vital advantages: home ground and perseverance. They were fighting on their own soil, land they knew in a way invaders never could. Familiarity gave them a constant edge. Second, as reflected in the enlistment *terms of Confederate soldiers, the Southern people, for the duration of the war, had a dedication to gaining independence that the sixty-day or even the three-year men in the Union ranks could not match. That dedication manifested itself in the astoundingly high percentage of fighting-age men in the South who were in the military, a trend that went a long way to eliminating the manpower advantage that the North had on paper. That dedication could endure suffering or setbacks or other privations to an extent the North would never fathom. What dedication could not overcome, the bishop left unmentioned, was the exhaustion of the South's fighting-age pool through the terrible attrition of three years of war. That this was a real and present danger was apparent in the Confederacy's most recent expansion of draft eligibility both by age as well as occupation. For the middle-aged manufacturer Francis Lynch to be made draft eligible was a clear sign of the South's growing shortage of fighting men.*

As the head of a girl's academy, Baptista Lynch experienced firsthand the consequences of sagging morale: parents calling their daughters home for fear of being cut off from them during the next—and final?—season of the war. Fortunately, for every student withdrawn, at least another appeared, wanting to enter the academy. The Ursuline school continued to flourish and build upon its rapidly rising reputation; the number of students converting and/or wanting to become nuns themselves increased along with the enrollment. Baptista made no attempt to mask her pride in the growing stature of the institution she headed, largely the consequence of the high status of the students it attracted. For the larger community the academy functioned as a regional social center for the elite émigrés from the lowcountry. All this social and religious success had, she sensed, engendered a backlash of envy in the community and of resentment among some parents distressed at the aggressive proselytizing and cultivation of vocations by the Ursulines. The price, she feared, would likely be a decline in enrollment for the next academic year. Then, too, the nuns were beginning to feel the full effects of isolation from the North; the texts and ritual aids that Catholic publishing houses in Baltimore and New York annually supplied were no longer to be had.

The Confederate government's announcement in February of a devaluation of its currency by a third forced the nuns to convert their old currency into goods they could barter for needed food and supplies once the new currency took effect, with the hope of thereby maintaining financial stability. Francis Lynch pursued a different road to financial security by continuing to speculate in cotton as a counterbalance and supplement to his shoe production, even as the Union blockade tightened around the dwindling number of ports available to the Confederacy.

At the beginning of February, Patrick Lynch learned that the Confederate government intended to commission an agent for a special mission to Rome, or, in formal terms, to the States of the Church. Still to be decided was whether that agent should be a layman or prelate. If the latter, they wanted the Charleston bishop for the position. Three weeks later Lynch traveled to Richmond, once again on his way to Montgomery White Sulphur Springs. While in the capital he met with Secretary of State Judah Benjamin, who informed him that he was President Davis's choice for the mission.[1] Patrick Lynch's life was about to change in a big way.

෴

BAPTISTA LYNCH, URSULINE CONVENT & ACADEMY COLUMBIA, S.C., TO PATRICK LYNCH, JAN 2D[2]

. . . Who ever heard a Profession taking place in the afternoon—? Unless you can say your Mass in the after-noon, for it [is] at the communion of the Mass, that the solemn vows are pronounced.[3]

We are *very much* disappointed at your arrangement of time—Our programme of time was to have the examination of Sister Etienne & Sister Gertrude on the evening of the 5th & professed at early Mass on the Epiphany, leaving us the middle of the day to arrange every thing for Sister Fannie's[4] reception in the afternoon at 4 P.M.—her father will arrive for the occasion on the day previous—.

Now you have overturned all our plans—Do if you can, come in time for an early Mass on the Epiphany— . . .

Sister Etienne may have her friends—we will be disappointed in having Mother & Father, as we wrote to them begging them not to run the risk—Sister Fannie's Father may invite his friends—But I expect many will work their way in—

The church was crowded to excess on the occasion of John Bauskett's marriage the other evening—I suppose you know he married Miss Helen Nürncey— it was a grand turnout—

Sister Gertrude & Sister Ursula & all the Sisters join in wishing you a very happy new Year & many joyous returns of the festive season.

We may well call it a festive season, for despite the war, the suffering which necessarily must exist, I hear of nothing this Christmas but festivities & there seems to be a forgetfulness of every thing else. I see by letters from the soldiers, that they too know how to take better care of, & for themselves now than formerly. . . .

BAPTISTA, URSULINE CONVENT, COLUMBIA TO PATRICK LYNCH,
JANUARY 9, 1864[5]

And so you got off this beautiful morning, my dearest Brother. I hope you
had a good fire in the Cars and arrived home safely as well—John tells me you
speak of going to Richmond next week. I hope, if you do, you will have a pleasant time—I enclose a letter from, I presume, Jacob Barrett, since I got one by
the same mail written from the same place & in the same hand, concerning
his little daughter. If he is a Catholic, we will perhaps take her, though I cannot
promise—but if not a Catholic as I suspect, we do not wish to receive any Protestants or Jews under fifteen years of age—these little ones are great trouble &
little profit either spiritually or temporally. . . .

Should you meet while in VA a Miss Kirk, niece of Mr. Lewis, I would be
very glad, as I have my eye on her as a Postulant.

ANNA LYNCH, CHERAW, TO PATRICK LYNCH, JAN 10TH[6]

We were sorry to hear through Sister Ellen that you were sick, when in
Columbia, and hope that you are better & will not venture on to Virginia [in]
this severe weather which renders the fireside the most comfortable place. As
wood is scarce in Charleston, you had better come up here where it is more
plentiful. . . . Mr Blain goes down in the morning & I send this by him with a
small package, which you will please hand Sister De Sales, or Miss Brennan
when you go on to the springs, for me. Sister De Sales was kind enough to offer
in Ellen's last letter to bring on anything from Baltimore to Father & Mother if
she succeeded in getting there, so, I suppose, she still hopes to do so. She mentioned that she would hand the box to Sister Catherine to have filled. As Father & Mother are in want especially of winter clothing they would gladly avail
themselves of her offer if you approve. . . .

FRANCIS LYNCH, CHERAW, TO PATRICK LYNCH, 15 JANY[7]

I received you welcome letter and am glad to learn you are well in the pelted
city. The Yankees seem determined to see what virtue there is in shells. Today I
deliverd a portion of the cotton to Mr. Roper, and paid 70,000 on the debt. The
remaining purchase money to be paid next week. I might have paid the remaining 10,000$ had I not made some other purchases of cotton, which I am
holding. . . .

❧

BAPTISTA LYNCH URSULINE CONVENT & ACADEMY, COLUMBIA, S.C., TO PATRICK LYNCH, JAN 15TH[8]

Do you remember that lady that came here in such a terrible fuss & hurry to see her daughter—& saying that she was hurrying on with Mr Barksdale, to exculpate a friend of her's who was suspected of being a government spy &— Well the friend is convicted & she herself implicated & for running off Negroes to the Yankees—!!! Did you ever hear of such a horrible thing!

It was awful to see her like a maniac running from justice, & we had to pack up every thing of the poor childs & let her go with her unfortunate Mother!— They may be hanged—!

This evening I had a very pleasant conversation with Antoinette Huchet who asked me to see her—She has made a formal demand to enter our noviciate —& we are much pleased for she is a steady sensible girl—I will speak to her mother about it on tomorrow—. It is too late to write more—When will you leave for Va—?

❧

JOHN LYNCH, COLUMBIA S.C., TO PATRICK LYNCH, JAN 18TH[9]

I send you at once Mr Buffs letter to me. I have not sent him answer, except that I would write to you. I think if he leaves the best thing you can do will be to advertize the place for rent for the year, as a place of refuge There is accommodations [*sic*] for at least 40 or 50 negroes besides the dwelling which is in tolerably good order; it would rent for as much as would (with what help the negroes could give themselves) support them and pay their taxes, I think if it did it is more than they can do there. Move the negroes to Murphys, hire out some of them, the balance let him work to the best advantage, he goes down to meet the cars tomorrow, I gave him $300 more today, so that he may fill the car he missed getting the rotten corn he spoke of, it was sold in the family. Mr Murphy says if Mr Kelly has to leave Charleston, he would like to get the Lexington place for him, but if you wish to offend no one—put it into the hands of Phillips or Mordecai to find a tenant and fix the price. . . .

❧

JOHN LYNCH COLUMBIA S.C., TO PATRICK LYNCH, JANY 18TH[10]

I have no doubt you will think on the recpt of this, that there is a screw loose about one, or that something wonderful is about to happen (perhaps peace) receiving three letters from me in two days, first about the corn, next about Mr

Buff, and now about M[rs] Proctor. I will enclose her note to Eliza, which will explain itself, as far as M[rs] P is concerned, but Eliza wishes to make an explanation also, she says M[rs] Proctor entirely misunderstood her, if she means by her note that Eliza ever intimated that *she* had the [the authority of] allowing any one to take possession, in sending the note to you she wishes this explained, as it might appear she was making too free with what did not belong to her, in conversation she did mention that she thought it would be very pleasant if they could get possession of one half of the house occupied by Genl Blanchard as it was a large house and could easily accommodate two families, this she thinks is what M[rs] Proctor alludes to, the conversation was brought about by M[rs] Proctor complaining of the high rate of rents which had been raised on them, and her inquiring if Eliza knew of any place they could get. In answering her note Eliza will mention that the Blanchards are now occupying the greater part of the house, but will write to you and see if you have made any arrangement, about the place, or can rent them a part of the house. I spoke to Ellen about it this evening who said she thought you would be glad to be able to do anything to oblige Genl Beauregard's sister, and she would not ask the Blanchards whether it would be agreeable to them or not, if they have taken the whole house, it is more than was given to them, and more than they need, I am afraid I put my foot into it when I let them take the place. As mentioned to you at the time I left the compensation entirely with you, I have never mentioned rent to them since, in the present case if you let M[rs] Proctor and her friend, the Miss Manigault have a part of the house, I would have it understood what rent they would pay, as I understand they are able to pay some. . . .

᭢

JOHN LYNCH, COLUMBIA, S.C., TO PATRICK LYNCH, JANY 21[11]

I recd word from M[r] Murphy tonight that he had the corn on the platform and that the car had not arrived, asking me to telegraph to you, which I have done. I have also written to him if he does not get the car by tomorrow night to turn the corn & pens over to the post quarter master and take his recpt in the name of Capt Coit by me, Coit is the collector of tax in kind here, and will make the exchange, I have been troublesome in the way of letters this week, still I will trouble you a little further. Mr P McKenna came down with Ned yesterday, and offers to hire him for $4000 a year and find him in clothes, pay his taxes &c—if you move Danl over, it would be a good arrangement to take his offer, for he could not possibly make you that much where he is, and if the others are moved over I would hire some of them out also, write and let me know your views for I do not know exactly how to act without instructions, and do not want to take too much responsibility on my own shoulders.

HENRIETTA LYNCH, CHERAW, TO PATRICK LYNCH, JANUARY 26TH[12]

I received your letter on Friday. I would have written to acknowledge the cloth you sent but I have been indisposed for a long time. I am exceedingly obligated to you for the cloth. The color is very pretty but I am sorry you had to buy it. I sent you six yds of cloth by the sisters and will send 9 again tomorrow by express.

We all hope you are quite well. I understand you are coming to Cheraw to lecture in a short time. Rev Mr Brown gives his lecture tonight. Mr. John Harrington and the Joleys have been giving large parties but the people of this town were not generally invited. Mr Feugas wrote me that they wanted to come & board with us. They think us rather unkind for not taking them as boarders. We told them they were welcome to come & live but will not take them that way. I am not going to be bothered with boarders but if they choose to come & live just so I know they cannot find fault with things. . . . We have cause to regret the death of Dr. Malloy. He is the only physician in whom confidence could be put. He died last Tuesday. I hope you are out of the way of the shells. . . .

BAPTISTA LYNCH, URSULINE CONVENT & ACADEMY COLUMBIA, S.C., TO
    PATRICK LYNCH, JAN 26TH[13]

I have a letter on my desk partly written to you & dated 24th but thinking you were in Richmond I took my time in finishing it—Today John recd your letter by Capt. Keitt undeceiving us on that position. What has kept you so quiet in Charleston all this time—? Bishop McGill ask[ed] Sister Etienne in a short congratulatory letter which he wrote her: "What has become of the Bishop of Charleston? We have been expecting him for the past week."

John received a long letter from Robert on Saturday, for which he had to pay $5.00—It was dated in March & I am sorry to say breathed little or nothing of the spirit of the ministry—I do not consider myself a judge of a student for the Priesthood but if a novice of ours breathed such spirit of vain conceit & condemnation of Superiors—such proud & worldly expressions—such unconstrained passion, I would soon decide her vocation, & send her to her family & the society of the world for which she seemed fitted—

I wish you could see this letter—& you could judge for yourself as he seems anxious to leave the college.

John seems disappointed, but if he has no vocation it is better that he should never be ordained—I had a visit from Mrs Proctor, for whom I feel great sympathy. She now resigns the idea of sharing your house with the Blanchards, as she has succeeded in getting some music pupils in town which she should lose if she went out in the country—. I'm afraid we shall lose several of our pupils at the close of this session Mademoiselle Le Salle of N.O. was sent for last Sunday, but she may return since she begs & pleads to do so—M I. Robinson was telegraphed for & written to, that she might return to Montgomery Ala this week, but she wrote back & telegraphed begging to remain until June—She also prayed and fasted to obtain her request, & to her great joy succeeded—. Mr Woodruff of Tuscaloosa says that if he had forty daughters to educate he would send them all to the Ursulines of Columbia, for *they* know how to train both mind & manners—! We have yesterday & today a counterbalance to that— We have had on our list of applicants for whom we have reserved places Miss Carter, Miss Murdoch & Miss Mitchel from Montgomery Al—well, they arrived yesterday & stopped with their friends Dr. Goodwyn's[14] family who prejudiced them against the convent to such an extent—at least so I judge, by their saying that since they came to C— they had heard so much against the Convent &c—that they have gone elsewhere & also taken away much against her will a very interesting young lady Miss Mitchel their cousin, who has been with us for some months. I suppose they fear our influence, for she told her sister that she wanted to be a Catholic & did not want to leave the convent—

The unfinished letter to you was to tell you of this terrible fright Md[m15] gave us, by arousing us in the quiet of the night by her cries in a regular crazy fit— fortunately it was a cold night, the windows closed, but if it had been in the warm weather, when she could have been heard for nearly a square, this would ruin the reputation of our house, & perhaps injure religion.

I wrote at once to Bp Verot—so that he may be prepared to see her at any time but it is to our interest to keep her, as long as we can, on account of her talents—these paroxysms last about twelve hours, but they are sometimes a week in coming on, or rather in reaching their culminating point—

You cannot imagine what a time we have had with our *quasi postulants*[.] I mentioned to M[rs] Huchet, as I said I would, after Antoinette's formal request to be admitted—. She took it very well so long as I was present, but when she went home, started off for Charleston to bring Mr H home & take Antoinette out of the convent right away. But the cars were gone.

She telegraphed however, & Mr H—arrived the following day. They both came & poor Antoinette had a time of it—She assured them however that we would not receive her into our noviciate without the consent of her parents, & so that gave a *quietus* to the matter—. M[r] Barbot too opposes the step. Gov. Lowe says if Ann. has a vocation both he & her Mother will be happy, but she must return to the world & test it, at least until she is twenty years of age—She is now seventeen.

Mrs Blanchard will not listen to her daughter! on the subject—& Jane Semmes from whom Sister Ursula got a letter today, will I suspect be a second. . . . Ah! me.—man proposes but God disposes—I'm sure it is all for the best, tho it puts me a little in the cellar we call depression of Spirits—

We read with anxiety of the advance of the enemys shells & trust that you will keep in a place of safety—

Rev Dr McGee was disappointed in getting off to Nassau but Genl Whiting[16] very kindly sent our letters without examining them. I will write again to Sister Antonia about our Boxes which M^r LaFitte says were not in Nassau Jan 10th. I'm afraid they are lying in the port of N. York & will be spoiled before we get them—having no one there to look after them— . . .

P.S. I have made it no better or worse than to ask Miss Goodwyn what was the objection &c to our academy &c for she is now in the parlor—and she assures me that her family have had nothing to do in the matter—That Miss Mitchell was highly pleased until her sister told her she wished to be a Catholic, then they all took the alarm—& are all going to the Methodist College! Much to the chagrin of Sallie.

᠅

John Lynch, Columbia, to Patrick Lynch [February][17]

I am having the things and the negroes moved over to the Keitt place, Mr Buff left last week, I do not know whether I can get more than $600 for the place for the year, the house is not so comfortable as I thought, and the amt of land not sufficient for a large gang of negroes, do you think I should take 600 if I cannot get more. I have offered Mr. McKenna, Ned for $400 for the balance of the year, he clothing & paying all expenses. Mr Murphy tells me since that Mr Keely is anxious to hire him & will give more than any one else, and will buy his wife, if it is not dangerous, it will be a good place for him to perfect himself in his trade.

I have furnished Mr Murphy with money to purchase corn & peas. to a larger amt than you would need, he succeeded in buying enough for yours & perhaps my own use for the year, before they began to raise on him, the last time he went down he did not get any. They were unwilling to sell, I will be able to exchange what he gets below, with Capt Coit of this place.

Let me know if you wish me to hire out many of the young hands. . . .

ᘓ

PATRICK LYNCH, CHARLESTON, TO TIMOTHY BERMINGHAM,[18]
1ST FEBRUARY[19]

Your letter & enclosing by Mr. Mottet, dated 21st November reached me yesterday. The previous bill for £240 is safe in Richmond. I mention . . . in the beginning of this letter to put that important matter straight, and as it may be a month before I can send this letter off, I may as well set out to write you a long tho irregular one, on all things about this poor distracted country, as well as about our own particular things. But about your letter by Mr. Mottet. He arrived here a few days ago, *without the letter* and told me it was in the hands of the Yankees. So I gave up all hopes of it. It seems that Mr. Mottet reached Bermuda safely.—had to stay there a fortnight and more, and then sailed in the Blockade running steamer Virginia Dare for Wilmington, N.C. as they came near they were discovered and chased by several Yankee Gunboats. The Dare had to run for it, which she could do in style—15 knots an hour—but they were too many—they kept her in shallow water along the coast and were firing at her. The passengers Mr. Mottet among them took each a valise, were put in a small boat, and rowed to the shore about 3 miles off—while the Dare continued her flight. They landed about ten miles south west of Cape Fear. She kept on half way to Georgetown—but being unable to get out to sea or escape her Captain ran her aground, and with the crew escaped in boats. The Yankees came in four rowboats and took possession and loaded two of their boats with trunks &c but overturned and some men drowned, and the others had to come ashore and were captured. The Gunboats fired shells into the hull to set it afire.—The waves battered it but the weather moderated, our men went off to the wreck and got much of the cargo and articles aboard—and perhaps are still at it. Among the things recovered was Mr. Mottet's trunk. But the patriotic Soldiers exercising the right of salvage broke open the trunk and took out all the clothing— save *one shirt*. That too has since then disappeared. Mr. Mottet had a good many papers in that trunk, among them your letter for me. All the papers are gone save that letter which looked so big and respectable, and was so grandly addressed to so well known an individual, that they were pleased to leave it in the trunk to be transmitted to Mr. Mottet—for which they have my profoundest acknowledgements. But you must allow Rev Dear Sir that this is corresponding under difficulties. We are now closing the third year of this cruel war and the country is in a state in which neither of us ever looked to see it. The first year was a year of glory for the South. On the whole we were everywhere victorious The second year was one of earnestness, and hard struggle in which we lost a little, but still could look at our signal victory. The third year was one of hard fighting, of suffering and of some severe losses. This coming fourth campaign will be, I think the last campaign on a large scale and may be the decisive one. On the part of the South it will be one of desperate and herculean effort. What it will be on the part of the North, of course, we cannot tell. They are inclined to do their best to crush us out, but inclination is one thing ability is another. If they can induce a large number of their tired troops to re-enlist this Spring, they will have soldiers as good as last year. If they do not, and are forced to depend on raw recruits in a great measure, they can effect nothing against our men, who are in for the war, and have had two or three years training.

The whole is a matter of endurance. The South is numerically the weaker party, but it is at home and it is wonderful how men take to camp life and fighting. Nearly every able bodied man—at least 19 out of 20—is in the army and we count about 250,000 on our muster rolls this month. But this development of the Army, has sadly crippled Agriculture. To be sure little or no cotton or tobacco is planted, "Corn, wheat, provisions," is all the cry. But even so the supply is getting limited, and this coming year I fear may be much more so. Should the North gain territory from us the coming campaign, as they did the last, and force our army to be more concentrated and to depend for its supply on only a part of our present area, and that devastated by Yankee raids or plundered by our own troops, I fear the words of "Handsome Charlie" (do you remember him?)[20] will be true, and "General Starvation will have something to do in settling the dispute" not very favourably to us.

If on the other hand we hold our own in the field, it is probable that the politicians at the North will make *peace* or war a question for the Presidential election next fall; The Abolitionist Yankees of course are the hottest for continuing the war, and are very earnest that the Northern Armies should be kept full, but personally they keep out of them as far as they can. Our troops say that the Irishmen in the Northern Armies fight best, the Kentuckians next best (indeed they are more dangerous because more wily) the Northwestern Men and the Germans are next, and are good troops. But as for a pure New England regiment. All they [Confederate troops] have to do is to face it, and to halloo, and it will break and run. Our men like to meet such a regiment because it is easy work—and for the fun of the chase, and for the plunder too. For the Yankees always throw away in their precipitate flight, a full stock of their ingenious contrivances and notions for the comfort of camp life. [ends]

Baptista Lynch, Ursuline Convent & Academy Columbia, S.C. to
Patrick Lynch, Feb 2d[21]

Sister Theresa has asked me to let her write you a private letter, to which I
have consented, & I only accompany it with a few lines to let you know that we
are generally well—enjoying this fine weather & doing finely. At the opening
of this session we are losing some & gaining other pupils—

Yesterday Miss Pizzini returned from Richmond, her father told her he had
heard several Protestant gentlemen say that ours was the best institution in the
Confederacy—Don't you feel proud of having founded—or rather I should have
said grateful for having founded it—? "Deo Gratias for all things"

You ought to have seen how heartily ashamed I made Miss Mary Mitchel
for having taken Sallie away from us & put her at the Methodist College & so
pleasantly I did it too—it was really amusing & rich—She is now sorry that she
was so precipitate & said she was astonished & pained to see Sally so weaned
from her & so attached to the convent & that she could not stand it so she took
her away before it would go any further—But I think she will return—A Miss
Rhett, about seventeen years of age, has registered her name to enter as a day
scholar in a few days & we have received within the last week about $3,000.
We have the daughter of Col. Jas. Davis of Barnwell & niece of Mr James Ash-
ley Green (name enough) of the same place. Col[n] J.J. Ryan brought them on
Saturday.

Do you know anything of a Dr Cobb who is a convert, & wants to send
his daughter to us to be prepared for the sacraments? He lives up on the Charlotte R.R.—

I recd a very satisfactory & grateful letter from Mr Edwd Conigland who
says that altho very thankful to us for our kind offer—he never intended to ask
a deduction in terms & will pay the whole fee—he will bring Ali next week
when Court is over—My hand is so shaky today from the effects of neuralgia
that I can hardly write. I miss the ether that I had to relieve myself with by
inhalation.

I don't believe I have written to you since the death of Abp Hughes. R.I. P.
was known to us. I read the full account & saw the lithograph of the funeral
service in a N. York paper. Everything was highly complimentary & I believe
the city defrayed the expenses of the funeral rites.

The biographical sketch was not calculated to excite the admiration of
Southerners—. When it speaks of his going to France at the request of Seward
& succeeding in dissuading the Emperor from acknowledging the Southern
Confederacy. What good does all the meddling politics do him now—?

Bishop McGill says "What a place vacant & what a pity for the man called to fill it—! May God give rest & glory to this deceased prelate, who wore his panoply becomingly & with great effect, & who, in all but his late move in diplomacy, deserved well of Catholics in this country. He fought a good fight, & I hope he's won the crown." I like so much this eulogism—I presume all will agree that Abp Hughes has been one of the Master Spirits of his age—.

When do you intend visiting Va? Mr Pizzini met the ex-Jesuit Revd. Mc-Mullen on his way to Georgetown, or rather to the wreck of that vessel ran ashore—to get a barrel of altar wine which had been presented to Bp McGill, if he would send for it—Have you plenty of wine—? . . . Where do you live now—way up town, I hope. I think you'll have to come up to Columbia after all for Miss Cohen tells us the Charleston Library is to be moved up here soon. Home news I do not pretend to give you & John has written so often lately that I write only they are all moving to the Keitt place. Mrs. Proctor has plenty of pupils now & will remain in town. I admire very much her energetic character & so devoid of that silly pride. . . .

ᘒ

BAPTISTA LYNCH, URSULINE CONVENT & ACADEMY, COLUMBIA, S.C., TO
   PATRICK LYNCH, FEB 7TH[22]

There are two things particularly that I wanted to write for, so I will do it before frequent interruptions make me forget it. The first is that Mary Michel —the daughter of Judge Michel of N. Orleans, has the written permission of her parents to be baptized & become a practical Catholic, which she has long desired, & as she is well instructed & very anxious to observe this Lent in a Christian like manner free from mortal sin, can you come up soon & receive her into the church; at the same time little Minnie Ryan could be baptized also. M. Michel who is seventeen years of age has joined the class of first communicants for instruction & will D.V. be prepared for Easter.

2nd is a temporal matter—Will you please write to Mr. Brown or whoever it is that refused last summer to receive our payment on the "American Hotel" (saying that Mrs Boatright (or somebody) had been offered 20 per cent on the Bond, but she refused it, prefering to hold it as an investment—) & by writing procure from him a written testimony to this effect, that at some future day, we or you may not be forced to pay interest on a debt, which he refused to let us liquidate. . . . If you want money we have plenty—I hope neither [sic] you will lose by this new change which is to be effected in the currency—. Two more little girls (Memphis) came to us as boarders since I wrote, making up for some of those who left. We have also received the daughter of Capt T. R. S. Elliott who spoke of your being down at Pocotaligo lately to marry somebody.—His daughter is a very interesting girl of fifteen—.

Mademoiselle La Pen says our school is going up since we have Miss Elliott-Heywood, Jabon, & Rhett! What do you think? Dr Marks is going to resume his school at Barhamville next October (never mind we will get that place yet) & poor Madame Togno has taken it into her head that she is going to die—but that is not the reason why she gives us Barhamville.

You do not know what a way we are in for an "Ordo" Has any one published one in the South? Or could you spare us one like you did last year? . . .

᪐

Baptista Lynch, Ursuline Convent & Academy, Ash Wednesday
[February 10][23]

Enclosed I send you a letter which I have recd from Miss Josephine South-all, Wilmington N.C. applying to enter our Convent—

Although I would be very happy to receive some pious sensible & well-informed postulants I must say that the tone of this letter is too much like Miss Lancaster's—too inflated to please me.

I never like these vocations that arise from disgust of the world, or in other words from wounded pride unacknowledged. I prefer those who can enjoy society—admire its beauties & love them too, but love God more—. I wrote a vague answer & invited Miss Southall to make a retreat with us so as to decide her future plans & I also wrote to Dr. Corcoran for information concerning her, as he is the pastor at Wilmington. My dislike to N. Carolinians & experience of Miss Jones cools my ardor in this case—which may after all be a very satisfactory one— . . .

I heard from Anna yesterday. All at home are well—we expect a Miss Harmon to enter as a pupil upon the recommendation of Francis. I hope that is only a start from about home & that we may get many more.

What are you doing with your money—? If you don't spend it before the *new currency* comes in, you will be apt to lose—we are buying with a view of bartering for provisions in the summer! Mrs Horlbeck is going to get us some salt—we are far from being out, but it will keep better than some things—Mrs Huchet & Mr Barbot save us a great deal by making purchases for us & at the same time leave Isaac at the garden. All the negroes are at the Keitt place now.

Please don't forget Mary Michel's Baptism & little Miss Ryan's—

I'm afraid you are in want of the necessaries of life down in Charleston where we are told the poor soldiers are half starved—I pity Dr. Northrop, who's so much censured— . . .

Mr Weed wonders how I will be able to get provisions for our numerous family—but the Methodist College has fully twice or I believe three times as many boarding pupils as we have—As yet we get meat regularly, but have to pay for it—! We can only repeat to ourselves "in patientia possedebitis animas vestras"[24] & we are so much better off than many others—. Please don't forget to write to Mr Brown about the payment offered & rejected last August &c—

&

BAPTISTA LYNCH, URSULINE CONVENT & ACADEMY COLUMBIA S.C., TO
PATRICK LYNCH, FEB 21ST[25]

Perhaps you will not thank me for this, but I want to give Miss Preston an excuse for calling at the Bishop's[26] & making his acquaintance & yours, since I think she is half a Catholic already & I hope may ere long be one in reality. I need not say anything of her as you have so often & secretly heard me express very great admiration for her character & disposition. I believe she is engaged to be married to Genl Hood—[27]

You will be glad to hear that Alice Conigland is an inmate of our academy again & seems quite happy to get back—she will be instructed for first Communion. Mr. Edw Conigland seemed very anxious to meet you in Halifax indeed he said it was almost of necessity that he should do so. Brother John is in Cheraw—he did not get off until yesterday at noon.

We are all well (DG) as when you left us—. Col Aldrich brought his daughter to us, the same evening that you left. She seems a very fine girl—. Col. J. J. Ryan lost one of his little daughters—a most interesting precocious child & one that was very pious. I trust this grief & bereavement may lead the parents to seek strength & consolation in the practice of our Holy Faith, which alone can give them.

Of course while in Richmond you will see M^r and Mrs Ferrall to whom you can say that Sister Stanislaus enjoys very good health, &c—

And to Mr Weed that Sister Charles is as good as ever—I am sorry to say she is suffering from a severe cold, which affects her head & chest.

Sister Etienne's friends are so numerous that the mere name of "Miss Vassar" seems to possess a charm in Richmond.

The Misses Cowarden, Dooley & Pizzini are all well.

And what shall we say to Bishop McGill—? Of course present our respects & compliments &c &c—& say that we propagate his tract "The True Church" & obtain for *him merit*, as well as a share for ourselves. We pray that the hearts of his hearers may be prepared to receive the good seed, & that it may produce a hundred fold—.

Have you not any "*quasi postulants*"? . . .

⚘

FRANCIS LYNCH, CHERAW, TO PATRICK LYNCH, 24 FEBY[28]

Your welcome letter reached me this morning, apprizing me of your visit to Virginia. And in order to avail myself of an exemption, I have today written to Col[n] Northrop, enclosing to him a copy of my original application, the substance of which is the same of [*sic*] my application now forwarded by the Ex. Officer, for the consideration of the Hon. Sec[ty] of War.[29] In order it was sent last week by the off. here to Maj. Milton[,] Columbia to be by him forwarded to Richmond. I hope it will fare well.

I have requested the influence of Col Northrop. Hon S. R. Mallory[30] kindly proffered to serve me when he could do so, altho I appreciate this offer, I have not applied to him—I trust it will not be necessary in this case. His wife made the proffer to Henrietta in exchange for attention to Mrs. Scannell.

I will send you some lard. Bro John left for home today. The tax will be heavy when considered together, the state & Confed[y]. But it is satisfactory to think it is all "pro patria"

⚘

PATRICK LYNCH. GENERAL HOSPITAL, MONTGOMERY SPRINGS, VIRGINIA,
    TO JUDAH BENJAMIN, SEC. OF STATE, 3 MARCH[31]

Sir,

The proposition which you made to me, that I should go to Rome as Commissioner of the Confederate States to the Holy See, has demanded my most serious consideration.

After mature reflection, I conceive it to be my duty to accede to the desire of the Government, and to accept the position.

I do it with the understanding that I will not be required to prolong my stay in Europe beyond six months; and in case, which I do not now anticipate, urgent reasons should require it, the Government will consent to my return at an earlier period.

In accepting this position, I yield my personal feelings to a sense of duty. Should it appear to you that the public interests will be as well or better served by the appointment of another, it will give me personally much pleasure to be relieved of a duty which I feel to be very responsible, and for which no previous training has prepared me.

I will require three weeks to arrange my ecclesiastical and personal affairs in view of an absence which may possibly be very protracted. I will lose no time and shall endeavour to be ready to start by the end of this month. Next week I hope to be in Richmond when I will do myself the honour of paying my respects in person.

෴

BAPTISTA LYNCH, URSULINE CONVENT & ACADEMY, COLUMBIA, S.C., TO
PATRICK LYNCH, MARCH 7TH[32]

Although we have not heard from you we have heard of you through letters from Richmond from Mr Ambler Weed. Some of our pupils' friends went to call on you, but your stay was so short that you had left almost as soon as they knew of your arrival—We were very glad that Mr Weed saw you for we feared he had left before you reached Richmond which would be a great disappointment to him as he anticipated your visit so long—. Mr Weed is not the sort of man I had fancied him to be, but I like him very much indeed, & have no doubt were he a Priest, he would do much for God's glory by his mild manner & patient sympathetic nature; something like Bishop Wood of Phila [Philadelphia]—. We had quite a number of inquisitive visitors lately, which is enough to make us wish we were not so convenient to them! but on the other hand, if it does good, I suppose it is all right—

I'm afraid you feel the cold very sensibly up in the mountains—I was so fortunate as to get the cloth for your cloak—you know Mr Jackson asks $100 per yd but at the *Bee* Store, I got some for $60 per yd Cornelia bought it for me & it was she who recommended saying that she, her mother, & sisters had all gotten cloaks of it. I can find no tassel yet, but may by the time you get home, where Sister Theresa's little friend will make it beautifully when once it is cut out. I wish you could have had it before going to Richmond. But you can trample on the world & wear your old cloak. How many poor fellows are there now in the hospital who are in want of the commonest coverings & I'm sure you would rather appear meanly clad while with them & sympathize in their distress, than be otherwise & at the same time unable to assist them.

. . . Poor Mademoiselle Marnier was here yesterday—& so sad—If she only had the means to go to France! Apropos have you read this new currency act? & have you not some money, that you want funded, &c—take care you do not lose—(it is too dark to see) Monday morning[.] I have not time this morning to do more than say we are all well. Thank God .There is quite a panic here about the small-pox, but I trust it may not spread. We have as many pupils in the house as we can accommodate & more than will be agreeable in warm weather. It would be dreadful to have it among them.

What about the payment of your taxes? John spoke to me about paying them. Shall I do so? Is it not mean of persons who have been dilatory in paying their bills to hasten now, since this bill on the currency act has passed & pay now? Some are doing this, *while* others so honorably have written to give us an opportunity of making the discount. I'm sick & tired of money matters—& sincerely pity those who have to be mixed up in it all the time. Everybody is so selfish too—!

Dear me one half hour's meditation before the Blessed Sacrament is such a treat—! I received a long letter from Sarah Beard giving me a graphic description of the effects of the late battle in Fla—where Finegan has been victorious over the enemy—.[33] The Sisters [of] Mercy often witness such dreadful effects —May our Lord sustain & protect them. It must be dreadful! I'm afraid we shall hear of dreadful battles soon. No wonder that in these troublous times people envy us our seclusion—I received another letter from Miss Josephine Southall which I liked very much, & have recommended her to call on D[r] Corcoran for advice & guidance & come to our Academy. Since then, I have received a similar application from another Protestant Lady to enter our noviciate, Miss Slater of Dalton Ga. She is an Episcopalian, but would be a Catholic were it not for the confession necessary. I was much pleased with her letter, & trust we may be instrumental in leading both of these ladies into the Church— they both seem to desire earnestly to do what is right & good. Miss Clem Keitt, niece of Col Lewis of Va has been here for a few days—She left yesterday for Pocotaligo, where she will be a governess in the family of Mr. Peeples—a situation which I procured for her. I had hoped by my correspondence with her that she had a latent vocation & we are so much in need of assistant teachers but I was mistaken—I am afraid Miss Blanchard will soon leave, & I regret it very much for our young sisters are over pressed with music lessons & as the warm weather comes on, they feel it all the more.

Revd L. O'Connell told Mr A. Weed that he thought we ought to buy Barhamville at any price & Mr Weed was led to think with him until John & myself spoke with him & we showed him the class rooms [here]—Father Lawrence told him we should be sick living so confined & so many together, but when he saw the high rooms he said such a house as this was not to be got any day—I told him we also, kept "in peto" the desire of purchasing Barhamville or some extensive place in a retired situation, but it must be the work of time for even if we had plans your first care would be the erection of your Cathedral & a "Boy's Manual Labor School" both of which were greater needs & justly claim your attention—I was interrupted __

We have just received a Miss McMahon who is from Memphis whose father is Maj. & Q.M. in the army & whose mother is Cuban Spanish, educated in [a] New Orleans convent—Catholic but not prepossessing—Well it is all A.M.D.G I hope—I hope you will write soon & let us know that you are enjoying the fresh mountain air—I am not anxious that you should return to Charleston, but, if you could get a house in Columbia, & live here, I would feel that you were safe—are you contemplating your trip to Europe? M Lafitte is still in Wilmington

Goodby for the present— . . .

Baptista Lynch, Ursuline Convent & Academy, Columbia, S.C., to Patrick Lynch, March 10th[34]

We wish you many, very many happy returns of this your natal anniversary —& offer for you our Holy Communions, praying that by this time next year, you may be giving glory to Almighty God by erecting your new cathedral, Orphans Boys Manual Labor school &c &c, as you now are, by your cheerful submission to His holy will, in the privation of these *& other goods*—the consequences of this trying time—. I wrote to you only a few days since—on "Laetare Sunday" when the novices begged for recreation in honor of your consecration, which of course I could not refuse, & shared with them between the times of our observances.—You are nearly six years a Bishop—!—& I superioress—! If you are as tired of superiority as I am—! But I suppose it will not do to say we are tired, since it is for God we work, but if it were not for Him, we would be tired. For him, labor & fatigue cease to be such.

Our dear parents & family are very well. There was a letter from Anna this week, she is the feeblest of them all.—John is very busy just now, with a man who was shot here in cold blood. A Mr. Hicks express man—who is a very respected & worthy man of family—his murderer is a low fellow, once a constable here, & is now a soldier—who concealed himself & shot Hicks with a double barrelled musket. It is a dreadful affair, & Morris, the assassin is in jail.

Among the recent visitors whom we have had was Mrs Semmes, the wife of Commodore (Pirate) Semmes.[35] She is a native of Cincinnati & altho her children are Catholics, she has never been received into the church, but now, she is converted by the miraculous cure of one of her daughters which took place in Mobile about three weeks ago, & of which Bishop Quinlan could give you the exact account since it was effected by his offering the Holy Sacrifice for her recovery. —Miss Semmes says that her daughter had the varioloid but I suppose it must have been small-pox, since she describes her as being one mass of corruption on the seventh day & very ill—When she saw herself in the glass, she exclaimed oh what an object—My dear Papa will never recognize his daughter (it seems she was very beautiful & his favorite child)—but she immediately added Oh God "not my will, but thine be done."

The physicians were coming the following day to put Mercurial ointment on, as a preventive to her being marked which is considered a risky thing to do—& the sisters of this sick young lady, said "Mama let us have Mass offered first for sister: "Well, said Mʳˢ Semmes" I have no faith in it, but you may—So the daughter went to Bp Quinlan, & told him the state in which her sister was, & he offered the Holy Sacrifice for her recovery—Miraculously the places healed —the scales fell off & in two days she was perfectly well without any medical aid—! Mʳˢ S, a cousin of hers who is a bigoted Presbyterian, & many others Protestant & Catholic can testify to this wonderful case. Mrs S says "seeing is believing" & now she is a Catholic for the spirit of God must be with the Catholics after that!

The young ladies were both educated at "Eden Hall," near Phila [Philadelphia] —& the one who had the Mass said is *very* pious, the other not so much so, but will be a more practical Catholic now. She was married two days after the Mass was said—that however was hurried, because the Yankees were attacking Mobile. . . .

A very respectable, even distinguished officer called here today to ask if we would receive a young lady in whose fathers house he had often visited, when in Va—& who had been induced to run away with a young man, who promised to marry her, but instead of doing so, left her at a Hotel in Columbia. I admired very much the young man who offered any sum, if we would only shelter her until he could write to her Father, & get her proper protection, but of course we could not receive such a one. What a trying time this must be for parents —many of whom I hear are suffering through their children—. They are now reaping the sad fruits of the irreligion & independence in which they brought them up.

Capt. T. R. S. Elliott of Pocotaligo, brought us his eldest daughter a few days since, & Maj. McMahon's daughter of Memphis has also arrived—both seventeen years of age & well advanced in their studies—.

Mʳˢ Horlbeck whose Harp practice is often interrupted by visitors, told me the other day, that our convent was equal to the President's House—that we had regular levees—that is, we were visited by the most distinguished personages of the present day, whose names would figure in our history—all of whom, seem to have sisters or daughters among our pupils—, & that a very bigoted Presbyterian gentleman of Columbia told her a few days ago, that, at first they were very much opposed to having such an Institution—as a convent established in Columbia, but, that by our urbanity of manner &c &c—we had won everyone.

"Deo gratias," for all things—but I think we shall suffer next year, for that very thing, since already we are accused of attaching our pupils too much to ourselves. The Catholic parents will object to us because they say we will make Religious of their daughters & the Protestant because we made Catholics of theirs, so I am prepared to have a smaller school next year—Dr. Marks & Madam Sosnowski will enter into Co. at Barhamville next term.

ANNA LYNCH, CHERAW, TO PATRICK LYNCH, [MARCH] 20TH[36]

Mr Drake informed us, that he met you at Florence, on Friday last, on your return from Virginia. . . . I hope you're quite well, & enjoyed your visit. I suppose we may expect you soon after Easter. Mother has made up her mind & is making preparations to accompany you on your foreign trip, as you once promised her she could do & is anxiously awaiting your answer, when you come up. Of course, we have never spoken of it to any one. We understand there was an explosion at the arsenal yesterday, killing some and wounding many & would like to know if Mr. Laughlin is hurt.[37] His wife has heard nothing of it yet. This is the anniversary of poor Brother Hugh's death. It appears as an event of yesterday, in its sad effects desolating heart & home. . . .

FRANCIS LYNCH, CHERAW, TO PATRICK LYNCH, 21 MAR[38]

Your letter to Father was received as also, the one written before leaving the city to which I replied to you at Richmond. I also wrote to Col. Northrop as yet have had no reply. Though I suppose the Govt will exempt myself and my workers within my establishments or they must be closed.

You are aware the State Legislature passed an act taxing manufactured objects in kind. The liberal definition placed on this act by our worthy Atty. Gnl[39] led me to hope it would work fairly. In my own case, the claim made to the Board showed the production of shoes and boots &c amounting to over 15000 pr. The gross income of the sale of shoes and some leather amtd to 186,500$. The shoes of last year having been sold I respectfully submitted to the Board that for their representative value (the sum they brot me as above) I was taxable 5 pct making a tax of $9,325. This I proposed to pay in money, or if more desirable furnish womens Boots at 20$ pr pair in payment of it. The Board suggested 700 pr of these shoes for the tax, to which I assented. At this period of the proceedings, one of the members of the Board took the ground that the Board was entitled to Boots, Shoes and everything else in the like, to the extent of 5 prct in quantity regardless of what they produced in sales—and argued that the sale of such articles (when not suited to the wants of soldiers' families) would bring a large amt of money at the present value of them, and by a bare majority of the Board carried his point—There will be an effort at the next meeting to set the matter right, for some members of the Board are men of business and see the wrong its present action would create—by requiring a tax in value of near $30000—on sales of 186,500—while of this amount included in sales 2300 pr that I have furnished to the Govrmt in exchange for Hides, rating 1 pr shoes for every 6 to Hides—and fixing the price 20$ is $48,300. The interest you have evinced in this matter has led me to apprize you of its working. If the view entertained by me in regard to it is correct I would like to have the approval of the Atty Genrl unofficially. . . .

1864 April–July

"Father . . . is very hopeful about your mission."

In the fall of 1863 Confederate authorities had asked John Bannon, the Irish Catholic chaplain to Missouri units in the western theater, to undertake a mission to Ireland to counteract the recruitment that Union agents were conducting there. Bannon's initial destination was to be Rome, to obtain a papal blessing for his mission. Such an emblem of approval, it was hoped, would make the Irish more receptive to Bannon's message about keeping out of America's civil war. For whatever reason the emigrant priest went straight to the homeland he had left a decade earlier. Bannon did, however, suggest to Judah Benjamin, Confederate secretary of state, that the government should send a highly placed figure of the Catholic Church to Rome to cultivate the favor of the Holy See, which, in turn, could be valuable in shaping opinion among the Catholic powers of Europe.[1] Whether Bannon specifically mentioned Patrick Lynch as a natural figure for the mission is unknown. Certainly Lynch stood out as the Catholic prelate who had forcefully asserted his commitment to Southern independence in his well-known exchange with John Hughes two years earlier. His extended Roman education and connections there also set him apart from the other Southern prelates. Adding his skills as polemicist and orator, no one was better qualified than Lynch to represent the Confederacy to the Holy See.

On April 9, five weeks after accepting the Confederacy's commission, Patrick Lynch boarded a blockade runner in the last open port of the Confederacy, Wilmington, North Carolina. He carried with him a letter from Secretary Benjamin to his counterpart in the Holy See, Cardinal Giacomo Antonelli, identifying Lynch as "one of our most esteemed and trustworthy citizens, [now] Special Commissioner of the Confederate States of America to The States of the Church, and I . . . ask for him a reception and treatment corresponding to his station and to the purposes for which he is sent. Those purposes he will more particularly explain to you."[2] In fact, the secretary had instructed the bishop that he was not to be explicit about his ultimate goal in Rome: papal recognition of the Confederacy. In no way was Lynch to press papal officials on the matter. Instead he was to be alive to seizing "opportunities . . . afforded for enlightening opinions and molding impressions . . . with signal benefit to the cause of our country." If the occasion should arise, in Lynch's judgment, for raising with papal officials the question of recognition, he was to pursue it if he thought the prospects good for a positive response. His primary charge was to be an ambassador promoting good will toward the Confederacy, which might eventually express itself in formal recognition.[3]

Knowing that his mission would likely keep him abroad for a considerable length of time, probably the six months he had set as a maximum in his acceptance letter, Patrick Lynch had to weigh fully the contingencies that might occur over the course of that time in providing for the governance of the diocese in his absence. Presuming the likelihood that Charleston and its environs would fall to Federal forces in the near future, he named a French immigrant priest as the administrator of the city and whatever territory the United States might reclaim within the Carolinas. In effect he was naming Leon Fillion the bishop of the occupied portion of his see. Over the rest he appointed someone whom Federal authorities would hardly have been well disposed toward: the fire-eating James Corcoran.

Lynch had two other persons in his party: a Confederate soldier who had received a furlough to visit a seriously ill parent in Italy and a seminarian being sent to the newly established American College in Rome for his theological studies. The trip took them to Bermuda, Nova Scotia, Ireland, England, France, Germany, and Italy.[4] *In Bermuda, in the kind of implausible encounter that Charles Dickens made routine in his novels, the bishop discovered his nephew Robert Lynch on his way home to enlist, a plan that Patrick Lynch quickly scuttled. With Robert added to the group as the bishop's unofficial secretary, they arrived in Halifax, Nova Scotia, on April 21, where the cream of the province's ecclesiastical, political, and professional worlds toasted Patrick Lynch at a dinner. Lynch, for his part, assured his well-disposed listeners that he had every confidence in "the ultimate success of the Southern Confederacy."*[5]

Then it was on to Cork, Ireland, in the first week of May, just as Grant was beginning the Overland Campaign west of Fredericksburg. Over the next month, savage fighting at the Wilderness, Spotsylvania Courthouse, North Anna, Cold Harbor, and Petersburg produced casualties that shocked and sickened the nation, North and South. Once again Lee won the tactical victories. In the end Grant laid siege to Petersburg and Richmond, Lee's ultimate fear. Without room to maneuver, the Confederate commander knew that the fall of the Army of Northern Virginia—and with it the Confederacy—was only a matter of time.

In Ireland Patrick Lynch met with Confederate agents, including John Bannon who accompanied him to England and the Continent. While in Ireland, the bishop conducted his own investigation into the emigration issue that had driven Confederate officials to send Father Bannon to Ireland. Patrick Lynch visited various sites on the island and interviewed as many people as would let him. His subsequent report to Benjamin was a penetrating analysis of the socio-economic-ecological-political origins of the stream of Irish males making their way to Northern shores. He also found time to journey, with his nephew, to northern Ireland, to Rosslea, his family's home, where they visited with Peter Conlaw Lynch's ninety-three-year-old brother Luke and other relatives. This side trip may well have been the fruit of a promise made by Patrick to his mother, who had very much wanted to accompany her son to Europe. Given the circumstances, that was out of the question. But Patrick may have solaced her by assuring that, while there, he would visit the family and homestead, as he had done a quarter century earlier, on his way home from Rome.[6]

England was the next destination, where he spent ten days, meeting with more Confederate agents and church officials, including Cardinal Nicholas Wiseman. Then, in early June the quartet crossed the English Channel to France. Two weeks later and a little more than a hundred miles south of where they crossed, the Confederate cruiser Alabama was sunk by the Union warship Kearsarge, ending the economic havoc Alabama had inflicted upon Northern maritime commerce by sinking or capturing scores of commercial vessels over the past two years.

Paris surpassed Halifax in the warmth of its reception for the Confederate agent. The bishop, as a blockade runner and the survivor of several months of Union shelling in Charleston, had become something of a celebrity. Lynch gained introductions to the archbishop of Paris, Georges Darboy, as well as the papal nuncio, Archbishop Flavio Chigi. The latter's reception could not have been more cordial and supportive. The nuncio even accompanied him to meet with the minister of foreign affairs, Drouyn de Lhuys,[7] whose overt sympathy for the South made him particularly appreciative of Lynch's natural command of the intricacies of diplomatic discourse. From the minister they secured a virtually immediate audience—the next day—with the emperor, Napoleon III. That meeting proved promising, as Napoleon expressed the hope that a decisive victory by Confederate forces during the current campaign in Virginia would provide the opportunity for France at last to recognize the South as an independent nation.[8] With this psychological tailwind Lynch and his party headed for Rome, where his mission would ultimately succeed or fail.

꩜

LYNCH TO HIS CLERGY [MARCH] (COPY)[9]

I have to inform you that diocesan and other reasons[10] require me to visit Europe at an early day, and that I contemplate starting before the middle of next month.

It is necessary before going to make some regulation for the Administration of the Diocese during my absence, which will extend over several months, perhaps until winter. . . . The Diocese of Charleston is divided into two parts.

The first will embrace the city of Charleston and the missions immediately dependent on the clergy of the city. Should Charleston fall under the power of the Federals, then all other portions of the Diocese also in their hands and with which there may be easy communication will be considered as annexed to this portion.

The second will embrace all the interior of the Diocese.

I have appointed as Vicar General of the first, V. Rev. L. Fillion V.G. who, to his good qualities of a zealous and pious clergyman, adds the very important and I may say, almost indispensable one of being a foreign subject. His French citizenship will exempt him from many annoyances to which a citizen of S. Carolina might be subjected, at the hands of the Federal military and civil authorities. I have appointed as Vicar General of the second, V. Rev. J. A. Corcoran, D.D. now Pastor of Wilmington.

꩜

PATRICK LYNCH. SAINT GEORGE'S, BERMUDA, TO BAPTISTA LYNCH,
15 APRIL[11]

. . . The passage cost me $200 in gold. The accommodations were such as they ought to pay me two hundred dollars in gold for enduring.—I got aboard of the Steamer Minnie, opposite Smithville N.C. in the Cape Fear River about 6 P.M., Saturday last.[12] —It was a misty drizzling afternoon, the guard looked sharp at our passes; but they were quite right. I had a letter for the captain which as he could not see me, I sent in by the mate, and waited on deck. After a while the mate returned, and said the captain would not take us. After a while I went to the captain, whom I found a stiff Englishman, quite curt and surly. As I had a point to gain, I soon talked him down into good humor, and we took a glass of wine together, and it was settled that we would go. . . . We waited there for a couple of hours, expecting the boat [to] start, but at length we found that the night was so dark and boisterous that the pilot refused to take us out. Then like rats we commenced feeling about for enough room to stretch ourselves out for some kind of a nap. . . . Sunday night at 11 P.M. we started. All windows of the ship were closed. All the dead light shutters were put in, in addition, and then to make sure, all the lights inside were extinguished, I went out on deck and sat on a cotton bale, holding a little hand valise with all the papers I wished to destroy in the event of capture,—and well laden with oyster shells to ensure its sinking, when thrown overboard. On we went, at our game of naval bo-peep. . . . Our vessel is small, has only one mast, is all over of a dull white colour, almost invisible by starlight and there are no lights aboard, as we go on silently and swiftly. Twenty pairs of practiced eyes are peering out into the darkness ahead and on either side, to descry the dark hulls the rigging, or the twinkling lights of the blockading vessels—we know there are *nine* of them or were at sunset. "There is one," says a look out. "Starboard your helm," cries the Pilot and we keep away from him. "there's another" on the other side. "Port helm" and we keep at a respectful distance from him too. Soon they are behind us, and have not noticed us. "There's another nearly right ahead." "Starboard helm" . . . Another! Rather near this time not half a mile off, . . . give her a full head, says the captain and the Minnie fairly jumps— . . . On we go and soon that blockader is far astern of us. Some say they saw a fifth far off, but by 12 ½ the captain and pilot came down, and took a drink on their success.[13] We were out at sea and out of immediate danger, and away we went toward Bermuda. I emptied out the oyster shells,—fixed my papers, crawled back to my sofa, and went to sleep. . . . On Monday, we had a clear day, a strong favorable westerly wind, and a rough sea, and we rolled along 8 and 9 knots an hour. . . . On Tuesday the weather was still the same, the sea a little smoother, and our speed about the same. . . . While at dinner, I noticed that the Minnie changed her course, and I went up on deck. Away in the distance about 18 miles off, was a Yankee Cruiser, firing up at a great rate and pursuing us. We turned off our course, and ran away as fast as we could 11 miles an hour. After three quarters of an hours trial, he gave it up and jogged on his first course, and we turned our head again to the eastward, and hurried on. In the afternoon still other vessels under sail. That night was exquisitely calm and beautiful. I staid on deck until 11 by which I lost my sofa and slept in consequence on a cotton bale. Next morning we had a gale, which lasted with showers all day, making it quite uncomfortable to stay out on deck, and the vessel rolled horribly, enough as a Pilot said to me, "enough to roll a chaw of Tobacco out of your mouth." That day still other sailing vessels in sight, sometimes three at a time. Night came on boisterous and tempestuous, we were approaching the "vexed Bermoothes"—I could not sleep and did not like to stay in the cabin, hot and close, with the chance of a cotton bale tumbling over on me, so I sat most of the time on the quarter deck, enjoying the scene, and taking shower baths as the spray dashed over the vessel. . . . Next morning, through the mist and rain, we saw *hills* at 8 A.M.—and for a couple of hours ran along the coast, as the weather cleared we saw that it was a cluster or range of islands with hills from 50 to 250 feet high with numerous snow white little houses dotted about. The shores were rocky, and the water underneath, was a clear transparent light green showing the sea weed and corals twenty feet under us, and even the fishes swimming about, or the crabs on the rocks at the bottom. At 10 A.M. the pilot who had come on board and taken charge,—a consequential *Negro*, turned the bow of the Minnie into a gap between two rocks.— In we went through it— . . . and in half an hour, had anchored in the Bay of St. George and I went ashore.

Having some dispatches to deliver, I soon found out Major Walter of Va, the chief Confederate agent here, a very gentlemanly man. He said he was intimately acquainted with Rev. Monsignor Virtue,[14] the Catholic clergyman of this place, (The same who accompanied Mgr. Bedini)[15] and at once sent him word of my arrival. But Mr. Virtue was absent on a mission, to some other of the Islands and has not yet returned (Saturday 10 A.M.) Accommodations being very hard to get in this place, Major W. Invited me to his house, where I am in clover. His wife a very amiable lady is the daughter of Judge Gholson[16] of Virginia, now a member of Congress.

I have remained quiet resting myself, and feasting on books published since the war, and which I had not been able to get a sight of before. I am now waiting for the Alpha, steamer from St. Thomas, which touches here and goes on to Halifax. She is expected some time to day so do not be surprized if this letter closes abruptly. . . .

. . . Who do you think I met here? Our nephew Robert, well and hearty, and finely grown. His dissatisfaction at Cambreé increased and his troubles likewise. Add to that serious doubts as to his vocation and a longing for home. He applied to Mr. Slidell[17] in Paris and got passage on a government vessel to this place, and reached here two days before me, and in a fortnight was to try to run the blockade to Wilmington. Of course this would only distress his parents, and for himself I do not think he ought to enter the army. Any how this would do him much evil, render worthless all his previous study and do the Confederacy no good. So I have resolved to take him back with me, and if he really has no vocation he can either return with me, or some other arrangement can be made.—He is a good boy.

When in Petersburg I learned that Miss M. Jones had made another attempt to go north, and had been forced to return, and was again in Wilmington. Poor Child! She said as she was starting, that she would soon be either in a convent or married, I think the alternative itself a decision.

John Lynch. Columbia, S.C., to Robert Lynch, June 6th[18]

I received your letter enclosed in one from your uncle, I was very much surprised at hearing from you from Bermuda, as much so no doubt as you were to hear that your uncle the Bishop had arrived, at the same port. . . . I am satisfied as things have terminated, and that you should have the privilege of filling a Secretaryship to the Bishop. I do not know how others may view the circumstances, nor do I know whether it has struck either the Bishop or yourself, but to me, the hand of Providence is as plainly shown in your meeting at Bermuda under the peculiar circumstances, at the particular time, without any previous notice, as in any case, I have ever heard of. . . . you should show by your acts, your thanks to Almighty God, for . . . he surely destined you for some special duty, or he would have allowed you to follow your own will, in which case you would now be exposing your life in the battlefield, with a fine prospect of being killed, or being maimed for life. . . .

There has been nothing new in the family circle since I wrote to you by the Bishop, only that your Aunt Anna and brother John are over to attend the distribution at the Convent. . . . Conlaw could not get a furlough to come up although he is still on the coast, your sisters came off in flying colours at the distribution, . . . The Governor of the State presided. . . .

I think I wrote you that a Capt William Lord was killed sometime ago in battle in Virginia. Since then Capt Len Henderson has also been killed. Mr Allemorige has received a serious wound in the neck. How serious we havent heard, but I expect it is quite so; Col Keitt & Col. Dansler who were both of the same regiment with Conlaw are killed; it is awful to think of the number of our best men who are cut off by this cruel war; God grant it may soon cease. . . .

John Lynch, Columbia S.C. to Patrick Lynch, June 5th[19]

. . . I am very glad to see you have progressed so far safely in your mission, but to tell you the truth, I expect more from you, than I suppose your modesty proposes yourself, and have never for a moment felt the least uneasiness on account of . . . the effect to be produced from your mission. . . .

In the case before us, taking all the circumstances into consideration, what conclusion can we arrive at than that Robert *has had* a vocation, whither it will develop itself, or whether it has been crushed in the bud, is to be seen. In the first place his father & mother, ignorant of the many graces conferred by self-mortification, before his birth, consecrated him if a boy to the priesthood,

Jefferson Davis,
President of the Confederate States of America,
To all to whom these Presents shall come, Greeting:

Know Ye, That, for the purpose of establishing friendly relations between the Confederate States of America and The States of The Church, and reposing special trust and confidence in the integrity, prudence and abilities of the Right Reverend P. N. Lynch, I have appointed him Special Commissioner of the Confederate States of America to The States of The Church, and have invested him with full and all manner of power and authority, for and in the name of the Confederate States, to meet and confer with any person or persons duly authorized by the Sovereign Pontiff of The States of The Church, being furnished with like power and authority, and with him or them to agree, treat, consult and negotiate concerning all matters and subjects interesting to both governments, and to conclude and sign a Treaty or Treaties, Convention or Conventions, touching the premises; transmitting the same to the President of the Confederate States for his final ratification by and with the advice and consent of the Senate of the Confederate States.

In testimony whereof, I have caused the seal of the Confederate States to be hereunto affixed.

Given under my hand at the City

Bishop's Lynch's commission from President Jefferson Davis, 1864. Courtesy of the Roman Catholic Diocese of Charleston Archives.

after his birth, dedicated him to the service, and as soon as he was old enough educated him to that belief, which always seemed agreeable to him, still this last move, where he at least places a plausible reason (patriotism) as an excuse for his movement I cannot say that I am pleased with his patriotism, but there is no necessity for mortifying him, . . . I therefore pass it over quietly, leaving it entirely in your hands, . . . [and if] you are satisfied he has no vocation; . . . I will expect him home with you.

ANTONIA LYNCH, MOUNT CARMEL [BALTIMORE], TO PATRICK LYNCH,
    10 JUNE[20]

Although it has not been a month since I wrote you asking many favours, still we have so many things which we require instruction upon, & we know you being from this country could better explain our position than one could by letter. I mean certain questions we would like you to ask our General. . . . We pray very much for you. Every day we say in the Choir the Litany of our Blessed Lady for your protection. . . . I hope you will see much of our General.[21] I do not think we will ever be satisfied until we have a Visitor from Rome. If you think there will ever be that blessing in store for us, I should think now would be as good a time as any other could you not talk it over with the General. Even though we are not under the order, still the Visitation would be productive of much fruit, for every thing would be submitted to the Bishop. We could obtain that knowledge which we ought to have but which no one in this country can give us, for they know nothing of the practice of the Order. Ever since I have been in this Community we have been under the Direction of the Redemptorist Fathers who have ever been most kind to us, more than Fathers—but in points of discipline they cannot but advise whereas should a Visitor once instruct us, it would save us a world of uncertainty. . . .

FRANCIS LYNCH, CHERAW, TO PATRICK LYNCH, 15TH JUNE[22]

. . . On the second return trip the "Minnie" was seized by the Blockade Squadron. Soon after you left, two replies to your note in reference to my application were sent to me from Charleston.—However the matter was formally considered by the Enrolling officer & Council here—

But all my hands have been conscripted. Still with my negroes and a few workmen I will try and pursue the even tenor of my way. The five Bales of Cotton were sent to Mr. J. Brown and I trust they will reach safely their destination in Nassau.

The attention you received at Halifax afforded us much pleasure and hope your whole tour will be as agreeable to you. The accounts that have reached us of the failing health of our holy Father Pius IX impress us with fear that he may not survive your reaching Rome. . . .

🕊

ANNA LYNCH, CHERAW, TO PATRICK LYNCH, JUNE 18TH[23]

. . . Your last letter, the second Father has received from you, reached us about ten days ago. (written on the steamship "Asia" when within a day's sailing of Cork, on the 6th of May). . . . The steamer Minnie was captured on her return trip & I suppose you will consider her a small loss.

Mother has been suffering from a severe cold since you left, but is now quite recovered. Father is as well as usual and is very hopeful about your mission. I am sure we have all a great reason to pray for its success for we have had some of the hardest fighting of the war within the last month attended with great loss of life. General Lee has been successful in every engagement & the disparity in killed & wounded between the two armies is unprecedented because of Grant & Butler[24] leading their men into battle so intoxicated that many are unable to reload their guns or surrender as prisoners when necessary and our army have no alternative but to kill them.

These accounts were not at first believed but officers from the field confirm them. Capt. Henry McIver[25] returned home wounded a few days ago & says there is not the slightest fear felt in the army of Richmond's ever being taken, altho' Grant is said to declare that he will sacrifice every man of his army rather than give up the attempt so far unsuccessful. From all accounts he appears as equally regardless of their lives, when leading them to battle & indifferent to their sufferings when wounded.

Eustace Pinckney called to see us for a few hours when on his way to Virginia. He was looking well. . . . Col. Keitt was killed the day after his arrival in Virginia. Conlaw's company were detained in Charleston but expect daily orders to join their regiment. We expected him up this week to accompany John to Columbia but he was disappointed in getting a furlough. Father & Mother were much grieved & disappointed to hear of the step Robert had taken & consider it a great blessing to his family & himself that he met you in Bermuda . . .

🕊

PATRICK LYNCH, PARIS, TO JUDAH BENJAMIN, JUNE 20[26]

. . . I left Bermuda on the evening of the 17th in the British Mail Steamer Alpha, and reached Halifax on the evening of the 21st, and learned that the

Cunard Steamer from Boston to Liverpool was not expected to call for passengers at Halifax for a week to come.

My stay in Halifax was made exceedingly agreeable. I can only add my statement to the many which you have already received of the deep interest which the inhabitants take in our affairs, and their earnest wishes for our success. They omit no occasion of expressing and of acting on their sympathy. I was the guest of his Grace, Most Rev. Dr. Connelly, Catholic Archbishop, the Chief Justice, the Attorney General, several members of the Assembly by then in session, and many of the prominent citizens called to pay their respects, and I was invited to a complimentary dinner given me by the Halifax Club.

The Acting Governor, General Doyle,[27] on whom I called with His Grace the Archbishop, and who was very cordial, spoke to me at length of his course in the matter of the then recent capture of the Chesapeake by the Ella and Annie of the Federal Navy, in Sambro Bay, and of his requiring the surrender of the captured prisoners to the British Authorities.[28] He said, he was in the happy position of having received the approval of all parties concerned. His own Government had fully sanctioned his action. This was exceedingly gratifying to him as an officer. The Federal Government at Washington had conveyed to him their satisfaction at his course. This was a mystery which he did not precisely understand, for he had looked for some remonstrances from them, on what appeared to him a very peremptory course, though under the circumstances, the only honourable one open to him. From the tone of the papers, and the assurances of gentlemen with whom he had spoken, he was sure the Confederate Government was also satisfied with his action, the results of which, as far as it had any, were in our favour. In making this statement, General Doyle was not aware of my official position. I believe he had said the same, perhaps more fully, to Mr. Holcombe,[29] who had come from Virginia to defend the prisoners, and I presume you were at once informed of it.

Among our friends in Halifax, next after the Archbishop, the most active and the most influential is, I think, Dr. Almon, whose son is an Assistant Surgeon in the Confederate Army. He had gone so far as to render himself liable to a prosecution; and at the time I saw him, was under bail to appear at the next sessions. Such however was his standing, and so great the sympathy for the South, that it was thought the prosecution would come to nothing.

On the 29th of April, I left Halifax in the Asia; and on the 8th of May I landed in Queenstown. I was soon made aware of the rapidly increasing tide of emigration to the United States, and thought it proper to examine the subject attentively and to see if anything could be done to arrest or to diminish it.

I accordingly put myself in communication with several Bishops and Clergymen and conversed with them freely on the subject. I also made a short tour into the interior that I might see the people at home and judge from my own observation of their actual state and learn from their own lips, their motives and feelings. I also saw Rev. Mr. O'Bannon in Dublin, and Lieut. J L. Capston[30] in Cork. Both seemed to have been working earnestly in the matter and were able to give me important details and valuable information. I was much aided in my intercourse with the clergy on this subject by the timely appearance in the papers of a strong letter from Bishop Lynch[31] of Toronto, Canada, to the Irish Bishops, deprecating this wholesale emigration on religious and moral grounds. I found the clergy, to a man, opposed to what they characterize as an insane phrenzy. They are using all their power to withstand it. But I fear the torrent is, for the present at least, too strong even for them.

The reasons of this exodus are very clear. The immediate one seems to be this. The greater portion of the tilled and the waste lands, belongs to proprietors who reside abroad, and frequently live up to, if not beyond their income. They consequently exact from their tenants the very highest amount of rent, which a farmer, naturally attached to the house and field his family have lived in and cultivated for centuries, can be induced to promise. This is usually an amount he cannot pay, except when the year's harvest is good, and then, only by stinting his family in every way, and denying them many comforts which in America we are accustomed to look on as almost necessaries of life. The wife of an industrious farmer told me, that she sent to market every year butter to the value of over twenty pounds Sterling; but could not afford to put it on her own table five times a year.

It is calculated that by this single system of Absenteeism as it is termed, Ireland loses every year over thirty millions of dollars, for which she receives no return. In consequence, waste lands are not reclaimed; on the contrary they are increasing. The tenants make scarcely any improvements, and studiously avoid any exterior show of comfort. The first would be an outlay for the benefit of the Landlord, for which a tenant would generally look in vain for any adequate, often for any compensation. Perhaps he might not even have the use of it. For he is a tenant at will and may be dispossessed next year, if he will not pay a higher rent. The second would be an evidence that he can afford to pay more for his farm and a higher rent will be surely exacted. If a farmer is able to save a few guineas, he conceals the fact, hides them away and dresses perhaps more poorly than ever. They have an instinctive dread of the Landlord and his agents, such as one might find among the helpless victims of a rapacious cad in a Turkish village, who seek protection against the Spoiler in the garb of abject poverty.

For the last four years, the Seasons have been unfavourable, and the crops scanty and of bad quality. Hence the tenant farmers have been gradually sinking more and more deeply into debt, until at length they are in despair, and are quitting the country in crowds, some to Australia, some to South America, some to Canada, but the greater portion to the United States.

This movement is further aided by the action of another class—those of the proprietors and wealthier farmers, who after the late bad crops, seem to think the climate of Ireland has undergone some material change and that henceforth grazing will be more profitable than tillage. The poorest class, of course very numerous, was heretofore accustomed to eke out the little they made on their farms of a few acres, by their earnings as laborers in harvest or spring, on the farms of their wealthier neighbours. They now find the demand for this labour far less and rapidly diminishing and they say, that go where they may, they cannot be worse off than they now are. On the other hand, the graziers are by no means reluctant to obtain possession of these holdings in order to convert them into meadows and paddocks.

The reason so many go to the United States is also very clear. Most of the emigrants are of themselves utterly unable to pay their passage. They receive letters from their friends and relatives already in the United States, enclosing passage tickets, or funds to pay their passage, accompanied with pressing invitations to come, and assurances that they will find ready and remunerative employment on farms, or perhaps places waiting for them. Though I heard many strong though vague statements to that effect, I did not myself come on the trace of any agent of the United States in Ireland. But several of the more intelligent clergymen seemed to think there was a concert between the members of the Feenian [sic] Brotherhood in the United States, and their fellow members in Ireland. The former can easily be acted on by the government and politicians of the United States who can thus attain their purposes more safely and more effectually than could be done by the employment of direct emissaries. The Feenian newspapers however deny this and oppose the Emigration.[32]

In the meantime the Catholic clergy acting on religious and moral grounds, and also because they are naturally unwilling to see their flocks dwindling away, oppose the Exodus strongly. When they cannot withstand it, they fail not to warn the emigrants of the dangers and snares they will encounter on their arrival. These on their part are determined, at least now as they start, to stand firmly on their guard; they declare that they go to seek honest work and are firmly resolved not to become soldiers. In their own words, if they were willing to take blood-money, they could at once enter the British Army. It is a fact stated by the English Government that recruits are so scarce in Ireland, that several Irish Regiments are being denationalized and are now being filled up in England.

It is however to be feared, that this resolution may too often be broken. And that, if the war lasts long, too many of these emigrants will ultimately be found, by draft or otherwise, in the Federal ranks.

On the 24th of May, I crossed over to Liverpool; and after making the proper pecuniary arrangements with Messrs Frazier, Trenholm and Co. touching my salary, I passed on to London where I stopped for several days.

I called on His Eminence Cardinal Wiseman, with whom I dined—[called] on several of the Catholic clergy—met several members of Parliament, and of course both in Liverpool and in London saw the chief agent, and friends of the Confederacy.

I heard every where expressions of admiration for our valour, and of Sympathy for our cause. But it seemed to me, that all minds were so engrossed by the Danish Difficulties, in which England might very soon be involved, that American affairs were entitled to only a complimentary notice. It also seemed to me that it would require weeks for me [to] enter a circle where anything I would say could have any real weight. Moreover Mr. Spence,[33] Mr. Hotze[34] and our other friends in England seemed to be so active, to know so well what they were aiming at, and how it was best to proceed, that I felt that I a Stranger could scarcely be of any assistance. And I concluded to go on to Paris, which city I reached on the 4th inst.

Immediately on my arrival I called His Excellency Monsignor Flavio Chigi Apostolic Nunzio at Paris,[35] and on the Archbishop[36] of the City with the former, whom I have seen very frequently since, my relations have been very intimate and friendly. He seemed well-pleased with my coming and has written to Cardinal Antonelli announcing my early arrival in Rome. I expressed to him my desire of having an Audience with the Emperor. He offered to ask one for me, but stated that as the Imperial Family was at Fontainebleau, it might be attended with some delay, perhaps some difficulty; and enquired if I wished a private interview. I replied that I much desired an opportunity of freely and frankly speaking to the emperor. He said he would take the necessary steps. And had no doubt it could be arranged.

Some days after I received a note from the Nunzio saying that M. Drouyn de Lhuys,[37] Minister for Foreign affairs was desirous of knowing me—and appointing Monday 13th, at 1 P.M. as a convenient time for calling on him. At the appointed time, I called on the Nunzio, and we drove together in his carriage to the Ministère des Affaires Etrangères. While we were waiting in the minister's antechamber, Lord Cowley[38] entered. The Nunzio introduced me, and we fell into conversation on the American war. . . . He was surprised to learn that Sherman's Army was over six hundred miles distant from that of Genl Grant. He had thought them sufficiently near to cooperate which under the actual circumstances was certainly out of the question.

The Nunzio and myself soon entered the Cabinet of the Drouyn de Lhuys, and I was introduced. As both speak English very well, the conversation was continued in that language. M. Drouyn de Lhuys first remarked that I had come from a country in a very sad state. I replied that it was true that we felt the war, but that I had left all filled with hopes and with confidence. He said that the latest accounts seemed to indicate success on the part of the Confederates. I replied that it was quite clear to me, such was the case, that Gen[l] Mosby under Gen Lee having destroyed the bridges and railroads in the rear of the Federal Army, Grant had been obliged to move his army to the Northeast of Richmond, in order to establish new lines of communication and supplies, by the rivers of the Peninsula;[39] and now stood with his left in almost the identical position occupied by McClellan's right, two years ago; that this was the side of Richmond best prepared for defence by manifold lines of fortification, and that I anticipated that in two or three weeks, we would hear of his discomfiture and retreat. And with that, I hoped the war, at least on a grand scale, would terminate. He said, that long ago the French government was disposed to intervene, and propose terms of peace. Unwilling to act alone, it had proposed a concert of action in the matter to the English Government. But the proposal was not accepted. The French Government was still of the same mind, and officiously informed the English Government to that effect.

I replied that I thought the time had come or would soon arrive, when in the interests of Religion, and of Humanity, something should be done by those who had the ability to put a stop to a war, the only aim and principle of which was at present, on the part of the North, the gratification of their hatred, and which can have no other result than the death of hundreds of thousands on the battlefields or in the hospitals. If the Northern Government should succeed in conquering the South, which I thought out of the question; the result would be a confiscation of the property of everyone in the South, in order to pay in some degree the expenses of the war and to gratify the rapacity of men who especially in the matter of money, are without principle. No man at the South who could . . . would consent to live under their rule, and there would be an exodus like that of the Circassians[40] from the rule of the Russians in their country. But in point of fact they could not subjugate us. The war was continued in a spirit of hatred and could only produce loss of life and destruction of property. Religion and Humanity alike called for its termination.

He said that at the beginning of the War, the subject of Slavery was identified in the minds of men, with the cause of the South, and on that account the French natives felt opposed to us. But our gallant course in the War, had had the influence of winning them all to our side. That the Government had proposed to the English and the Russian Governments to interfere and to propose terms of a settlement, and if necessary to impose them. But found those governments unwilling to cooperate. France did not think proper to assume the responsibility of acting alone.

. . . The minister then went on to say that he was not in the government when the blockade was recognized. If he had been he would not have been so ready to admit it. He had lists of vessels that had passed in and out, some of them many times. The traditions of France were all against recognizing a paper blockade. But it had been done.

Here during a slight pause, His Excellency the Nunzio mentioned the official character of my journey to Rome. M. Drouyn de Lhuys expressed his pleasure and offered to mention it to the French Minister at Rome, that when I arrived he might extend to me the courtesies that would be proper. Of course I expressed my thanks. The Nunzio likewise asked for me an audience of the emperor which M. Drouyn promised to ask at once by telegraph, either for the next day when the Emperor was to come to the City for a meeting of some council, or as soon after as it could be granted.

We rose to leave. But before we left he said, I wish your Alabamas and Floridas that have so brilliant a reputation on one side and so bad a one on the other, would not come so very frequently to our ports. Once in a while is very well. But to come so frequently is embarrassing and might lead to an express prohibition. . . ." I said I would convey his Excellency's statement to Mr. Slidell for which he thanked me, and added, The Alabama has come, and I may have Mr. Dayton[41] down on me in a few days, with embarrassing questions. I said that as a Bishop I was not at all acquainted with the laws of maritime warfare[;] . . . —that in England the courts had pronounced decisions in our favour; but the *personel* of the Government being opposed to us, practically set them aside. The Confederates felt assured that in France they would always meet with kindness and justice, and that explained, perhaps, why they liked to come to France. He replied that he felt flattered; but for all that, it was to the Government an embarrassing course.

The same evening the Nunzio sent to me a note he had received from the minister, stating that the Emperor would receive me the next day at 10. A.M. and requesting him to notify me.

Accordingly at the appointed hour I went to the Tuilleries, robed as a Bishop. . . . In a quarter of an hour I was conducted to the immediate antechamber of the Emperor's Cabinet, and soon after was ushered into his presence.

He came forward to meet me, saluted me, first in French and then in English, asked me to be seated, and then commenced to speak of the brilliant defence of Charleston, and its future prospects. I said that the day before my departure Gen[l] Beauregard had told me he considered Charleston now perfectly safe against any attack from the front. He spoke of Fort Sumter, the present state of which I explained to him; of the blockade which is so often broken, my coming through being one instance, enquired of President Davis' health which he understood had been bad. I was happy to assure his Majesty that the President's heath was comparatively reestablished, and that I thought him good for twenty years work. He enquired about the demeanor of the negroes, which

I said had never been more quiet and submissive; that the tumult of the war seemed to me to have oppressed them with awe. Certainly they were never more docile and obedient. He spoke of the length of the war, and I stated to him that I deemed Grant's effort to take Richmond the last that would be made by the North, explained my views of his actual position, and my anticipation of his defeat. He said he hoped there would soon be some decisive battle so that England and France might at once recognize the South. . . .

I also spoke with respect of what he had done in Mexico in the interest of good Order; Civilization and Religion. But on this subject, he was reticent, and the hour of the Meeting of the Council having arrived, he politely bowed me out. As I was leaving he enquired how long I proposed staying in Paris, and said if I staid any time, he would be pleased to see me again. . . .

I have had the pleasure of meeting a number of French Bishops, Clergymen, and laymen of distinction. Having been in Charleston during months of its bombardment, and having run the Blockade, I found myself everywhere an object of some interest, and was able to give some serviceable information as to our real state.

If we could smooth down their prejudices on the subject of slavery, our task would be easy. Our gallant fighting,—the highest glory of a people in French eyes,—has put Slavery, for the present, in to the back ground. But I apprehend it will reassert its importance, whenever French Sympathy passes into action Something has been done,—much more remains to be done on this point, in a very delicate and prudent manner if we would disabuse the French mind even partially of its deep prejudice against Slavery.

I must acknowledge the kind manner in which I have been received by Hon. J. Slidell, Mr Hotze, Mr. Spence, Com. Barron,[42] Hon. J Elvard, Baron Erlanger,[43] Mr. De Leon,[44] and other Southern gentlemen and friends of the cause in England and France, especially in this city, where every attention has been lavished on me.

I shall leave on Wednesday, and hope to reach Rome by Sunday.

⟡

PATRICK LYNCH, ROME, TO JUDAH BENJAMIN, 5 JULY 1864[45]

Leaving [Paris] on the 23rd of June I reached Rome on the 26th.[46] Soon after my arrival I called on Cardinal Barnabo,[47] with whom I had already some acquaintance. . . . To him I explained the character and purpose of my visit to Rome. He entered at once into my views and offered to see Cardinal Antonelli,[48] and to arrange for a private and special audience with His Holiness for me, in my character as Bishop.

Accordingly, on the 28th, I called by appointment on his Eminence the Cardinal Secretary of State. He received me with marked warmth of manner, saying "Your Excellency comes from a country sorely tried, but, so far as I can judge from the latest news holding out bravely, and gaining advantages." He . . . had endeavoured to make himself acquainted with the real condition of affairs in the Confederate States, and keep himself informed on the progress of events. In fact I have not, thus far, found any European on the continent who seemed to be so well informed on the merits of the American question as Cardinal Antonelli.

In the course of conversation his Eminence observed, that when His Holiness wrote the letter on Peace, which he addressed to the ArchBishops of New York and New Orleans, he had thought that matters had not gone so far but that some terms of peace and settlement might then be proposed and accepted; and that, His Holiness having no political interest to subserve, but actuated by motives of peace and good will, wrote these letters thinking he might fittingly suggest and inaugurate such a settlement. Ulterior events have proved, and subsequent events have demonstrated that in the ruling condition of popular feeling such a settlement was then impossible. Sooner or later he deems an arrangement must conclude the contest.

Some time after the publication of His Holiness' letter to President Davis, the American Minister had taken and expressed exceptions to the terms in which President Davis had been addressed by His Holiness. "But the matter was simple enough," Cardinal Antonelli went on to say. It was an incontestable fact that the Confederate Government had an existence and exercised the functions of a government, and President Davis, its chief could be properly addressed by the title which his country gave him. So had the Cardinal replied to the American Minister; and he added, laughing, that the only remedy for the North was to conquer the South, and suppress the Confederate Government, *if they could.*

I explained, informally, to the Cardinal Secretary of State the purport and character of my visit to Rome, and the purpose of the Confederate Government in sending me as Commissioner to the States of the Church. He listened with attention and seemed pleased, but did not make any direct reply. I spoke to him of my interview with the Emperor of France and repeated the expressions that he had used to me in relation to the confederacy. These expressions of the Emperor, the Cardinal considered very strong and then proceeded to express his own views on the policy of England and France in our regard. "England," he said "had become jealous and rather fearful of the growing power of the United States, and, if she were not to be held accountable for having stirred up or fomented our dissensions, she certainly looked on them with satisfaction at reducing for a time, and perhaps for a very long time, the only power which could compete with her in commerce. "England," he said "is willing that the enfeebling process should grow, and she will, when necessary, step in to recognize the South when such a recognition may prove the means of preventing a reunion, and the reestablishment of the U.S. Government in its olden integrity, with a likelihood of its reasserting its former maritime pretensions.

"France," he said "will hold it necessary that the Confederacy should be independant [sic] of the North for the purpose of carrying out her policy in Mexico." So clear were these connections to the mind of Cardinal Antonelli that he had, when the Emperor Maximillian was in Rome on his way to Mexico, taken the liberty of a friend of former days and strongly presented this view to his Majesty, and recommended him, as one of the chief points of his policy on Mexico to cultivate intimate and friendly relations with the Confederacy. . . . The interview lasted nearly an hour, and the Cardinal's manner was very cordial. . . .

On Monday, July 4th, at 11½ o'clock A.M I had an audience with His Holiness. It was private and special, and in my quality as Bishop. After replying to his inquiries regarding the condition of Charleston and the amount of the damage realy [sic] done by the long bombardment, I said that I came charged by his Excellency President Davis to present to His Holiness the expression of his respect & veneration and good will; and for my self, I expressed the general sentiments of the people of the Confederacy, in regard to his letters on Peace and his letters to the President. His Holiness expressed his gratification in receiving such assurances of the kindly feelings entertained toward him in the Confederacy: enquired concerning the Presidents health, the general state of the country and the progress of the war, deploring in strong terms the immense destruction of life, and enquired how many I thought or had calculated to have fallen on both sides from the beginning of the War. I placed my estimate at 120,000 who had fallen in battle, or died of their wounds, in a few days after the conflict, and that more than three times that number had died of wounds or camp diseases contracted in the war that in all, over half a million had been sacrificed. . . .

. . . Genl. Rufus King, the American Minister at Rome, having lately requested the Holy Father to attach his autograph to some photografs of His Holiness destined for sale at a sanitary fair in a Northern city the Holy Father of course complied but above his signature he wrote: "Mitte gladium tuum in vaginam, et Deus pacis erit vobiscum,"[49] (John XVIII.11 & Phillippians IV.9) and finished his narration of this incident to me by observing playfully, "valeat quantum valeat! May the admonition have its weight." . . .[50]

I then stated that I had been sent in an official character and that at a proper time I hoped to present myself before him as the minister of the Confederate

States, and that my government had thought it would be agreeable that the first representative of the new nation at the Holy See, should be a Bishop. He replied that he highly appreciated, and was truly grateful for this manifestation of the sentiments which characterized the Confederate government in this regard, and went on to speak of the future, when terms of peace will have to be settled between these two nations, "for," added he most emphatically, " it is most clear that you are two nations." In this relation he added, "when some foreign power will perhaps have to be called in as umpire, when, perhaps, by a miracle, for it would be a miracle if the North should consent, that I might be called on as umpire, I wish it to be understood beforehand that I could not say anything directed to confirm and strengthen slavery. I hold that Christianity has bene-fited society as to the position of woman and as to the position of the slave. The first has been elevated and made equal to man and has her appropriate sphere of action. I am happy to believe that on both sides your women have done and are doing immense good in the hospitals."

". . . As to your slaves, I see clearly that it would be absurd to attempt, as it were to cut the Gordian Knott; by an act of Emancipation. But still something might be done looking to an improvement in their position or state, and to a gradual preparation for their freedom at a future opportune time. I have al-ready said this much to several Americans from the South and they seemed to agree with me."

On this point I did not deem it opportune to offer my reply.

. . . I am now engaged in drawing up a paper on the actual condition and treatment of slaves at the South, at the request of Msgr. Nardi,[51] one of the judges of the Rota or supreme court of the Papal States. I presume it will find its way into the press. As I said in my last dispatch, it seems to me a very im-portant matter to arrest, in every way that it can be done, the erroneous ideas which prevail in Europe on this subject, and to produce if possible a more fa-vourable or rather a less unfavourable feeling on the subject of African Slavery in the Confederate States.

1864 July–September

"The fundamental danger . . . is the Antagonism of Races."

In his June report to Secretary Benjamin, Patrick Lynch had noted that the key to securing French recognition lay in changing the negative image of slavery that dominated popular opinion in the country: "If we could smooth down their prejudices on the subject of slavery, our task would be easy."[1] The following month in Rome, a sympathetic judge of the supreme court of the Papal States asked Lynch to compose a report on the condition and treatment of slaves in the South. Shortly afterwards, the bishop began a pamphlet designed principally to be not merely an exposition of the South's peculiar institution but an apologia for it, intended not only for the marketplace of French opinion but for that of all the Catholic powers, including the papacy. A Few Words on the Domestic Slavery in the Confederate States of America, under the generic byline "a Catholic Clergyman," appeared subsequently in three languages: Italian, French, and German.

The most receptive audience, in the summer of 1864, was the papal curia. The Roman attitude toward the American Civil War had shifted from identifying with the right of the United States government to defend itself against rebellion (Rome was contending with its own insurrection in the Papal States) to growing sympathy for a people seeking independence. When Bishop Lynch had a private audience with Pope Pius IX in early July 1864, the pontiff remarked, "It is clear you are two nations."[2] The catalyst for changing the Holy See's position on the war was the Emancipation Proclamation, which had implicitly made the abolition of slavery a war goal. In Rome that tended to be interpreted as a call for an uprising of the slaves and all the horrific evils that would follow. That sentiment was enforced by a long letter written by the Bishop of Louisville, Martin Spalding, to the prefect of the Congregation for the Propagation of the Faith (Propaganda Fide), which had jurisdiction over the Catholic Church in the United States as a mission country. What the Emancipation Proclamation had done, Spalding warned, was to convert a war to "restore the broken Union" into "a war of confiscation of property, of violent emancipation of the Negroes, of threatened and encouraged slave insurrection, of destruction and desolation of the vast and fair territory of the South, and finally of extermination of all the whites, and perhaps at the same time also of the Negroes themselves."[3] In October 1863 the semiofficial L'Osservatore Romano published it anonymously. Six months later Rome appointed Spalding to succeed Francis Kenrick as archbishop of Baltimore, the premier see in the United States.

Spalding, in his dissertation, had admitted the intrinsic evil of slavery. The problem was how to abolish it without doing greater evil in the process. For Spalding the only practical moral recourse that Catholics had was to wash their hands of the whole bloodbath that the war had become. That, of course, was unacceptable to Lynch. Censuring American Catholics for advocating abolition or adopting a noninvolvement policy would do nothing to win independence for the Confederacy. Rather, the key issue to be confronted was the moral status of slavery. Three years earlier two of Lynch's fellow prelates in the South, Augustine Verot of St. Augustine, Florida, and Auguste Martin of Natchitoches, Louisiana, had issued pastoral letters in which the French-born bishops affirmed the compatibility of slavery with Christianity but found the actual order of bonded labor in the South falling far short of what God intended slavery to be. In January 1861 Bishop Verot delivered a sermon on slavery and abolitionism in which he contended that the abolitionists were to blame for the collapse of the Union that was becoming more evident by the day. In calling for the end of slavery, the abolitionists had left Southern states with no other option but to secede in order to protect the peculiar institution that scripture, law, and tradition all sanctioned. The just course for slavery in the South was not abolition but reform of the institution so that the inherent rights of those in bondage would be honored.[4] The following August, with the South now at war to preserve the independence they had secured through secession, Bishop Martin had issued his pastoral on the war and slavery. He, too, laid the principal responsibility for the conflict at the abolitionists' feet. But Southerners shared some of the blame as well, insofar as they failed to fulfill their duties as Christian slaveholders. For Martin slavery was the providential way through which Africans became Christians. The scandal was the sorry record of slaveholders in nurturing Christianity among their slaves. The upshot was a war for which both sides bore blame.[5]

Neither pastoral, unlike Spalding's "Dissertation," got any circulation in Europe, including Rome. There was a compelling need, so Lynch concluded in the summer of 1864, for a defense of slavery that demonstrated its essential moral—indeed, Christian—character in providing the ideal environment for Africans. Such a domestic institution, far from rendering a nation illegitimate,

A Few Words on the ~~State of~~ Domestic Sla=
very in the Confederate States of America
By a Catholic Clergyman

To the Reader,

The following pages are not intended as a discussion or a defence of Slavery, but as a statement of facts. To say that freedom is better
than slavery, is to my mind very like saying that
health is better than sickness. Yet this world is
so unfortunate that both sickness and slavery
have existed, do exist, and will continue to exist.

I have never heard that any sane man proposed
to banish all sickness, by slaying the Doctors and
burning all hospitals. But I have met Philanthropists
who in their horror of slavery and their blind zeal
against it, would rush into measures almost equally
absurd, and far more destructive. The Federals in
America have of late gone farther. They are killing
the sick. They consenpt the liberate negro men, and
use them in the front ranks, and the most dange=
rous positions, where they are slain by thousands.
Women and Children are left to die of disease or
starvation at home.

To treat a case correctly and skillfully, it is necessary to have a correct diagnosis of it. In these
pages is here given, if the reader pleases, a diagnosis of Slavery.

First page of English draft of *A Few Words on the Domestic Slavery in the Confederate
States*. Courtesy of the Roman Catholic Diocese of Charleston Archives.

rather should make it particularly worthy of recognition by the Christian nations of the world.

Casting the tract as a scientific report by an impartial observer, Lynch assured his readers that it was no apology for slavery but rather a simple "statement of facts." It was, in fact, a classic manifestation of the art of propaganda in which Lynch wove selective facts, racist suppositions, fanciful history, and wishful thinking to compose his idyllic profile of Southern slavery. In this telling, despite persistent efforts by the now Confederate states to contain and suppress it, the peculiar institution had been forced upon the region by outside groups, including the North, driven by economic interest and greed. Despite its dark origins, slavery in the South provided the opportunity for Africans to be Christianized as well as the moral restraint that their excess-prone character required. At the core of Southern slavery were the mutual obligations of master and slave that ensured productive plantations and well-cared-for slaves. The remarkable fidelity that slaves displayed, amid the upheavals of war, to their often absent masters was the best testimony to the slaves' basic satisfaction with their place in Southern society. Unlike obligations, fidelity was not mutual. Owners were free under the law to sell and will their slaves to others; indeed, in Southern society such practices were regarded as integral to the institution. Tradition, in effect, bested any moral considerations. Freedom for the slaves, on the other hand, was unthinkable. With climate shaping character, the slaves' African origin rendered them unfit to provide for themselves through the industrious application of intelligence. Hence freedom for the slaves would inevitably bring misery, pauperization, and a race war that would threaten their very survival. The ideal post-slavery state for them would be an isolated colony in a tropical land, such as Santo Domingo, where a vastly larger-scale replica of the California missions or Paraguay Reductions could be instituted by a religious order, such as the Society of Jesus. That quasi utopia being politically unfeasible for the foreseeable future, the only practical alternative, Lynch concluded, was to accept the status quo, with which the slaves themselves seemed happy enough.

A FEW WORDS ON THE DOMESTIC SLAVERY IN THE CONFEDERATE STATES OF AMERICA BY A CATHOLIC CLERGYMAN [1864][6]

To the Reader

The following pages are not intended as a discussion or a defence of Slavery, but as a statement of facts. To say that *freedom is better than slavery* is to my mind very like saying that *health is better than sickness.* Yet this world is so unfortunate that both sickness and Slavery have existed, do exist, and will continue to exist.

I. Introduction

In the Confederate States there are about eight millions of white inhabitants, descendants of Europeans, and four millions of negroes, descendants of Africans, living, the greater part of them, in a state of Slavery subject to the former. These slaves were ordinarily spoken of as a race kept in chains by force, subjected to every kind of cruel usage, yearning for liberty, and so ready for revolt that the Southern States were often compared to "a slumbering volcano," the fires of which might burst forth, any day.

The war came. The armed vessels paraded the coasts of the South, sailing in sight of the plantations. Armies took possession of much of the sea shore. On the northern and western boundaries other armies entered the Confederacy from the adjoining states of the Union, taking possession of cities and towns and entire districts of the country. They all sent out expeditions or moveable columns of troops, which entered every state of the Confederacy. By proclamation of the Federal President Lincoln, the slaves of the south were declared free. The Generals of those armies,—some of them through a spirit of Abolitionism,—some through obedience to the order of their Government, some from military motives, wishing to weaken the South by cutting off our agricultural supplies, and to demoralize us by the dangers of threatened servile disturbances,—all invited the negroes to flock to them for protection. This has been going on for over two years.

The Northerners undoubtedly expected the appeal to be successful. Many in Europe have looked for the same result. This is what would have happened, had their preconceived notions been true. The downtrodden negroes would have hailed with transports of joy the day of their liberation.

What has been the fact? The negroes have paid no attention whatever to the Federal Proclamation; and so far as they could have kept out of the way of the Federal forces. Thousands have followed their masters faithfully to the war, sharing with them the fatigues of the march, the discomforts of camp, and the dangers of battle. Tens of thousands of them work in the erection of the earthen fortifications, which throughout the Confederacy, protect every Railway bridge, and every pass. . . . The great mass have desired and desire nothing more than to be left quietly at home, pursuing, as their fathers did, the easy cultivation of the fields, under the guidance and discipline of their masters. I do not believe that five out of a thousand have voluntarily gone to the Yankee Armies. The Federals have come into possession of many thousands of them, living in towns and villages and districts which they have occupied, and who could not move off. Of these many seize the opportunities that offer, of getting back to their masters within the Confed. lines, and voluntarily return to that state of Slavery, from which it was thought they were so anxious to escape.

III. Historical Sketch of the African Slave Trade

The Slave Trade has been almost entirely suppressed within the last half century.

. . . it is honourable to our century that, even if late, the voice of Divine Truth and Justice has been listened to, and the Traffic has been suppressed. Still one may believe that it was no injury,—perhaps on the contrary a benefit,—to these captive negroes themselves, that they were not left to be slain on some funeral pile, at some savage debauch, or in some demoniacal heathenish rite; but on the contrary were transferred, even though roughly, to a Christian land, where, if slaves, they might live in peace and security, and, if forced to earn their bread in the sweat of their brow, they might at least obtain a knowledge of the true God, and might save their souls.

V. Domestic Slavery

Domestic Slavery . . . I define it to be essentially a system or state of mutual claims and obligations between the owner and the slaves, whereby the latter is bound to give to the former the produce of his reasonable life long labour under the owner's direction; and the owner is bound in return to give to the slave a reasonable support according to his condition, from infancy to death. . . .

In the Southern States the owner has the further right of transferring his claims and obligations to another owner, without consulting the slave, or as it is said, of selling him. They also pass from one owner to another by will or inheritance. . . . In practice, in the Southern States, it is looked on as essential to the system.

VI. Various Classes of Slaves

The House servants do not differ in their treatment and work from the house servants in every civilized country, except that unfortunately three of them will not do as much work as one European or Northern white servant. To foreigners coming into the South their idleness, slothfulness and awkwardness render them unbearable. It is among masters coming from abroad, and for this cause, that nine tenths of the instances of sever[e] punishment or cruelty will be found to occur, when they really happen. . . .

Another class, sufficiently numerous in cities and towns, consists of those who "hire their own time," that is, who pay a certain sum every month, generally a very moderate one, to their owners, and beyond that live and work and earn for themselves very much as they please. Such negroes may be said to enjoy, at least to some extent, the privilege of freedom. But as a class they are not looked on with favour. There are exceptions among them, but it is generally found that they become idle and dissipated, and plunge into drunkenness and other vices. . . .

VII. Agricultural Labourers. Their Work, Food, & Condition

Nine tenths of the slaves constitute the third class, employed in the interior in agricultural labours. . . .

Here too we meet varieties depending on the character of the country, the various kinds of agriculture and especially on the number of blacks in any special district, compared with that of the whites. . . . In those parts of the interior, where the climate is healthy and where the whites can labour with impunity, and where consequently the slaves are comparatively fewer, and are usually found in smaller groups, and more intimately associated with the whites, their condition and treatment approximates to that of the House Servants. . . . In the rice plantations, on the contrary, where no white man can labour, . . . while on the contrary the. . . negro exults in the fullness of health in a tropical heat; on the cotton plantations of the coast, . . . the slaves live together in villages, working under the direction of a white superintendent, and governed by a special police. . . .

Each family lives in a small house of a suitable size, and ordinarily has a small plot of ground attached to serve as a garden. They all work, men and women according to their capacity, unless prevented by illness. . . . An industrious man can ordinarily accomplish his work by two or three o'clock. In that case the remainder of the day is at his own disposal. . . . On Saturdays only half the usual quantity is assigned to be done, in order that the slaves may have half a day to prepare for Sunday, which is always a day of entire rest. . . . Ordinarily their tasks are fixed, and are very light, at least they would be trifles in the hands of an English or Irish farm labourer. . . .

The negroes receive strong solid food, fully as much as they [can] consume, and have something over to satisfy a negro's natural inclination to waste. In addition they enjoy with pleasure the fruits of their fishing and hunting, of the latter of which they are very fond. They also have their poultry, their hogs, if they raise any, and the products of their gardens . . . ; they may either consume them as luxuries, or sell them in order to purchase whatever else they please.

In addition to this, the master is bound to give them a sufficiency of suitable clothing . . . two suits a year, one for summer and one for winter, with hats and shoes, as may be necessary. There is also a Physician, employed to attend the negroes regularly when ill. Large plantations have a regular hospital for the sick. . . . There is also a playground for the younger children, who are left under the charge of the aged negroes, while their parents are away at work in the fields.

VIII. Punishments

Cases of cruelty are rare, and are punishable by law. . . .

For grievous offences against society, the negro is answerable to, and is judged by the tribunals of the country, but for neglect of work, pilfering from his fellow slaves, or minor offences, his master is his judge. . . . As it is, flagellation is used for slaves as for children, because it pains without inflicting injury, and punishes without incapacitating for work. Where a negro is insubordinate, or vicious to an extent to demoralize the other negroes, and cannot be reclaimed by ordinary punishments, he is sold away from the scene of his offences. . . . It certainly restrains the negroes from many of the offences, which are so common among the free negroes, and those who hire their own time, and which so often make the members of these two classes the pests of society.

IX. Education of the Slaves

[B]y the laws of several of the slave states, it is forbidden to teach them to read. Such laws do exist, and although favorite negroes may, not infrequently, be taught to read and write, by the planter's children, there are no schools for the education of the slaves, nor are any allowed. . . .

During the warm discussion of Abolition in England, and the agitation of the same question in the Northern States, hot headed men undertook to circulate tracts among the slaves in the South inciting them directly to servile insurrection. Plots were in fact formed, even on a large scale, and were detected. In one instance, the insurrection broke out.[7] Murders, arsons, and outrages of every kind marked its brief progress to a bloody end. In order to guard against such attempts to subvert society, various measures were taken, one of which was the enactment of the laws in question, which were not intended to oppress the negro, but to destroy the mode by which evil agents could most artfully and secretly work among them from a safe distance. The propriety of such laws depends on the question, whether the whites have a right to take such means to protect themselves.

X. Religion of the Negroes

. . . The various Protestant denominations, especially the Methodists and Baptists, have laboured assiduously for the religious instruction of the negroes. But the results so far have not been as great as were anticipated. Essentially a sensuous race, loving the excitement of an hour, and having generally good voices, and a natural sense of music, the negroes love to join in prayer meetings or assemblies of their own, where much of the service consists of all singing hymns together; where the discourses are generally rude and impassioned; and where, at times, each member of the Church, man or woman, is allowed to rise up in turn and preach a ludicrous exhortation, or to scream forth a wild untutored extempore prayer, as often blasphemous in its phraseology, as it is hypocritical in its meaning. The audience in the meantime is in a tumult of sobs and groans, and shrill hysterical exclamations. . . . With strong passions, and prone to give them license, the negroes run readily into Antinomianism,[8] and think that if they "belong to the Church," and have a good standing among their brethren, especially if they have the gift of praying aloud in their reunions, or still more, of being easily thrown into convulsions or hysterics, which they think a physical effect of the power of the Holy Ghost on them, all is well, whatever their customs or deeds in other times and places. . . .

Although they are very ignorant of the doctrines of Christianity, still they believe firmly in the Divinity of our Saviour, and in the Redemption. . . . Our holy religion has . . . wonderful power over the negroes, when they yield to God's grace. . . . But the number of them is yet so small, that while it gives us hope for the future and tells us what might be done, still in speaking or judging of the actual character of the mass of negroes as at present, we need not take the Catholics into account.

XI. The Morality of the Slaves

. . . The negroes are, as a race, very prone to excesses, and, unless restrained, plunge madly into the lowest depths of licentiousness. . . .

It does not appear to me that it is caused by Slavery. For, in the first place, the free negroes are far more immoral than the slaves. . . . They are exceptions, but "drunkenness, theft, and promiscuous sexual intercourse are quite common amongst them." . . . The negroes who live on the plantations, under the restraints and discipline of the owners and superintendents, show less immorality, at least in its grosser forms. The best of all are the house servants, for whom a good character is a special commendation, and who know that unless they comport themselves with a certain degree of outward virtue at least, they are liable to be sent in disgrace to labour on the plantation. . . .

The passions of men exist and will seek their gratification whether Slavery exist or not. As far as the intercourse between the two races exists, it will be found that the whites who indulge in it are . . . mostly young unmarried men, who consequently are not yet, ordinarily, owners of slaves, and that the partners of their guilt are generally free coloured women. It should be further noted as a fact, that just as such females abound, and debauchery [is] thrown into that channel, the white females are exempted from its influence. Nowhere save in Ireland are they so pure as in the South. . . .

There is unfortunately too much libertinism between the white race and the negroes, whether free or slaves, in the South. . . . More probably, by putting the negro under a special authority, and still more by so largely uniting them in villages apart, it tends to repress this evil to a very large extent. I really think if the negroes were free, this immorality would assume infinitely greater proportions.

XII. Marriages of the Negroes

. . . [I]n the Southern States, the negroes themselves have very loose ideas on the subject, and very little regard for the sanctity of marriage. . . . A large number of [the free blacks] live without marriage at all, giving themselves up to every form of immorality,—a thing which the owners do not allow among their slaves on the plantations, where it can be prevented. . . . The slaves who hire their own time, living as they please in the towns and cities, are similar to the free negroes, in their matrimonial relations.

XIII. Marriages of Negroes, Continued

. . . It is urged against the system of Domestic Slavery, that according to the laws the owner may, and in point of fact habitually does, sell his negroes at will, separately; thus dividing husband and wife, even though faithful to each other, warmly attached, and most solemnly and validly married,—that in point of fact there is no legal protection for the marriage of the negro. . . . The matter from the beginning has been left in the hands of the master, who can have the fullest knowledge of each case, and whom the force of public opinion,—the interests of morality,—and generally his own pecuniary interests also will lead to act in the matter with more justice and truth than would be obtained from any merely civil tribunal appointed to judge such cases. . . .

So far as Catholic owners are concerned, they recognize and are guided by the teaching of the Church, and hold it to be a sin to separate man and wife legitimately married.

. . . in fact, the custom is to respect and preserve the marriage relation, even when of the mere informal character. . . .

XVI. The Future of Slavery

Not infrequently the negroes refuse to accept the [offer of emancipation]. They actually possess the good will of a kind owner and protector, to whom they are attached; and they prudently decline to exchange the comfort and the certainty of their present position, for the uncertainty and misery to which they would be exposed as free negroes.

Thirty years ago such instances of liberation were much more frequent than they have been of later years. But as the number of free negroes increased and the libertinism and viciousness of that class, and their evil influence on the slaves became more evident, the governments of the several states made laws on the subject. Some of the Northern free states made laws, prohibiting under severe penalties, the further entrance of such freed negroes within their borders, and providing for their expulsion. In the South it was first enacted that a master freeing his slaves should give bonds that the freed negroes should not in course of time become a charge on the public charity. This law was intended to protect the negroes and strike at such owners as, after reaping the fruit of a negro's work while in health and strength, would under the specious pretext of freeing them, aim at freeing themselves from the burden and duty of supporting him in his old age.

Later laws based on the character of the free negroes, and especially on the fact that they sometimes become the agents of the Abolitionists at the North, required that when an owner freed his slave, he should send him away to some Northern State where the negroes are free. Under this regulation freedom is not very acceptable to the negroes. They are unwilling to leave their homes; and many of them are well aware of the miserable condition to which they would be reduced, if they were to go to the Northern States.

XVII. General Emancipation. Antagonism of Races

. . . I will briefly discuss some of the proposed plans.

The first . . . is to imitate England and France, to declare by enactment the cessation of Slavery, with or without compensation to the masters, and to leave the negroes in the country. This plan would be every way disastrous, and to no party more so than to the negroes themselves, whom it is intended to benefit. Its first and immediate consequence would be to put two races face to face, in the most deadly Antagonism and to inaugurate at once an inhuman war unparalleled in the history of the world. There are now in the Southern States two distinct races, the whites, descendants of Europeans, eight millions in number, and the blacks, descendants of Africans, four millions in number. At present there is no Antagonism between them. The latter are subject to the former. But set them free, let them claim an equality with the whites, let them come into competition or be felt as an obstacle in the way of the whites, and this antagonism of races at once springs into active power.

We may lament, but we cannot deny facts. Such Antagonism manifests itself wherever two races come into social collision. . . . Such an antagonism contributed to the utter extinction of the original population which the early European settlers found in the West India islands, and is seen in the perpetual revolutions of Mexico, Central America, and the Spanish settlements of South America, as the Europeans on one side with intellect, and the Indians on the other with numbers, contend for the possession of the Government. . . .

Certain it is, that no people is so fierce and inexorable in such an Antagonism, as the Anglo Saxon and cognate races, which people the English settlements of North America. No race would be more relentlessly pursued than the unfortunate African, marked by his colour and features, and so different in traits of mind and habits of body. Hence the unfortunate lot of the Free negroes in the Northern States and in Canada. They are the Pariahs, and worse than the Pariahs of these countries. It is only the insignificance of their numbers which saves them from incessant outbursts of violence, such as have been seen at New York and Philadelphia.[9] As it is they are perishing. . . . their condition is in every way vile and abject.

. . . There would be a war of cruelty, of rapine, murder, tortures and countless horrors, of which no mind can measure the depth, or foretell the duration. Where the negroes would for a time obtain the upper hand, the attrocities [*sic*] of San Domingo would be reënacted; where the infuriated whites, from superior numbers and superior intelligence, would conquer, no mercy would be shown. The contest would cease only from exhaustion, to be renewed until the negroes approached extinction. I apprehend the Abolitionists have little conception of this Charybdis of destruction into which they would plunge the negroes, in the endeavour to save them from the Scylla of Slavery. . . .

XVIII. Financial Difficulties

. . . The slaves now represent property of individuals to the amount of at least 9.000.000.000 francs. . . .[10] [W]ould not their emancipation be, in fact, the confiscation by the state of the property of individuals to that vast amount, and the disposal to other purposes at the will of the Civil Government? What compensation would or could be given to those, who thus lose their property? The very amount forbids any such compensation.

. . . [W]ho would guarantee that the country would not be ruined pecuniarily? At present, and under the system in force, these four millions are profitably employed. If emancipated they would at once sink to the level of the free negroes, and become unproductive and a load on the community. . . .

. . . [M]en may well pause before the proposition [of emancipation] and ask for some way of escaping these evils.

XIX. Preparatory Apprenticeship

. . . It would be necessary to devise some plan, which would purify and change the negro character. . . . As the world goes, it would be folly to look for such from a civil government of this age. . . .

During the war, which now desolates America, the Federals have taken possession of New Orleans, and a portion of the States of Virginia, North Carolina, South Carolina, Georgia, Florida, and Louisiana, where there were many plantations or villages of negroes. At least 250,000 have fallen into their hands, by such capture, or have sought their protection, and have all been declared free. These were to live and work under the care and guidance of certain teachers and superintendents specially sent by the Government for that purpose. . . . Their own journals have been filled with accounts of the horrible condition into which the negroes fell. . . . They were dependent on charity for food and raiment. Diseases ravaged them. They lay ill for days without medical attendance. They died uncared for of fever, or of starvation, or of cold. In a word, it is calculated that of the 250,000, not one half are now living. Is this the apprenticeship and preparation for freedom offered to the negro?

But even if such a plan were carried into effect successfully, at its conclusion at least, and when the negroes would enter on the possession and exercise of freedom, if not before, would not the Antagonism I spoke of break out? And if the previous preparation had elevated the negro character, would this do more then, than to render the struggle less unequal, longer, more bloody, and more horrible?

XX. Transportation of the Negroes to Africa

Another proposal is to assign some tract of country, sufficiently large to receive the negroes as they become free, and in which they might live in a community apart, either under their own government, if they were capable of it, or of white governors, if it were necessary. . . . But here too, we are met by serious difficulties. What country shall be selected? It must be large enough to receive a population of millions; . . . It must be separate by strong natural boundaries from any land inhabited by the whites; else the war of extermination may sooner or later set in. It must be under or near the tropics; for there only do we find a clime naturally suited to the negro race.

Some have proposed Africa, which is large enough, distant enough, and tropical. Sierra Leone and Liberia were intended to commence such communities. To the latter place, two or three vessels a year, if so many, have been sent from America carrying over Free negroes. It is said that in the course of time thousands of them or their children have passed or fallen into the hands of the savage tribes around them.

But however successful these efforts may be, they are on too infinitesimal a scale to accomplish any thing of importance. The annual increase of the negroes in the Southern States is about 100.000. If there were two hundred and fifty vessels, each making three round trips a year from America to Africa, and each carrying three hundred and fifty passengers at a time, engaged continuously in transporting Africans to the land of their ancestors, fully thirty years would be required for the total work. . . . Does anyone dream that any one nation could, or that all nations combined would, subject themselves to this labour and tax upon their resources and commerce, for thirty years, for mere charity, without any pecuniary return, and simply out of a desire that the negroes now in the Confederacy, instead of continuing to live as they now are, may live in Africa under such government as they can devise? . . . The negroes must perforce be left to themselves. It needs no prophet to foretell that they would soon sink below the level of Hayti.

XXII. General Considerations

. . . The fundamental danger, in great measure to the whites, & absolutely to the blacks in America, is the Antagonism of races.

. . . Even if the two races were such that they could intermarry, and thus become gradually merged in an intermediate race, the difficulty might perhaps be lightened. But this is not so. The differences between the two races are such as to forbid their regular amalgamation. Only on a very small scale, and mostly through libertinism, has it occurred. The consequences of it on a considerable scale would be, as in San Domingo, to produce a third class, with the faults of both races, and equally inimical to both. . . .

. . . At present the negroes are well provided and well cared for, happy and content. I know of no condition in which the Abolitionists would place them, in which they would be equally so. . . . most of the plans they advocate would lead to internecine war of the most atrocious character, and would end either in the bloody reënslavement of the negroes, or more probably in their utter extinction.

XXIV. Conclusion

. . . Those who wish to prepare for their freedom, and would wish to save them from extermination, should prepare homes for them elsewhere, apart from the white race, either sufficiently large at once, or capable of extension, and under the tropics, to be suited to the physical character of the negro. A government must be provided, suitable to his moral and intellectual character. At the South we believe that the government of a master is eminently such. . . . Self Government, they are incapable of. . . .

. . . Such a nascent [patriarchic] community might be put under the entire charge of some religious body, like that of the Society of Jesus. The negroes would yield readily to this religious, almost theocratical rule. . . . It is only in such a way that these communities can be successfully and prosperously governed. It is only doing on a larger scale what was done so well in the Indian Missions of California and of Paraguay in the last century. . . . What a home for the negroes there now, and for the millions that might in course of time be sent there, would San Domingo . . . be, were it under such beneficent rule. . . .

But there is nothing in the heart of the nineteenth century, which would support, or even tolerate, such an effort.

At least then, the slaves of the Confederate States may ask to be left in their present state of quiet and content, awaiting the future which God only knows; and not be doomed at once to ruin, if not speedy extermination, for the sake of a mere theory.

1864 October–December

"A miracle—a standing miracle"

Patrick Lynch's tract on slavery appeared first in Italian in the early fall of 1864. The Rome-based Jesuit journal of opinion, La Civiltà cattolica, *pronounced Patrick Lynch's* Few Words *the convincing work of an "impartial, superbly well-informed" man of "broad and just views," revealing the "true condition of slavery in the American South."[1] If he was hoping that* L'Osservatore Romano *would give it a similar review or even print excerpts of it, as the semiofficial journal had done for Martin Spalding's "Dissertation" a year earlier, he was disappointed. By the time* Few Words *appeared in its Italian edition, the winds within the Holy See were clearly moving against Lynch's mission and the Confederacy.*

Over the past year the Papal States' consul in New York City, Louis Binsse, apparently at the behest of the Paulist priest, Isaac Hecker, had been pressuring Propaganda Fide, as the governing body over the Church in the United States, to take a public stand of support for the Lincoln Administration's war goal of emancipation. Rome, he contended, could no longer remain silent about the issue that clearly was the reason for the break-up that had plunged the country into a war of such unprecedented carnage and destruction. The congregation's decision to examine the 1861 pastoral of Bishop Auguste Martin of Louisiana was seemingly its response to Binsse's urgings. That fall the Propaganda official charged with its examination issued his report. It condemned the pastoral as completely at odds with Catholic teaching and wildly wrong in its arguments about the symbiosis between Christianity and slavery. The report was a thorough repudiation of the chattel slavery practiced in the South. Pope Pius IX accepted the report's recommendations and placed the pastoral on the Index of Forbidden Books. All this was to remain secret, however, until Bishop Martin had the opportunity to retract his condemned assertions.[2] Thus Patrick Lynch could only wonder what had gone wrong when his Few Words *failed to gain any traction in papal Rome and changed no opinions towards the Confederacy and its peculiar institution.*

Securing recognition for the Confederacy from the Papal States as well as other Catholic European governments had been the major goal of Patrick Lynch's trip. But if his official status was as an emissary of the Confederate government, Patrick Lynch was still very much an apologist for his church. Wearing that hat, he headed south from Rome in September 1864 to Naples, for the festival of St. Januarius, to observe the reputed flowing of the saint's blood. Forty years earlier, Patrick Lynch's mentor and model, John England, had been drawn to another widely reported wonder, the dramatic cure in Washington, D.C., of the mayor's sister, Ann Mattingly, who had been at death's door, according to many around her. England, like a good scientist, studied the cure for nearly six years, interviewing Mattingly, witnesses, and doctors. Here was an extraordinary event that many had observed; there was abundant evidence open for scrutiny. Following his lengthy empirical investigation, England concluded that all the evidence pointed to the cure being the result of "an immediate and miraculous interference of the Creator himself."[3]

Like his distinguished predecessor regarding the Washington miracle, Patrick Lynch was drawn to the phenomenon of Januarius's flowing blood because of the opportunity it afforded for clinical observation and the objective examination of the meticulous records of it kept over the centuries. Moreover, there was something particularly special about Januarius's blood. It was, as the bishop put it, "a standing miracle." Like any phenomenon that science studies, this one was not a "once and for all" event, as had been the Mattingly cure. It occurred predictably, again and again during the three occasions in the calendar year when the relic was exposed. These were the ideal circumstances for identifying a "scientific miracle," one that could be observed and logically confirmed. And so Patrick Lynch arranged to be in the very midst of those conducting the elaborate ritual over the saint's relics. What ensued was to the American bishop a dramatic confirmation of God's dominion over nature, through his wonder-working with this barbaric relic of the dark ages, verified by the very scientific methods that supposedly liberated humankind from religion's cage. He would have to wait five years to bring his faith-affirming discovery to the American public through a five-part article in the Catholic World *in 1871–72.[4]*

cℛ

FRANCIS LYNCH, CHERAW, TO PATRICK LYNCH, 14 OCT[5]

Since the letter you had written to father, while on board the stmr [steamer] Asia, I am without anything direct from you. The newspapers gave notice of your visit to Paris and Rome.

A report has reached me, that you have been sick at Paris. I hope you are quite well again. Soon the time will elapse, you had contemplated for your tour and anxiously will your return be looked for and hailed. Father & Mother are enjoying their usual good health. D.G. as are all the members of the family. Henrietta boasts another son, since 1st of Spt. We have named him James. He is a promising boy. The children are growing fast. A letter from Bro John tells of the good health of his family and of Sister Ellen and Ellen Spann. The school at the Convent is most prosperous. I need say nothing of political affairs, as I presume you are "well informed." Genl Beauregard has command of the Armies of Tennessee and Miss. Before his appointment the Federal Gen. Sherman had penetrated Georgia and taken Atlanta. Genl Hood in command of our forces there has taken position in his rear, much is expected from that quarter soon. I suppose the election in the northern states will force a crisis in this eventful war.

A stockade prison has been made near Florence and I learn that from 8 to 10000 prisoners are there. It is truly lamentable that the Exchange of Prisoners is so tardy, resulting doubtless to much suffering to ourselves and to the enemy. I consider the Federal Authorities entirelly blameable in this matter. The shelling in Chston has been severe, the last few days, somewhat abated supposed to result from the exhaustion of the guns. . . .

Patrick Lynch, Florence, to Antonia Lynch, 4th Nov.[6]

. . . [I write to tell you of] my trip to Naples to witness the miraculous liquefaction of the blood of St. Januarius . . . bishop of Benevento . . . put to death by being beheaded . . . in 305. . . . It was the custom at such executions to gather the sacred blood of the martyr and to preserve it, generally in small glass vials. . . . For many centuries past the liquefaction of the blood in one of those Ampullae or vials has been a standing miracle. . . . From 1400 down the mention of it is very frequent and for the last two hundred and fifty years and more, there is a diary—perhaps several—of every time the relics were exposed—and what happened.

. . . On the 17th Sept. Saturday I went to Naples. On Sunday morning I went to the Cathedral to say Mass, and to take a preparatory look at the Church, and to see how things were prepared. I looked, made all sorts of inquiries, and made arrangements to be there the next day (the festival.)

On Monday morning at 8½ I was in the Chapel, and went back of the Alter [*sic*], where the day before I was shown two armories in the solid stone wall of the church, in one of these the head of the Saint is kept; in the other his blood. They are closed by strong metal doors, each having two locks. The keys of the upper locks are kept by the Archbishop, those of the lower locks by laymen called Deputies on behalf of the city authorities.—Neither can open the Armories without the consent of the other. . . . Inside, and between . . . plates of glass, are seen the two vials When the chaplain took it out of the Armory, he said, *It is hard*, and *it fills the Ampullae*. In fact as I saw it, the Ampullae was full to the very top, of a dark red substance, whether hard, or fluid I could not say, for it was so full that as he slowly moved it from side to side, or turned it upside down, I saw no change. . . . The Chaplain first showed the relic to those who had crowded around the Alter, on the steps, and were pressing . . . against me. The second chaplain held the light about 6 inches off behind it, so that all could see clearly. The Ampullae was full.—He then turned to the Alter, and leaning on it with his elbows, and holding the reliquary, about a foot from the Bust; or perhaps more, and the assistants kneeling he commenced the *Miserere* and other Psalms. It is impossible to describe the scene. . . .

The Tesoro Chapel was completely packed, and through the Archway you saw the crowd stretching away across to the other side of the vast Cathedral. The furthest off must have been nearly a hundred yards off looking to see what they could, at that distance. . . . Of course there was a vast number of strangers, especially in the chapel nearer the alter. It was curious to see the combination of piety and curiosity. As for the crowd of Neapolitans themselves, they were even more interesting. They were praying aloud hundreds on their own . . . — others together in groups forming a chorus. Here a hymn in a chanted chorus, there the Rosary. . . . It was a perfect Babel. . . . Meanwhile, after the recitation of the *Miserere* and other Psalms, the chaplain ever holding the Reliquary, turned again with it towards the people and showed it as before; then back to the alter, and more Psalms, hymns, litanies, and prayers, then he showed it again as at the first time then turning to the alter, came still other prayers. So a half hour passed. It was a hot day, and steaming hot in that crowd. So far no liquefaction took place. . . . The Chaplain bearing the Reliquary went down with it from the steps of the Alter, and out of the Sanctuary, into the dense mass of people, shewing it to all on either side of him, and giving them an opportunity of kissing it.—then he came back to the Alter. More Psalms and prayers followed, then he showed it again to us on the Alter steps.—Still more prayers litanies, and Psalms, and again he descended the steps of the Alter with it. Again he returned to the Alter for more Psalms, prayers, hymns, and litanies, and exhibitions to us around every five minutes. Thus more than a second half hour passed, and still no change.

At last, I saw a change, I think I was the first to see it. I saw a dozen times before, that the vial was completely full to the top, at this time I saw a mere streak of light between the top of the vial, and the substance within. . . . As the Chaplain again came round the circle . . . Again it came round and the line was a quarter of an inch broad, the blood was sinking down in the Ampullae. . . . The Chaplain tilted the Reliquary from side to side, and the air in the vacancy now above the blood, ran from side to side freely like the air bubble in a spirit level. *Miracolo, Miracolo,* said some, others shed tears. The Chaplain waved a white handkerchief. The organ pealed forth Te Deum, the vast Italian crowd joined in one full swelling chorus almost drowning the fullest tones of the Instrument. The mighty bells of the Cathedral sent their peals over the city to the mountains and valleys and the still waters of the Bay. The cannon of the distant Castle of St. Elmo took up the refrain in a national salute. . . . Hundreds came up in succession, as if to communion each one saw and attentively looked at the liquid blood in the Ampullae which yielded to every motion of the Reliquary, as would so much water, and reverently kissed the Relic. At the end of [a] half hour the blood had sunk about an inch. It with the Bust was reverently taken from this Chapel in procession to the main Church, to the Grand Alter. I staid to say mass on the Alter where the miracle occurred. . . .

Next morning (Tuesday) I went to say Mass on the same Alter at 7½ and was ready at the door of the armories at 9 o'clock. The Bust was extracted as before. Then the Reliquary of the blood was taken out. It was solid this time, and only filled the Ampullae about two thirds. . . . It was borne in procession as yesterday to the Alter. . . . after just 16 minutes, I noticed that as he held the Reliquary reversed, the surface of the hardened or coagulated blood, which in this position, was underneath seemed to sag down in its middle. Soon after (a minute or so) I noticed that along the edge of the surface, where it touched the glass, it became a brighter red and was liquefying. In fact, as he would move the Reliquary, the whole mass would slide like a soft jelly from side to side. Soon it became liquid, with a lump unmelted floating in the middle. This after a while melted also. . . . I staid a full half hour to examine the blood, and then went to see other relics, and some antiquities of the city.

. . . [W]hen liquid, it is often *seen* to change in quantity under the very eyes of the observer, increasing or diminishing ten or twenty per cent. Sometimes as a liquid it is quiet and level, sometimes it apparently boils a bubble up and shows a froth. It sometimes liquefies in cold weather, and sometimes remains hard in the hottest day, sometimes it has been found liquid every time it was extracted from the Armory for more than a year, and sometimes two years have passed over without any liquefaction at all, at any of the Expositions. In fact all the physical laws of liquefaction, dependant [*sic*] on temperatures and volume, are all set aside. The more one examines it, the more clearly it is seen to be a miracle—a standing miracle, most glorious and useful in the days of proud physical science, when men puffed up by the amount of their knowledge of natural things, almost reject God, or at least would explain away all miracles, and the revealed supernatural religion. They may shut their eyes to the facts of the case, they may give it the go-by with a sneer. So much the worse for them. God has vouchsafed to the World this standing miracle, a scientific one so to speak, just in the line of their studies, that they may be without excuse. Not one of recent origin, but coming down to us undoubtedly from those ages when natural sciences were at their lowest ebb, and from what they call the dark ages. . . .

1865 February–April

"This last news was a terrible stroke."

In late January, William Tecumseh Sherman began the third—and final—leg of his expedition that had begun in Chattanooga nine months and 370 miles ago. As expected, he headed north to give South Carolinians a full taste of the total war they had unwittingly set in motion and, having fulfilled that hope-sapping objective, to link up with Grant around Petersburg and checkmate Lee. Most Carolinians thought that Sherman would make Charleston his prime destination in South Carolina. That city, after all, had been widely viewed by both North and South as the heart of the rebellion. For nearly two years Federal land and naval forces had been frustrated in their efforts to capture Charleston. When Sherman's grand army headed out of Georgia into South Carolina, their chosen path through the lowcountry seemed to confirm conventional expectations. It was a feint. The main body of Sherman's troops headed for the uplands. Columbia and Cheraw, it turned out, were the two main targets Sherman had selected: Columbia, as the site of the drafting of the first ordinance of secession; Cheraw, as a vital transportation center, the feature that had attracted the Lynches forty-five years before.

To Columbia and Cheraw, the two main havens for lowcountry refugees over the past four years, the war finally—and so suddenly—came. Two years before Columbians had vowed to burn their city rather than have the Yankees occupy it. Burn it they did on an apocalyptic scale. At least a third of the city was destroyed by fire. As South Carolina's most celebrated author, William Gilmore Simms, saw it: "It has pleased God . . . to visit our beautiful city with the most cruel fate which can ever befall States or cities. He has permitted an invading army to penetrate our country almost without impediment; to rob and ravage our dwellings, and to commit three-fifths of our city to the flames."[1] To Simms, Sherman's army were neo-Vandals, epitomized by their barbaric looting and burning of the "shrine" of piety, learning, and culture that was the Ursuline convent and academy. In the Ursulines' own account, the Federal marauders were far worse than their ancient counterparts, who, barbarians though they were, had the decency to respect the persons and sacred spaces of the religious virgins of their day. The language of the Ursuline annalist evoked the evangelists' description of the Passion. In the harrowing events experienced during the night of February 17–18, the Ursuline Community and their young charges were participating in the most sacred mystery of their faith.

If the Ursulines' account caught the horror of their experience, the burning of the city itself had no such Manichean explanation. The fires themselves (at least some of them—there was no single one but a series of blazes over the course of two days) probably started with the burning cotton ignited by fleeing Confederates. Despite persistent efforts by some Federal troops to combat the fires and protect property, the Yankees, left to their drunken, revengeful devices by superiors taking their cue from General Sherman's contentment to let the Columbians experience the horrors of hard war and thus hasten its end, spread it randomly but widely over the city.[2] In the end, it was less than the climax of the hard-war policy pursued by Sherman and more than an "accident of war," as the fire's chief historian has termed it.[3]

"[W]hen they had . . . brought [Columbia] to ruin," Simms noted, "they gave [the] towns of Camden and Cheraw [along with the villages], to the flames, and laid waste all the plantations and farms between."[4] In truth the looting and general destruction of property north of Columbia was on a much smaller scale than what had befallen the capital, but that was scant consolation to owners such as Francis Lynch, who watched most of his industrial operations succumb to the flames of the Federal avengers. Claudian Bird Northrop, managing the bishop's Malta Plantation at Lancaster in the Edgefield District, fared worse. Bummers among Sherman's advance cavalry ransacked and burned the mansion. When Northrop refused their demand for money and valuables, they hanged him as his wife looked on in horror.[5]

As the vise of the Federal armies closed upon the Confederacy, Patrick's family correspondence became restricted to the two members outside its shrinking borders: his sister Antonia in Baltimore and his nephew Robert in France. Robert had returned to Ireland with Father Bannon in the hope of securing a foothold in another line of labor in which an uncle had done so well by: tanning. From Antonia, Patrick heard the grim news that "the sack of Columbia" had not spared Baptista or the Ursulines. Even Robert, who had been the family member most insulated from the war, was deeply shaken by the reports of the terrible sufferings that had proven to be the fate of both Columbia and Cheraw. Antonia's letters, meanwhile, became a litany of ever-grimmer news: the fall of Richmond, Lee's surrender, the assassination of Lincoln. Where all this would end, Antonia knew no more than anyone else but dreaded the unspecified evils *that people predicted would befall the country in the wake of the president's murder. She urged her brother to remain in Europe "until all dangers are over."*

ROBERT LYNCH, HÂVRE, TO PATRICK LYNCH, 2ND FEBRUARY[6]

. . . all our efforts to find a situation in Ireland were useless, not from the want of places, but by the selfishness of all the leading tanners. . . . [A]fter having hunted during three weeks without any results, Father Bannon advised me to return to France, and to rely on the help of God and my own strength of mind to live as I should live.

I returned then, immediately to France. On my arrival here, I found out an old school mate of mine, an American who is employed in a large and extensive ship-broker's office. I explained to him why I had come to Havre, and asked him to help me. . . . He spoke of me to his employer, M^r E Frangue

. . . Mr Frangue is one of the most influential men of France, being president of all the ship-brokers of France. . . . He offered a berth in his office of fourteen hundred francs. . . . If I do not receive this berth, well then I will try the tanners of . . . Normandy, for that is the great tanning country after Bordeaux. . . .

ANNALS OF THE URSULINE CONVENT, COLUMBIA, S.C., FEBRUARY[7]

When the city was taken possession of by Genl Sherman's Army on the morning of February 17th—a guard of protection, one man, was obtained for the Convent by Rev. Father O'Connell. . . . About noon a Cavalry officer rode up to the Convent and, after a few words to the man on guard, rang for admittance. The door having been opened by the Portress & her attendant, the officer asked to see the Superioress, Mother Baptista Lynch, to whom he introduced himself as Major FitzGibbons, and a Catholic, offering to render any assistance to the Nuns, . . . earnestly insisting, . . . "Columbia is a doomed City:—at least such was the talk of the Army—and he did not know if a house would be left standing!" Such an announcement startled the Religious, . . . yet the Superioress, and her companion, assured the Officer that such threats could not apply to the Convent since General Sherman had given a lady in Savannah, whose daughter was in our Institution, an assurance that she was in a place of perfect safety. "Of course," replied Major FitzGibbons, "I do not say that your Convent will be burned, such a thing as that would happen only by accident but added he, significantly, "we all know what accidents are"— . . . —Major FitzGibbons listened with apparent interest and then said, "Sisters, I wish you would write all that to the General, I know that he will do all he can for you."

... Some of the Religious had lived previously in Ohio, where, in their Convent several of General Sherman's relatives had been educated.... Accordingly the letter was written. ...

True to his word, Major FitzGibbons returned to the Convent about 3 o'clock P.M. accompanied by 7 guardsmen. "Here" said he, ... [g]iving to the Mother Superior at the same time the envelope of their letter to Genl Sherman upon which was pencilled—"Commanding Officer near, protect carefully this convent Sherman, Maj. Genl.— ... Now said the Major, with a joyful air, "I can assure you of the safety of all in this Convent, I bring with me 7 men, picked guards, upon whom you may depend, I have chosen them for a purpose, American Protestants, as best suited to meet those with whom they may have to contend, and should you want me to give you assistance at any time, you will find me at Rev. Dr. O'Connell's house."[8]

... For the first time the Religious now perceived that some mysterious evil threatened them.—they had been very anxious about some 40 of their pupils ... who, with a small band of Religious, had been sent by the Superioress, to "Valle Crucis"[9]—a country house some 3 miles from Columbia,—that they might escape the shells which fell over and near the Convent, during the previous day.—Now that the city had been taken by the Federal troops, the Mother Superior found it impossible to obtain a passport for an escort to bring them into the City—Judge then of the surprise of the Religious when the Band of Sisters and pupils rang for entrance at the Convent-door, having for escort a Cavalry officer in front and another in the rear of their ranks! —It appears that while the Nuns & children at Valle Crucis were awaiting a proper escort into the City, two horsemen galloped up the Avenue leading to the house, brandishing their fire arms and shouting, "Burn it, burn it, the Hampton house, burn it: One man dismounting, rushed under one of the octagon rooms adjoining the main building, to set it on fire, while the other ran up the steps and on to the front piazza—The Religious in charge immediately advanced to meet the man, who ... at seeing here a Nun, bowed most politely and apologized saying. "Pardon me, Sister, is not this the Hampton place?—No," replied the Nun, pointing to the Cross and the Words "Convent Valle Crucis" which had been placed over the roof of the house as a precautionary measure, "did you not see that this is a convent?" "I did not, Sister," he replied, had I done so, I would not have approached, much less have entered as I did. Excuse me. Is there any thing I can do for you?" "Certainly" replied the religious, "and I will avail myself of your kindness and accept your escort into town, if you will be good enough to give it to us and our pupils . . ."—"Certainly, sister:"—and the horsemen placing themselves—one in front, & the other in the rear of the ranks, brought the Sisters and pupils in safety to the Convent in town.

While walking into the City they were alarmed by cries of terror as they passed homesteads already enveloped in flames—soldiers dashing about as they had done at Valle Crucis, and in one place, a young girl, almost frantic, ran and clung to one of the Nuns for protection.

Judge of the gratitude which filled the hearts of these uncloistered Religious when the Convent door opened to them. The officer politely handed in a sister's satchel which he had insisted on carrying for her, and left. —wild work was going on in the City, altho' unknown in the Convent. . . . They, it is true, had feared that as some government buildings were near their Convent, their safety might be endangered, therefore, they had filled some bags with clothing &c &c—which could be removed conveniently—but they never could have imagined the awful scenes which they were to witness that night— . . . — Scarcely had the Nuns finished giving supper to the seven guardsmen placed in and near the Convent yard, and assembled in their Community room, where they were amusing themselves over the 3 miles promenade from "Valle Crucis" and congratulating themselves on their safe reunion,—the shelling also being over, when one of the Nuns entered saying that she thought there was a fire in town. "Now, don't disturb us," said one of the Sisters. . . . "I think you must be mistaken"—said another, "we have heard no alarm bell nor engine"—But, rising they went to see.—Judge of their amazement on seeing the heavens lurid with the flames, which, altho' far distant, looked fearful—A breathless silence seemed to pervade— . . . as, looking out upon the doomed city, they saw the soldiers and officers, walking or riding triumphantly to and fro thro' the Main St.—

But near the depot and where the fires were set, all was not so calm, and when the citizens were prevented from working their fire engines by the soldiers, who, finally pierced the hose with their bayonets—there confusion reigned. —In the stillness of this terrific night nothing was heard by these cloistered inmates of the convent—but the approaching roar of the flames, the crash of falling buildings—while the fires which were being set with great rapidity in various parts of the City, borne on by an impetuous wind, seemed hastening toward one another. —Calling to their guards the religious asked one to go for Major FitzGibbons,—He refused, saying in a surly manner, that he did not know where to find him. The other guardsmen were then asked to go on the top of the house where the roof was flat, and see what could be done in case the fire came near—A number of bail buckets had been placed conveniently filled with water, and the Nuns showed the guards where the water would be most [put to use] should the house catch on fire and also showed them the bath tubs filled in the second & third stories, ready for any emergency. The Sisters soon saw, however, from the cool indifference of the one, and the real enjoyment of the scene manifested by the other,—that nothing was to be hoped for from them.

Early in the evening Rev. Dr O'Connell and Rev. Father McNeal had called to remove the blessed Sacrament from the Chapel, but the Religious, hoping against hope, had begged them not to deprive them of so great a blessing, as they saw no immediate danger.—Now, however, when the Rev. Clergy called a second time, they could no longer hesitate.

With lighted candles in their hands the Sisters led the way to the Chapel, where the Rev. Chaplain gave them, in perfect silence, the Benediction of the Blessed Sacrament, for the last time in their beloved Convent home. The suppressed sobs of the younger Sisters were but a feeble index of the deep emotion which filled all hearts. Silently the Clergy passed out and the only home of the blessed Sacrament on that eventful night in Columbia, was upon the person of that fervent young priest, who was obliged to bear insult and to fly from street to street with his Sacred Charge. —As the fire neared the Convent Parents came running for their children—and friends to inquire where all would seek safety. . . . the Sisters endeavored to save their bags of clothing &c by dragging them into the middle of their large yard. The guardsmen, seeing them laboring beyond their strength, said reproachfully "You deserve it, you brought it on yourselves"—and, with a sullen air, refused to help them.—Three of the men at length, seemed touched, perhaps by the silent meekness with which the Religious bore their rudeness, and came forward to help a little—Meanwhile the danger became so imminent and the crowd of soldiery gathered around so great, that it was thought expedient to send the pupils and younger Religious to a place of safety—if such could be found. Each young girl had given to her, a small bundle containing a change of clothing, and all were desired to take their ranks,[10] this being a precautionary measure to prevent straggling—[or] a panic among them, by which any might be lost. . . . Rev. Father O'Connell accompanied them to the Catholic Church which was situated to the west of the great fire and from which point a strong wind blew. Shortly after flakes of fire fell thick and heavy and the Nuns who remained at the Convent were admonished to leave, as it would soon be impossible to find egress thro' such a sea of fire. —Happily, none of the Religious were aged, but there was one, Sister Loretta,[11] a Lay Sister and a cripple from inflammatory rheumatism. What were they to do with her? She was not able to walk, nor could the Sisters carry her—and a conveyance was not to be had—Great was their distress, when their anxious hearts were relieved by a young officer, who, aided by others, kindly placed her in a buggy, and took her safely to the Church. . . . "I am truly sorry" said an Army Surgeon, Dr. Gallagher, "that my corps is not allowed to come into town, it is all Catholic and would have helped you—but it is stationed some two miles below here."—

All the Religious had now left the Convent, excepting a few Seniors who still labored to save some of their effects. —Several of the Lay Sisters were

Ruins of the Ursuline Convent and neighborhood, Columbia, 1865. Courtesy of the South Carolina Library, University of South Carolina.

disappointed and pained by the conduct of the guards. One, from Connecticut, had lost two nephews in the Federal Army. Another, from Cincinnati, who supposed her brother to be still in the ranks, said aloud, "Well, I did not think such mean people lived in Cincinnati. Sure, I never saw them there." "Are you from Cincinnati?" Asked one of the guards; "then I'll help you, I'll take care of you."—"God will take care of me" she replied. But he did assist her, for the danger from fire was imminent— . . . —Now, about midnight and by the light of the approaching flames, the plundering of the Convent was begun. The guard, thinking perhaps that the house was vacated—rushed upstairs opened the Pianos and strummed upon them—-danced about and finally ran up to the Young Ladies' dormitory. One came running down stairs, with a fancy Holy Water font dangling on his fingers, which he jeeringly shook in the face of the religious. Starting towards the Nuns dormitory, he was stopped in the corridor by a venerable old gentleman, Mr Isaac Cohen, whose daughter was in the Institution, and who was protecting the remaining Religious, "Know," said he, that those apartments are sacred, You must not enter there!" The snowy locks and noble bearing of Mr Cohen deterred for a time this riotous fellow, who, with others, bent his steps in another direction. Prudence and safety suggested the immediate departure of the remaining Nuns—[12]

Hatchets and axes were now brought into play—doors were staved in— beautiful dresses strewn along the yard and streets, books and apparatus,— music &c scattered in every direction, trunks cut asunder and emptied of their contents, &c &c. Of the contents of their well stacked storerooms only a small box of coffee was brought to the Nuns by Dr. Gallagher of Ohio. To this gentleman the Nuns acknowledge themselves as much indebted for kind services during that eventful night. . . . [I]f in the Middle Ages Vandalism respected and spared the Vestal's Shrine, assuredly all that is beautiful, pure and innocent— would not be less honored now. But, we behold this Institution laid in ashes! —Weakness unsupported—the defenceless unprotected and religion disregarded! What a contrast between our era and that of the falsely called "dark Ages"! . . . —when the first band of Sisters with their pupils left the Convent, . . . at about 11 o'clock P.M. they were firmly persuaded that they were leaving only for a few hours—The first salutation they met, as they stepped out on the pavement was, "Well Sisters, what do you think of the Yankees—cruel, are'nt they?" This was, however, only from the rabble—for, as they proceeded on their way, they were not only undisturbed, but treated with respect.— . . . They met a band of horsemen galloping triumphantly yet leisurely along who reined in their horses as politely and composedly as they would have done on an ordinary occasion—and seeing the hesitation of the Nuns, who were evidently strangers to the streets of their own City—one of the horsemen called out, "Follow me, sisters, I will conduct you to a place of safety."—The flakes of fire fell so thick and fast, as to burn holes in veils and habits of the Sisters as they hastened to join those of their number who had already taken refuge in the Catholic Church yard.—[13] . . . they . . . lost in that one night all that they possessed of this world's goods. It was not until about 3 o'cl, A.M. that the Cross upon the cupola of the Convent fell and not until every building around had succumbed to the raging element. . . . the Nuns finding that houses around them were being fired, and feeling the heat very sensibly, began to fear that they should not be left unmolested even among the tombs.

Meanwhile the guards paced to and fro outside the Church yard railing, groups of soldiers stood at Mrs Ringold's door adjoining the Church; (Mrs Ringold was the widow of a United States Officer and her house was made a sort of headquarters)—straggling soldiers, half intoxicated, passed by and puffed their cigar smoke contemptuously over the railing,—while some remarked, sneeringly—"Hurrumph! Sanctified! I'm as sanctified as you are!"

2 men entered the church with a fire ball and combustible material in hands—but finding themselves closely watched, passed on to the rear of the yard, embedded the ball in one of the graves and, after a little hesitation, left.— Col Curley who had defended the Church with his life, walked with a troubled mien from place to place.

The fears and anxiety of the Nuns increasing, two of them walked aside under the shade of a cedar tree, where, unobserved, they might confer as to whether it were advisable or safe to remain where they were, or better to betake themselves into the woods below near the river. The two Religious were startled by a voice near them saying, "I am sorry for you, Sisters." An officer was leaning against the tree and upon his musket, and had overheard their anxious conversation. His voice betokened deep emotion . . . "Are you a Catholic?" Asked the Sister. "No Madam." "From what state are you?" "From Indiana" — The Religious expressed their surprise and gratification at this manifestation of sympathy.—"There was a time" said he with evidently suppressed emotion, "there was a time when I was proud of being an United States Officer, but when I look upon such a scene as this," and turning, he looked upon the crowd of Nuns and children, "I am ashamed of it!" . . .

The following morning broke upon the Nuns and children as they grouped around the Church door, cold, cheerless, and hungry—without a house to shelter them, a morsel to eat, or a bed whereon to rest after so much exhaustion and some were even without a change of clothing!

Crowds passed by, gazing upon them, some with emotion, others with mingled surprise and curiosity.— . . . Three of the neighboring families, who, fortunately were not burned out of house and home, Mrs. Ringold, Mrs Bollin, and Mrs. Dr. Lynch,[14] sent their servants over to the Church yard, with trays bearing cups of hot coffee and breakfast for the Nuns and their pupils, of which they partook gratefully— . . . These kind friends wished the Nuns and pupils to go to their respective houses, but, they unwilling to be separated, preferred to remain where they were until some refuge for all could be obtained.—Several of the private solders, who were good honest Irishmen came to ascertain if there would be Mass in the Church, and seeing the condition of the Nuns and their pupils, would exclaim, "Oh! This will never do! Sure, if the General saw Ye, he'd never let ye be in this way, at all—at all! Sure, and just go to the General and tell him your condition and he'll help ye" &c &c— . . . Just then, Genl Sherman, with several officers, rode past, and reined in his horse at Mrs. Ringold's door. "There's the general now," exclaimed the sympathizing soldier, "do go and speak to him"—Remembering that he had sent word that he would call on them the following day, which message had been delivered to them by Major FitzGibbon—together with a promise of protection, two of the Senior religious, were sent to let the General know that he would find the Nuns in the Church yard. Quite a crowd of officers and soldiers, with Mrs. Ringold and her family, were conversing from and near the porch. —Genl Sherman was seated on horseback and smoking a cigar, apparently in high spirits. —He received very graciously the Sisters who were introduced to him by Mrs. Ringold, and said that it was his intention to call on the Religious—A few minutes later he dismounted and entered the Churchyard where the Mother Superior, Mother Baptiste Lynch, came forward to meet him. As he approached with extended hand, he said, in a bright and cheerful tone and manner. "Ah! Sister these are times in which to practice Christian fortitude and patience." "You have made them thus to us, General," she replied, extending her hand in an equally cordial and cheerful manner. "I am sorry, truly sorry that your Convent was burned" said he, and a short interview followed, in which it was beautiful to witness such an absence of passion and resentment between the injured and the injurer—

. . . — Officers had respectfully dismounted and held their bridle reins— children and Nuns alike drew near to see one of the greatest Generals—the Attila of the Age— . . .

The remarks of some ladies near by seemed not very agreeable to the General, who, raising his voice, exclaimed, "This is the fault of your negroes, who gave whiskey to my men! It is the fault of your Mayor, who ought to have destroyed all the liquor before the Army entered your town."[15] Then, turning to the Nuns, he offered in the kindest manner, to give them any house in town they might choose for a Convent, to take them there and to place around it a strong guard of protection.—Had this been done the day before, they might have had goods to protect and a home to guard, but, unfortunately, it was now too late.[16]

However, the offer was kindly meant, and as such received.—General Sherman, moreover, deputed his aide—Col. Charles Ewing,[17] to contribute in whatever way he could to the comfort of the Sisters—and the General certainly evinced for them great sympathy and kindness of feeling for which they expressed their sincere gratitude. Having learned that the Nuns had been advised to take refuge in the "Methodist College," he (Col Ewing) came to the Church with several ambulances to carry them and their pupils thither—and when upon arriving there, he found an unwillingness on the part of its present occupants to admit them, he not only insisted, but, demanding the keys of the house, turned them over to the Mother Superior. This act, together with placing a strong guard of protection for the Religious, gave great offense to some of the Trustees of this Methodist College, who afterwards refused to rent it to the Nuns, and, after many painful disagreeabilities finally notified them to leave by a certain date, fearing they would take advantage of the preceding act of confiscation by the United States Army. Before leaving Columbia, Col Ewing, who had daily visited the Nuns in their destitute and uncomfortable condition, observed that the college was crowded to excess, having in it about forty families who had been burned out—these had taken possession of the first and second stories, that in the event of the College being set on fire—which was expected on account of its having been used as a Confederate hospital—they might more readily save themselves by flight—consequently the Nuns and their pupils were forced to occupy the third and fourth stories—where fifteen were crowded together in rooms measuring 15x20 ft. and even of these, many were divested of furniture and bedding. The Nuns had neither kitchen, yard room, nor the

Burned area of Columbia, looking north from capitol. Courtesy of the South
Carolina Library, University of South Carolina.

ordinary comforts of life.—For weeks after the fire they had no table from which
to eat their frugal meals. They supplied the place alike of spoons and forks, by
little wooden paddles, which they cut with their pen knives—the remainder of
their table furniture was equally recherché!!

. . . On the morning of the army's departure from Columbia, Captain
Cornyn[18] of the commissary Dept, who happened to be an old acquaintance of
some of the Nuns, brought them "eight or ten day's rations"—as he was pleased
to term a generous offering of meat, flour, coffee, sugar &c—Had it not been
for this and the timely aid of the people of Augusta, Ga., and of Sumter, S.C.
who sent provisions the Nuns would have suffered from hunger—Col. Ewing
and Capt Cornyn having called to see the Religious, and observing how crowded
together they were reminded them of General Sherman's offer to give them any
house they might choose for a convent. "We have thought of that," answered
the Mother Superior, "and of asking for General Preston's Mansion."[19] "Is that
where Genl Logan has his headquarters?' inquired Col Ewing. "Yes," was the
reply "That building, I know, has been ordered to be burned on tomorrow
morning when the Army leaves the City, but if you will take it—for a Convent,
I will speak to the General and the order will be countermanded"—Accordingly
this was done, and on the following morning, some of the Religious took possession of the house; the officer in charge having sent them word that his orders
were to fire it, unless the Nuns were in actual possession—When the detach-
ment of Nuns hastened around, they found the fire already kindled near, and

the servants carrying off the bedding and furniture, in view of the house being consigned to the flames. Indeed, with the exception of the parlor, they had divested the house of all that rendered it comfortable. Then, however, as at all times, kind and sympathizing friends were ready to share with them the little which had been spared.[20]

&

ROBERT LYNCH, RENNES, TO PATRICK LYNCH, 14 MARCH[21]

. . . I am now in the tannery of Mr. Penault of Rennes. It is the finest in this city and one of the best of France— . . . M[r] Penault . . . is under–mayor of the city. . . .

You have already heard of the fall of Charleston and the evacuation of Columbia.

Well I will try and bear up to the end, although, it is hard to know ones parents in the hands of the Yankees, and I here taking it comfortably.

Write soon my dear Uncle if you please, for this last news was a terrible stroke for me. . . .

&

ANTONIA LYNCH, MT. CARMEL, TO PATRICK LYNCH, APRIL 9[22]

. . . Most of your friends rejoice much that you think of remaining in Europe until the end of the war. I am afraid you will be much surprised at the many changes in S.C. I was much grieved to hear of the death of Rev. Mr [Leon] Fillion who died at Florence I think in Feb. also of the two Fathers of the name of O'Neill.[23] Revd Mr Moore,[24] the Archbishop told me would be until your return the V G. Letters have been written to the Abp. and to me from Charleston. All are so anxious about your return as their [*sic*] are many reports. But I think they would rather be deprived of the consolation of your presence than that you would return when there are so many difficulties. I also heard from home. Anna wrote by an officer who passed thro' Baltimore on furlough. He had staid three nights at Father's house during the time Shermans army was resting in our peaceful little town. She said they were all in good health but begged many prayers for strength to support their many trials. No one was left more [than] ten days provision. The whole of Front Street was burnt-down including all of brother Francis's property in that section. I am happy to learn that he did not enter military service, as they would miss him so much at home. Rev Father Cullinan[25] standing at the Church gate was robbed of his watch and five hundred dollars in gold[;] in his fright he thought he might be taken prisoner and would provide himself with what money he had. . . . At [the] same time she told me that the Nuns' since the Convent was burned were living at your house two miles from Columbia S.C. As they had lost everything. Sister Ellen had some idea of moving to Savannah. I do not think she could have gone or else she would have written. I have not been able to write to them as there is no communication with the interior. The Federal troops only made a "Raid" they did not hold possession of the places that they passed thro. Brother John's house was not destroyed. I do not let myself be much troubled at the many reports we have. Could I hear from them directly it would be a great relief, but now we can only *pray for them.*

. . . Our friends in this city are at the present time making collections to relieve the sufferers in Charleston and Savannah but this prospect of a speedy subjugation of the South has made such a shock upon the money market that many merchants will not be able to meet their bills so they cannot be very liberal in their contributions. I hope my dear Brother you will not let all this I have written have an effect upon you, do not let it trouble you. I am afraid I am saying too much, but I suppose you can form a more correct state of things than I can give you. I trust we may all strive to submit in all things to the "Will of God" & to what He permits should befall us. . . .

My dear Brother you will be pleased I am sure to know how much satisfaction we find in our Archbishop.[26] He is a very kind Father to us & thinks very much of you and of those you have charge of (but cannot now be with.) I cannot express what are my feelings I am glad for *your own* sake that you will remain in Europe, but I at the same time would wish that they could have you in their midst at home—then again if they are suffering so much at home I know you *can* procure for them some assistance in Europe which you could not whilst in the South. . . . I suppose you know ere this of the evacuation of Richmond and Petersburg but I do not feel discouraged. . . .

❦

ROBERT LYNCH, [RENNES], TO PATRICK LYNCH, APRIL 17TH[27]

. . . oh if peace would only come I could see my parents also, for seven years have now passed since I saw them last. . . .

Since my last letter nothing has changed at Rennes. I go to the tannery ever day to work five or six hours; Mr Penault told me the other day that I would be soon able to act as contre-maître [foreman]; I now work at the most difficult [tasks] and the only difference between the workmen and myself is that they work faster; from the first I gained the affection not only of Mr Penault but also of all the workmen, and now they all take the greatest pleasure in showing me everything. . . . Do you think we will have peace soon, my dear uncle? Oh, if I could only go home when you will! I will work hard at any rate so as to be ready.

ANTONIA LYNCH, MT CARMEL, TO PATRICK LYNCH, APRIL 20[28]

You will find me troublesome, but as I have learned something from the Community in Columbia, I felt that it would be cruel not to tell you especially as they have no way of communicating with you. This child I saw, was one of the boarders, she rode thirteen miles on horseback, & then walked twenty five before she reached the cars which took her to Charlotte, N.C. She then came on to Richmond, was there at the time of the evacuation of that city, and is now in Baltimore with her mother. . . . She told me when that city was bombarded in the evening Sister E. with two companions and all the children each carrying a blanket & pillow walked out to your house in the country. Then they returned in hopes nothing would befall them. Genl Sherman was sent for, he sent six men to protect them but they were their worst enemies. For one of them carrying a burning torch up to the third story, soon had the house in flames. They saved three Harps, two pianos one piece of Habit-stuff & flannel. Loosing [*sic*] all their books &c they at present occupy two houses the Preston House, and the Methodists College. They are using every exertion to lessen their number of scholars. In the Preston House they have a regular chapel & chaplain. Every other morning they have Mass in the College. They were in hopes when their number would be smaller to only occupy the first named house but now that they have left Richmond (I mean the Preston family) I do not know what they may do. . . . Other things I might tell you but I think as you cannot change them it [is] better not to be imprudent. It is a great blessing that they passed thro' so much trouble and anxiety with presence of mind. They have still to live on "rations" sent them by friends in Augusta and other parts of the country, but as the roads are all out of order, and so difficult to transport supplies, they are obliged to use very great economy to live at all. This child said also that it was Sister E.'s intention or expectation to open a day school in September. So my dear Brother you see how God protects us all in most trying circumstances. Your own position is very trying but I hope you will have courage to meet with all that may cross your path. Your absence is most painful but we do not see how you could return. For some time we all thought you were spending the months until Spring with sister Mary & family, but a few days since I positively heard that [you] were still in Rome but much embarrassed about your return. Our country is at present in a very great excitement from the murder of the President and other persons in authority which took place on the night of the fourteenth. What the consequences may be no one can imagine, but I suppose you will learn more than I can tell, but generally it is thought much evil will come from it. I have written that part about the community losing all their clothing, because as I learned they *imported* their worsted goods & I thought perhaps you might make some agreement, so that when the ports are opened they might again obtain some more. My dear Brother I have not been able to write or to hear from Cheraw since the letter Anna wrote in early March. Our only consolation under all these cruel circumstances is to pray for one another. . . . We all send you our greeting this holy Season. Praying that our Lord may so arrange things that you may soon return home, but hope that you will wait until all dangers are over. . . .

1865 May–December

"By the destruction of the South, all this is lost."

When Patrick Lynch submitted his resignation to the Confederate government in the waning days of 1864, he expected to return to South Carolina early the next year. But there remained work to do in getting his pamphlet on slavery printed in German as well as in French. Overseeing the translations (the original manuscript was in English) and the mechanics of publishing, first in Germany, then in France, delayed his departure by several months. By the time the last of the three editions, the French, appeared in February 1865, sixty thousand Union troops were marching through South Carolina. Worse, Fort Fisher, the bastion at the mouth of the Cape Fear River that had allowed blockade runners from Wilmington relatively free access to the sea, had finally fallen to the Federals, effectively closing the last functioning Confederate port. There was no longer any way open for Patrick Lynch to return. He was trapped in Europe, effectively a prisoner of the blockade that had finally become the anaconda Winfield Scott had envisioned four years earlier.

By April there was no longer a Confederacy to come home to; moreover, officials of that defunct nation were suspected of involvement in Abraham Lincoln's assassination. No one in Washington was likely to excuse the bishop for his involvement in the rebellion, merely because he had submitted his resignation as a Confederate agent in the dying months of the war. A prison stay was the best prospect Patrick Lynch could imagine for himself should he return to America. Back again in Rome, he decided to put himself at the mercy of Federal officials. He appealed to Martin Spalding, the archbishop of Baltimore, as well as to James Wood, the Bishop of Philadelphia, to use their influence with the government to secure permission for him to return home with impunity. He met with Rufus King, the United States minister to the Papal States, to ascertain what he would have to do to be allowed back into the country. "I told him," King informed Secretary of State Seward in late June, "that the first thing to be done was to take the oath of allegiance, and make his peace with the federal *government. This he was willing and ready to do, if that would suffice; but he seemed apprehensive that if he returned to America he might be proceeded against criminally. I told him that the President's proclamation, which was daily expected, would no doubt contain full information on this point."* When the text of President Johnson's Amnesty Proclamation reached Europe, Bishop Lynch found that it did not apply to him. So his only recourse was to petition the U.S. government for a formal pardon.

The bishop's effort to secure a pardon is a painful exercise in disingenuousness regarding his supposed noninvolvement in political matters. Purporting, in his scientific fashion, to present merely "the facts" in the case, Patrick Lynch recast his war experience as that of a man of the cloth, whose motivations transcended partisan actions. The war, he insisted, was merely an extraordinary opportunity to exercise his ministry, particularly with wounded and dying soldiers, North and South, something he had begun on Fort Sumter while it was yet in Union hands. Without doubt, Patrick Lynch's ministry to the sick and wounded of both sides was more than commendable. But forgotten in this résumé of his involvement in the war was the Te Deum in his cathedral following the attack on Fort Sumter; the blessing of battle flags and cannon; the assuring prediction of ultimate Confederate victory to a pro-Southern audience in Halifax, Nova Scotia; the extensive apologia for slavery, aggressively distributed throughout Europe to sway continental thinking to the side of the Confederacy about the main casus belli. As for the polemical exchange of letters with the late Archbishop Hughes in 1861, inasmuch as it was intended for the New York prelate's eyes only, it did not count as a political statement. In his rewriting of history, the Confederate agent became the irenic prelate undertaking his dangerous mission abroad in a desperate attempt to engage a mediator, either in Rome or elsewhere, whose services Union and Confederacy, bone weary of the mutual destruction three years of warfare had inflicted, would at last accept.

For Robert Lynch the war's end brought not anguish and despair but relief that he could—at last—return home after a biblical sabbatical in Europe. In Columbia the Ursulines had taken up new quarters at the Methodist College. To the new order of things still taking shape in South Carolina as throughout the former states of the Confederacy, Baptista surprisingly displayed a serene resignation. Trust in a loving Providence was at the heart of her outlook. Confirming it was the generous assistance Federal military occupiers provided for the nuns trying to make a new start in makeshift quarters after having lost virtually everything to the February holocaust. And the friendly appointments to local government positions that President Andrew Johnson made toward the South's self-reconstruction also served to encourage Baptista's plan to start satellite academic communities in other southern cities where they had alumnae until they could secure the funds from government compensation and private benefactors, both Catholic and Protestant, to rebuild in Columbia.

Baptista had much greater difficulty in dealing with the radically changed status of the former slaves. African Americans may have been freed by law. They were, in her mind, still servants, now ones to be paid rather than cared for, but still subservient to their old masters and mistresses. For a former slave to seek to be self-sufficient and acquire land for himself and his family was unthinkable, a shattering of the natural order that slavery ideally preserved. Her bishop brother, while sharing Baptista's estimation of the proper status of blacks within Southern society, had a larger patriarchal vision for the freedmen: to re-create for his former "people" and other ex-slaves in the state cooperative communities in the Sea Isles such as the ones Jesuits had so successfully established in Paraguay. For the Lynches, Africans could survive in America only in a protectorate, be it slavery or some more benevolent form of control.

By the fall of 1865 the Methodists had succeeded in reclaiming the property the Ursulines had occupied since February. The nuns' only alternative was the former Keitt plantation, renamed Valle Crucis, three miles outside of Columbia. During the move, death struck the community once more. Sr. Gertrude (Ellen Spann), Baptista's beloved niece, became the latest Lynch whom tuberculosis claimed.

Patrick Lynch, despite his enforced absence from the diocese, was trying to do what he could from afar. What Europe had that South Carolina and the South in general sorely lacked was money. So Bishop Lynch made a fund-raising tour across the Continent for his devastated diocese, a forerunner of the begging tours to the North that would for the remainder of his life annually keep him out of South Carolina for as much as half the year.

෴

PATRICK LYNCH, ROME, TO MARTIN SPALDING, MAY[2]

The recent events in the United States have left me stranded, in a position of some embarrassment, and at this distance, I scarcely see how to steer my way. You are aware that last year, in April, I came to Rome as a commissioner of the Confederate States. Of course the Confederacy no longer exists, and you see the difficulty of my returning at once. Probably I would go to some fort or prison, or other inconvenient place of residence.

Why I consented to come in that capacity I need now scarcely state. The true reason was this. It seemed to me that we were doomed to many years of destructive and internecine warfare, unless some word would be spoken from abroad which might pour oil on the waters. I did not anticipate that the Confederacy would be conquered in one year more. The only way of procuring an early peace, seemed to me to depend on some influence exercised from Europe. Of what kind, or under what circumstances, I had no clear opinion. But I supposed that after some more drawn battles, both parties would be willing to listen to a friendly voice.

However events have turned out otherwise and I now wish to return home to the peaceful and exclusive discharge of my duties, and I beg that you will try to see Mr. Seward, or the President, or those you think proper in the matter, to obtain, if necessary, their consent to my doing so without molestation.

I really do not think they ought to class me among the "heads of secession" For I was personally disinclined, to say the very least, to such action on the part of the South, and deprecated it, and used such little influence as I had, against it. On the abstract right I did not enter, for I was not a politician. But I very much doubted its prudence. When the State of S. Carolina acted, I felt that her action, prudent or imprudent, bound me. In the war I took no part, save this, of ever inculcating, by word, and by example, that everyone was bound, to mitigate its horrors.—hence I made it a rule to omit no occasion in my power of shewing kindness to the Federal prisoners whom I could visit or benefit. . . . —I may refer to Genl Meade, whose nephew was, I believe, the last officer I tried to aid.

I think my sole action in the war was attending to the sick & wounded and suffering,—of either side as occasion presented them.[3]

Of the letter to Abp. Hughes, published in Sept 1861, if I remember ought, I must say, that I wrote it to *him* and that he published it, without my knowledge.[4]

ہ⋟

ROBERT LYNCH, RENNES, TO PATRICK LYNCH, PENTECOST SUNDAY [JUNE 4][5]

The last events of the war in America raised greatly my hopes of returning home & I await only your permission to do it, as I have now learnt the tanning trade, and think that I could be of service to Uncle Francis. . . .

My dear Uncle, have you received any news from home? Have my dear brothers escaped the war? Father & mother are all well? Ah, my dear Uncle, if you know any thing let me know; if the news are bad, God will give me the streangt [*sic*] to support them, if good to thank him.

ہ⋟

ANNA LYNCH, CHERAW, [TO ANTONIA LYNCH], JUNE 15TH[6]

[Beginning of letter missing] that destroyed the city & he hopes to get on. Notwithstanding the Times so does Bro Francis who has lost extensively but retains his cheerful & buoyant disposition. I hope they may realize their expectations. The Nuns occupy the Methodist Female Academy at present. I suppose you know they were burnt out, & lost everything in the fire. They have a pretty fair school & Sister Ellen writes quite cheerfully. Conlaw is at home a paroled prisoner, came over here a few days ago to remain with Bro Francis. We hear nothing from Sister Mary-Brother we understand is soon expected home. That Revd Mr Moore received intelligence to that effect from Archbishop Spaulding. We would all be rejoiced to have him at home, again, under other circumstances, but in the present state of affairs would *much prefer* his remaining away—a *few months longer* since he . . . has been away so long. . . . he may risk a great deal in returning to the city in Yellow Fever season. I regret very much now that he went away at all, except that his health will be benefitted by the change & recreation and he has escaped witnessing much that is disagreeable & distressing at home. Of course I do not mean in his immediate family alone. We have been favored in never having been deprived of our wants either during the war or since. . . . I hope communications will soon be resumed & we will hear from you. None of our negroes left us but as they are free now we may not keep all in our employment. . . .

ᜒᜒ

ANTONIA LYNCH, BALTIMORE, TO PATRICK LYNCH, JUNE 23[7]

I send you a part of a letter I received today from Anna. I thought you would like to hear what they think of your return at the present time. I hear your friends or Sympathizers are exceedingly mortified at the effort made for your return to the country in this mornings' papers[8]—but we have to pass thro' many hard things in the life. I am happy to find all doing so well at home. I would be very sorry myself were you to endanger your life by returning until after this season of Yellow Fever is past. But of course you are able to judge your own case.

We are all in our usual health—but our weather is quite warm and dry, with much sickness. In the first part of this letter Anna mentions that all are well at home. Cornelia is boarding at home—her mother's home was burnt—Conlaw a paroled prisoner is visiting Cheraw. Mother de Sales & Sr. Agatha called to see us when passing thro' Baltimore. . . .[9]

ᜒᜒ

PATRICK LYNCH, ROME, TO WILLIAM SEWARD, 24 JUNE [COPY][10]

I have just learned the tenour of the Proclamation of Amnesty, issued by the President, on the 29th of May, and in accordance with it I respectfully make this "Special Application," in order that I may be allowed to return to Charleston, for the quiet discharge of my ecclesiastical duties.

I was a Citizen of S. Carolina at the time of the Secession of that State. I took no part whatever in that movement. Standing aloof from politics, and not even having voted for years I did not feel called on to judge the political questions involved. But I feared that the act would lead to war and to great evils, and I thought it was one to be deprecated. So far as a clergyman might with propriety, I expressed these opinions in private. In the pulpit, I have always scrupulously avoided all political questions.

When the State seceded, I was bound by the act. But as I dreaded the war before it came, so now I conceived that it was my duty to labour in every way I could to mitigate its evils.

When Fort Sumter was first invested in 1861, I communicated with Major (now General,) Anderson and Captain, (now General) Foster, and gave the Garrison of the Fort the Services of Religion, sending them a clergyman regularly until their departure. I need not say here what I did in the Hospitals of the South and among those whom the war left at home poor and suffering. But I may say, that in 1862 and 1863, I laboured both personally and through my clergy and the Sisters of Mercy in the Hospitals of wounded Federal Soldiers in Charleston, giving them, both blacks and whites, every attention in our power. For this, I had the gratification of seeing in 1863, the thanks of the U.S. Surgeon Craven, and through him, those of Genl. Gilmore,[11] to whose forces they belonged. I believe my course became known at the North, for I received not a few letters from Boston, New York, and elsewhere requesting me to seek out and to aid friends of the writers, who were, or were thought to be, prisoners at the South. In all such cases I endeavoured to comply w the requests.

Besides this, I was accustomed to visit the Military Prisons, especially in Charleston and Columbia, to afford the Federal Prisoners the consolations of Religion and to give them such aid in money or otherwise as my means allowed. This I commenced the first week that any Federal Prisoners were brought to Charleston in 1861, and continued down to the Spring of 1864. As opportunity offered I endeavoured to do the same in Salisbury and in Richmond. Federal officers confined in Charleston and Columbia have stated to me, repeatedly, that they were treated in those places, with a courtesy and kindness, which they could not but appreciate. I have since seen the same statement made by many correspondents of Northern papers. I cannot but feel that the course I openly adopted & defended from the beginning, and which was sustained by others, was not without its influence in producing this result.

When there was question in 1863 as to the status of the Coloured soldiers, taken prisoners near Charleston, I earnestly cooperated with Honorable Nelson

Mitchell,[12] since deceased, who acted as their legal friend and counsel, in settling the question.

In the early months of '64 it seemed to me, as it seemed to many others, North and South, that three years of war had so intensified the passions on both sides, that neither was willing to take any steps acceptable to the other by which hostilities might cease, and that each had the means of continuing the war for years to come. In common too with many I could not help entertaining the hope that a friendly disinterested voice from abroad, spoken on some fitting occasion during the war, might be listened to by both parties, as it counselled peace and reconciliation.

Entertaining this opinion of the future and this hope, and earnestly desirous of peace, I acquiesced in an official proposal unexpectedly made to me, and I came to Rome, having left the South in April 1864.

Contrary to my anticipations, the progress of the struggle presented no such fitting occasion, and the war has come to a close in a space of time very different from what many at that period, and I among them thought likely.

Hence, I have to say, that I am not conscious of ever having said or done anything to originate the war, to exacerbate it, or to prolong it an hour. On the contrary I regretted the steps that led to it, during its continuance I did what I could to mitigate its evils, and my motive in coming abroad was the hope it might be shortened.

I desire now to return home for the quiet discharge of my ecclesiastical duties. In the discharge of them I will feel bound in conscience, to accept in good faith, the altered social state of the country, and to act in a manner to promote, so far as in me lies, the peace and good order of the community in which I labour.

ᐛ

PATRICK LYNCH, ROME, TO MARTIN SPALDING, 1 JULY[13]

I enclose to you, a special application which I have addressed to the Government at Washington, for the benefit of the Amnesty Proclamation which should you approve of it, I beg you to forward to Mr. Seward,—and at the same time to support it as strongly as you can.—I send a rough copy of the same to the Archbishop of New York, asking him to give the same his support.

. . . Abp. Hughes published in the papers a letter I wrote to him in 1861.— The letter was a *private* one.—such a one as I sometimes wrote to him,—But although he had previously published extracts of my letters in the *Metropolitan Record,* and I thought he might perhaps do the same in that case, I was completely surprized at finding the letter published entire in the northern papers, under my name. Had I been consulted, I would not have consented. For I never wrote politics even in the Miscellany—except against the Know-Nothings.

I want to get home as soon as possible.—You of course must feel how necessary it is that I should be there at the earliest day possible. If I hear that the Yellow Fever breaks out, I do not know but I would be strongly tempted to go to Charleston anyhow. . . .

P.S. I may add as a complement of my case, though I do not know that it will be considered of any importance, that since I came abroad, *I have not sought to present myself,* and in fact have not *ever presented myself* in any official capacity. This was my own decision, based on the state of things in America—Whatever authority I might have had remained in my pocket.[14]

༒

BAPTISTA LYNCH, URSULINE CONVENT AND ACADEMY, (AT METHODIST F. COLLEGE) COLUMBIA S.C., TO PATRICK LYNCH, JULY 17TH[15]

You will be gratified to hear that things here begin to assume quite a cheerful appearance—the mails, so long interrupted, are becoming regular again— Business letters are passing pretty briskly—express wagons running as before —Merchants going north to buy their stock of goods—the war &c ignored &c &c I have just received a letter from our old friend Henry F. Baker replying to one of mine, saying he would with pleasure do business for us as heretofore—& and then from one of our pupils gone north—a Miss Kate Harris, niece of Mrs Dr Robert Emmet,[16] of New York, saying she had shipped us a box of goods which I sent for by her, in lieu of the payment of her bill—I expect that this winter will be a very busy & brisk one, especially with merchants & mechanics— We have met with so much kindness & sympathy that we cannot feel sufficiently grateful & when you return to us next spring, you will be delighted to hear it all—more than I can write— . . .

Francis has taken Conlaw into partnership with him—& both are much pleased with the arrangement—Conlaw is a fine manly Boy—Both tanyards were burned & since the Freedmen walked off with themselves, Francis will concentrate his labors & work only one yard—He is very cheerful as usual. If Providence has sent adversity to the South He has certainly given it a beautiful spirit of cheerful submission to His holy will—Sister Antonia tells me that she wrote to you lately. . . . I also wrote to you telling you that I hoped you would remain in Europe until the military & civil authority would decide between them, what we shall consider as "the powers that be"—this is I suppose until next spring—

You will be gratified as every one else is, to learn that the Governor appointed under our present regime is Mr Perry[17] of Greenville—the friend of Mr

Dudley[18] of Marlborough & your friend too. John says: I suppose he will soon put things to the satisfaction of all concerned.

We have our school still in operation & do not intend to suspend it this summer, unless Father Gache who is stationed in Charleston now, will visit us & give us a partial retreat—. We have only thirteen boarding pupils, nor do I expect we can well take more until we build, which will take us about two years at best—. In the mean time we will accept the offer of Genl Preston to take his house for our convent while his family are travelling in Europe & we hope by the time they will want it, our convent will be completed.

. . . We have written a circular to all the Bishops in the United States—mentioning the burning of our Convent & asking aid to rebuild as speedily as possible—. We have also written to Washington representing the fact, & asking our indemnification for our losses—I am assured that both will meet with a favorable hearing & response.[19]

Many kind friends—(all Protestants) have told us to count on their assistance when we begin to build—they are particularly anxious that we would not accept any invitation to go elsewhere—

You do not know how very polite Genl. A. S. Hartwell[20] whose Hd Qrs are at Orangeburg—has been to us,—when Genl Hatch[21] from Charleston advised us to go north & offered free transportation, Genl Preston said with indignation —"What, they are not content with robbing us of our silver but would also rob us of our Nuns—! Col Siebels also offered us the use of their house for a while & have been very kind[.] Mrs Col Bauskett offered hers to us for the summer. We thanked them all, but as yet have kept ourselves quiet & our school going on the best we could—the day school was very good until the heat became excessive, & will no doubt be again in the winter—It has occurred to me to establish day schools in one or two other places temporarily until our Convent was built—by sending "detachments" of Sisters—say three in number, two choir & one Lay, to Macon, Ga (with permission of Bp Verot)—another to Raleigh, N.C. (spiritual aid will be wanting there I fear) & in that way, support ourselves & disseminate our Holy Faith—our mission seems to be, making converts, in which we continue with God's blessing to succeed.

One of our pupils returned to us yesterday, more to be instructed in our holy faith, than to study her books—She is 19 years of age & has the consent of her parents.

It occurred to me that if we could not raise immediate funds to carry on the work of our convent, for I apprehend no difficulty in two years hence, we could do as the Ursulines of Brown County did—they borrowed $10,000 in specie from the Visitation Convent of Paris at .6 percent with the privilege of paying it when Convenient, & they took 15 years to do it. I do not think we would require as many.

Oh! How I would like to talk all this over with you—Mr *Kenny* is my man of business but we have only planned as yet—to begin soon however, for no time is to be lost every one says.

Do write me a long letter—I have never received one line from you since you left Halifax—! And we have been for nearly a year before peace was declared, before we heard a word of, or from you— . . .

Today Genl Blanchard & family have vacated Valle Crucis & I do hope the Jesuit Fathers will soon be in possession of it—giving to the diocese what it so much needs—& a new railway is being cut or rather surveyed near the "Wallace farm" by Captain Hayden which John says will render it more valuable. I hope the Christian Brothers will soon come & establish their manual-labor school—I think John had done [as] well as you could expect in these times & will be relieved when this property is in others good hands—. Daniel & his family as just & good & faithful servants as ever but Isaac is thoroughly trifling & ungrateful—I suppose from what Dr. Cummings[22] says you will take a tour before you return on a questing expedition, but if so & you succeed in raising funds to rebuild your Cathedral &c, be sure & leave it over in Europe for it is not advisable or safe to own property on this side of the Atlantic—Mr Trenholm & many others are assured of that fact—(a word to the wise &)— . . .

⚓

BAPTISTA LYNCH, URSULINE CONVENT & ACADEMY, VALLE CRUCIS NEAR COLUMBIA S.C., TO PATRICK LYNCH, SEPT 25TH[23]

Yesterday evening we had a visit from bishop Verot, & we were so happy to hear *directly* from you. But you had not heard of your pardon when he left [for] home, although we have long since known it was granted—& Bp Verot thinks we may expect you now very soon—God grant it may be so—. We pray for a safe & speedy return for you—. Robert told me that your health had not been good, but I was happy to learn from Bp. Verot, that you were looking well— Our dear parents long to welcome you home, their health is feeble, but their hope & faith are strong. Of course you have heard a thousand & other rumours of the dreadful ravages made in the south by the war, & are prepared to see desolation on every side. I have often written to you in many ways, but fear none of my letters have made known to you our affairs, since, *not one line* from you has reached me since your arrival on the Continent, except a few lines written in Paris—. Being thrown entirely on our own resources after Shermans destruction of Columbia we endeavoured to manage the best we could, & after much writing & telegraphing (all at a snail's pace) we arranged with the approbation [of] the Abp of Baltimore & Bp of Savannah or his vicar general, to establish a branch institution in Macon—To make arrangements for this, I set out

ANDREW JOHNSON,

PRESIDENT OF THE UNITED STATES OF AMERICA,

TO ALL TO WHOM THESE PRESENTS SHALL COME, GREETING:

Whereas, *P. N. Lynch, D. D.,* of Charleston, South Carolina, by taking part in the late rebellion against the Government of the United States, has made himself liable to heavy pains and penalties;

And whereas, the circumstances of his case render him a proper object of Executive clemency;

Now, therefore, be it known, that I, ANDREW JOHNSON, President of the United States of America, in consideration of the premises, divers other good and sufficient reasons me thereunto moving, do hereby grant to the said P. N. Lynch, a full pardon and amnesty for all offences by him committed, arising from participation, direct or implied, in the said rebellion, conditioned as follows, viz: this pardon to begin and take effect from the day on which the said P. N. Lynch shall take the oath prescribed in the Proclamation of the President, dated May 29th, 1865, and to be void and of no effect if the said P. N. Lynch shall hereafter, at any time, acquire any property whatever in slaves, or make use of slave labor; and

Patrick Lynch's pardon from President Andrew Johnson, 1865. Courtesy of the Roman Catholic Diocese of Charleston Archives.

with Sister Charles as my travelling companion & went to Macon via Augusta & Atlanta—, having free transportation partly from government & partly from the R.R. superintendent—.

We were very kindly received in every place & at Macon, where the V.G. of Sav. had twice telegraphed about our coming. We were treated with the utmost courtesy—We found a house already rented for us & vacant, but such is the demand for houses in the South where whole cities have been destroyed, that our friends prefer retaining this for us, to running the risk of losing our Institution—The house rents will be paid for us during the first year. Our furniture will be supplied gratuitously & a collection made in the city for us, which if we do not go to Macon will be sent to Columbia, but if we settle there, will be given to supply us with provisions &c—

We propose to send three sisters there to establish a day-school until we can rebuild our convent in Columbia—which arrangement seems advantageous to our interests & to those of religion—especially as our school is so broken up here—Living, as we do, out at the Keitt place we can have no day school here —& the house will not admit of many boarding pupils. Therefore we think it advisable for our sustenance to establish this branch house & day school so as not to call on the contributions which we may receive for the rebuilding of our convent, which we desire to begin as soon as possible—. All these arrangements & plans were laid, when we could not procure ourselves the happiness of welcoming you home for a long time—they now, only await your consideration & permission to consummate them, for which my dearest Brother, I lay them before you in writing—Oh! How I will enjoy talking to you—! My heart is big with the expectation— I enclose this to the care of Abp. McCloskey hoping you may receive it before your arrival—.

❧

[Patrick Lynch], Rome, to [Charles G. Schwarz], Sept. [copy][24]

My dear Sir,

The diocess of Charleston is now truly desolate. During the cruel civil war which raged for four years and which has just closed, I have seen almost everything that my two predecessors had accomplished, or that I had undertaken, gradually perish. In December 1861, the Cathedral which after years of toil had been finished by my predecessor in 1855, was entirely consumed by fire. At the same time perished also, in the same conflagration, the residence of the Bishop, the diocesan Seminary, with its theological Library, a Boys Orphan Asylum which I had just completed, and an adjoining house which I had purchased in order to be able, when necessary to enlarge the asylum. The convent of the sisters of Mercy was also badly injured, and a House which they used as a school for poor girls was completely burned.

All this perished in a few hours, in a conflagration which destroyed over one sixth of the city. The books of the Library and much of our moveable property perished after they had been moved to places which we thought safe but which the flames afterwards reached.

After the fire came the bombardment of the city which lasted for over fifteen months. In this the convent of the Sisters of Mercy again suffered having been repeatedly struck and shattered by the bombs. An Orphan Asylum for girls was also repeatedly struck, and three out of the four Catholic Churches remaining were severely injured likewise, and, in addition one house, in which the clergy resided.

These are the losses in property in the city of Charleston. To them must be added the losses in the interior of the Diocess. One church was destroyed, another was injured. In the city of Columbia the capital of S. Carolina, the Ursuline Convent and Academy was burned, as also another building which had been used as a convent and girl's school, and also the residence of the clergymen of that place, and the house in which was a school for boys under their charge. I fear that other property has likewise been destroyed. But I have not certain knowledge of it.

At the date of my appointment as Bishop of Charleston, early in 1858 and until the war commenced in earnest, things looked very bright in the Diocess of Charleston. The conversions were frequent. Amid the general prosperity, the Catholics were liberal in their contributions, and I had been able with God's blessing to do something and had prepared to do much more in the course of a few years in the Diocess. The Ursuline Convent in the city of Columbia had been established. A Boy's Orphan Asylum, as I stated, had just been finished, and five new churches had been built in various parts of the Diocess. I was making arrangements for the introduction of the Christian Brothers and the establishment of a Reformatory school like that of Mettray in Belgium, for opening a Catholic Hospital under the sisters of Mercy, and I hoped to be able to do much more in the course of time

A portion of the funds necessary for this, I had already put in the Public Stocks, and when the war arrested everything, I put the remainder of what I had, or that came into my hands, together with what I had of my own, in the same securities. By the destruction of the South, all this is lost. I scarcely hope to get five per cent. from it. Later in the course of the war, fearing the result, I purchased cotton, with the money already depreciating, hoping when the war was over to sell it, and have thus means to provide for the emergencies that would press on us. I placed about one hundred bales in one place, and a small quantity in another, both one hundred and fifty miles away from all armies, and in as secure places as I could find. But the troops of General Sherman, in their march across the interior of the State, came on both of them, and burned all the cotton, as they did every where.

You see, my Dear Sir, with how much reason I said that the Diocess of Charleston has been truly desolated in this war. The estimated money value of our losses may be summed as follow:

Cathedral burned	$106,000
Bishop's residence	$7,000
Episcopal Seminary	$10,000
Diocesan Library (17,000 volumes)	$20,000
Boys Orphan Asylum	$15,000
Adjoining house	$5,000
Girls School	$2,500
Damage to Convent of Srs of Mercy	$9,000
Further damage to Do. by shells	$3,500
Damage to girls Orphan Asylum	$2,000
Damage to St. Mary's Church	$2,500
Do St. Paul's Church (German)	$1,000
Do St. Joseph's Church	$4,500
Do parsonage of the same	$1,500
Two churches in the interior destroyed Or injured @$2,000	$4,000
Ursuline Convent burned	$33,000
Furniture, vestments &c burned in it	$4,000
Old Convent burned	$7,000
Pastor's residence & school burned in Columbia	$15,000
Total	$252,500

Add loss by depreciation of Bank Stocks, Railway shares & Public Securities	$43,000
Also, loss on Cotton burned	$21,000
Final total	$316,500

I have now before me the duty and the task of commencing to repair those losses. I say of commencing, for I cannot hope that in the few years that remain to me, I can do much towards restoring what it took my venerated predecessors and myself forty years to accomplish. Did I not put my trust in God, I should shrink in despair before the labour.

Patrick Lynch, Lyons, to Martin Spalding, 7 Oct 1865[25]

I have not yet thanked you for your kind and successful effort in my behalf at Washington. I received your letter giving me the news on the 9th of September.[26] I had already settled to make a spiritual retreat. This over I packed up—got leave from His Holiness to start, (altho' some cardinals thought it still at least premature, but Cardinal Barnabò stood for my going.) and on this day a week [ago] I started from Rome. The cholera and the Quarantine being both in force at Marseilles, I came thru Switzerland and got here two days since, where I am devoting a few days to the Propagation of the Faith, in behalf of Charleston and to replenishing my episcopal wardrobe, wh[ich] Gen[l] Sherman kindly reduced to ashes. This done I go to Paris to see the Council of the Propagation of the Faith, there, and then on homeward through England and by steamer. Perhaps I may have an opportunity of taking the "oath" in Paris. I have already written to Mr. Seward, from Rome.

Baptista Lynch, Convent "Valle Crucis" near Columbia, S.C., to Patrick Lynch, Oct 28th[27]

I have not heard from sister Mary for a long time, & I fear they have had much to suffer out there from the presence of the army.

I have not had the courage to write to her since it pleased our Lord to take our Ellen to Himself—.

We have in her I believe a powerful intercessor in Heaven—May she there repose on the SS.[28] Heart of Jesus—

Oh! How often have I wished you back since then—But all is for the best, & you will I do hope & pray soon write & telegraph us that you are coming.

You know I cannot bear surprises,—I am expecting daily the news of your arrival.

In December, almost twenty-one months after he had departed from Wilmington in the dead of night aboard a blockade runner, Patrick Lynch returned to South Carolina. He came back to a society entering a radical new phase of the revolution in which he had played a larger part than he ever imagined he would. The grim harvest of war surrounded him. "I am like Marius amid the ruins of Carthage, he told a fellow Southern bishop.[29] *In the remaking of the South he saw, as he told a potential European benefactor, but the most modest role for himself. The destruction that natural disaster and war had wrought throughout his diocese seemed to have drained out of him all the ambitious plans and strategy that had marked his early years as bishop. Almost all that he and his two predecessors had built over the past forty-five years lay in ruin. Even for a relatively young man like himself, not yet fifty, making a beginning in the vast work of restoration in the diocese seemed the outer limit of what he could accomplish in what remained of his episcopacy.*[30]

It was his Ursuline sister who gave voice to the embattled optimism that had marked the Lynches in Ireland and America. In the unsettled condition of the conquered South, between war and reconstruction, she sensed an extraordinary moment for the diocese: not only to rebuild and repair what the war had devastated but to enter upon the most ambitious program of institutional expansion. This would be a new and larger girls academy, a Jesuit college, an industrial school, a hospital, a model African-American community—all this in the service of advancing the Faith in the Carolinas. The ravages of defeat had not destroyed, but actually deepened her conviction that she and her brother had been called to spread Catholicism in their home country; her special mission, she was more sure than ever, was to make converts through the academic institution that had survived the worst the war could do to it. Inherent in the Lynch tradition was the belief that tragedies bred opportunities. Tragedies on the scale of the just-completed war created opportunities of equal magnitude. What remained for them was to seize the moment and find the means to convert hope into reality, for the Catholic Church and Carolina, if no longer for the Confederacy.

NOTES

INTRODUCTION

1. Robert Manson Meyers, ed., *Children of Pride: A True Story of Georgia and the Civil War* (New Haven, Conn.: Yale University Press, 1972; repr., 6 vols., New York: Popular Library, 1977).

2. Joseph Jones to Rev. and Mrs. C. C. Jones, Savannah, November 3, 1856, in Meyers, *Children of Pride* (Popular Library ed.), 1:355–56.

3. His mission became the building of a biracial community anchored in the church. In Liberty County he led the way in establishing congregations in Presbyterian and other Protestant churches that were models of interracial participation. See Donald Mathews, "Charles Colcock Jones and the Southern Evangelical Crusade to Form a Biracial Community," *Journal of Southern History* 41 (1975): 299–320.

4. 1840 U.S. Census, Chesterfield County, South Carolina.

5. For a three-generation history of the Jones family, see Erskine Clarke, *Dwelling Place: A Plantation Epic* (New Haven, Conn.: Yale University Press, 2005).

6. Charles Colcock Jones, Maybank, to Charles Colcock Jones, Jr., October 3, 1859, in Meyers, *Children of Pride* (Yale ed.), 522–23.

7. Baptista Lynch, Columbia, to Patrick Lynch, April 19, 1862, 14G8, Charleston Diocesan Archives (hereinafter abbreviated CDA).

8. Lincoln A. Mullen, "The Contours of Conversion to Catholicism in the Nineteenth Century," *U.S. Catholic Historian* 32 (2014): 13–22.

9. Charles Colcock Jones, Montevideo, to Charles Colcock Jones, Jr., November 7, 1859, in *Children of Pride* (Yale ed.), 527.

10. C. C. Jones Jr., Savannah, to C. C. Jones, January 28, 1861, in Meyers, *Children of Pride*, 648.

11. C. C. Jones to Rev. David H. Porter April 30 1861, in Meyers, *Children of Pride,* 670.

12. C. C. Jones Jr., Savannah, to C. C. and Mary Jones, August 6, 1861, *Children of Pride,* 733–34.

13. Baptista Lynch, Ursuline Convent, Columbia, to Patrick Lynch, June 4, 1862, 14 H11, CDA.

14. This document is housed in the Archives of the Ursuline Community of Louisville. In 1938 the Ursulines of Columbia, South Carolina, merged with the Ursulines of Louisville, at which time the archives of the Columbian Ursulines were made part of the Louisville collection.

15. Patrick was even worse at visiting his family. At one point in the mid-1850s, five years passed between his visits to his parents' home in Cheraw. He was forever disappointing family by failing to make promised visits.

PROLOGUE

1. Perhaps the most famous descendant of the expatriate MacMahons was the French President Edmonde Patrice MacMahon (1808–1893), whose ancestor had served with the Irish Brigade in the French Army in the seventeenth century. So long lasting was the family's exalted place in Irish memory that as late as the 1850s the nationalist group, the Irish Revolutionary Brotherhood, attempted to exploit McMahon's heritage by securing his support for their movement (Patrick Steward and Bryan McGovern, *The Fenians: Irish Rebellion in the North Atlantic World, 1858–1876* [Knoxville: University of Tennessee Press, 2013], 22).

2. Archives of the Ursuline Community of Louisville (hereinafter abbreviated AUCL).

3. "For hearth and home" (Cicero).

4. Hugh O'Neill (ca. 1550–1616), Earl of Tyrone and head chieftain of the Gaelic tribes of Ulster Province. In 1594 he led an uprising against the English occupiers to reverse the seizure of land and Anglicization of the province that had become English policy since Henry VIII. It took the English government nine years to put down the revolt. For the Irish it meant further loss of land, frame of government, and culture.

5. To the penal colony in Australia.

6. Daniel O'Connell (1775–1847), lawyer, who led the movement to abolish the penal laws that had marginalized Catholics in Ireland since the sixteenth century. In 1829 the Emancipation Act repealed most of the statutes that had so severely restricted Catholics' civil and political rights.

7. A fictional government agent in William Carleton's eponymous novel (Dublin, 1845).

8. "Orangeman": a supporter of William of Orange (1650–1702), the Dutch prince to whom the English Parliament offered the crown in 1688 in defiance of the sitting monarch, the Catholic James II. William's subsequent triumph over James restored a Protestant to the throne and hence became known as the "Glorious Revolution."

9. Literally "Saxon," the Irish term for "English."

ANTEBELLUM YEARS

1. David C. R. Heisser and Stephen J. White Sr., *Patrick N. Lynch 1817–1882: Third Catholic Bishop of Charleston* (Columbia: University of South Carolina Press, 2015), 8–10.

2. James Henley Thornwell, *Arguments of Romanists from the Infallibility of the Church and the Testimony of the Fathers in Behalf of the Apocrypha. Discussed and Refuted* (New York, 1845), 72, quoted in James Oscar Farmer Jr., *The Metaphysical Confederacy: James Henley Thornwell and the Synthesis of Southern Values* (Macon, Ga.: Mercer University Press, 1986), 191–92.

3. Heisser and White, *Patrick N. Lynch,* 32.

4. A priest in his diocese described his preaching style as that of "grand simplicity." Lynch had, he added, the imposing presence ("tall, full, and senatorial mien") and "absolute self-possession to command immediately the attention and good-will of his listeners." Starting in a deliberately dry, almost pedestrian manner, Lynch would gradually and subtly broaden the scope and emotional intensity of his discourse, while still maintaining a plain style of speaking. His oratorical ability proved to be a very reliable medium for

fund-raising, particularly after he became a bishop (J. J. O'Connell, *Catholicity in the Carolinas and Georgia: Leaves of Its History* [New York: D & J. Sadlier, 1879], 127).

5. David T. Gleeson, *The Irish in the South, 1815–1877* (Chapel Hill: University of North Carolina Press, 2001), 118–19.

6. Eliza's grandfather, John Steele, had been comptroller of the Treasury in Washington's administration.

7. John Lynch to Patrick Lynch, Cheraw, S.C., June 22, 1848, 6 C2, CDA.

8. John Lynch to Patrick Lynch, Cheraw, January 24, 1854, 8 A4, CDA.

9. John Lynch, Cheraw, to Patrick Lynch, July 24, 1846, 5 G2, CDA.

10. Mary Lynch Spann, Washington County, Tex., to Patrick and Ellen Lynch, September 10, 1847, 5 S4, CDA.

11. "Annals of Ursuline Convent, Valle Crucis, Columbia South Carolina," AUCL.

12. Baptista Lynch, Ursuline Convent (St. Martin's Fayetteville), Brown County, Ohio, to Patrick Lynch, April 15, 1854, 9 B1 CDA.

13. Patrick Lynch, Baltimore, to Mother (Teresa Sewall), October 12, 1858, Archives of the Baltimore Carmel (hereinafter ABC).

14. March 25, 1857, Profession Book, March 25, 1857, ABC.

15. Ursuline Convent, Brown County, Ohio, April 22, 1856, 9 R6 CDA.

16. Francis Lynch, Cheraw, to Patrick Lynch, July 13, [1850], 6 W1 CDA.

1858

1. Decree of Propaganda Fide, December 13, 1856, *Lettere e decreti*, vol. 347, fol. 654 v, in Finbard Kenneally, O.F.M., *United States Documents in the Propaganda Fide Archives: A Calendar*, 1st ser., vol. 4 (Washington, D.C.: Academy of American Franciscan History, 1981), 318; Francis Kenrick to John McCaffrey, July 1, 1857, quoted in Mary E. Melina and Edward F. X. McSweeney, *The Story of the Mountain: Mount Saint Mary's College and Seminary* (Emmitsburg, Md., 1911), chap. 46.

2. The prelates of the Baltimore Province had not been urging Rome to press McCaffrey to accept. Instead, they drew up a new terna, with Lynch in the first position. Rome, citing Lynch's administrative record, integrity, orthodoxy, and, as a native Carolinian, seasoning against the area's fevers that victimized too many episcopal transplants, happily ratified their choice (Heisser and White, *Patrick N. Lynch,* 49).

3. *Charleston Daily Courier,* February 9, 1858, 2, cited in Heisser and White, *Patrick N. Lynch,* 49.

4. Annals of Ursuline Convent, Valle Crucis, Columbia, S.C., 1–3, AUCL.

5. Annals of Ursuline Convent, 2–3, AUCL.

6. Patrick Lynch, Baltimore, to Mother [Teresa], October 12, 1858, ABC. St. Charles College, located on a portion of the historic Carroll estate fifteen miles west of Baltimore, had opened under the direction of the Sulpicians a decade earlier.

7. 10 R4, CDA.

8. Mary Catherine Montague, daughter of Charles Montague, married C. J. Bollin.

9. John Bauskett, son of Colonel John and Sophia Crane Bauskett.

10. Oscar Montgomery Lieber (1830–1862), a geologist who headed South Carolina's Mineralogical, Geological, and Agricultural Survey. In 1857 he issued the first of his annual reports. His father, Francis Lieber (1798–1872), was a renowned jurist and political

scientist who had taught at the University of South Carolina for two decades before the increasingly repressive intellectual climate in the South drove him in 1856 to Columbia College in New York.

11. 10 W3, CDA.

12. William Rice, judge of the City Court of Charleston and his (second) wife, Caroline Spann Rice, 28. They had been visiting the Spanns in Texas.

13. Louisa Macnamara, twenty-six-year-old sister-in-law of John Lynch, who was contemplating joining the Sisters of Our Lady of Mercy. She entered the community eventually and became in religion Sister Mary Agnes.

14. A reference to the custom of candidates for the Ursuline communities in the South bringing slaves as part of their dowry.

15. "Ad Majorem Dei Gloriam": "for the greater glory of God," the motto of the Society of Jesus, which Baptista frequently used, especially at the heading of her correspondence.

16. Edgefield: a town fifty miles southwest of Columbia, South Carolina. At the beginning of the decade, Bishop Reynolds had approved the erection of facilities for a female school to be operated by religious (O'Connell, *Catholicity in the Carolinas*, 233–34).

17. Frederick William Faber (1814–1863), English convert by way of the Oxford Movement, who, as a priest of the Oratory, gained an international influence through his writings on the spiritual and devotional life.

18. 10 W4, CDA.

19. Lucius Bellinger Northrop (1811–1894), a career military officer and doctor who had converted to Catholicism upon his marriage to Maria De Bernalieu.

20. John Bellinger (1804–1860), a renowned Charleston physician who held the chair in surgery at the Medical College of South Carolina and was one of the many converts in this long-established family in the state.

21. 10 Y 3, CDA.

22. Francis Patrick Kenrick (1797–1863), Irish-born archbishop of Baltimore who had consecrated Patrick Lynch as bishop of Charleston in the Cathedral of St. John and St. Finbar on March 14, 1858.

23. Outsisters: those sisters in the community who were allowed outside of cloister to fulfill their duties of providing for the material needs of the house. Like many religious orders, male and female, the Ursulines had two classes of members: choir nuns and lay sisters.

24. 13 A1, CDA.

25. 13 A2, CDA.

26. The Ninth Provincial Council of Baltimore held in May 1858.

27. The Brown County community had extended an invitation to the nuns of the original Charleston community who had relocated to Springfield, Illinois, to join their sisters in returning to South Carolina, but they did not take up the offer, apparently because their local bishop refused to release them.

28. 13 A4, CDA.

29. General James Jones, chairman of the Board of Visitors of the Citadel from 1842 to 1865.

30. 13 A5, CDA.

31. 13 A6, CDA.

32. 13 A7, CDA.

33. 13 A9, CDA.

34. Louisa Blain, mother of Henrietta Blain Lynch.

35. 13 A10, CDA.

36. "Stella Coeli": "Star of Heaven," one of the titles given in Roman Catholic devotional literature to the Virgin Mary.

37. John Breckinridge (1821–1875) of Kentucky, vice president under James Buchanan.

38. Sister of Henrietta Blaine Lynch, wife of Francis.

39. 13 B1, CDA.

40. Twenty-two-year-old daughter of the planter, John Brownfield, and his wife, Pauline (Sumter) Brownfield of Charleston. Mary did indeed become a religious, a member of the Sisters of Our Lady of Mercy.

41. 13 B2, CDA.

42. 13 B3, CDA.

43. Robert Macnamara, Eliza Lynch's younger brother, whom John had been supporting since the 1840s.

44. 13 B4, CDA.

45. Michael O'Connor (1810–1872), bishop of Pittsburgh.

46. 13 B6, CDA.

47. 13 B8, CDA.

48. Ross Winans (1796–1877), inventor and builder of railroad engines and cars, chiefly for the Baltimore and Ohio Railroad.

49. 13 B9, CDA.

50. John Joseph Murphy (1812–1880), Irish-born, Baltimore-based printer, who became a major publisher of Catholic books in the nation.

51. 13 B10, CDA.

52. The 103-mile Northeastern Railroad ran between Florence, South Carolina, and Charleston.

53. 13 C1, CDA.

54. 13 C2, CDA.

55. 13 C3, CDA.

56. 13 C4, CDA.

57. Agnes Coffey, originally from the Charleston community.

58. 13 C5, CDA.

59. December 16.

60. A merchant of Barnwell Court House, married to a niece of the Bellingers.

61. 13 C6, CDA.

62. The islands of the Bahamas were under the jurisdiction of the bishop of Charleston, hence Patrick Lynch's obligation to visit them periodically.

63. 13 C7, CDA.

1859 JANUARY–JUNE

1. 13 D2, CDA.

2. Sophia Crane Bauskett, wife of Colonel John Bauskett of Columbia, a lawyer. Her father was a co-owner (together with his brother) of the American Hotel.

3. Reverend Jeremiah J. O'Connell, who held a doctor of divinity degree.

4. Joseph O'Connell, youngest of the three brother-priests in the diocese.

5. The other two O'Connells.

6. 13 D3, CDA.

7. 13 D5, CDA.

8. Unclassified document, CDA.

9. Thomas Quigley, stationed at St. Mary's Church in Charleston.

10. 13 D6, CDA.

11. 13 D7, CDA.

12. Edward Sourin (1818–1893), a priest of the Congregation of the Holy Cross and founder, in 1842, of the College of Notre Dame, in South Bend, Indiana.

13. Angelo Paresce.

14. 13 D8, CDA.

15. 13 E1, CDA.

16. John Cullinane, who had been appointed pastor of St. Peter's Church, Cheraw, in 1856.

17. Claudian Bird Northrop (1813?–1865), a Charleston lawyer and convert.

18. 13 E2, CDA.

19. Probably Sister Augustine.

20. "Exhibition": The ceremonies that marked the end of the academic year.

21. On Holy Thursday, it was a custom in many churches and chapels to have an altar of repose for the Eucharist, after it was removed from the tabernacle at the conclusion of the liturgy, before which altar worshippers could pray and meditate.

22. From the Latin, meaning "commandment," a reference to Jesus's instruction to his disciples at the Last Supper to wash one another's feet, as he had just washed theirs. The Holy Thursday liturgy included a remembrance of this by having the priest wash the feet of twelve persons representing the disciples. In a convent, the "disciples" were typically the nuns.

23. 13 E2, CDA.

24. Lawrence O'Connell, the youngest brother of the three O'Connells.

25. *"Omnes homines me deserent"*: "all have abandoned me," a reference to Isaiah's prophecy about the Son of Man's being abandoned by all those he had done so much for, a fickleness that the crowds acclaiming Jesus's entry into Jerusalem displayed when a few days later they demanded his crucifixion.

26. 13 E3, CDA.

27. 13 D10, CDA.

28. Caroline Wadlington Keitt, wife of Ellison Keitt.

29. 13 E4, CDA.

30. 13 E6, CDA.

31. 13 E10, CDA.

32. 13 E7, CDA.

33. "Relic": a fragment of wood from the cross on which Jesus was supposedly crucified.

34. 13 E8, CDA.

35. 13 E9, CDA.

36. Bernard had died three days earlier, on May 13. Baptista is alluding to Patrick's travel by train to and from Cheraw.

37. "Distribution" of prizes for academic achievement at the close-of-year ceremonies.

38. 13 G1, CDA.

39. Home of the Richland County planter, Jesse DeBruhl (1795–1859).

40. Henry Barnard (1811–1900), Connecticut educator who became a national figure in the movement to reform the common school. In 1859 he was serving as chancellor of the University of Wisconsin.

41. 13 G2, CDA.

42. "Gospel": a scapular or two small blessed cloths with sacred images embossed on them, connected by strings, to be worn over the chest and back.

43. Elias Marks (1790–1886), founder of the South Carolina Female Collegiate Institute at Barhamville, outside of Columbia.

44. 13 G3, CDA.

45. 13 G4, CDA.

46. Julia Lynch's marriage to Eustace Pinckney.

47. 13 G5 CDA.

48. 13 G6, CDA.

49. 13 G7, CDA.

1859 July–December

1. Allen J. Green, mayor of Columbia from 1859 to 1861.

2. William K. Scarborough, ed., *The Diary of Edmund Ruffin*, vol. 1 (Baton Rouge: Louisiana State University Press, 1972), 442–43.

3. Scarborough, *Diary of Edmund Ruffin*, 1:348–51.

4. 13 G9, CDA.

5. Samuel Fair, a prominent physician in Columbia. His residence was on Gregg Street in Columbia.

6. 13 G10, CDA.

7. Jeremiah O'Connell, with whom Baptista was ever at odds.

8. Charles J. Bollin (b. 1824), a railroad agent and real estate broker.

9. 13 H1, CDA.

10. Probably Bernard Reilly, a local real estate broker.

11. 13 H2, CDA.

12. Since 1848 the United States had had qualified diplomatic relations with the Papal States, with an American minister in Rome but no reciprocal representation by the Holy See in this country. From the beginning there was heavy opposition in Congress to this arrangement, with periodic attempts to discontinue the Roman ministry. Francis Lynch was alluding to the latest failure of opponents in Congress. The relations continued until 1867, when they were brought to an end by the Republican-dominated Congress, which refused to provide any funding for the maintenance of the minister in Rome.

13. 13 H3, CDA.

14. A reference to Pope Pius IX's tenuous sovereignty over the Papal States in the wake of the loss of the protection that Austrian troops had provided for the territories, as a result of Austrian's defeat by combined French-Sardinian forces in 1859. The French emperor, Napoleon III, was offering to replace Austria as the protector of the pontiff's temporal domains. In the end Napoleon provided a garrison for Rome and its environs, an arrangement that survived until the emperor's downfall in 1870.

15. 13 H4, CDA.

16. John H. Boatwright (1816–1865), physician who served as mayor of Columbia from 1861 to 1863.

17. 13 H5, CDA.

18. Sarah W. McAully (b. 1810), a widow with an estate in Richland County assessed at $25,000 (1860 Census).

19. 13 H6, CDA.

20. A key component of the Spiritual Exercises promoted by Ignatius Loyola and the Society of Jesus, which he founded, the examen is a reflection made twice daily of one's behavior and dispositions amid the changing circumstances one encounters from rising to retiring.

21. Paul J. Semmes (1815–1863), bank agent of Muscogee, Georgia.

22. 13 H7, CDA.

23. 13 H8, CDA.

24. 13 H9, CDA.

25. The laws enacted in Ireland to restrict the rights and practices of Roman Catholics.

26. The Pharisee member of the Sanhedrin who, in Luke's Acts (5:34–39), successfully appealed to that body not to prosecute Jesus's disciples but to leave their fate in God's hands.

27. 13 H10, CDA.

28. Edmund Bellinger, a lawyer and convert to Catholicism who was representing the bishop in the case.

29. 13 K1, CDA.

30. 13 K2, CDA.

31. 13 K4, CDA.

32. 13 K6, CDA.

33. Patrick Lynch apparently thought it best to leave non-used titles undisturbed. Neither "The Academy of the Immaculate Conception" nor "St. Charles Institute" became the common title for the school. It remained simply "Ursuline Academy," the term Baptista normally used in identifying the place in her correspondence.

34. The pledge to abstain from alcohol.

35. 13 K5, CDA.

36. Mary Otis Weed, who as an Ursuline became Sister Mary Charles.

37. Elizabeth Dummett Hardee, wife of William Joseph Hardee, a lieutenant colonel of cavalry in the U.S. Army.

38. 13 K3, CDA.

39. 13 K7, CDA.

40. Fire companies were notorious for instigating or at least being enthusiastic participants in nativist vigilante actions. In this case, they were deterred by an imposing force for law and order headed by the mayor himself.

41. The Sisters of Our Lady of Mercy of Charleston.

42. 13 K8, CDA.

43. 13 K9, CDA.

44. 3 K10, CDA.

45. 13 M1, CDA.

46. 13 M2, CDA.

47. 13 M4, CDA.

48. 13 M5, CDA.
49. 13 M6, CDA.
50. 13 M7, CDA.
51. 13 M8, CDA.

1860 JANUARY–JUNE

1. 13. N1, CDA.
2. Allen J. Green, mayor of Columbia.
3. Possibly William J. Shields, planter of neighboring Kershaw County.
4. Horace E. Nichols (b. 1811), Columbia merchant.
5. George Huggins (b. 1820), Columbia bookkeeper.
6. 6 S1, CDA.
7. 13 N2, CDA.
8. Eli Stephens, fifty-three, a wheelwright. 1860 Census, Columbia, Richland Co., S.C., 65.
9. Unclassified, CDA.
10. "Second turnout": a reference to the Ursulines' departure from Charleston in 1845.
11. Maximillian LaBorde (b. 1804), professor of logic at South Carolina College, and president (chairman of the faculty) from 1861 to 1865.
12. 13 N10, CDA.
13. "Permissions for Lent": The need for religious superiors to obtain the bishop's dispensation from the strict observance of the Lenten regimen of fasting and abstinence.
14. M. I. Kelly, P. J. Hedian, and John B. Piet, Baltimore publishers who edited the *Catholic Mirror,* official newspaper of the Archdiocese of Baltimore, as well as of the Dioceses of Richmond and Wheeling.
15. 13 N4, CDA.
16. John Hughes, archbishop of New York.
17. 13 N5, CDA.
18. The Ursuline Convent and Academy in Galveston.
19. St. Scholastica, the sister of St. Benedict. Once, according to tradition, when her brother was visiting her, she implored God's aid in keeping her brother from departing as early as he intended. A fierce storm ensued, which forced Benedict to extend his stay.
20. 13 N6, CDA.
21. Timothy Bermingham (1797–1872), Irish-born pastor of St. Mary's Church in Edgefield, fifty-five miles southwest of Columbia.
22. A suit against the bishop in the county court was taking Patrick Lynch to Lancaster. William McKenna, the wealthiest Catholic in the state, had left virtually his entire estate, valued at more than $250,000, to the diocese of Charleston. McKenna's family contested the will, and the matter ended in court. See Baptista Lynch's letter to Patrick Lynch of July 31, 1860, for the outcome of the suit.
23. 13 N7, CDA.
24. Mary Borgia McCarthy, one of the members of the Blackrock Ursulines in Ireland whom Bishop England had brought to Charleston in 1834 to establish a foundation there. Borgia served consecutively as superior and novice mistress of the community from 1840 to 1852.

25. 13 N8, CDA.

26. The Lynch home in Columbia was on the east side of Assembly Street between Taylor and Blanding Streets, a block from the Ursuline Convent and Academy.

27. 13 P9, CDA.

28. "According to the [Ursuline] rule."

29. The Charleston Sisters of Our Lady of Mercy.

30. "Disinclination to going out": that is, to be a lay sister or outsister, unlike the choir nuns who were strictly cloistered.

31. 13 P1, CDA.

32. Edward LaFitte (b. 1820), a Catholic merchant of Charleston.

33. Joseph Glover Baldwin (1815–1864), lawyer and writer. In 1853 Baldwin had published *Flush Times in Alabama and Mississippi,* a work that gained him renown as a regional humorist.

34. St. Peter's Church, approximately three blocks from the Ursulines' location.

35. 13 P2, CDA.

36. The former convent and school that the Sisters of Mercy occupied in Columbia before Bishop Lynch transferred them to Charleston.

37. Edward LaFitte kept a home in Sumter, about forty miles east of Columbia.

38. John Loughlin (1817–1891), Irish-born bishop of Brooklyn.

39. Catherine Semmes, wife of Thomas Semmes, a planter of Madison County, Mississippi, and mother of Jane Semmes, fourteen, student at the Ursuline Academy.

40. 12 P3, CDA.

41. 13 P7, CDA.

42. John McGill (1809–1872), Philadelphia-born third bishop of Richmond.

43. 13 P8, CDA.

44. 13 R1, CDA.

45. 13 R2. CDA.

46. 13 R3, CDA.

47. James W. Baskin (b. 1821) of Columbia, a railroad agent.

48. 13 R4, CDA.

49. St. Crispin, the third-century martyr who, as a reputed shoemaker, became the patron saint of tanners and shoemakers.

50. 13 R5, CDA.

51. 13 R7, CDA.

52. 13 R8, CDA.

53. 13 R9, CDA.

54. Patrick O'Neil, pastor of St. Patrick's Church in Charleston.

1860 July–December

1. "It Has Come At Last," *U.S. Catholic Miscellany,* November 10, 1860.

2. 13 S2, CDA.

3. William McKenna, an Irish immigrant merchant-planter, at his death in 1859, was the richest Catholic in South Carolina. In his will McKenna left virtually his entire estate to the Diocese of Charleston, most of it for the establishment of a male orphanage. McKenna's family contested the will and the county court of Lancaster found in the family's

favor. The family offered three-eighths of the estate (which exceeded $250,000) to the diocese; Patrick Lynch thus became the legal owner of Malta Plantation and its eighty-five slaves.

4. Alexander Hitzelberger, a former diocesan priest who had joined the Maryland Province of the Society of Jesus in the 1850s, was teaching English and Latin to seminarians at the Jesuit novitiate in Frederick, Maryland.

5. 13 S3, CDA.

6. 13 S6, CDA.

7. 13 S4, CDA

8. 13 S5, CDA.

9. "Via illuminata": the second stage (of three) in the spiritual journey of Christians, in the course of which the person gains insights into the mysteries of the faith.

10. 13 S7, CDA.

11. 13 S8, CDA.

12. 13 S9, CDA.

13. Addie Lowe was a professional actress and a recent convert to Catholicism. When a stagecoach carrying her to a theater engagement had overturned and left her with severe injuries, she made a full recovery in a hospital operated by the Sisters of Charity. That experience led her to profess the Catholic faith and to seek admission to the Ursuline community. Permission was granted for her to enter the following month; she was subsequently given the name in religion of Mary Pauline (Annals of Ursuline Convent, 13–14).

14. 14 N2, CDA.

15. 13 S10, CDA.

16. 13 T1, CDA.

17. 13 T2, CDA.

18. 13 T3, CDA.

19. Georgetown in the District of Columbia. Presumably Ryan sought to remove his daughter from the convent school that the Visitandines conducted there.

20. 13 T 4, CDA.

21. 13 T6, CDA.

22. Felix J. Carr, a diocesan priest stationed in Charleston.

23. 13 T7, CDA.

24. 13 T8, CDA.

25. 13 T9, CDA.

26. 25 Y2, CDA.

27. Henry Wilson, Republican senator of Massachusetts.

28. Samuel Chase, Republican senator of Ohio.

29. Charles Sumner, Republican senator of Massachusetts.

30. Owen Lovejoy, Republican representative of Illinois.

31. George W. Julian, Republican representative of Indiana.

32. Lewis D. Campbell, Republican representative of Ohio.

33. Hinton Rowan Helper's 1857 book, *The Impending Crisis,* indicted slavery as the root of the South's economic stagnation, which was most harmful to the non-slaveholding class. Helper's volume was a call for non-slaveholders to unite in ending "the peculiar institution" as the backbone of the economy and allowing free white labor to compete on an equal playing field.

34. Lynch's argument was that the states of the Deep South could save $50 million by no longer having to pay the heavy tariffs imposed by the U.S. government on the import of foreign manufactured products in order to protect Northern industries.

35. "In not shaking things up."

1861 JANUARY–JUNE

1. Diocesan tradition identified the bishop as the second figure from the right in the photograph. We do know that Patrick Lynch took part in a later tour of local fortifications by dignitaries, including President Davis, on November 2, 1863 (Richard C. Madden, *Catholics in South Carolina: A Record* [Lanham, Md.: University Press of America], 89).

2. *Charleston Daily Courier*, September 21, 1861, quoted in David T. Gleeson, *The Green and the Gray: The Irish in the Confederate States of America* (Chapel Hill: University of North Carolina Press, 2013), 151.

3. David C. R. Heisser, "Bishop Lynch's People: Slaveholding by a South Carolina Prelate," *South Carolina Historical Magazine* 102 (July 2001): 243–44.

4. 13 W1, CDA.

5. Thomas W. Radcliffe (b. 1815), Columbian jeweler and watchmaker.

6. Given the length of time it would take students who lived at a great distance from the school to make the journey home and back again, it was customary for such students to remain at the school during summer vacation. Thus studies could resume with the year-round boarders and local students.

7. 25 A2, CDA.

8. Catholics made up a substantial minority within the U.S. military. Among the eighty-three who surrendered were nineteen Irish, the vast majority of whom would have been Catholic.

9. 13 W2, CDA.

10. Felix J. Carr, diocesan priest stationed in Charleston at the Cathedral of St. John and St. Finbar.

11. 13 W3, CDA.

12. William McGuinnis, real estate broker in Columbia.

13. 13 W4, CDA.

14. 30 M17, Kenrick Papers, Associated Archives of St. Mary's University and Seminary, Baltimore.

15. Benedict Joseph Spalding, diocesan priest of Louisville and brother of Martin Spalding, bishop of Louisville.

16. "Let them consult the approved authors."

17. "One would be better off."

18. 13 W6, CDA.

19. 13 W8, CDA.

20. 13 W9, CDA.

21. 13 W10, CDA.

22. 13 Y1, CDA.

23. 13 Y2, CDA.

24. 13 Y3, CDA.

25. 13 Y4, CDA.

26. Ellison Keitt, a convert of Newberry and planter.

27. 14 A1, CDA.

28. 14 A2, CDA.

29. In July 1856 Conlaw Peter and Ellen Neison Lynch had traveled by train to New York City for Ellen to have experimental surgery for an ailment from which she had long suffered. Surgical complications prolonged their stay there into September. While there Jeremiah Williams Cummings (1814–1866), who had studied with Patrick at the Urban College in Rome, hosted them at St. Stephen's, the church he had established in midtown Manhattan.

30. 14 A4, CDA.

31. James Wallace (1787–1851), English-born priest who, as a Jesuit, had been assigned in 1817 to work in Charleston. He eventually became a diocesan priest and taught, until his death, mathematics and the sciences at the College of South Carolina in Columbia.

32. 14 A6, CDA.

33. 14 A7, CDA.

34. 14 A8, CDA.

1861 JULY–DECEMBER

1. 14 A9, CDA.

2. The forty-five-year-old Joseph Ardia, a Jesuit refugee from the revolution in Italy in 1848, was at the novitiate in Frederick, Maryland. Although Maryland was formally outside of the Confederacy, Baptista, like a great many in the South, regarded it as a likely twelfth state in the new republic. As the native Marylander James Ryder Randall predicted in his piece "Maryland, my Maryland," which became one of the signature songs of the Confederacy, "She'll come! She'll come!"

3. 14 A10, CDA.

4. 14 B1, CDA.

5. *New York Daily Tribune,* Thursday, September 5, 1861, 6. Under the title "Catholic Bishops on the War For the Union," the paper in an editorial ("Bishops in Politics") saluted the exchange of letters between Archbishop Hughes and Bishop Lynch as a valuable manifestation of the right of prelates and other religious authorities to participate in the public discourse on matters of vital importance to society. Indeed, the *Tribune* noted the responsibility of religious leaders to speak out on issues involving moral principles, as the origin and the prosecution of the present war clearly did. Its major criticism was leveled at Hughes for being too condemning of the abolitionists and too tolerant toward the slaveholding South, attempting to avoid the moral judgment that slavery cried out for.

6. "Stonebridge": the Battle of Bull Run or Manassas, which had ended in a humiliating rout of the Union forces. The stone bridge over Bull Run had been a focal point of the fighting on July 21. The bishop's prediction about a Maryland invasion was a year premature. Following the second Battle of Bull Run in August 1862, the Army of Northern Virginia crossed into Maryland days after its second decisive victory on the plains of Manassas.

7. A reference to the Republican Party's commitment to oppose the spread of slavery to the territories, a key element of the party's platform adopted at their convention in Chicago in 1860.

8. The pressure of Northern governors was not decisive in setting the Lincoln administration's policy regarding Sumter. President Lincoln in his inaugural address had stated plainly that he was resolved to hold *all* possessions of the United States that happened to be in territory claimed by the Confederacy. The assurances the Confederate commissioners had received in Washington about the evacuation of the fort reflected the intention of Secretary of State William Seward, not that of Lincoln, who in the end directed that Sumter be resupplied. The subsequent expedition of the resupply fleet provided a rationalization for the Confederate government to attack the fort, in the miscalculation that the Lincoln administration would simply accept Sumter's capture as a fait accompli and take no further action (see Brian Holden Reid, *The Origins of the American Civil War* [London: Longman, 1996], 310–59).

9. "With what little wisdom the world is governed."

10. A reference to the "personal-liberty" laws passed by several Northern states to nullify the enforcement of the Fugitive Slave Law of 1850.

11. In fact, Great Britain turned to its own colonies, specifically Egypt and India, as alternate suppliers of cotton.

12. This charge that the abolitionists were cynically using the Irish to fight the war they had not the stomach to wage themselves was one that the Irish in the South would invoke with greater frequency as the casualties of the war mounted to more and more horrific levels. There is no indication that Bishop Lynch or any others who made this argument ever questioned whether the Southern Irish were being similarly exploited. Archbishop Hughes, in his response, denied there was a plot to use the Irish as cannon fodder. And he could not resist quoting the English journalist William Howard Russell, who had been reporting on the war for the *London Times* from both North and South, to provide evidence that in the matter of the Irish as cannon fodder, the South's hands were no cleaner than the North's.

13. In his lengthy response, Archbishop Hughes argued that the original compact made by the states in the Constitution that created the republic of the United States preempted secession as a course of action by any of the signatory states. Even conceding the right of secession, Hughes could see no justifying cause for invoking it. The archbishop reminded his Southern friend how thoroughly the South had dominated the United States government over its first eighty-plus years. The current situation in which they confronted a "Black Republican" in the White House was an anomaly, the consequence of the Democrats' own disunity, which had resulted in the Democrats, in effect, running three candidates against the sole Republican. What was needed on the part of the South was a little patience that would allow the normal political calculus to reset. Lacking that, Hughes suggested that both sections, even in the midst of war, might undertake simultaneously the calling of conventions, North and South, to examine the Constitution of the United States and determine what amendments needed to be made so that it would continue to be a viable life source for a nineteenth-century republic.

14. Richmond Diocesan Records, University of Notre Dame Archives, microfilm.

15. Lucius Bellinger Northrop (1811–1894), a career military officer from Charleston and a Catholic convert. Northrop, upon resigning his army commission after his state seceded, was appointed commissary general by Jefferson Davis with the title of colonel.

16. John Bankhead Magruder (1810–1871), a Virginian who resigned in March 1861 from the U.S. military. Having commanded the Confederate force that gained the first

notable victory for the Confederacy the following June at Big Bethel on the lower peninsula (between the James and York Rivers), he was promoted from colonel to major general.

17. Pierre Gustave Toutant Beauregard (1818–1893), from an old Creole Catholic family in Louisiana. Together with Joseph Johnston, Beauregard commanded the victorious Confederate forces at Manassas in July 1861.

18. John Teeling was one of three seminarians recruited by Bishop John McGill from All-Hallows in Ireland at the outset of his episcopacy (1850). Teeling, as pastor of St. Patrick's in Richmond, became an early, outspoken supporter of the rebellion. The all-Catholic company of the 1st Virginia Regiment voted to have Teeling as its chaplain. The regimental commander, Colonel Patrick Moore, subsequently named Teeling chaplain of the regiment itself, a move he was quickly forced to retract after the unit's Protestant majority protested having a Catholic chaplain. Teeling was subsequently named chaplain for the Catholics in the regiment (Gerald P. Fogarty, S.J., *Commonwealth Catholicism: A History of the Catholic Church in Virginia* [Notre Dame, Ind.: University of Notre Dame Press, 2001], 148–49).

19. Joseph Eggleston Johnston (1807–1891), another Virginia career military officer who resigned following that state's secession in April 1861. At the end of August, a week after Lynch's letter was composed, Richmond raised Johnston's rank from brigadier general to full, with command of the Confederacy's major army, now concentrated at Centreville.

20. 14 B4, CDA.

21. Georgetown Visitation Academy in the District of Columbia.

22. 14 B6, CDA.

23. Sister Augustine England.

24. The report was false. In early June three Daughters of Charity had set out from their motherhouse in Emmitsburg in response to an appeal from Confederate authorities for nurses to work with the wounded in the military hospital just outside of Harpers Ferry. Without incident the three reached the Potomac town and worked in the hospital there until the Confederates pulled out. From there they followed the Southern forces to Winchester, where they resumed their nursing, reinforced by three additional sisters from Emmitsburg (George Barton, *Angels of the Battlefield: A History of the Labors of the Catholic Sisterhoods in the Late Civil War* [Philadelphia: Catholic Art Publishing, 1898], 37–43).

25. 14 B7, CDA.

26. William Dougherty (1814–1867), a Northern stonemason. South Carolina officials had contracted with his firm, Sisson & Dougherty, to do the stone work for the new state house, then under construction.

27. 14 B8, CDA.

28. 14 B9, CDA.

29. Over the past year Baptista had noted Augustine's mercurial temperament, but her behavior took a sudden turn toward the dark side in the summer of 1861. This abrupt change Baptista traced back to their retreat the previous month. Augustine's sudden hostility toward Baptista may well have been triggered by another event that occurred around that time: the entrance of Baptista's niece, Ellen Spann, into the community as a novice. Baptista doted on her namesake, as would have been painfully evident to Augustine in the year that Ellen had been with them as a student. Augustine may well have experienced Ellen's entry as a threat to her own relationship to Baptista and even, in a warped way, as the superior's rejection of herself in favor of the niece. That would explain Augustine's loss

of faith in her ability to persevere in the religious life, shorn, as she felt, of Baptista's loving support. Baptista herself never gave any indication of having such suspicions about the origin of Augustine's turn against her.

30. 14 B10, CDA.

31. 14 C1, CDA.

32. Intended in retaliation for the Confiscation Act, passed by the U.S. Congress in July 1861, authorizing the seizure of property, including slaves, used in the prosecution of the rebellion against the U.S. government, the Confederate Congress's Sequestration Act of the following month declared that all goods and credits held by citizens of the United States within the borders of the Confederacy were to be the property of the Confederate government for the duration of the war.

33. Baltimore would hardly seem to qualify as the "land of Lincoln," with the president having finished a poor fourth in the city and state in the election of 1860. Anti-Republican feelings ran deep, probably more so than vestigial Southern loyalties. It all made for an explosive mix that blew up on the nineteenth of April when mobs attacked Massachusetts troops making their way through the city to Washington. There were sixteen fatalities: four soldiers and twelve civilians, the first bloodshed in the undeclared war. In the ensuing days, secession fever ran unchecked. Pressure mounted on Governor Thomas Hicks to call a special session of the legislature to provide a legal path for the state's withdrawal from the Union. Hicks resisted. Then, in early May, Federal troops occupied the city, the first in the greater South to fall under federal military control. Slowly the occupiers sucked the air out of any movement to make Maryland the twelfth state of the Confederacy. Francis Lynch had that repressive situation in mind in warning his brother, who had clearly marked himself as a Confederate advocate, about visiting a city under Union military control. With Bluecoats everywhere, their cannon on Federal Hill trained on the heart of the city below, Baltimore indeed had become "the land of Lincoln."

34. 30 M19, AASMUS.

35. Augustine Verot (1804–1876), French-born Sulpician and, since 1857, vicar-apostolic of Florida, a position he continued to hold after being named the third bishop of Savannah. In the previous January, Verot in a sermon had defended slavery as an institution but called for major reforms to make it compatible with Christianity.

36. Martin Spalding, bishop of Louisville, and his priest-brother, Benedict.

37. 14 C2, CDA.

38. Alexander Gregg (b. 1819), bishop of the Texas Diocese of the Protestant Episcopal Church in the Confederate States. The bishop was in town for the denomination's annual convention. Gregg previously had been rector of St. David's Church in Cheraw (*Charleston Courier,* February 10, 1860, and October 25, 1861; 1850 Census, Chesterfield, S.C., 111).

39. Even in the early months of the war, with relatively little campaigning by Federal armies, the war was generating refugees, particularly in the border and coastal areas of the Confederacy. Upcountry South Carolina was a natural destination for those seeking a safer location. John Lynch, for one, was quick to respond to the forced migration, finding space in his already crowded home for those fleeing the war, while securing other housing to take advantage of a seller/leaser's market.

40. 14 C3, CDA.

41. Louisa Susanna Cheves McCord (1810–1879), daughter of Langdon Cheves, planter, judge, and U.S. congressman (Speaker of the House of Representatives).

42. 14 D8, CDA.

43. Likely Martha Huchet, wife of the Charleston merchant Thomas Huchet. They had two daughters, Mary (12), and Jane (9) (Census of 1860, Charleston Ward 4, Charleston, SC, 101).

44. 14 C5, CDA.

45. 14 C6, CDA.

46. Mary Purcell (b. 1825), Irish-born widow and seamstress. Her sister, Mary Ryan, was forty (1860 Census, Charleston Ward 6, Charleston, S.C., 4).

47. William Hume (b. 1802), professor of experimental science at the Medical College of the State of South Carolina (1860 Census, Charleston Ward 6, Charleston, S.C., 97).

48. 14 C7, CDA.

49. 14 C8, CDA.

50. 14 C9, CDA.

51. Esther Winder Lowe (1824–1918), wife of Enoch Louis Lowe (1820–1892), former governor of Maryland, who had gone south to Richmond early in the war.

52. 14 D1, CDA.

53. James Louis Petigru (1789–1863), a lawyer, politician, and intellectual who, in his twenties, had changed his name from "Petigrew" to "Petigru" to highlight his Huguenot, rather than his Scotch-Irish roots. Petigru and Patrick Lynch were both members of the informal literary set that met regularly in the 1850s at Russell's Bookstore in Charleston.

54. 14 D2, CDA.

55. 14 D3, CDA.

56. 14 D4, CDA.

57. "God's will be done."

58. 14 P1, CDA.

59. 14 D5, CDA.

60. Albert Gallatin Blanchard (1810–1891), brigade general in Benjamin Huger's division in John B. Magruder's command of the Army of Northern Virginia.

61. 14 D6, CDA.

62. 14 D7, CDA.

1862 January–June

1. Claudian Bird Northrop (1820–1865), another Catholic convert from a prominent Charleston family.

2. 14 E1, CDA.

3. The bishop had purchased 130 acres of land from a convert Catholic, Ellison Summerfield Keitt, as the future site of the Ursuline convent and academy. For the present he intended to farm it, hence the transfer of slaves from the Lexington plantation to the new one, Valle Crucis, about three miles northwest of Columbia.

4. 14 E2, CDA.

5. Likely A. Fillette (b. 1810), a Spanish immigrant (1860 Census, Charleston Ward 6, Charleston, S.C.).

6. John Auchincloss Inglis (1813–1879), Maryland-born lawyer and Presbyterian elder in Cheraw. One of four chancellors of the state courts. Served as a delegate to the convention in 1860 and wrote the Ordinance of Secession that the delegates unanimously adopted.

7. 14 E5, CDA.

8. 14 E6, CDA.

9. 14 E7, CDA.

10. The name by which the Army of Northern Virginia was known until Robert E. Lee assumed command.

11. 14 E8 J, CDA.

12. 14 E9, CDA.

13. At the close of the school year of 1861–62, Rosalie Acelie Guillon Togno (1813–1913) moved her school from Charleston to the more secure environs of Barhamville outside of Columbia.

14. John Le Conte (1818–1891), professor of physics and chemistry at South Carolina College. His wife was Catherine Graham. His younger brother, Joseph (1823–1901), taught geology and chemistry at the college.

15. 13 W5, CDA. Henrietta dated this letter "29th January 1861," but the context of the letter clearly indicates that the year was 1862.

16. Ellen Posi (b. 1840), wife of Julius Posi (b. 1834), who had taught Italian and ancient languages at schools in Charleston and Columbia, including St. Mary's College. The American-born Posi had gone to Italy.

17. 14 E11, CDA.

18. 14 E10, CDA.

19. Charles J. Bollin (b. 1824), railroad agent.

20. The younger sister of Cornelia O'Reilly Lynch.

21. 14 G1, CDA.

22. 14 G2, CDA.

23. Alice O'Reilly.

24. Claudian Bird Northrop had agreed to manage the two-thousand-acre Malta Plantation in Lancaster country that the bishop had acquired from the William McKenna estate in 1861. When Bishop Lynch decided to honor the government directive to discontinue the cultivation of cotton and restricted the agriculture at Malta to the growing of foodstuffs, less labor was needed and Northrop apparently chose to lease out his slaves as best he could (Heisser, "Bishop Lynch's People," 244–49).

25. John C. Coit (b. 1800), Connecticut-born Presbyterian minister, who had been pastor of an Old Side church in Cheraw in the 1850s. The 1860 Census listed him as a resident of Goldsboro, Wayne County, North Carolina.

26. 14 G3, CDA.

27. H. C. Guerin (b. 1830), Charleston physician.

28. 14 G4, CDA.

29. 14 G5, CDA.

30. "Scarletina": a mild form of scarlet fever.

31. A reference to the fund-raising by South Carolina women toward the construction of a Confederate vessel—CSS *Palmetto State*—which inspired the popular name of the "Ladies Gunboat" for the ship.

32. The *Virginia*, formerly the *Merrimac,* which had been converted into an ironclad at Norfolk, and on March 7 had wreaked havoc with the blockading Union ships around Hampton Roads before being neutralized the next day by a Union ironclad, the *Monitor.*

33. 17 G6, CDA.

34. 14 G7, CDA.

35. 14 G9, CDA.

36. 14 G10, CDA.

37. M. Ferrall, an Irish-born merchant and widower with two children, including a daughter Harriet, aged seventeen (1860 Census, Halifax County, N.C., 83).

38. 14 H1, CDA.

39. 14 H2, CDA.

40. 14 G8, CDA.

41. Francisco Jimenez de Cisneros (1436–1517), Franciscan who became Archbishop of Toledo and held several offices under King Ferdinand II, including grand inquisitor.

42. 14 H3. CDA.

43. 14 H4, CDA.

44. 14 H5, CDA.

45. Rose Russell, who had joined the Columbian community on Christmas Eve 1858, died three days after Baptista wrote this letter.

46. 14 H6, CDA.

47. Sophie Vassas, a French immigrant who had joined the community as a postulant the previous March.

48. John Teeling, an immigrant priest and vicar general of the Diocese of Richmond.

49. Robert H. Andrews, of Alexandria, Virginia, a convert and priest, stationed at the cathedral of the Diocese of Richmond.

50. Sr. Mary Charles: Mary Otis Weed, who had entered in October 1859.

51. 14 H7, CDA.

52. The three days immediately preceding the feast of the Ascension in the liturgical calendar, marked especially by fasting and prayers for a successful harvest of the newly planted crops and other needs.

53. 14 H8, CDA.

54. A Corsican who had been the Italian consul in Richmond.

55. 14 H9, CDA.

56. 14 H10, CDA.

57. Louis-Hippolyte Gache (1817–1907).

58. Elias Marks (b. 1795), physician and principal of the South Carolina Female Collegiate Institute at Barhamville.

59. Natalie Dowell, aged thirty, wife of J. R. Dowell, thirty-nine, a telegraph operator. They had one daughter, Josephine, eleven.

60. 14 H11, CDA.

61. 14 K4, CDA.

62. On June 16, in what became known as the Battle of Secessionville, Confederate forces turned back a Union attempt to establish a beachhead on one of the islands surrounding Charleston harbor.

63. As a cloistered order, the Ursulines could not undertake the ministry of nursing. The Sisters of Our Lady of Mercy of Charleston had no such restrictions. Indeed, their initial nursing ministry dated back to 1852, when they had opened a relief hospital during the yellow fever epidemic. Early in the Civil War, sisters from the Charleston community had nursed in the hospitals of Richmond. Then, in December 1861 they took over a military hospital in western Virginia at Greenbrier. Fighting in and around the upper Shenandoah

Valley in April of the following year forced them to relocate the facility farther west to Montgomery White Sulphur Springs (Madden, *Catholics in South Carolina,* 64, 84; Heisser and White, *Patrick N. Lynch,* 91–92).

64. Minerva Clark had entered the order from the academy in 1861 and received her veil under the name of Mary deSales.

65. 14 K3, CDA.

1862 July–December

1. 14 K5, CDA.

2. 14 K6, CDA.

3. Joseph Bixio, an Italian Jesuit who had come to the United States in 1848 as a refugee from the revolution.

4. 14 K7, CDA.

5. Halifax, North Carolina, was the home of Michael Ferrall, an Irish merchant, and friend of the Lynches. He had two daughters. One, the seventeen-year-old Harriet (Nannie), was a troublesome student at the Ursuline Academy in Columbia. Ferrall in his will named Patrick Lynch as executor of his estate, the bulk of which was left to his two daughters in the form of a trust that the bishop was to manage. This matter would seem to have been the bishop's "business" that took him out of his way to Halifax on his return to Charleston from Montgomery White Sulphur Springs (Edward Conigland, Halifax, N.C., to Patrick Lynch, August 13, 1869, 46 S7, CDA).

6. 14 K9, CDA.

7. 14 K10, CDA.

8. Lucius Cary Polk (b. 1838), native of Somerset County, on the Eastern Shore of Maryland, who, in 1861, crossed the Chesapeake into Virginia to enter Confederate service.

9. Enoch Louis Lowe (1820–1892), British-educated Maryland Catholic, a lawyer who served as governor of Maryland from 1851 to 1854. Lowe went south following the outbreak of war in 1861 and made his residence in Richmond, Virginia.

10. Darius Hubert, S.J. (1823–1893), chaplain of the 1st Louisiana Regiment.

11. 14 M1, CDA.

12. Mathew S. Reeves (1817–1862), Charleston-based musician and singer, whose patriotic concerts were popular fund-raisers throughout the state during the first year or so of the war until his death from a stroke on August 10, 1862.

13. 14 M2, CDA.

14. 14 M3, CDA.

15. 14 M4, CDA.

16. Florence Dooley, daughter of John and Sarah Dooley of Richmond. John owned the Great Southern Hat and Cap Manufactory and Depot in that city.

17. Thomas Mulvey, Irish-born pastor of St. Joseph's Church in Petersburg.

18. Peter Augustus Aveilhé (b. 1827). His wife was Mary D. Aveilhé.

19. Daniel J. Quigley (1831–1903), the brother-in-law of the late William McKenna, who, as a layman sought to catechize the slaves on McKenna's plantation, who had been given to Bishop Lynch in the settlement of the McKenna estate. See section 1864 April–July.

20. 14 M5, CDA.

21. 14 M8, CDA.

22. Jeremiah O'Neill, Irish-born priest of the Savannah Diocese and staunch Confederate nationalist.

23. Peter Whelan. An Irish cleric recruited by Bishop John England for Charleston, Whelan became a priest of the Diocese of Savannah when it was organized in 1850. He was another firmly committed Confederate patriot (Gleeson, *Green and the Gray,* 153).

24. 14 M7, CDA.

25. After two of the most complete victories of the war at Manassas and Richmond, Kentucky, at the end of August, Confederate armies, so many in the North feared, would soon threaten Baltimore and/or Washington in the East, and Louisville and Cincinnati in the West. All four cities went on a war footing to prepare for the worst.

26. 14 M9, CDA.

27. Samuel Cooper (1798–1876), inspector general of the Confederate States Army.

28. 14 M10, CDA.

29. 14 N1, CDA.

30. 14 N3, CDA.

31. Lawrence O'Connell.

32. The military hospital in western Virginia conducted by the Charleston Mercy sisters.

33. Brigadier General William Duncan Smith (1825–1862), commanding officer of the Charleston Military District, died of yellow fever on October 4.

34. 14 N4, CDA.

35. Thomas Jordan (1819–1895), aide to General Beauregard.

36. 14 N5, CDA.

37. 14 N6, CDA.

38. 14 N7, CDA.

39. Zebulon Baird Vance (1830–1894).

40. 14 N8, CDA.

41. 14 P2, CDA.

42. A District of Columbia native and Harvard Law School graduate, Thomas Jenkins Semmes (1824–1899) had moved to New Orleans at the end of 1850. He was a drafter of the Secession Ordinance that Louisiana adopted and a member of the Confederate Senate from 1862 to the end of the war.

43. 14 P3, CDA.

44. 14 P4, CDA.

1863 JANUARY–JUNE

1. 14 R1, CDA.

2. 14 R4, CDA.

3. 14 R5, CDA.

4. It is not known what took Julius Posi to Italy or how he came to be jailed.

5. 14 R6, CDA.

6. Thomas Jenkins Semmes.

7. Alexander Jenkins Semmes, a brother of Thomas Jenkins Semmes and a surgeon with the 1st Louisiana Volunteers.

8. 14 R7, CDA.

9. Public dissatisfaction with the Lincoln Administration's prosecution of the war and its issuance of the Emancipation Proclamation had led to Democratic victories in the fall of 1862 in several western states, including Ohio, Illinois, Minnesota, and Wisconsin. This emboldened Democrats in the region to launch a peace movement calling for an immediate cessation of the fighting as the first step toward a resolution of the sectional differences and eventual reunion.

10. Louis Napoléon Bonaparte (1808–1873), emperor of France, had long been considered sympathetic to the South's quest for independence.

11. Semmes's information was false. None of the three could be honestly described as "violent Know-Nothings." Nathaniel P. Banks (1816–1894), to advance his political career, had briefly supported the Know-Nothing party in Massachusetts. John Pope (1822–1892) was a career soldier uninvolved with the ethnic-religious politics of the 1850s. Abraham Lincoln was known for his opposition to nativism. But Semmes's comment points up the pervasive tendency among Catholics, not just in the South, to equate Republicans with Know-Nothings.

12. 14 R8, CDA.

13. 14 R9, CDA.

14. Baptista was referring to St. James (Jacob) of Nisibis, fourth-century bishop of Nisibis in Mesopotamia.

15. 14 S1, CDA.

16. 14 R10, CDA.

17. A "blue stocking," or bookish woman.

18. 14 S2, CDA.

19. In February, Confederate newspapers reported that scores of women and children had been banished from St. Augustine as punishment for their refusal to take the oath of allegiance to the United States. The previous September about 150 women and children had been forced onto a steamer, without any provisions, and sent up the St. Johns River beyond the lines for the same offense.

20. Amelia Lancaster, aged twenty-two, daughter of John J. and Amelia Lancaster. The Lancasters were an old Catholic family with seventeenth-century roots in southern Maryland.

21. 14 S4, CDA.

22. Aloysius Gonzaga (1568–1591), canonized Italian Jesuit known for his piety and service to the poor and sick.

23. 14 S5, CDA.

24. 14 S6, CDA.

25. 14 S10, CDA.

26. On April 6 Union ironclads attacked Fort Sumter but retired after two hours, with several vessels severely damaged by devastating fire from forts on the islands guarding the harbor.

27. 14 T1, CDA.

28. 14 T2, CDA.

29. John Quinlan (1826–1883).

30. 14 T3, CDA.

1863 JULY–SEPTEMBER

1. 14 T6, CDA.
2. C. E. Engelbrecht, principal of Belle Haven Institute on Laurel Street in Columbia. The school had relocated from Alexandria, Virginia, in 1862 to escape Union occupation.
3. 14 T4, CDA.
4. Unclassified, CDA.
5. 14 T5, CDA.
6. The Cotton Planters Loan Association of South Carolina, chartered by the state legislature in 1862, was a cooperative venture by which funds were made available to member planters who had subscribed to the association a certain portion of their cotton production or its currency equivalent.
7. 14 T8, CDA.
8. 14 T11, CDA.
9. 14 T9, CDA.
10. July 16 was the feast day for Mary under the title of Our Lady of Mount Carmel.
11. 14 T10, CDA.
12. 14 W1, CDA.
13. J. D. B. DeBow, the founder and editor of *DeBow's Review,* had moved his eponymous journal from his native Charleston to Columbia when Charleston first faced the prospect of a Union attack in April 1863.
14. 14 W2, CDA.
15. Fort Wagner, on Morris Island, guarded the southern approach to Charleston Harbor. The Confederate bastion was the target of two Union infantry attacks, a week apart in July, both of which the Confederate defenders repulsed with heavy losses for the Union forces and minimal casualties to the Confederates. Two months later, the Confederates abandoned the fort and retreated to inner defenses of the harbor and city.
16. 14 W3, CDA.
17. John McGill (1809–1872), a Philadelphia native who had been named to the see of Richmond in 1850.
18. 29 H1, CDA.
19. "Translation": moving a bishop from one see to another, whether on the same level (diocese to diocese) or to a higher level (diocese to archdiocese).
20. Richard Vincent Whelan (1809–1874), bishop of Wheeling since 1850. The Baltimore native was as much of a "Southern man" as any of the suffragans within the Confederacy, as Lynch surely knew.
21. 14 W4, CDA.
22. 14 W7, CDA.
23. 14 W8, CDA.
24. 14 W10, CDA.
25. John T. Monroe (1823–1871) had been mayor of New Orleans from 1860 to 1862.
26. Major General Thomas Carmichael Hindman (1828–1868), then in command of forces in the Atlanta area.
27. 14 Y2, CDA.
28. 14 Y4, CDA.

29. Set off by the imposition of a draft, rampaging mobs, a large portion of them Irish immigrants, terrorized New York City for five days in mid-July. Archbishop Hughes, his own health rapidly failing, made a feeble attempt to pacify the rioters by addressing them as members of his flock outside his episcopal residence.

30. Baptista presciently identified the West rather than the East as the source of their mortal danger.

31. Major General William Starke Rosecrans (1819–1898), a convert like his brother, Sylvester, auxiliary bishop of Cincinnati, commanded the Army of the Cumberland in Tennessee. In 1857 William had suffered severe facial burns when an oil lamp exploded during a test he was conducting as head of a coal-oil refinery in Cincinnati (William M. Lamers, *The Edge of Glory: A Biography of General William S. Rosecrans, U.S.A.* [New York: Harcourt, Brace & World, 1961], 17–18).

32. 14 Y5, CDA.

33. A reference to the 12.75-inch-bore Blakely rifled cannon produced in Liverpool in the summer of 1863 for the Confederate government. Two of these massive weapons were shipped through the Union blockade into Wilmington, North Carolina, where they were transported to Charleston to provide weapons with the range and firepower to destroy the ironclads attacking the city.

Also on the Liverpool docks the Laird shipbuilders were in the final stage of constructing two customized ironclads for the Confederate Navy, with the power to more than neutralize their counterparts in the Union fleet besieging Charleston. They never made it out of England. The warning of Charles Francis Adams, the U.S. minister to Great Britain, that the British government's failure to prevent the ironclads from taking to sea would be regarded by the United States as an act of war, persuaded the Palmerston administration to effectively confiscate the vessels by forcing Laird to sell the ships to the British government.

34. 14 Y6, CDA.

35. 14 Y7, CDA.

36. 14 Y8, CDA.

37. The Federals had begun their full-scale bombing of the city from Morris Island on August 22. Day and night the powerful guns poured their deadly loads upon lower Charleston. Its only purpose, Bishop Lynch firmly believed, was to terrorize the inhabitants, "to destroy houses needlessly, to harass and exterminate women, children and noncombattants" (Patrick Lynch to Conseils Centraux de la Société de la Propagation de la Foi, Lyon, June 17, 1864, Archives of the University of Notre Dame, MPFL, 31, reel M10, cited in Heisser and White, *Patrick N. Lynch*, 86).

38. 14 Y9, CDA.

39. The huge cannon was eventually repaired, but neither it nor its mate ever proved to be the super weapon the Confederates had hoped would end the siege.

40. 15 A2, CDA.

41. 15 A3, CDA.

42. Mary Charles Curtin, a Charleston Sister of Mercy, had written Mother Baptista, to express her desire to be admitted to their novitiate. Baptista had discouraged her from transferring from an active to a cloistered religious community in which she would know much less freedom than she did in her present life. If, however, she was intent on becoming an Ursuline, Baptista informed her, she would need a testament of her good character as a religious from her current superior. The enclosed letter presumably was Baptista's

request for such a reference from Mother Theresa at the Mercy Convent (Baptista Lynch, Ursuline Convent and Academy, Columbia, S.C., to Sr. Mary Charles Curtin, September 15, 1863, 15 A1, CDA).

43. 15 A4, CDA.

44. 15 A5, CDA.

1863 OCTOBER–DECEMBER

1. 15 A7, CDA.

2. The Sisters of Our Lady of Mercy daily brought food and other supplies to Union soldiers in the makeshift prisons and hospitals, where they wrote letters for them and provided other measures of comfort and the lifting of spirits (Heisser and White, *Patrick N. Lynch*, 87).

3. 15 A8, CDA.

4. Georgetown Visitation Academy, established in 1799, was the oldest Catholic school for females in the original thirteen states.

5. Translation: according to the rule.

6. Albert Gallatin Blanchard (1810–1891), brigadier general. The Massachusetts-born Blanchard was a West Point graduate (Robert E. Lee was a classmate), served in the Mexican-American War, and made a permanent home in New Orleans, where he was a civil engineer. His second wife (his first had died in 1836) was Herminie Benoist de la Salle, by whom he had fifteen children. In the summer of 1863 he had been transferred from the Trans-Mississippi Department to that of the Carolinas.

7. 15 A9, CDA.

8. Daniel Heyward Trezevant (1796–1873), a Columbia physician.

9. Felix Joseph Barbelin (1808–1869) had emigrated in 1831 from France to the United States, where he joined the Jesuits. From 1838 on he was stationed in Philadelphia, where in 1851 he founded St. Joseph's College; for a time, in the 1850s, the college was located in St. John's parish.

10. S. I. Mahoney, *Six Years in the Monasteries of Italy and Two Years in the Islands of the Mediterranean and Asia Minor: Containing a View of the Manners and Customs of the Popish Clergy in Ireland, France, Italy, Malta . . . etc. With Anecdotes and Remarks Illustrating Some of the Peculiar Doctrines of the Roman Church* (Hartford, Conn.: Andrus & Son, 1851).

11. 15 B2, CDA.

12. 15 B7, CDA.

13. 15 B4, CDA.

14. 15 B5, CDA.

15. 15 B6, CDA.

16. The alpaca Henrietta was inquiring about.

17. The Halifax, North Carolina, lawyer Edward Conigland, who was handling the disposition of the Ferrall estate.

18. 15 B8, CDA.

19. It is surprising that a seasoned religious such as Baptista took no account of the need for the approval of the Jesuit superior of Father Gache for him to make any move from the Army of Northern Virginia to the Ursuline Academy in Columbia. Presumably she simply expected her brother to arrange all such matters.

20. A reference to the siege of Chattanooga that the Confederates had imposed following their decisive victory at Chickamauga the previous September. Ironically, the very night Baptista wrote, the news turned bad for Bragg and the besieging Confederates as they were driven from their supposedly impregnable position on Lookout Mountain and then the next day from the even more formidable defenses of Missionary Ridge. With Bragg's army in retreat, the way was open to invade Georgia and create a second front deep within the Confederacy.

21. 29 Y7, CDA.

22. 15 B9, CDA.

23. 14 N9, CDA.

24. 15 B10 CDA.

25. Videlicet (by custom).

26. John Ingalls (b. 1834), clerk.

27. Pat Flannigan (b. 1820), shoemaker.

28. "West": Cincinnati and Ohio.

29. 15 C1, CDA.

30. Likely John E. Tobin (b. 1822), planter, who had a ten-year-old daughter, Rosa.

31. John Caldwell (b. 1801), president of the South Carolina Railroad.

32. 15 C2, CDA.

33. John Mitchell (1815–1875), Irish nationalist exile who had become a fire-eating advocate of Southern independence. He was at this time editor of the *Richmond Enquirer*.

34. 15 C3, CDA.

35. 15 C5, CDA.

36. January 6, the feast of the Epiphany, a holy day in the liturgical calendar for Catholics.

37. 15 C6, CDA.

1864 January–March

1. Heisser and White, *Patrick N. Lynch,* 99–100.

2. 15 D1, VCD.

3. Masses, by canon law, were to take place normally during the morning hours.

4. Fannie Fennel had entered the novitiate in 1863. She was given the name in religion of Sister Mary Stanislaus.

5. 15 D3, CDA.

6. 15 D4, CDA.

7. 15 G6, CDA.

8. 15 D5, CDA.

9. 15 D7, CDA.

10. 15 D6, CDA.

11. 15 D8, CDA.

12. 15 D9, CDA.

13. 15 D10, CDA.

14. Thomas J. Goodwyn (b. 1800), physician with six children, including Margaret, aged thirteen.

15. Madam Laure de Bertheville.

16. Major General William Henry Chase Whiting (1824–1865), a Catholic and career military officer.

17. 15 G8, CDA.

18. Timothy Bermingham (1804–1872), a priest of the diocese, was in Europe at the time to raise funds for the diocese.

19. CDA. Letter printed in Willard E. Wright, ed., "Some Wartime Letters of Bishop Lynch," *Catholic Historical Review* 43 (April 1957): 27–29.

20. Likely a reference to Charles Lever's eponymous protagonist in his Napoleonic Wars novel, *Charles O'Malley: The Irish Dragoon*, 2 vols. (Dublin: William Curry, Jun. and Co., 1841).

21. 15 E1, CDA.

22. 15 E2, CDA.

23. 15 G1, CDA.

24. "Through patience you will find peace for your spirits."

25. 15 E3, CDA.

26. Bishop John McGill's residence in Richmond.

27. John Bell Hood (1831–1879) had that very month been promoted to lieutenant general for his valiant performances at Gettysburg and Chickamauga, where he had lost use of an arm and a leg respectively. He indeed had been courting Sallie Buchanan Preston, but his marriage proposal the previous fall had failed to muster a commitment from the South Carolina socialite.

28. 15 E5, CDA.

29. James Seddon (1815–1880).

30. Stephen Russell Mallory (1813–1873), Confederate secretary of the navy and a Catholic.

31. Photostat, CDA.

32. 15 E6, CDA.

33. On February 20, outside of Olustee in north central Florida, 5,500 state militia under the command of Brigadier General Joseph Finegan, an Irish immigrant, routed a Federal expeditionary force of about equal size.

34. 15 E7, CDA.

35. Raphael Semmes (1809–1877), Maryland-born Catholic who gained international notoriety as commander of the *Alabama*, which for over two and a half years from 1862 to 1864 wreaked havoc with the maritime commerce of the North by capturing or sinking more than sixty ships.

36. 15 G9, CDA.

37. On Saturday, March 19, there had been an explosion in an arsenal building where rockets were stored. Damage was limited to that building. There was one casualty, a mortal one (*Charleston Mercury*, March 21, 1864, 2).

38. 15 E8, CDA.

39. George Davis (1820–1896).

1864 APRIL–JULY

1. See Leo Francis Stock, "Catholic Participation in the Diplomacy of the Southern Confederacy," *Catholic Historical Review* 16 (1930): 1–18.

2. Judah P. Benjamin, Richmond, to Cardinal Antonelli, April 4, 1864, Box 6, CDA.

3. The secretary further instructed him, "At Paris, Madrid, and Vienna we are inclined to think your presence would be very useful," but left it to Lynch's discretion to include any or all of them in his diplomatic stops on the continent. Lynch was also to decide, according to the particular circumstances, whether to present himself formally to officials as bishop or commissioner (Judah P. Benjamin to P. N. Lynch, Richmond, April 4, 1864, in James D. Richardson, ed. *Messages and Papers of the Confederacy,* vol. 2 [Nashville: United States Publishing Company, 1905], 471–73). As a special commissioner of the Confederacy, Patrick Lynch received a salary of $1,000 a month, plus $500 for a secretary and other expenses (Benjamin to Lynch, Richmond, April 4, 1864, Records of the Confederate States of America, Container 17, Library of Congress (hereinafter LOC) Manuscript Division).

4. Willard E. Wright, "Bishop Patrick N. Lynch, Confederate Propagandist" (paper, Annual Meeting of the American Catholic Historical Association, Philadelphia, December 1963), copy in CDA; Heisser and White, *Patrick N. Lynch,* 104–5.

5. *Charleston Mercury,* May 18, 1864, quoting *Halifax Reporter,* April 28, 1864.

6. Seán Corr, "Bishop Patrick Lynch of Charleston and His Visit to Roslea in 1864," *Clogher Record* 20 (2010): 359–72.

7. 1805–1881.

8. Wright, "Bishop Patrick N. Lynch, Confederate Propagandist."

9. 34 U1, CDA.

10. Bishop Lynch's opaque allusion to the reasons taking him to Rome notwithstanding, his papal mission was common knowledge, at least among the clergy and religious of the diocese.

11. Unclassified, AUCL.

12. April 9.

13. Captains who so chose could look forward to a celebratory toast with fair confidence since the success rate in slipping the Federal blockade was approximately 85 per cent.

14. John Virtue (1826–1900), English priest.

15. Archbishop Gaetano Bedini, papal legate to the United States in 1853–54. Virtue had been the archbishop's secretary during his riot-filled tour.

16. Thomas S. Gholson (1800–1868), had given up his judgeship in 1863 when he was elected to the Confederate Congress.

17. John Slidell (1793–1871), Confederate minister to France.

18. 15 G2, CDA.

19. 15 G2, CDA.

20. 15 G3, CDA.

21. The Superior General of the Discalced Carmelites who had his headquarters in Rome.

22. 15 G5, CDA.

23. 15 G4, CDA.

24. Benjamin Butler (1818–1893), commander of the Army of the James in the Bermuda Hundred area east of Richmond.

25. Henry McIver (b. 1827), a state solicitor before the war, had been a member of the 12th Battalion of the 4th South Carolina Cavalry (1860 Census, Cheraw, Chesterfield, S.C., 177; Confederate Soldiers Compiled Service Records, 1861–1865, Ancestry.com).

26. Patrick Lynch Papers, photocopy, CDA.

27. Charles Hastings Doyle (1804–1883) served as lieutenant governor of the province from 1863 to 1865.

28. In December 1863 a Confederate privateer captured the S.S. *Chesapeake* off the coast of Nova Scotia. It was subsequently recaptured by the U.S. Navy in Sambro Bay, about ten miles south of Halifax.

29. James Philemon Holcombe (1820–1883), a Virginia representative in the Confederate Congress who, like Patrick Lynch, received a commission from the Confederate government in 1864. Holcombe's mission, however, was not merely a legal one, to represent the Confederate naval crew imprisoned for seizing the *Chesapeake,* but military as well: the organization of Confederate prisoners who had escaped to Canada. Eventually Holcombe became involved in espionage in Canada (Jon L. Wakelyn, *Biographical Dictionary of the Confederacy* [Westport, Conn.: Greenwood Press, 1977], 234; William A. Tidwell, James O. Hall, and David Winfred Gaddy, *Come Retribution: The Confederate Secret Service and the Assassination of Lincoln* [1988; repr., New York: Barnes & Noble Books, 1997], 188–89).

30. James L. Capston (1831–1893), an Irish Protestant immigrant and graduate of Trinity College, Dublin, whom Confederate Secretary of State Judah Benjamin had sent to Ireland in July 1863 to change public opinion about the war from pro-Union to pro-Confederate and thus reduce Irish enlistments for service in the Union military (William Barnaby Faherty, S.J., *Exile in Erin: A Confederate Chaplain's Story; The Life of Father John B. Bannon* [St. Louis: Missouri Historical Society Press, 2000], 127–29; Paul R. Wylie, *The Irish General: Thomas Francis Meagher* [Norman: University of Oklahoma Press, 2007], 199–200).

31. John J. Lynch (1816–1888), bishop (1860–1870), then archbishop (1870–1888) of Toronto.

32. Irish immigration to the United States had tripled in 1863 (94,000 from 33,000 the year before) but the causes of the enormous spike were primarily the symbiosis of two factors: the push factor of a highly productive agricultural season that provided many farm laborers with the opportune means to pay their passage to America; the pull factor of the Northern states' labor shortage. Overt recruitment had little to do with the size of the traffic from Queenstown to New York or Boston, much less any conspiracy between the Fenians and the U.S. government (Joseph M. Hernon, Jr., *Celts, Catholics & Copperheads: Ireland Views the American Civil War* [Columbus: Ohio State University Press, 1968], 23–25; Steward and McGovern, *The Fenians,* 61–65).

33. James Spence (1816–1905), Liverpool industrialist who became a propagandist for the Confederacy, notably through his best-selling book *The American Union,* as well as the Confederacy's official financial agent in Great Britain (Amanda Foreman, *A World on Fire: Britain's Crucial Role in the American Civil War* [New York: Random House, 2012], 585).

34. Henry Hotze (1833–1887), early in the war, had secured an appointment from Secretary Benjamin as a special agent to Great Britain, charged with cultivating the press so as to shape public opinion in favor of the Confederacy. In 1864 he had moved to France to expand his operations to continental Europe (Foreman, *World on Fire,* 215–16, 671–72).

35. Archbishop Flavio Chigi (1810–1885).

36. Georges Darboy (1813–1871).

37. Édouard Drouyn de Lhuys (1805–1881).

38. Henry Wellesley Cowley (1804–1884), British Ambassador to France.

39. The peninsula running between the York and James Rivers from Fortress Monroe to Richmond.

40. A Muslim ethnic group in the western Caucasus whose leaders had, just weeks earlier, ended their resistance to Russian rule by taking oaths of loyalty to the Czar. The "exodus" that followed, however, was not a voluntary one. The victorious Russians forcibly dispersed the Circassians throughout portions of the Ottoman Empire.

41. William Lewis Dayton (1807–1864), U.S. Minister to France.

42. Commodore Samuel Barron (1809–1888), commanding officer of Confederate naval forces in Europe.

43. Baron Frédérick Emile d'Erlanger (1832–1911), the German-born head of the French banking house which, in 1863, had agreed to issue $15 million in Confederate bonds in the European market.

44. Edward De Leon (1818–1891), a journalist whom Judah Benjamin in April 1862 had appointed as a "Confidential Agent . . . supplied with twenty-five thousand dollars as a secret service fund to be used by him . . . both in Great Britain and the continent for the special purpose of enlightening public opinion in Europe through the press" (Benjamin to de Leon, April 14, 1862, Records of the Confederate States of America, Container 11, LOC Manuscript Division).

45. Unclassified Lynch Papers, copy. CDA.

46. In the Campo Marzo district of Rome, Patrick Lynch took an apartment for himself, his nephew, and John Bannon, on the Via Condotti, close by the Spanish steps and a short walk from the Congregation of Propaganda Fide.

47. Alessandro Barnabò (1801–1874), cardinal prefect of the Congregation of the Propagation of the Faith (Propaganda Fide).

48. Giacomo Antonelli (1806–1876).

49. "Put your sword back into its sheath and the Lord's peace will be with you."

50. According to Odo Russell, the British representative in Rome, in his meeting with the pontiff toward the end of July, Pius made no attempt to "conceal from me that all his sympathies were with the Southern Confederacy and he wished them all success" (Odo Russell to Earl Russell, July 30, 1864, in Noel Blakiston, ed., *The Roman Question, Extracts from the Dispatches of Odo Russell from Rome, 1858–1870* [London, 1962], quoted in Paul J. Schmidt, *Patrick N. Lynch, Bishop of Charleston, South Carolina, Commissioner of the Confederate States of America to the States of the Church (1864–1865)* [Rome: Pontificia Universitas Gregoriana Faculta Historiae Ecclesiasticae, 1967], 24).

51. Francesco Nardi.

1864 July–September

1. Lynch, Paris, to Benjamin, June 20, 1864, Confederate States of America Records, microfilm, Box 17, Reel 10, MD, LOC.

2. Lynch to Benjamin, July 5, 1864, copy, Edward James Wallace Papers, CDA.

3. Martin Spalding, "Dissertation on the American Civil War," quoted in Thomas M. J. Spalding, C.F.X., ed., "Martin John Spalding's 'Dissertation on the American Civil War,'" *Catholic Historical Review* 52 (1966): 78.

4. *A Tract for the Times: Slavery and Abolitionism, being the Substance of a Sermon, Preached in the church of St. Augustine, Florida, on the 4th day of January, 1861. Day of Public Humiliation, Fasting and Prayer, by the Right Rev. A. Verot, D.D., Vicar Apostolic of Florida* (Baltimore: John Murphy and Co., 1861).

5. *Lettre Pastorale de Mgr. L'Eveque De Natchitoches A l'occasion de la guerre du Sud pur son Indépendance* (August 1861).

6. Text from David C. R. Heisser, ed., "A Few Words on the Domestic Slavery in the Confederate States of America by Patrick N. Lynch," *Avery Review* 2 (Spring 1999): 64–103, and *Avery Review* 3 (Spring 2000), 93–123. Although written in English, there was no English version published, as there was no English target audience.

7. The Nat Turner uprising in tidewater Virginia in August 1831.

8. The doctrine that those Christians possessed by the Spirit are not bound by the law.

9. A reference to the riots in lower Manhattan in July 1863 and the nativist attacks on Catholics in Philadelphia in May and July 1844.

10. More than $1.7 billion in U.S. currency.

11. 15 G7, CDA.

1864 OCTOBER–DECEMBER

1. Quoted in David Heisser, "Bishop Lynch's Civil War Pamphlet on Slavery," *Catholic Historical Review* 84 (1998): 694.

2. See Robert Emmett Curran, "Rome, the American Church, and Slavery," in *Shaping American Catholicism: Maryland and New York, 1805–1915* (Washington, D.C.: Catholic University of America Press, 2012), 106–10.

3. Sebastian G. Messmer, ed., *The Works of the Right Reverend John England: First Bishop of Charleston* (Cleveland: A. H. Clark, 1908), 6:156.

4. "Liquefaction of the Blood of St. Januarius," *Catholic World* 13–14 (1871–72): 772–84, 33–49, 201–12, 391–400, 526–49.

51. 5 G7, CDA.

6. Copy in Antonia Lynch's hand, ABC.

1865 FEBRUARY–APRIL

1. William Gilmore Simms, *Sack and Destruction of the City of Columbia, S.C.* (Columbia, S.C.: Power Press of Daily Phoenix, 1865), 3.

2. In his memoirs Sherman noted:

> it was to me manifest that the soldiers and people of the South entertained an undue fear of our Western men, and, like children, they had invented such ghostlike stories of our prowess in Georgia, that they were scared by their own inventions. Still, this was a power, and I intended to utilize it. Somehow, our men had got the idea that South Carolina was the cause of all our troubles; her people were the first to fire on Fort Sumter, had been in a great hurry to precipitate the country into civil war; and therefore on them should fall the scourge of war in its worst form. Taunting messages had also come to us, when in Georgia, to the

effect that, when we should reach South Carolina, we would find a people less passive, who would fight us to the bitter end, daring us to come over, etc.; so that I saw and felt that we would not be able longer to restrain our men as we had done in Georgia.

"... I would not restrain the army lest its vigor and energy should be impaired; and I had every reason to expect bold and strong resistance at the many broad and deep rivers that lay across our path" (*Memoirs of General William T. Sherman,* vol. 2 [New York: D. Appleton & Co., 1875], 254).

For Sherman the subduing of Columbia was key to ending the rebellion. "I suspect," Sherman wrote Ulysses Grant, just as he began his march through South Carolina, "that Jeff. Davis will move heaven and earth to catch me, for success to this column is fatal to his dream of empire. Richmond is not more vital to his cause than Columbia and the heart of South Carolina" (Sherman, Pocotaligo, S.C., to Grant, January 29, 1865, quoted in *Memoirs of General William T. Sherman,* 2:260).

3. Marion Brunson Lucas, *Sherman and the Burning of Columbia* (Columbia: University of South Carolina Press, 2000), 165.

4. Simms, *Sack and Destruction,* 57.

5. Heisser, "Bishop Lynch's People," 260.

6. 15 H1, CDA.

7. AUCL. This manuscript seems to date approximately from 1886. Immediately before the section on the burning of Columbia, it notes, "This account was written immediately after the burning of our Convent and while recent events were fresh in the minds of the chief sufferers thereby." Its author is most likely Baptista Lynch, who, in the year following the end of the war, prepared for publication an insider's story of the convent burning and the events surrounding it. Much of the language and general style are unmistakably those of Mother Baptista.

8. In his *Memoirs* Sherman related, "I received a note in pencil from the Lady Superioress of a convent or school in Columbia, in which she claimed to have been a teacher in a convent in Brown county, Ohio. At the time my daughter Minnie was a pupil there, and therefor asking special protection. My recollection is, that I gave my note to my brother-in-law, Colonel Ewing, then inspector-general on my staff, with instructions to see this lady, and assure her that we contemplated no destruction of any private property in Columbia at all (2:279–80).

9. "Valle Crucis": "Valley of the Cross," the Keitt plantation that Patrick Lynch had acquired the previous year.

10. In Catholic educational institutions it was a common practice to assign "ranks" to students, that is, to appoint a fixed place within the line of assembled students that they would form to process into the dining hall or chapel. The most common criterion for ordering the students when they processed seems to have been height.

11. Loretta Moran, one of the band of six Ursulines who had come from Brown County in 1858 to establish a foundation in Columbia.

12. In his study of the burning, Marion Lucas concluded that of the many guards assigned to protect properties, perhaps a majority attempted to carry out their orders. Madame Sophie Sosnowski, who had taken over the Barhamville property for her school when

the Ursulines declined to do so, managed to preserve her building, thanks to the guard she had received (Lucas, *Sherman and the Burning of Columbia*, 111–15).

13. Three blocks distant from the academy and convent.

14. Eliza Macnamara Lynch.

15. Sherman in many venues, including his *Memoirs*, singled out local authorities, as well as local African Americans, as the culprits bearing chief responsibility for the conflagration that leveled most of the town: authorities for giving the order to set cotton bales afire; blacks for providing liquor to the troops.

16. Neither Sherman in his memoirs nor Simms in his account mentions any encounter between the commanding general and the religious superior. Simms, who interviewed Mother Baptista among many eyewitnesses, did report an aide to Sherman being present in the churchyard, purportedly in the early morning of the 18th. Simms identifies him as a "Colonel Ewell." Sherman notes in his memoirs that he had designated his brother-in-law, Colonel Thomas Ewing (a Catholic), of his staff, to assure Baptista that she had nothing to fear regarding school and convent (Sherman, 2:279–80). He also acknowledges that he authorized General O.O. Howard to make the Methodist College available to house the "Sisters of Charity" (whom he took the Ursulines to be) (Sherman, 2:286–87). Was the encounter in the graveyard depicted by the Annals, written more than two decades after the event, actually one between Baptista and Ewing or Howard, but not Sherman? That conclusion is tempting but there is evidence of Sherman's presence in the graveyard the morning after. One bit of near-event affirmation comes from a member of the commander's staff, George W. Nichols. Writing in *Harper's New Monthly Magazine* in August 1866, Nichols described General Sherman movements before, during, and after the burning. The morning after the conflagration, the general's party headed for St. Peter's Church on Assembly Street, in response (according to Nichols) to a request from the superior of a local convent. When they found the superior with her fellow sisters and pupils still clustered together in the graveyard, Sherman sought out Baptista. The nun-superior "thanked the General for his kindness, and expressed especial gratitude for the efforts" of Sherman's brother-in-law, General Ewing (Nichols, "The Burning of Columbia," *Harper's New Monthly Magazine* 33 (August 1866), 363–66). [I am indebted to one of the anonymous reviewers for bringing this article to my notice.] Somewhat weaker testimony comes from Lieutenant William White of the 90th Illinois Volunteers, who had been at St. Peter's the night of the burning and had a heated argument with Father O'Connell over Sherman's responsibility for the inferno sweeping through the capital, wrote his wife that afterwards he was "glad to hear the General [Sherman] called on them next morning, and did what he could to alleviate their condition (James B. Swan. *Chicago's Irish Legion: The 90th Illinois Volunteers in the Civil War.* [Carbondale: Southern Illinois University Press, 2009, 208). Strongest of all is a deposition which Sherman himself gave in 1872 in which he recounted visiting St. Peter's Church the morning after and promising "the Lady Superior" a replacement for their convent/academy (Deposition of William T. Sherman, December 12, 1872, No. 103, Wood and Heyworth vs United States, No 2292, Cowlam Gravely vs. United States, *Mixed Commission on British and American Claims. Appendix: Testimony,* xiv, 92, cited in Lucas, 133–34).

17. Ewing (1835–1883), a Catholic, was William Tecumseh Sherman's foster brother as well as his brother-in-law.

18. John W. Cornyn, captain of Company K, 78th Ohio Infantry Regiment.

19. The residence of Brigadier General John Smith Preston (1809–1881), the son-in-law of Wade Hampton Sr., who headed the Bureau of Conscription in Richmond.

20. Among the official Federal records of the war is the following order:

> Head Quarters 15th Army Corps
> Columbia, S.C. February 18th 1865
> To all whom it may concern:
> The Protection of the United States is extended to the Branch of the Ursuline Convent of Columbia, S.C. at Valley Crusa.
> All officers and soldiers are hereby ordered to respect the same.
> By order of
> Major General John A. Logan
> Maxwell Woodhull
> Major and Asst. Adjt. Genl.
> Madame Blanchard
> Superintendent of Convent

Victoria Blanchard, the daughter of the Confederate brigadier general Albert G. Blanchard (1810–1891), was teaching music at the Ursuline Academy at the time, a quasi postulant (as Baptista referred to those who were considering joining the order). The mother superior may have chosen Victoria to approach the local Federal commander as their best hope for securing a written order of protection, a day after a verbal promise had proven less than worthless. If so, the outcome could not have been more satisfying. The place the Ursulines were to call home for the next eleven years was left untouched. The two generals, Blanchard and Logan, were themselves involved in the battle of Bentonville a month later. Blanchard commanded a brigade in McLaws' Division in Hardee's Corps; Logan commanded the 15th Corps.

21. 15 H2, CDA.

22. 15 H11, CDA.

23. Patrick O'Neill of the Charleston diocese died in that month. There is no recorded death of any other O'Neill then serving in either Charleston or Savannah or having served there (as in the case of Father James O'Neill, who left Savannah for Illinois in 1864). Mother Antonia had apparently been wrongly informed. See Rita H. DeLorme, "Looking for the elusive 'other' Father O'Neill," *Southern Cross*, December 1, 2005, 3.

24. John Moore (1834–1901) was of a famine refugee family that settled in Charleston in 1848 and, like Patrick Lynch, an alumnus of the Urban College. When Fillion died in February 1865, Moore succeeded him as vicar-general.

25. John Cullinane, longtime pastor of St. Peter's, Cheraw.

26. Martin Spalding, formerly bishop of Louisville, named as successor to Francis Kenrick.

27. 14 H3, CDA.

28. 15 H12, CDA.

1865 May–December

1. Rufus King, Rome, to William Seward, June 24, 1865, in *Papers Relating to Foreign Affairs of the United States,* vol. 2, 1865, part 3 (Washington, D.C.: Government Printing Office, 1866), 160, quoted in Corr, "Bishop Patrick Lynch," 371–72.

23. 4U3, Associated Archives of St. Mary's University and Seminary (hereinafter AASMUS).

3. The disingenuous character of this statement notwithstanding, Patrick Lynch's record of ministering to the servicemen of both sides, without regard for creed or race, was unquestionably outstanding. Even before the outbreak of war, when Fort Sumter was under siege, he sent a priest to provide religious service to the many Catholics in the fort's garrison (see section 1861 January–June). From the first establishment of prisons in the Charleston area, Lynch was a regular visitor, as Colonel Michael Corcoran of the New York 69th Infantry regiment discovered in Castle Pinckney in Charleston harbor. "Bishop Lynch . . . never leaves us with a shadow on our countenances," he noted in his diary. "He is a dear man, and truly and zealously devotes himself to his high and holy calling" (October 13, 1861, Corcoran Diary, quoted in Michael Corcoran, *The Captivity of General Corcoran: His Twelve-Month Imprisonment in Richmond and Other Southern Cities* [Philadelphia: Barclay & Co., 1864], 62). In the summer of 1863, when Confederate officials were threatening to treat African American prisoners as escaped slaves or even insurrectionists, the bishop intervened to ensure that members of the 54th Massachusetts who had been taken prisoner in the failed attack on Fort Wagner received the same treatment as white prisoners. That same summer he was responsible for President Davis's sparing the lives of two Union prisoners who had been designated for execution in retaliation for the Union's execution of two Confederate chaplains charged with spying. He was also on several occasions asked to oversee the exchange of prisoners (Heisser and White, *Patrick N. Lynch,* 87–88).

4. Since the District of Columbia was within the ecclesiastical jurisdiction of the Archdiocese of Baltimore, the archbishop of Baltimore frequently acted as the liaison with the government on matters affecting Catholics. Martin Spalding was especially well positioned for such missions, having an old Louisville friend, James Speed, serving as the attorney general of the United States. Despite a natural dislike of any sort of ecclesiastical lobbying of government, Spalding did write in behalf of Lynch to Speed; he asked Jacob Walter, the pastor of St. Patrick's, close by the president's house, to deliver that letter to the attorney general. Walter reported in late June that Speed had presented Lynch's petition at a cabinet meeting, but the Johnson administration had decided, rather ambiguously, that the bishop ought not to return to the states until "affairs are settled South" (Walter to Martin Spalding, Washington, June 9, 1865, 36K5, AASMUS; Walter to Spalding, Washington, June 26, 1865, 36K7, AASMUS).

5. 15 H4, CDA.

6. 14 H5.

7. 15 H6, CDA.

8. On June 22, 1865, the *Baltimore Sun* reported: "Pardons asked for: It is stated that among the applications to the President . . . was that of Bishop Lynch, the Catholic Bishop of Charleston. The petition is drawn up and signed by [Arch]Bishop Spaulding of Baltimore and the Bishop of Buffalo, N.Y. [John Timon]."

9. Sisters of Our Lady of Mercy (Charleston) who had been stationed at the military hospital in Montgomery White Sulphur Springs for the past three years.

10. 34 U4, AASM.

11. Quincy Adams Gillmore (1825–1888), commanding officer in 1863–1864 of the Department of the South, which included the Carolinas, Georgia, and Florida.

12. Nelson Mitchell (d. 1864), Charleston lawyer.

13. 34 U6, AASMUS.

14. A formally true statement. Bishop Lynch never presented his credentials as a Confederate agent to any state official with whom he met, but he made clear to most, if not all of them, that he was there as an emissary of the Confederate government.

15. 15 H7, CDA.

16. Catherine Duncan Emmet, wife of Thomas Addis Emmet, grand-nephew of the Irish nationalist Robert Emmet and a renowned gynecological surgeon at the Women's Hospital in New York City.

17. Benjamin Franklin Perry (1805–1886), a late secessionist appointed by President Andrew Johnson as the provisional governor of South Carolina during its period of self-reconstruction.

18. C. W. Dudley (b. 1808), lawyer and former representative, from Marlboro, in the South Carolina general assembly.

19. Over the next eight decades the Ursulines would write many times to Washington for indemnification. For all their efforts, they received nothing.

20. Alfred Stedman Hartwell (1836–1912), Harvard graduate who had served as an officer of two of the earliest African-American regiments, the 54th and 55th Massachusetts. He was responsible for blacks being made commissioned officers in June 1865. As a breveted brigadier general, Hartwell at this time was commanding a combined force stationed in Orangeburg.

21. John Porter Hatch (1822–1901), career military officer who had been appointed commander of forces in the Charleston area after the city surrendered in February 1865.

22. Jeremiah Cummings, New York priest and friend of Patrick Lynch.

23. 15 H9, CDA.

24. Unclassified, CDA. Schwartz was an official with the Leopoldine Society in Vienna. Emperor Francis I had established the association in 1828 for the support of Catholics in the United States. By the Civil War it had provided over $430,000 in funds for the church in America.

25. 34 U7, AASMUS.

26. When Bishop Lynch had written Secretary of State Seward on July 1 for a pardon, Spalding had appealed directly to President Johnson, which finally brought a favorable response (Thomas X. Spalding, *Martin John Spalding: American Churchman* [Washington, D.C.: Catholic University of America Press in association with Consortium Press, 1973], 167–68, 170).

27. 15 H10, CDA.

28. Abbreviation for "sacratissimi" (most sacred).

29. Lynch to William Elder, January 10, 1865[6], cited in Brian Fahey, *Catholic Diocese of Charleston: A History* (Charleston: Office of the Chancery, n.d.), 30.

30. Patrick Lynch to Charles G. Schwarz, September 1865, Unclassified, CDA.

INDEX